"In this book Robert Letham offers an e
both ontologically as a divine person of
his operations in the life of the church a
for Eastern Trinitarianism, and being a sober critic of modern Pentecostalism, Letham guides readers through a panoply of texts and issues. In dialogue with a diverse set of authors from church history (ancient and modern), he engages a swarm of theological questions surrounding the Holy Spirit, including the Spirit as the third person of the Trinity, the procession of the Spirit and the *filioque* clause, and the Spirit's role in creation and salvation, along with such topics as the Spirit and baptism, the gifts of the Holy Spirit, the Spirit and the future, and many other related themes. Letham makes us exercise our flabby minds as he works through the biblical materials afresh, with the benefit that we are made more fit to contemplate how and where the Spirit is at work (or not at work) today. His volume is a most valuable contribution in the church's effort to embrace the Holy Spirit as the Lord and giver of life."

—**J. Mark Beach**, Professor of Doctrinal and Ministerial Studies, Mid-America Reformed Seminary

"This book is a gold mine of scholarship concerning the blessed third person of the Trinity. Robert Letham digs deeply into the classic doctrine of the Holy Spirit as it developed from the early church to the medieval period and beyond, extracting riches for students of classic Christian doctrine. Furthermore, he discusses the refined interpretations of modern biblical commentators on the progressive revelation of God's Spirit through redemptive history, a profitable study in biblical theology. It is a rare scholar who can write well in both historical and biblical theology, and Letham is eminently qualified to do so."

—**Joel R. Beeke**, President, Puritan Reformed Theological Seminary

"Dr. Letham has provided us with a clear and thorough examination of the Christian doctrine of the Holy Spirit, explaining how controversies have arisen and been debated over the centuries. He presents different views fairly and respects the positions taken by others, while at the same time he defends classical Reformed orthodoxy with grace and conviction. This volume will be an essential reference work for every pastor and student of God's self-revelation in the power of his Holy Spirit."

—**Gerald Bray**, Research Professor of Divinity, Beeson Divinity School, Samford University

"Historically informed, exegetically acute, sensitive to the contours of redemptive history, and responsive to the questions of the present day, this volume on the doctrine of the Holy Spirit by Robert Letham is a treat. It models an approach to Reformed theology willing to learn from the best of the Christian tradition as a whole, and will be profitably read by seasoned theologians, seminarians, and informed laypersons. We await the projected volumes on the Father and Son with anticipation."

—**William B. Evans**, Younts Professor of Bible and Religion, Erskine College, Due West, South Carolina

"Professor Bob Letham is too good a theologian and too sensible a Christian to think that even with his award-winning work on *The Trinity* and the publication of his *Systematic Theology*, he had spoken the last word about God. His new commitment to produce a trilogy of volumes on the Father, the Son, and the Holy Spirit is therefore welcome news indeed. Fittingly, this down-payment volume deals with the person and work of the Holy Spirit. It exhibits all the hallmarks that we have come to expect of its author—a rich combination of biblical, historical, and systematic theology coupled with shrewd analysis and insight, all placed in tribute to the triune Lord. If we may reapply Paul's famous words, those 'who have the firstfruits of the Spirit' will surely 'wait eagerly' for Dr. Letham to complete his theological triptych."

—**Sinclair B. Ferguson**, Chancellor's Professor of Systematic Theology, Reformed Theological Seminary

"This book continues the high-quality contributions on major theological topics we have come to expect from Dr. Letham. One need not agree at every point to greatly benefit from this sound and, in view of persisting controversies, balanced treatment of the person and work of the Holy Spirit. All told, an impressive accomplishment."

—**Richard B. Gaffin Jr.**, Professor of Biblical and Systematic Theology, Emeritus, Westminster Theological Seminary

"For a long time the Holy Spirit was called 'the forgotten member of the Trinity.' But surely the growth of charismatic Christianities and new forms of pietism prove that the neglect of the Holy Spirit is a thing of the past. Or is it? To a significant degree at least, the Spirit that has been 'recovered' is arguably not the Spirit of the church's confession. The Spirit remains deeply mysterious. And yet, isn't this the Spirit's way? Is it not the Spirit's desire to speak not of himself but of the Son, not to speak his own words but to speak only what he hears (John 16:13)? And is it not the Son's desire not to speak of himself but to reveal the Father? Our goal, then, is not to fully unveil all mysteries but to hear faithfully what the Spirit does say—of himself, of the Son and the Father, of all things. With characteristic breadth and depth, Dr. Letham in this work reminds us of—or perhaps introduces us to—key features of the person and work of the Holy Spirit. Shaped by long reading in the principal original texts of the Christian tradition and animated by a deep, confessional Reformed catholicity, Letham's survey is unfailingly interesting and edifying. Even those who may disagree with one or more positions taken here will undoubtedly appreciate the way in which the author makes his case. Above all, Letham provides yet another illustration of how a rigorous commitment to the authority and primacy of Holy Scripture is not only consistent with but generative and formative of a strong, charitable, yet not uncritical embrace of the rich tradition of the church. New theology students and long-seasoned ones will alike find Letham's work a welcome addition to the still sadly underwhelming library of works on the Holy Spirit."

—**Mark A. Garcia**, Associate Professor of Systematic Theology, Westminster Theological Seminary

"Anyone familiar with the writings of Bob Letham will look forward with delight to reading his newest book, *The Holy Spirit*. Letham, as to be expected, locates the person and ministry of the Spirit within the Holy Trinity, and proceeds to take us on a historical, biblical, and theological journey that wonderfully and engagingly presents to us the riches and richness of who the Spirit is, what he does, and what he continues to do in creation and redemption. This is a book written for the church—theologians and pastors will benefit greatly, but so will 'ordinary' church members. It is a pleasure to commend Letham's latest work."

—**Ian Hamilton**, President, Westminster Presbyterian Theological Seminary, Newcastle, England

"After his award-winning volume on the Trinity, Robert Letham has appropriately turned his attention to a volume on the Holy Spirit. This thorough and comprehensive study considers both the person and work of the Spirit. It expounds the historical development of teaching on the person of the Spirit within the Trinity, and then the teaching on the Spirit in the Bible. The concluding chapter is a brief but hard-hitting answer to the question of how to discern where the Spirit is at work today. Over the past century, the doctrine of the Spirit has been a subject of considerable attention and controversy, in terms of both theology and practice. One of the benefits of this book is that Letham confronts these issues head-on and gives his own incisive judgment on contemporary attitudes and practices, especially in the appendix on "Pentecostalism and the Charismatic Renewal." Not all readers will agree with all his conclusions, but all should take note of the serious issues that he raises. This is an excellent comprehensive study of the Holy Spirit, one that those with an interest in the topic cannot afford to ignore. Sell your shirt to buy this book!"

—**Tony Lane**, Professor of Historical Theology, London School of Theology

"This is a work of massive erudition, reflecting a lifetime of disciplined study, while at the same time excelling in analysis and evaluation. Yet it is also marked by appropriate humility, recognizing that it is hard to walk with confident sure-footedness through mysteries that have stretched human language and concepts to their limits. Students seeking light on such questions as the *filioque* and the gifts of the Spirit will turn to this rich source for years to come. And in case we forget that divine revelation is not only the source and norm of theology, but first and foremost a means of grace, the volume closes with a powerful chapter on the Holy Spirit at work (usually through the labors of the patient and the self-effacing)."

—**Donald Macleod**, Postgraduate Supervisor, Systematic Theology and Church History, Edinburgh Theological Seminary

"For many centuries, the church has lived and breathed Trinitarian doxology. While this trend largely dropped off in nineteenth-century Protestantism, there has been a most welcome resurgence of interest in the glory of the triune God as the heart of Christianity in recent years. Though welcome, this movement has brought some unwelcome ideas, such as social Trinitarianism and Pentecostalism. Robert Letham is well suited to write this first in a series of three books on the Father, the Son, and the Holy Spirit. *The Holy Spirit* wonderfully introduces readers to the third person of the Trinity by tightly wedding his person and work to the Father and the Son. Doing so makes all the difference in the world, cutting through debates over what it means to be filled with the Spirit. Readers will gain insight, clarity, and devotion to the Holy Spirit as they prayerfully digest this work."

—**Ryan M. McGraw**, Morton H. Smith Professor of Systematic Theology, Greenville Presbyterian Theological Seminary

"Letham, a significant contributor to our understanding of the blessed, holy, undivided Trinity, has undertaken an explication of each of the persons thereof, beginning in this work with the Holy Spirit. He employs his customary care, fairness, and brilliance in a first-rate biblical, theological, and historical treatment of the third person of the Godhead. This is a work not to be missed, especially the concluding brief, but insightful and encouraging, chapter on 'The Holy Spirit at Work.'"

—**Alan D. Strange**, Professor of Church History, Mid-America Reformed Seminary

"I warmly commend Robert Letham's book. He is very widely read in patristics, in biblical research, and in modern theology, in all of which he rightly cites primary sources. This gives a wide perspective and context. He produces very many insights into this crucial subject, even adding a useful evaluation of the modern charismatic movement. This book is not to be missed."

—**Anthony C. Thiselton**, Emeritus Professor of Christian Theology, University of Nottingham

"Bob Letham has written one of the most satisfying single works on the person and work of the Holy Spirit that I know. Bringing his fine scholarship into play, he presents the subject from the historical, biblical, and theological perspectives. This work demonstrates finely tuned sensitivity to other church traditions and also to the practical discernment of where the Spirit is at work. The six chapters presenting the biblical development have a hope-stimulating eschatological focus. The appendix with a balanced discussion of the Pentecostal renewal movements is a welcome bonus."

—**Paul Wells**, Editor in Chief, *Unio cum Christo*; Emeritus Professor, Faculté Jean Calvin, Aix-en-Provence, France

THE HOLY SPIRIT

Also by Robert Letham with P&R Publishing

The Holy Trinity: In Scripture, History, Theology, and Worship
The Lord's Supper: Eternal Word in Broken Bread
The Westminster Assembly: Reading Its Theology in Historical Context
Union with Christ: In Scripture, History, and Theology

THE HOLY SPIRIT

ROBERT LETHAM

P U B L I S H I N G
P.O. BOX 817 • PHILLIPSBURG • NEW JERSEY 08865-0817

Some of the material presented in chapters 1–4 was originally published in Robert Letham, *The Holy Trinity: In Scripture, History, Theology, and Worship*, rev. and expanded ed. (Phillipsburg, NJ: P&R Publishing, 2019), 131–352. Content has been edited and revised for this new format.

Material on pages 212–13 and 296–97 has been adapted from *Systematic Theology* by Robert Letham, Copyright © 2019, pp. 860–65. Used by permission of Crossway, a publishing ministry of Good News Publishers, Wheaton, IL 60187, www.crossway.org.

Italics within Scripture quotations indicate emphasis added.

Printed in the United States of America

Library of Congress Cataloging-in-Publication Data

Names: Letham, Robert, author.
Title: The Holy Spirit / Robert Letham.
Description: Phillipsburg, New Jersey : P&R Publishing, [2023] | Includes bibliographical references and index. | Summary: "Writing with care and reverence, Robert Letham develops a holistic and canonical view of the Holy Spirit in the context of the Trinity, the person and work of Christ, and redemption"-- Provided by publisher.
Identifiers: LCCN 2022029712 | ISBN 9781629953809 (paperback) | ISBN 9781629953816 (epub)
Subjects: LCSH: Holy Spirit. | Trinity.
Classification: LCC BT121.3 .L476 2023 | DDC 231/.3--dc23/eng/20220715
LC record available at https://lccn.loc.gov/2022029712

For Joan

Creator Spirit, by Whose Aid

Creator Spirit, by whose aid
The world's foundations first were laid,
Come, visit every pious mind;
Come, pour thy joy on humankind;
From sin and sorrow set us free,
And make thy temples worthy thee.

O source of uncreated light,
The Father's promised Paraclete,
Thrice holy fount, thrice holy fire,
Our hearts with heavenly love inspire;
Come, and thy sacred unction bring
To sanctify us while we sing.

Plenteous of grace, descend from high
Rich in thy sevenfold energy;
Make us eternal truths receive,
And practice all that we believe;
Give us thyself, that we may see
The Father and the Son by thee.

Immortal honour, endless fame,
Attend the almighty Father's name;
The Saviour Son be glorified,
Who for lost man's redemption died;
And equal adoration be,
Eternal Paraclete, to thee.

—John Dryden, 1693

Contents

Foreword

Robert Letham is well known through his theological writings, which include a widely acclaimed work on *The Holy Trinity* and his more recent magnum opus, *Systematic Theology*. Those who are familiar with these works will find that Letham's latest book—*The Holy Spirit*, his study on the person and work of the third person of the Trinity—exhibits several features characteristic of his other writings: careful attention to the catholic church's great tradition of theological reflection on the Holy Trinity, uncompromising respect for the testimony of the canonical Scriptures, and wise judgments regarding disputed questions. Those who are unfamiliar with Letham's works will be introduced to a theologian who combines theological acumen with lucid brevity, a rare combination not often found in books on important theological topics. I am delighted at the opportunity to introduce this new volume.

While reading Letham's *The Holy Spirit*, I could not help but recall a professor's sage advice during my graduate studies in theology. Clearly exasperated with the publication of theological studies that were, in his judgment, born more out of vanity ("publish or perish") than out of an acknowledged need to contribute clarity on a particular theological doctrine, my professor laid down three simple guidelines for would-be authors: (1) the book should make a genuine contribution or fill a gap in the present literature on its topic; (2) the book should present a mature, wise, and thoughtful treatment that exhibits a broad familiarity with its topic; and (3) the book should not be born out of a desire to be clever or innovative, a species of theological whimsy that does not enhance the church's witness to the truth.

By the measure of these guidelines, Letham's study passes the test with flying colors. Sympathetic readers of *The Holy Spirit* will discover a book that makes a much-needed contribution to our understanding of the doctrine of the Holy Spirit, especially in the context of the modern emergence of Pentecostal and charismatic views. They will also discover a book whose treatment is deeply rooted in the history of theological reflection on the person and work of the Holy Spirit. Far from being a piece of theological whimsy, Letham's handling of the topic is consistently thoughtful, wise, and mature. Readers will also encounter an author who respectfully engages in conversation with theologians who span the course of the history of theology.

The first part of Letham's book, entitled "The Holy Spirit and the Trinity," exhibits his familiarity with the history of theological reflection on the Holy Trinity. Letham views the church's confession of the Trinity as an expression of the "cumulative biblical exegesis of the whole church." While some readers may question Letham's decision to begin with a survey of the church's reflection on the doctrine of the Holy Spirit before treating the biblical witness to the person and work of the Holy Spirit in the history of redemption, Letham properly recognizes that the interpretation of Scripture's witness did not begin in the modern period. Accordingly, it is inappropriate to engage directly with the scriptural witness regarding the Holy Spirit, as though modern readers of the biblical text may ignore the church's engagement with this witness throughout the centuries. Thus, unlike many contemporary studies of the doctrine of the Holy Spirit, the first part of Letham's book lays a foundation for an understanding of the person and work of the Holy Spirit by taking readers on an extended tour through the history of confessional and theological reflection. Rather than beginning with contemporary voices and emphases, Letham welcomes his readers to join him in exploring the fruits of the church's historic reflection on the Holy Spirit.

In the course of his discussion of the Holy Spirit and the Trinity, Letham traces the development of the doctrine of the Holy Spirit on the road to the Council of Constantinople I (381). This council represented a kind of watershed in the early church's confession of the Trinity. In the aftermath of the critical decision of the Council of Nicaea (325) on the deity of the Son, the church reached a consensus that the Holy Spirit is consubstantial with the Father and the Son—the same in being, yet distinct in person or *hypostasis*. To the affirmation of Nicaea that the Son is consubstantial with the Father, Constantinople added that the church believes "in the Holy Spirit, the Lord and life-giver, who proceeds from the Father, who is worshipped and glorified together with the Father and the Son, who spoke by the prophets."

Two features of Letham's treatment of the church's historic consensus regarding the Holy Spirit are especially noteworthy.

First, on the dispute between the Eastern and Western church regarding the "double procession" of the Spirit from the Father and the Son (*ex Patre filioque procedit*), Letham steers a middle course. In Letham's estimation, the common Western objection to the Eastern church's denial of the double procession, namely, that it fails to affirm the intimate relation between the Spirit and the Son, is overstated. Since the Eastern church has expressed a willingness to affirm that the Spirit proceeds from the Father *through* the Son, the claim that the Spirit is not intimately related to the Son within the Eastern view is somewhat exaggerated. Moreover, by virtue of the Eastern church's acknowledgment that the three persons of the Trinity mutually indwell and interpenetrate one another, the procession of the Spirit from the Father is a procession from the Father of the Son, who eternally is "in and with the Father." Because the West's formulation affirms a common procession of the Spirit from the Father and the Son, Letham maintains that it tends to confuse the distinction between the persons of the Father and the Son in their relation to the Spirit. In order to clarify this possible confusion between the Spirit's procession from the Father and the Son, Letham proposes that we use the expression of Cyril of Alexandria (A.D. 378–444): the Spirit proceeds "from the Father *in* the Son." In Letham's judgment, Cyril's formulation better expresses the mutual indwelling of the three Trinitarian persons, avoids any residue of subordinationism (by excluding the Son in respect to the procession of the Spirit), and offers a sure basis for the economic mission of the Spirit in granting us communion through Christ with the Father.

Although Letham's proposal on the Spirit's procession from the Father in and through the Son will not likely bring about ecumenical consensus between East and West, it certainly deserves consideration as a credible contribution to the resolution of this long-standing controversy. And it does so on the crucial principle that what the triune God does in the history of redemption reveals God as he truly and necessarily is. The "order" of the eternal and necessary relations between the Father, the Son, and the Holy Spirit within the one being of God is revealed in the economy of all of God's works in creation, providence, and grace. Quoting John Owen, Letham affirms that "the order of operation among the distinct persons depends on the order of their subsistence" in the Trinity. The missions of the three persons in the economy of redemption correspond to the intra-Trinitarian relations between the Father, the Son, and the Holy Spirit. All things in creation and redemption come from the Father through the Son in and by the Holy Spirit.

Second, on the basis of his defense of the main axioms of historic Trinitarian theology, Letham critically engages with a diversity of "Spirit Christologies" that have emerged in recent theology. These Spirit Christologies proceed from the conviction that historic Christian theology has not given sufficient attention to the person and work of the Holy Spirit. Letham distinguishes between non-Trinitarian and Trinitarian Spirit Christologies. Non-Trinitarian Spirit Christologies tend to be unitarian in their doctrine of God and adoptionistic in their doctrine of Christ. The preexistence of the eternal Son is denied, and Jesus becomes merely an outstanding example of experiencing God by his indwelling Spirit. Trinitarian Spirit Christologies retain a semblance of the Christian doctrine of the Trinity but reverse the relation obtaining between the Son and the Spirit. Rather than the Father's sending the Son, and the Father and Son's sending the Spirit, Trinitarian Spirit Christologies ascribe priority to the Spirit as the one through whom the Son proceeds. Rather than viewing the Spirit's ministry as pointing to and glorifying Christ, Christ is subordinated to the Spirit, and his work is merely a prelude to the ministry of the Spirit. Letham's critical assessment of these Spirit Christologies demonstrates convincingly that a reversal of the proper order of the eternal relations between the Father, the Son, and the Holy Spirit has perilous consequences for the church's understanding of the nature of the Spirit's ministry. Rather than viewing the Spirit as the "bond of unity" between believers and Christ, as the "minister of Christ's liberality" whereby we are restored to life-communion with the Father through the Son (Calvin), the Spirit's ministry subverts or takes priority over the ministry of Christ.

In the second part of the book, entitled "The Holy Spirit in the Bible," Letham provides a comprehensive survey of the Spirit's work throughout the history of redemption. Letham's survey respects the progressive nature of the Bible's revelation of the person and work of the Spirit. Although the Old Testament provides hints of the unique person or *hypostasis* of the Holy Spirit, the New Testament provides a more clear and fulsome disclosure of the Holy Spirit's distinct person and ministry. Letham's treatment of the testimony of the New Testament follows the sequence of the great complex of events in redemptive history that include the ministry of Jesus Christ, the incarnate Son; the resurrection and ascension of Christ; the outpouring of the Spirit at Pentecost; the work of the Spirit through the apostolic ministry; the gifts of the Holy Spirit; and the Holy Spirit's work in bringing all things to their perfection in the coming kingdom of God. Throughout this part of his study, Letham offers a masterly and thorough account of the ministry of the Holy Spirit, one that confirms the truth of the church's historic doctrine of the Trinity. The New Testament's witness supports the Trinitarian axiom that the "works of the triune God are indivisible" (*opera Trinitatis ad extra indivisa sunt*). Letham also shows clearly that the work "appropriate" to the Holy Spirit is to bear witness to, and bring believers into fellowship with, the incarnate Son, whom the Father sent into the world for us and our salvation. The works of the triune God, particularly the work of the Holy Spirit, can be understood only in terms of the Trinitarian relations that the church confesses in the doctrine of the Holy Trinity.

Because Letham's study of the Holy Spirit is governed throughout by the church's historic understanding of the Trinity, several dominant themes emerge in his treatment of the biblical testimony regarding the Spirit's ministry. First, the ministry of the Holy Spirit is always tethered to the Word and apostolic testimony concerning Christ. The Holy Spirit's ministry is self-effacing in its focus on the Word of Christ. The Spirit is pleased to communicate, as the Spirit of truth, all those things he has heard from the Father concerning the Son whom he has sent (John 16:13–15). Where Christ is known and worshiped, you may be sure that the Holy Spirit is present. Second, Letham gently criticizes the overemphasis in theologians such as John Owen on the role of the Spirit in furnishing Christ in his human nature for his ministry as Mediator. Although Letham acknowledges the propriety of this emphasis (it comports with the Trinitarian axiom that the three persons of the Trinity act indivisibly in all their operations), he argues that it may reflect a "Nestorian tendency"to separate the human nature from the divine nature, thereby denying the "communion of the attributes" in one and the same Christ. And third, Letham strongly rejects the Pentecostal and charismatic claim that Pentecost involved a postconversion baptism of some believers and not others. In this connection, Letham offers one of the best, and most theologically grounded, critical assessments of the tendency within Pentecostalism to identify the Spirit's ministry with subjective experiences or empowerments that some believers enjoy in distinction from others. The outpouring of the Holy Spirit at Pentecost is the one baptism that grounds the incorporation of all believers into the one body of Christ. All believers are incorporated into union with the Father, the Son, and the Holy Spirit through baptism. Rather than associating baptism in the Spirit with subjective experiences of the Spirit's presence, we must view the ministry of the Spirit in theological and Trinitarian categories. Through the Spirit, believers are drawn into fellowship with the Father in and through the Son.

I make these observations about Letham's study to whet the appetite of any would-be reader to take up and read his fine contribution to our understanding of the Holy Spirit. Those who do so will discover a rich treasury of theological and biblical insight. If you are looking for a study of the doctrine of the Holy Spirit that makes a contribution to our understanding and genuinely fills a gap in contemporary literature on the topic, you will not be disappointed. Indeed, you will encounter a theologian who, in his engagement with the doctrine of the Holy Spirit, understands well the task of systematic theology as Herman Bavinck aptly describes it:

> Dogmatics [systematic theology] shows us how God, who is all-sufficient in himself, nevertheless glorifies himself in his creation, which, even when it is torn apart by sin, is gathered up again in Christ (Eph. 1:10). It describes for us God, always God, from beginning to end—God in his being, God in his creation, God against sin, God in Christ, God breaking down all resistance through the Holy Spirit and guiding the whole of creation back to the objective he decreed for it: the glory of his name. Dogmatics, therefore, is not a dull and arid science. It is a theodicy, a doxology to all God's virtues and perfections, a hymn of adoration and thanksgiving, a "glory to God in the highest" (Luke 2:14).[1]

Letham's study is indeed a "glory to God in the highest" that sheds fresh light on the oft-neglected and misunderstood glory of the Holy Spirit.

Cornelis P. Venema

1. Herman Bavinck, *Reformed Dogmatics*, vol. 1, *Prolegomena*, ed. John Bolt, trans. John Vriend (Grand Rapids: Baker Academic, 2003), 112.

Acknowledgments

It has been a great privilege to write about the Holy Spirit, one of the Trinity. I am greatly appreciative to John J. Hughes for asking me to do so and for his constant assistance throughout the process, as well as to Karen Magnuson for her usual eagle-eyed copyediting. The entire team at P&R is worthy of high praise.

I am thankful to Union School of Theology for providing sabbatical leave during the 2019–20 academic year, before the COVID pandemic, and covering expenses I incurred for travel and accommodation then and at other times. I am indebted to our former librarian at Union School of Theology, Donald Mitchell, who was tragically killed in a road accident in December 2020. Donald was unfailingly helpful, and his expert knowledge was put to use on many occasions. His successor, Marni Thurm, is following in that tradition. I am also thankful to the staff at Cambridge University Library for their kind assistance with material that was otherwise difficult to obtain. I am in debt to a range of readers, whose input has made this a far better book than it might otherwise have been, especially Keith Underhill, Jonathan Humphreys, Tony Lane, Mark Cartledge, Ryan McGraw, and Richard B. Gaffin Jr. My colleagues at Union School of Theology (erstwhile, in the case of Cor Bennema, and present, in Steffen Jenkins) have provided valuable assistance on particular points. I am also grateful to Raj Sangha for help with some references. No such faults as may be present in this book can in any way be attributable to them.

I thank Ian R. Hepburn for granting me access to a manuscript of lectures given by D. Martyn Lloyd-Jones at Westminster Chapel,

London, in the 1960s, typed by a "very reliable" fellow member of that congregation. Throughout our time in Wales, we have greatly valued the fellowship of Bethel Presbyterian Church, Cardiff, and the loving leadership of the session.

Above all, I am particularly grateful to my wife, Joan. She has been a constant support throughout my career and our current forty-six years of married life. It is exceedingly doubtful whether I could ever have done what I have done, such as it may be, without her. She has eminently exhibited the fruit of the Holy Spirit, in love, joy, peace, patience, kindness, goodness, faithfulness, gentleness, and self-control, not least in the last few months when, suffering herself from ill health, she has willingly tended to me following injuries and, additionally, side effects from surgery. Besides this, she has diligently ministered to the spiritual and material needs of members of our congregation. It is to her that this book is dedicated.

Blessed be the kingdom of the Father, the Son, and the Holy Spirit, now and ever, and unto the ages of the ages.

Veni, creator Spiritus
Lent 2022

Introduction

This book follows an invitation by the publisher to undertake a trilogy on the Trinitarian persons, stemming from my earlier work on the Holy Trinity (2004, 2019). Further volumes on the Son and the Father are projected. I contemplate this with a sense of overwhelming responsibility. Something in me tells me that it is too much for one individual to give an account of the Holy Trinity in all its uniqueness and glory, and yet also to write of the three *hypostases* or "persons" distinctly. This is literally an awesome task, too great for a mere human to undertake. Yet God has made himself known to us. He has come among us in the person of his Son, living as man. He has poured out his Spirit upon us and within us. We can so speak; indeed, we must speak, if only through trembling and stammering lips. One thing is certain: this book, as all others on the subject, will be nowhere near adequate. John Stott often quoted the words of Charles Simeon, who upon entering the pulpit would remind himself: "One thing I know, I am a fool; of that I am certain."[1] We are all fools, for such wisdom as we have comes from the Holy Spirit alone.

The book has the following outline. The first section is a historical survey of discussion in the church. The focus here is that the Trinity is indivisible and so the works of the Spirit are inseparable from those of the Father and the Son. The second section is biblical,

1. Heard on two occasions, at the Theological Students Fellowship conference at Swanwick in January 1969 and again at an informal gathering for graduates at Westminster Theological Seminary on May 25, 1976, to which Stott had been invited as he was passing through the area. Stott had a lifelong admiration for Simeon, and rightly so.

tracing the pervasive and increasing stress on the Spirit in creation, the history of redemption, the life and ministry of Christ, the work of the apostles, and the establishment of the church, ultimately extending to our own transformation and eventual resurrection. The book comes to its climax with a short chapter that asks how we are to discern where the Spirit is clearly at work. I hope readers will not miss this because, to my mind, it is the single most important chapter. Finally, I have included an appendix on modern developments relating to our understanding of the Spirit. Throughout the book, words that are included in the glossary are in bold at their first appearance in a chapter.

We start with the historical discussions in the church. This hammers home the vital point that the Spirit is God, one of the Trinity. Being so, he is indivisible from the Father and the Son. Moreover, in all the works of God, all three persons work together inseparably, and so when we consider the Spirit, we must not think of him as out on his own. These commitments, at the heart of the faith of the church for centuries, are vital to appreciate when we come to consider the biblical testimony. It is absurd to assume that we must ground everything on our own exegesis of the Bible, while ignoring the cumulative wisdom of the people of God down through the ages. That route invariably leads to disaster. It is an attempt to reinvent the wheel and frequently regurgitates old errors and heresies.

There has been a welter of discussion on the Spirit in recent decades, some of which is still a matter of debate, difference, and sometimes controversy, but I do not focus on such territory. Nor do I wish to be confrontational. The intention is to develop a holistic and canonical view of the Holy Spirit in the context of the Trinity, the person and work of Christ, and redemption. Not that we shy away from disputed matters. The appendix in part addresses these. We can surely disagree freely, as long as we recognize the reality of the one holy catholic and apostolic church.

Abbreviations

AugStud	*Augustinian Studies*
BAGD	Walter Bauer, William F. Arndt, and F. Wilbur Gingrich, *A Greek-English Lexicon of the New Testament and Other Early Christian Literature* (Chicago: University of Chicago Press, 1957)
BHS	Baptism of the Holy Spirit
C	Niceno-Constantinopolitan Creed
CD	Karl Barth, *Church Dogmatics*, ed. Thomas F. Torrance, trans. Geoffrey W. Bromiley, 14 vols. (Edinburgh: T&T Clark, 1956–77)
CO	John Calvin, *Calvini Opera* (*Opera quae supersunt omnia*), ed. Guilelmus Baum, Eduardus Cunitz, and Eduardus Reuss, 59 vols., *Corpus Reformatorum* 29–87 (Brunswick: 1863–1900)
Institutes	John Calvin, *Institutes of the Christian Religion*, ed. Ford Lewis Battles, trans. John T. McNeill (Philadelphia: Westminster Press, 1960)
JEPTA	*Journal of the European Pentecostal Theological Association*
JPT	*Journal of Pentecostal Theology*
LN	Johannes P. Louw and Eugene A. Nida, eds., *Greek-English Lexicon of the New Testament Based on Semantic Domains* (New York: United Bible Societies, 1988)
Lumière et Vie	*Lumière et Vie: Revue théologique d'information et de formation*
LXX	Septuagint

NPNF[1]	Philip Schaff and Henry Wace, eds., *A Select Library of the Nicene and Post-Nicene Fathers of the Christian Church*, 1st ser. (repr., Peabody, MA: Hendrickson, 1995)
NPNF[2]	Philip Schaff and Henry Wace, eds., *A Select Library of the Nicene and Post-Nicene Fathers of the Christian Church*, 2nd ser. (Grand Rapids: Eerdmans, 1988)
PG	J.-P. Migne et al., eds., *Patrologia Graeca* (Paris, 1857–66)
PL	J.-P. Migne et al., eds., *Patrologia Latina* (Paris, 1878–90)
Pneuma	*Pneuma: The Journal of the Society for Pentecostal Studies*
SJT	*Scottish Journal of Theology*
ST	Thomas Aquinas, *Summa Theologia*
StPatr	*Studia Patristica*
SVTQ	*St. Vladimir's Theological Quarterly*
Them	*Themelios*
WCF	Westminster Confession of Faith
WLC	Westminster Larger Catechism
WSC	Westminster Shorter Catechism
WTJ	*Westminster Theological Journal*

Part 1

The Holy Spirit and the Trinity

The Holy Spirit is one of the three Trinity *hypostases* or "persons," fully God without remainder, of one identical and indivisible being with the Father and the Son. The Spirit, together with the Father and the Son, is Creator and Redeemer. Together with the Father and the Son, the Spirit is to be worshiped and adored. In all of God's works, the Spirit is active inseparably with the Father and the Son. Yet since each of God's works is specifically the work of a particular Trinitarian person, so to the Spirit is attributed the effective power by which these works are accomplished. But we must always see this in the context of harmonious, united, and inseparable action.

All our thought about the Holy Spirit, in terms of both the inner life of the Holy Trinity and also his works in creation and grace, must proceed on this basis.

The church's recognition of these realities took time to develop and come to articulate expression. This section surveys that process. It reflects the cumulative biblical exegesis of the whole church. A knowledge of how that took place will help us to put in perspective questions that arise in our own day.

1

The Road to Constantinople

The Holy Spirit in the Church Fathers

In order to appreciate the presence and work of the Holy Spirit today, we need to ask how this has been seen over the past two thousand years of the church's existence. Such a search is not a merely antiquarian exercise. It is vital for us to ensure that our own thinking is within the parameters shaped by more than fifty generations of those who have gone before us. How else can we be clear that our experience is demonstrably Christian? We have two millennia of accumulated wisdom, biblical exegesis, and concentrated thought to guide us. While not all of it may seem fruitful, much if not most will. Besides, attempting to reinvent the wheel is a fruitless exercise and has frequently led to serious error or even heresy.

The first four centuries of the church involved a slow process through which a clearer grasp of the Holy Spirit's identity emerged. Because of controversial proposals that undermined Christ's divine status, the dominant focus was on the relation of the Son to the Father. Consequently, less attention was given to the Spirit. In the first two centuries, the Spirit was generally considered as the Creator.[1] By the late second century, a threat had emerged from forms

1. Michel R. Barnes, "The Beginning and End of Early Christian Pneumatology," *AugStud* 39, no. 2 (2008): 169–86; Mark DelCogliano, Andrew Radde-Gallwitz, and Lewis Ayres, *Works on the Spirit: Athanasius the Great and Didymus the Blind* (Yonkers, NY: St. Vladimir's Seminary Press, 2011).

of **monarchianism**, which excessively stressed the unity of God, "the one rule" or **monarchy**, eroding the distinctiveness of the three **persons**. In this, it was held that God's revelation as the Father, the Son, and the Holy Spirit was for the purposes of redemptive history only and did not represent eternal realities. The consequence was that if this were true, we could have no valid knowledge of God, since his revelation in human history would not disclose who he is eternally. This provoked a reaction from Irenaeus and especially Tertullian. Eventually the church rejected this form of **modalism**, known as **Sabellianism**, at the Synod of Antioch in 268.

Irenaeus (A.D. 130–200)

In his developed theology,[2] Irenaeus, bishop of Lyons, used a striking image that points to a triadic view of God. Writing against **gnosticism**, which posited a supreme entity, from which a chain of beings emanated, involving angelic intermediaries, Irenaeus repeatedly wrote of the Father's having created by his "two hands." Alluding to Genesis 1:26 and asserting **creation *ex nihilo***, he wrote that God stood in need of no angel to help him, "as if he did not possess his own hands. For with him were always present the Word and Wisdom, the Son and the Spirit, by whom and in whom, freely and spontaneously, he made all things, to whom also he speaks, saying 'Let us make man after our image and likeness.'"[3] The Son and the Spirit are both coeternal with the Father, he argued, and one with him, for they share in what is exclusively a work of God. So "the Father plans and gives commands, the Son performs and creates, while the Spirit nourishes and increases."[4]

2. Michel René Barnes, "Irenaeus's Trinitarian Theology," *Nova et Vetera* 7, no. 1 (2009): 67–106, presents a close and thorough case that only in his later works does Irenaeus take the Holy Spirit into consideration in relation to creation. This is largely due to his focus on God as Spirit and his need to defend the faith against gnosticism. Moreover, apart from Athenagoras, there was not a robust doctrine of the Holy Spirit at the time, nor did Irenaeus develop a clear idea of the distinct identity of the Spirit. In large measure, this was due to his living in the second century with the limitations that this imposed.

3. Irenaeus, *Against Heresies*, 4.20.1; *PG*, 7:1032.

4. Irenaeus, *Against Heresies*, 4.38.3; *PG*, 7:1107–8.

Irenaeus extended this metaphor to the creation of Adam and to the incarnation of the second Adam: "For never at any time did Adam escape the *hands of God*, to whom the Father speaking said, 'Let us make man in our image, after our likeness.' And for this reason in the last times . . . his hands formed a living man, in order that Adam might be created [again] after the image and likeness of God."[5] The translation of Enoch and Elijah followed a similar pattern, for "by means of the very same hands through which they were molded at the beginning, did they receive this translation and assumption. For in Adam the hands of God had become accustomed to set in order, to rule, and to sustain his own workmanship, and to bring it and place it where they pleased."[6] So for Irenaeus, God's whole work of creation, providence, and grace was carried out by his two hands, the Son and the Holy Spirit. At first sight, this seems to subordinate the Son and the Spirit as merely God's agents. In fact, before the Council of Nicaea (A.D. 325), some form of subordination was endemic. But Irenaeus did not consider the two hands external to God. They are unmistakably divine, always with the Father. There is but one God, while the Son "was always with the Father; and . . . the Spirit was present with Him, anterior to all creation."[7] Henry Swete remarks that as the hands of God, they are divine and coequal.[8] The Father has first place, however, and salvation focuses on union with him.[9]

Irenaeus considered at length neither the internal **relations** of God, of the Son and the Spirit with the Father, nor their preexistence.[10] But he did make a start, with the external works of God, particularly the baptism of Jesus. There the Holy Spirit, like a dove,

5. Irenaeus, *Against Heresies*, 5.1.3; *PG*, 7:1123.

6. Irenaeus, *Against Heresies*, 5.5.1; *PG*, 7:1134–35.

7. Irenaeus, *Against Heresies*, 4.20.2–4; *PG*, 7:1032–34; Irenaeus, *The Demonstration of the Apostolic Preaching*, 5.

8. Henry Barclay Swete, *The Holy Spirit in the Ancient Church: A Study of the Christian Teaching in the Age of the Fathers* (London: Macmillan, 1912), 88.

9. Basil Studer, *Trinity and Incarnation: The Faith of the Early Church*, ed. Andrew Louth, trans. Matthias Westerhoff (Collegeville, MN: Liturgical Press, 1993), 64.

10. Boris Bobrinskoy, *The Mystery of the Trinity: Trinitarian Experience and Vision in the Biblical and Patristic Tradition*, trans. Anthony P. Gythiel (Crestwood, NY: St. Vladimir's Seminary Press, 1999), 204; Studer, *Trinity*, 62.

descended on Jesus. Receiving the Spirit as a gift from the Father, Jesus then imparted him to his followers, sending the Spirit upon all the earth.[11] Jesus' anointing at the Jordan reveals the triad, for we see he who anoints (the Father); the Son, who is anointed by the Spirit; and the Spirit, who is the anointing.[12] The reverse movement is seen in our redemption, which Irenaeus understood as a form of ascent by steps like a ladder, through the Spirit to the Son, and through the Son to the Father.[13] Indeed, without the Spirit of God, we cannot be saved.[14]

Montanism

A second-century movement gained ground and posed a different sort of challenge to the church. Montanus, who was from Phrygia in Asia Minor and was a Christian convert, began to prophesy, in an ecstatic, trancelike state, joined by two women, Prisca and Maximilia. They claimed that this was direct revelation from the Holy Spirit. Moreover, they held that the return of Christ was imminent and would happen in Phrygia. Alongside these claims was a rigorous moralism, with fasting emphasized and marriage discouraged. The movement posed a threat to the church, since it implied that the Spirit was giving extra revelation additional to Scripture. Eventually, in A.D. 177, Montanus was excommunicated and Montanism as such became an independent sect.

Tertullian (160–220) shared some Montanist beliefs later in his career. But it is a matter of dispute whether he left the Roman Catholic Church and became a Montanist or, if he did, whether he remained one.[15]

11. Irenaeus, *Against Heresies*, 3.17.1–3; *PG*, 7:929–31.

12. Irenaeus, *Against Heresies*, 3.18.2–3; *PG*, 7:932–34.

13. Swete, *Holy Spirit*, 90–91; Irenaeus, *Against Heresies*, 5.36.2; 3.24.1; Irenaeus, *Demonstration*, c. 7. Later, John Calvin was to develop this theme; see Julie Canlis, *Calvin's Ladder: A Spiritual Theology of Ascent and Ascension* (Grand Rapids: Eerdmans, 2010).

14. Irenaeus, *Against Heresies*, 5.36.2.

15. Swete, *Holy Spirit*, 67–83; Augustine, *De haeresibus ad quodvultdeus*, 86, in *PL*, 42:47; Allan G. Fitzgerald, ed., *Augustine through the Ages: An Encyclopedia* (Grand Rapids: Eerdmans, 1999), 822. I am grateful to Tony Lane for some clarifying remarks on this.

The Third Century

Together with the modalist tendencies of monarchianism, there was a threat from the opposite direction. This was an unreflective form of **subordinationism** in which the Son and the Spirit were seen as clearly distinct from the Father but were accorded lesser status. In refuting Montanism, the move toward distinguishing the Son and the Spirit from the Father may have encouraged this development, since the linguistic tools did not exist to explain how the three could be distinct, yet one and indivisible. John 1:3 was commonly used in support, the Spirit seen as one of the things brought into existence by the Logos.[16] It is difficult to be precise because, in some form or another, this tendency was pervasive. Sometimes Origen (185–254) has been connected with this development, but this view is neither accurate nor fair. In one sense, before the fourth-century crisis, this endemic form of undeveloped subordinationism ought not to be equated with the later repudiation of the deity of the Son and the Spirit. Origen definitely held that both were to be regarded as God, not as creatures.[17]

The Fourth-Century Crisis

A third and crucial stage occurred from the middle of the fourth century, following the controversy provoked by **Arius**, who held that the Son was not coeternal with the Father but had been brought into existence by him. The crisis was later greatly exacerbated by **Eunomius**, who held similar views but was a bishop and far more able. The resulting controversy led eventually to the Trinitarian settlement at Constantinople in 381. The controversy was fueled by subordinationist groups such as the **Homoians** and **Heterousians**.[18] At first, the issues surrounded the relation of the Son to the Father, but in the years leading up to the Council of Constantinople, attention turned to

16. Lewis Ayres, "Innovation and Ressourcement in Pro-Nicene Pneumatology," *AugStud* 39, no. 2 (2008): 187–205; DelCogliano, Radde-Gallwitz, and Ayres, *Works on the Spirit*, 12–13.

17. See Swete, *Holy Spirit*, 127–34, esp. his wise comments to the foot of page 132; Robert Letham, *The Holy Trinity: In Scripture, History, Theology, and Worship*, rev. and expanded ed. (Phillipsburg, NJ: P&R Publishing, 2019), 100–107.

18. DelCogliano, Radde-Gallwitz, and Ayres, *Works on the Spirit*, 13–15.

the status of the Holy Spirit. The **Arians** drew attention to the work of the Spirit, but as a tacit suggestion of his inferiority to the Son, who in turn they regarded as a creature.[19] Lewis Ayres points out that in the fourth century, all sides recognized that there was an **order** among the three persons. Those opposed to the Creed of Nicaea (325) argued that this entailed that the Spirit was less than the Father and the Son. It was generally agreed that the Spirit's status was not immediately clear or explicit in Scripture. This was acknowledged by Basil and Gregory of Nazianzus, since they appealed to the "sense of Scripture" and in the latter's case to progressive revelation.[20] The crisis elicited some major works on the Spirit, which we will now consider.

Athanasius (A.D. 295–373)

Athanasius's *Letters to Serapion on the Holy Spirit* were the first extensive discussion of the Holy Spirit. He wrote them between 355 and 360 against the *tropicii* (trope-mongers), a small group in Egypt who, while accepting the deity of the Son, balked at ascribing the same status to the Spirit.[21] Serapion, a bishop, asked Athanasius for advice in dealing with this group. Athanasius called them *tropicii* because they appear to have specialized in biblical interpretation by tropes. Athanasius referred to their predilection for "modes of exegesis."[22] He countered their claims, based on Amos 4:13, that God had created the Holy Spirit,[23] and from 1 Timothy 5:21 that the Spirit is to be classed with angels.[24]

The Persons of the Trinity Are Indivisible

The indivisibility of the Trinity was central to Athanasius's argument. He stated that the Father and the Son are not separated,

19. Swete, *Holy Spirit*, 169.

20. Ayres, "Innovation and Ressourcement," *passim*.

21. Ayres indicates that the *tropicii* do not appear outside this context. Ayres, "Innovation and Ressourcement," 187–91.

22. Athanasius, *Letters to Serapion on the Holy Spirit*, 1.7.2. Quotations are from DelCogliano, Radde-Gallwitz, and Ayres, *Works on the Spirit*.

23. Athanasius, *Serapion*, 1.3.1f. Note that the Hebrew word *ruach*, translated "wind" in the ESV, is also the common word for "spirit." See chapter 5.

24. Athanasius, *Serapion*, 1.10.4f.

"but in their hands is the Spirit, who cannot be parted either from him that sent or from him that conveyed him."[25] This insistence on the inseparability of the persons of the Trinity was a constant theme. Following this, Athanasius regarded the Spirit to be inseparably one with the Father and the Son. Since he proceeds from the Father, he is ever in the hands of the Father who sends and of the Son who conveys him.[26] The Spirit is in Christ as the Son is in the Father. What is spoken from God is said through Christ in the Spirit.[27]

Against the argument of the *tropicii* that if the Spirit is from the Father he must be a second son, and brother to the Son, Athanasius replied that there is no other Father than the Father, no other Son than the Son. Hence the one and only Father is Father of a Son who is one and only. As the Son is uniquely related to the Father, so too is the Spirit.[28] The Spirit cannot change, fills all things, and is present in all things.[29]

The Relation between the Spirit and the Son

Athanasius turned to the relation between the Son and the Spirit. He stressed the connection, seen in Jesus' baptism, between the Spirit and salvation. There Jesus was anointed with the Holy Spirit, and in turn supplies the Spirit to his church. Since Jesus sanctified himself for our sake, the descent of the Spirit was a descent on us because Jesus bore our body. When he was washed in the Jordan, we were washed in him and by him. Underlying such a claim is the recognition that Jesus' baptism was theologically connected to his crucifixion (Matt. 3:13–15). When he received the Spirit, we received him. The flesh he assumed was anointed, and this for us. Since the Son had united us to himself in his incarnation, only he could unite us to the Holy Spirit, for the Spirit is his.

Athanasius affirms repeatedly that the Son is the giver of the Spirit. Elsewhere he writes, "Through whom and from whom was

25. Athanasius, *Defence of Dionysius*, 17; *PG*, 25:503–6.
26. Athanasius, *Statement of Faith*, 4; *PG*, 25:203–6.
27. Athanasius, *Serapion*, 1.14; *PG*, 26:564–65.
28. Athanasius, *Serapion*, 1.16; *PG*, 26:568–69.
29. Athanasius, *Serapion*, 1.26; *PG*, 26:589–93.

it appropriate that the Spirit should be given but through the Son, whose Spirit he is?"—since there was no other way that we could receive him unless through the Son, who was united to us in the form of a servant and, as such, received the Spirit for us. He continues, "Because as man he is said to have received the Spirit, the flesh being first sanctified in him, we subsequently receive the Spirit's grace from his fullness."[30]

The relation of the Spirit to the Son is the most distinctive aspect of Athanasius's discussion in these letters, one that sets his theology of the Spirit apart from others who came later. Clearly, the reason for this is that the *tropicii* held to the deity of the Son. Athanasius builds on this to demonstrate that the Spirit should therefore also be accorded deity; he does not mean to exclude the Father. As the Father is light and the Son his radiance, we see in the Son the Spirit by whom we are enlightened. In turn, when the Spirit enlightens us, Christ in the Spirit enlightens us. As the Father is fountain and the Son is called river, we are said to drink the Spirit. When we drink the Spirit, we drink of Christ. As Christ is true Son, so when we receive the Spirit we are made sons. When the Spirit is given to us, God is in us. When God is in us, the Son is in us. When we are quickened by the Spirit, Christ lives in us.[31] This mutual indwelling of the three underlies their inseparable involvement in the one work of God for our salvation. The Spirit is never apart from the Word, the Son, a point that Athanasius repeats time and time again.[32]

So for Athanasius, the Spirit is the image of the Son, proper to the Son, distinct from the creatures, and one with God. Since the Spirit joins creation to the Word, he cannot belong to the creatures, and since he bestows sonship on creation, he cannot be alien from the Son. He belongs to the Godhead of the Father, and in the Spirit the Word deifies creatures. Consequently, since he makes all things

30. Athanasius, *Against the Arians*, 1.46–50, here 1.50; *PG*, 26:105–18 (my translation).

31. Athanasius, *Serapion*, 1.19; *PG*, 26:573–76.

32. Athanasius, *Serapion*, 1.14, 17, 20, 31; 3.5; 4.4; *PG*, 26:564–65, 569–72, 576–80, 600–605, 632–33, 641–44.

divine, he cannot be outside the Godhead of the Father[33] and is indivisible from the Son.[34] As the Son is in the Spirit as in his own image, so also the Father is in the Son.[35] The Trinity is indivisible, so wherever the Father is mentioned the Son is also understood, and where the Son is the Holy Spirit is in him.[36]

Moreover, as the Son has his particular property—being **begotten**—in relation to the Father, so does the Holy Spirit in relation to the Son[37]; the Son is the image of the Father, but so also the Holy Spirit is the image of the Son.[38] Athanasius denies an obvious rejoinder that there are consequently two sons, maintaining the distinctiveness of the Holy Spirit in doing so, but the fact that he feels obliged to make such a point indicates how inseparable he understands the relation of the Son and the Spirit to be. Indeed, the Holy Spirit has the same order or rank (*taxis*) and **nature** (***phūsis***) toward the Son as the Son has toward the Father. The Son is in the Father and the Father is in the Son, and so also the Holy Spirit is in the Son and the Son is in the Holy Spirit. Thus, the Spirit cannot be divided from the Word.[39] So also the Spirit is in God the Father and from the Father.[40] As the Son comes in the name of the Father, so the Holy Spirit comes in the name of the Son.[41] There is one efficacy and action of the Holy Trinity, for the Father makes all things through the Word by the Holy Spirit.[42]

Similarly, the Spirit receives from the Word, while the Word gives to the Spirit, and whatever the Spirit has he has from the Word. Whatever the Word has in the Father he wishes to be given us through the Spirit.[43] Nothing could be clearer than the intimate, unbreakable relation between the Son and the Holy Spirit in

33. Athanasius, *Serapion*, 1.24–25; *PG*, 26:585–89.
34. Athanasius, *Serapion*, 3.5; *PG*, 26:632–33.
35. Athanasius, *Serapion*, 1.20; 3.1; *PG*, 26:576–80, 624–28.
36. Athanasius, *Serapion*, 1.14; *PG*, 26:564–65.
37. Athanasius, *Serapion*, 3.1; *PG*, 26:624–28.
38. Athanasius, *Serapion*, 4.3; *PG*, 26:640–41.
39. Athanasius, *Serapion*, 1.20–21; *PG*, 26:576–81.
40. Athanasius, *Serapion*, 1.25; *PG*, 26:588–89.
41. Athanasius, *Serapion*, 1.20; *PG*, 26:576–80.
42. Athanasius, *Serapion*, 1.20, 28, 30; *PG*, 26:576–80, 593–600.
43. Athanasius, *Against the Arians*, 3.24–25. See also 3.44; *PG*, 26:373–78, 415–18; *PG*, 26:373–78, 415–18.

Athanasius's thought. The three persons indwell one another, are in one another. This applies as much to the Son and the Spirit as to the Son and the Father or the Father and the Spirit.

These relations among the three persons being what they are, Athanasius understands the **procession** and giving of the Spirit to occur in the indivisible union of the triad. The Spirit, he says, proceeds from the Father, since he shines forth, is sent, and is given from the Word, who is from the Father. Furthermore, the Son sends the Spirit. The Son glorifies the Father and the Spirit glorifies the Son. So in order of nature, the Spirit bears the same relation to the Son as the Son to the Father. As the Son, who is in the Father and the Father in him, is not a creature, so the Spirit cannot be ranked with the creatures, since he is in the Son and the Son in him.[44] On the contrary, the Spirit is proper to the Word, and is of the holy triad.

> So, the Trinity is holy and perfect, confessed in Father and Son and Holy Spirit. . . . It is self-consistent and indivisible in nature, and it has one activity. The Father does all things through the Word in the Holy Spirit. In this way is the unity of the holy Trinity preserved. . . . It is not a Trinity in name alone . . . but in truth and actual existence. For just as the Father is "he who is," so too is his Word "he who is" and God over all. And the Holy Spirit . . . exists and subsists truly. And the Catholic Church does not entertain the thought of anything less than these three.[45]

Hence, while Athanasius does not state it explicitly in precise words, this demands that the ***homoousios*** is applicable to the Holy Spirit as well as the Son.[46]

44. Athanasius, *Serapion*, 1.20–21; *PG*, 26:576–81.

45. Athanasius, *Serapion*, 1.27–28; *PG*, 26:593–96. Unless otherwise mentioned, quotations of Athanasius's *Letters to Serapion* and from Didymus the Blind are from DelCogliano, Radde-Gallwitz, and Ayres, *Works on the Spirit*.

46. Athanasius, *Serapion*, 1.14, 16–33; 2.2; *PG*, 26:564–65, 568–612.

The Spirit and Our Salvation

In terms of our salvation, we are sealed by the Spirit, and so made partakers of the divine nature, as Peter puts it (2 Peter 1:4), and thus all creation partakes of the Word in the Spirit.[47] It is important to note that Athanasius normally uses the term *metochoi* ("partakers, participants") for the saints but reserves *idios* ("proper") to the relation of the Son and the Spirit to the Father in the indivisible Trinity. We are given to participate in the divine nature by grace (v. 4) and remain creatures, but the Spirit and the Son are **ontologically** one with the Father from eternity. The gifts of the Spirit are also given from the Father through the Son. For all things of the Father are of the Son also, and so those things given from the Son in the Spirit are gifts of the Father. These gifts are given in the triad, from the Father, through the Son, in the Holy Spirit. When we partake of him, we have the love of the Father and the grace of the Son and the communion of the Spirit himself. Once again, the activity of the triad is one, for all is originated and effected through the Word in the Spirit, for the Spirit is indivisible from the Word.[48] Referring to John 4:21–24, Athanasius says that true worshipers worship the Father in the Spirit and the Truth (the Lord himself), confessing the Son and in him the Spirit.[49] This powerful focus on the relation of the Spirit to the Son was not to be followed by the Greek church.

Didymus the Blind (A.D. 313–98)

Didymus's treatise on the Spirit was written only a few years after Athanasius's *Letters to Serapion*, in around 360–65. In it Didymus argues that the deity of the Spirit is demonstrated by his works. His main point is that the Spirit is the source of sanctification for all Christians and angels, which proves that he is not a creature, for a creature could never do such a thing. The Spirit is the fullness of the gifts of God. "If he sanctifies those who are

47. Athanasius, *Serapion*, 1.23; *PG*, 26:584–85.

48. Athanasius, *Serapion*, 1.30–31; *PG*, 26:597–605.

49. Athanasius, *Serapion*, 1.33; *PG*, 26:605–8. On the inseparability of the Spirit and the Word in Athanasius, see Ayres, "Innovation and Ressourcement," here 197.

capable of participating in him, then he should be placed with the Father and the Son."[50]

Indivisibility and Inseparability

Didymus agrees with Athanasius that the three are indivisible and work inseparably, for "the fact that there is a single grace of the Father and the Son perfected by activity of the Holy Spirit demonstrates that the Trinity is of one **substance**."[51] Consequently, the **attributes** of God, exemplified by love, are possessed equally by all three persons.[52] "Whoever has communion with the Holy Spirit immediately has communion with both the Father and the Son, [and] whenever anyone has the love of the Father, he has it as a gift from the Son through the Holy Spirit. In addition, whenever anyone is a participant of the grace of Jesus Christ, he has the same grace as a gift from the Father through the Holy Spirit."[53] Thus the activity of the Father, the Son, and the Spirit is the same, and so they are a single indivisible substance.[54]

The Spirit Is Clearly Different from the Creation

Consequently, the Spirit is uncircumscribed,[55] present to and indwelling the angels so that they are holy through **participation** in the Spirit.[56] The Spirit does not share the nature of the creature.[57] He is participated in by creatures and therefore is uncreated.[58] Baptism is incomplete if it is administered in the name of the Father and the Son only.[59]

50. Didymus the Blind, *On the Holy Spirit*, 19; DelCogliano, Radde-Gallwitz, and Ayres, *Works on the Spirit*, 149, see also 45. See also Swete, *Holy Spirit*, 221–25.

51. Didymus the Blind, *On the Holy Spirit*, 76.

52. Didymus the Blind, *On the Holy Spirit*, 77–78. See also 82–98.

53. Didymus the Blind, *On the Holy Spirit*, 80.

54. Didymus the Blind, *On the Holy Spirit*, 81, 103, 191.

55. Didymus the Blind, *On the Holy Spirit*, 23.

56. Didymus the Blind, *On the Holy Spirit*, 24–25.

57. Didymus the Blind, *On the Holy Spirit*, 29.

58. Didymus the Blind, *On the Holy Spirit*, 54. See our comments above on Athanasius, *Serapion*, 1.30–31; *PG*, 26:597–605, in note 48.

59. Didymus the Blind, *On the Holy Spirit*, 101.

There Is an Order among the Three

The Spirit has gone out from the Father[60] and is sent from the Son "without moving from one place to another."[61] "The Father does not send the Spirit without the Son sending him since he comes through the identical will of the Father and Son."[62] In all this, Didymus acknowledges, the Trinity is beyond all material substances, and so "everything we say is said καταχρηστικῶς, that is, in an improper sense."[63]

Basil the Great (A.D. 330–79)

A native of Cappadocia who became bishop of Caesarea, Basil is noteworthy for his organizational skill and his development of monastic life. He wrote a volume, *Against Eunomius,* in 364,[64] but his mature thought on the Holy Spirit and the Trinity is found in his magnum opus, the treatise *On the Holy Spirit* against the ***pneumatomachii,*** written around 376.[65] He writes most probably against his former mentor Eustathius, who had latterly taught that the Spirit is subordinate. This work is a staunch defense of the Spirit's deity. Basil has often been thought hesitant in affirming this, while Mark Larson undermined such an interpretation.[66] We will note below Christopher

60. Didymus the Blind, *On the Holy Spirit,* 111.
61. Didymus the Blind, *On the Holy Spirit,* 112.
62. Didymus the Blind, *On the Holy Spirit,* 117.
63. Didymus the Blind, *On the Holy Spirit,* 167.
64. For a detailed discussion of Eunomius's theology and Basil's response in addition to the literature cited above, see Thomas A. Kopecek, *A History of Neo-Arianism,* 2 vols. (Cambridge, MA: Philadelphia Patristic Foundation, Ltd., 1979), vol. 2. Milton V. Anastos, "Basil's *Kata Eunomiou*: A Critical Analysis," in *Basil of Caesarea: Christian, Humanist, Ascetic: A Sixteen-Hundredth Anniversary Symposium,* ed. Paul Jonathan Fedwick (Toronto: Pontifical Institute of Medieval Studies, 1981), 67–136, considers this work at length, which has neither been published in a critical edition nor been translated into a modern language. On Basil, see Philip Rousseau, *Basil of Caesarea* (Berkeley: University of California Press, 1994); Volker Henning Drecoll, *Die Entwicklung der Trinitätslehre Des Basilius von Cäsarea* (Göttingen: Vandenhoeck & Ruprecht, 1996); Johannes Quasten, *Patrology,* 4 vols. (Westminster, MD: Christian Classics, 1992), 3:204–36, esp. 230–33; John Behr, *The Formation of Christian Theology,* vol. 2, *The Nicene Faith,* pt. 2, *One of the Holy Trinity* (Crestwood, NY: St. Vladimir's Seminary Press, 2004), 263–324.
65. See Studer, *Trinity,* 148–51, for a perceptive summary.
66. Mark J. Larson, "A Re-Examination of *De Spiritu Sancto*: Saint Basil's Bold

Beeley's case that he stopped short of what became the Constantinopolitan settlement. Some have pointed out that Basil does not speak of the Spirit as *homoousios* with the Father and the Son,[67] in marked contrast to his friend Gregory of Nazianzus.[68] Larson, however, marshals evidence that Basil says the same thing in other words. Again, scholars have regarded it as read that he never explicitly identifies the Spirit as God.[69] Yet his comments belie this claim, and Gregory of Nazianzus's critical remarks to that effect may well apply to an earlier time.[70] It is probable that Basil was attempting to persuade his readers, including opponents, to align themselves with him and, in doing so, using subtle, diplomatic means to achieve his goal.[71] This is the opinion of Gregory.[72] John Behr adds that Basil may also have wanted, for those reasons, to stick to biblical language.[73] As a master administrator, Basil was more inclined to subtle persuasion than was the volatile Gregory, who was far more at home in scholarship and preaching and was an abject failure at church politics.

Liturgical Origin of the Dispute

Basil points to the liturgical origin of the dispute that occasioned the treatise. Opponents had attacked him for the prepositions he used in the doxology, in which he was accustomed to say "to the Father *with* the Son together *with* the Holy Spirit" rather than their approved form "*through* the Son *in* the Holy Spirit." They considered his addition a novelty, extrabiblical, and contradictory. Their preferred form

---

Defence of the Spirit's Deity," *Scottish Bulletin of Evangelical Theology* 19, no. 1 (Spring 2001): 65–84.

67. Thomas F. Torrance, *The Christian Doctrine of God: One Being, Three Persons* (Edinburgh: T&T Clark, 1996), 126; Quasten, *Patrology*, 3:232.

68. Gregory of Nazianzus, *Oration 31*, 10; *PG*, 36:144.

69. Quasten, *Patrology*, 3:231; Larson, "Re-Examination," 67–69.

70. Basil of Caesarea, *On the Holy Spirit*, 16.37; 19.49; 21.52; *PG*, 32:133, 155–60, 164–65 (all citations from Basil's treatise *On the Holy Spirit* are from Basil the Great, *On the Holy Spirit: St. Basil the Great*, trans. Stephen Hildebrand [Yonkers, NY: St. Vladimir's Seminary Press, 2011]); Larson, "Re-Examination," *passim*.

71. Lewis Ayres, *Nicaea and Its Legacy* (Oxford: Oxford University Press, 2004), 216–17.

72. Gregory of Nazianzus, *Oration 43*, 8; *PG*, 36:504.

73. Behr, *Nicene Faith*, pt. 2, 314.

allowed a clear subordinationist understanding, reducing the Son to an instrument and the Spirit to a creature, which Basil's expression offset.[74]

Distinction between *Ousia* and *Hypostasis*

These terms had been introduced at Nicaea. Their use in Greek thought was ambiguous and sometimes contradictory; much confusion resulted in subsequent years. For his part, Basil distinguished the *hypostases* clearly,[75] a development from Nicaea, where ***hypostasis*** and ***ousia*** were apparently interchangeable, the Father and the Son being said to be of the same *hypostasis*! By using *hypostasis* to denote the way in which God is three, and reserving *ousia* for the way in which he is one, Basil opened the way for clearer language to speak of the Trinity and thus of the internal **processions**.

The Son Is Inseparable from the Father

Basil strongly defended the Son as inseparable from the Father, against the pneumatomachian refusal to recognize the Son or the Spirit as together with the Father.[76] In nature the Son is with the Father, Basil insists, acting inseparably from the will of the Father.[77]

The Works of the Spirit Evidence His Nature

The commonly accepted doctrine concerning the Holy Spirit, Basil continues, is that he is of "the highest nature[,] . . . a necessary, intellectual substance that is infinite in power, unlimited in greatness, immeasurable by times or ages. . . . He perfects others, but himself lacks nothing. . . . He is the source of life[,] . . . complete all at once[,] . . . present everywhere. . . . He fills all things with power"—all terms and descriptions that can apply only to God. Those who are cleansed, he makes spiritual by fellowship with himself and conveys the gifts of "unending joy, remaining in God, kinship with God, and the highest object of desire, becoming God."[78]

74. Basil of Caesarea, *Holy Spirit*, 1.3–4. See to 4.6; *PG*, 32:72–73.
75. Basil of Caesarea, *Holy Spirit*, 5.7; *PG*, 32:77–81.
76. Basil of Caesarea, *Holy Spirit*, 6.13–14; *PG*, 32:88–89.
77. Basil of Caesarea, *Holy Spirit*, 7.16–8.20; *PG*, 32:93–105.
78. Basil of Caesarea, *Holy Spirit*, 9.22–23; *PG*, 32:108–9.

The Spirit Is Ranked with God

The Holy Spirit is ranked by our Lord with the Father and the Son in the baptismal formula (Matt. 28:19). What closer conjunction can there be than this? Basil asks. Our salvation is established in baptism through the Father and the Son and the Holy Spirit.[79] Thus the Spirit is ranked with God, inseparable from the Father and the Son "on account of the communion of nature (ἐκ φύσεως κοινωνίαν)."[80] This fellowship—possibly, some suggest, indicating that Basil had in mind a looser union—is evident in the work of creation. Here the **original cause** of all things made is the Father, the creative cause is the Son, and the perfecting cause the Holy Spirit. Yet the source of all existing things is "one, which makes through the Son, and which perfects in the Spirit." The work of all three (the Lord, the Word, the Spirit) is lacking in nothing, whether taken singularly or together.[81] This inseparable action entails a common **being**. The inseparable conjunction of the Holy Spirit with the Father and the Son is seen in that, referring to 1 Corinthians 2:8–11, "he is said to be related to God as our spirit is to each of us."[82] He is to be numbered *with* the Father and the Son, not under them as the heretics allege.[83]

The Monarchy Demonstrates That God Is One and That the Relations of the Three Are Distinct

This does not mean that there are three gods, for while the persons are distinct, they are not additions in a numerical sequence. We confess "the particularizing property of the persons and we stay

79. Basil of Caesarea, *Holy Spirit*, 10.24–26; *PG*, 32:109–13.

80. Basil of Caesarea, *Holy Spirit*, 13.30; 16.37; cf. 11.27; 23.54; *PG*, 32:120–21, 133, 113–16, 168–69. Beeley remarks that Gregory of Nazianzus never used communion language in relation to the intra-Trinitarian relations. Christopher A. Beeley, "The Holy Spirit in the Cappadocians: Past and Present," *Modern Theology* 26, no. 1 (January 2010): 90–119, here 100–101. This language of Basil's might undermine the assertion of indivisibility. Basil died, however, before the full resolution of the crisis and before Gregory's greatest work on the Spirit in his *Theological Orations*. But the phrase could be rendered as "common nature" or "commonality of nature." See note 91 below.

81. Basil of Caesarea, *Holy Spirit*, 16.38; *PG*, 32:136–40.

82. Basil of Caesarea, *Holy Spirit*, 16.40; *PG*, 32:141–44.

83. Basil of Caesarea, *Holy Spirit*, 17.41–43; *PG*, 32:144–48; Basil of Caesarea, *Letters*, 125; 159.2; *PG*, 32:545–52, 620–21.

within the monarchy." These are distinct persons, but there is only one object of worship, the one God. The Holy Spirit is one "joined through the one Son to the one Father, and through himself, he completes the famed and blessed Trinity."[84] The Spirit in his relations with the Father, however, is distinct from the Son.

Basil, like Athanasius, was concerned to offset the argument of skeptics that by asserting deity of the Spirit, he was positing a second Son.[85] The Holy Spirit is "from God" not in the way in which all things are from him, but "comes forth from God, not begottenly as the Son does, but as breath of his mouth." Basil distinguished this from human realities; this was to be seen in a way appropriate to God. The mode of **generation** is beyond our understanding. Styled "Spirit of Christ," he has as close a relation to the Son as to the Father.[86] He proceeds from the Father and is God, not something created or a mere minister of God.[87] Thus, according to nature, there is a movement from the Father through the Son to the Spirit, seen in creation and grace, while in terms of our knowledge of God we move in the reverse direction, from the Spirit through the Son to the Father. This order is not that of three separate beings in a hierarchy, which would effectively be polytheism.[88] Basil argued that the Spirit is in status God, for he has the same titles and shares the same works as the Father and the Son.[89] On the other side of the spectrum, his use of the preposition *with* in his doxology refuted Sabellianism by distinguishing the *hypostases*. The preposition affirms simultaneously "the particularity of the persons and the inseparability of their communion."[90] "He who fails to confess the community of **essence** (τὸ κοινὸν τῆς οὐσίας) . . . falls into polytheism [and] he who refuses to grant the distinction of the *hypostases* is carried away into Judaism."

84. Basil of Caesarea, *Holy Spirit*, 18.45; *PG*, 32:152; Basil of Caesarea, *The Hexaemeron*, 2.6; *PG*, 29:41–44.

85. Ayres, *Nicaea and Its Legacy*, 217.

86. Basil of Caesarea, *Holy Spirit*, 18.46; *PG*, 32:152–53.

87. Basil of Caesarea, *Letters*, 125; 159.2; *PG*, 32:545–52, 620–21.

88. Basil of Caesarea, *Holy Spirit*, 18.47; *PG*, 32:153.

89. Basil of Caesarea, *Holy Spirit*, 19.48–49. See 21.52; 23.54; *PG*, 32:156–60, 164–65, 168–69; Basil of Caesarea, *Letters*, 90.2; *PG*, 32:473–76.

90. Basil of Caesarea, *Holy Spirit*, 25.59; *PG*, 32:176–77.

Merely enumerating the persons is insufficient, for we must confess each person to have a natural existence in real *hypostasis*.[91] Thus, Basil insisted on the oneness in being of the Spirit with the Father and the Son, together with the distinction of *hypostases*; none of the three is subordinate to the others, but the Father is still the source or ultimate principle of the hypostatic relations. In talking of a "community of essence," however, Basil's language might allow for the possibility of a looser union than perhaps Athanasius would have allowed. But τὸ κοινὸν τῆς ουσίας can be rendered as "common essence." Moreover, read in the context of the earlier part of the letter, it is clear that Basil did not intend to posit a loose relation, since he was emphatic that "the Father and the Son and the Holy Spirit are the same in nature and one divinity (φύσις μὲν ἡ αὐτὴ, καὶ θεότης μία)."[92]

The Holy Spirit in Worship and Sanctification

Finally, Basil returned to where he started, with worship and sanctification. In a remarkable figure of speech, he wrote that the Holy Spirit is "the place of those being made holy[,] . . . the proper place for true worship." Referring to John 4:21–24, the place of Christian worship is the Holy Spirit, for "the Spirit is truly the place of the saints, and the saint is the proper place for the Holy Spirit, as he offers himself for indwelling with God and is called a temple of God." The Spirit is in the saints in different kinds of ways, but in relation to the Father and the Son he is not so much in them as with them, denoting that he, together with the Father and the Son, is to be worshiped and glorified.[93] Thus, even in our own worship, the Holy Spirit is inseparable from the Father and the Son.

The Limitations of Human Thought and Language

Basil insisted, in a letter to Gregory of Nazianzus, that no theological term is adequate to the thought of the speaker, for language is too

91. Basil of Caesarea, *Letters*, 210.5; *PG*, 32:773–77. The translation is from *NPNF*², 8:250. It could be rendered as "common essence." See G. W. H. Lampe, ed., *A Patristic Greek Lexicon* (Oxford: Clarendon Press, 1961), 761.

92. Basil of Caesarea, *Letters*, 210.5; *PG*, 32:773 (my translation).

93. Basil of Caesarea, *Holy Spirit*, 26.62–64; *PG*, 32:184; see 181–85.

weak to act in the service of objects of thought. Yet in turn, our thought itself—let alone our language—is too weak for the reality. Nevertheless, we are compelled to give an answer about God to those who love the Lord.[94] Basil's recognition of the limitations of human thought and language contributed to the relaxation of the strict semantic usage of the technical terminology that had bedeviled the Trinitarian question. As with Athanasius, he recognized that the claims of truth are paramount and that human language and logic must bow before it.

Ousia and *Hypostasis*

Thus, Basil made the vital move of disengaging *ousia* and *hypostasis*.[95] He wrote to Count Terentius that "*ousia* has the same relation to *hypostasis* as the common has to the particular." *Ousia* is common, like goodness or Godhead, "while *hypostasis* is contemplated in the special property of Fatherhood, Sonship, or the power to sanctify." These are perfect, complete, and real *hypostases*, while the *homoousion*, the identical being, is preserved in the unity of the Godhead.[96] Thus, he used *ousia* for the one indivisible being of God and *hypostasis* for the three "persons." This was a major step forward, and it helped in finding a way out of the conceptual maze that had been created by the varieties of ways in which these words had been used.

By his comparison of general to particular, however, Basil may have left the door open for a generic view of God, and a comparison to three men sharing a common human nature. He wrote to his friend Amphilochius that "the distinction between *ousia* and *hypostasis* is the same as that between the general and the particular." With God we confess one essence but a particular *hypostasis*, so that our conception of Father, Son, and Holy Spirit may be without confusion and clear. If we have no idea of the separate characteristics of fatherhood, sonship, and sanctification but form our conception

94. Basil of Caesarea, *Letters*, 7; *PG*, 32:244–45.

95. Occasionally Basil writes of *phūsis* rather than *ousia*, and *prosōpon* rather than *hypostasis*.

96. Basil of Caesarea, *Letters*, 214.4; *PG*, 32:789. See Dragos A. Giulea, "Divine Being's Modulations: *Ousia* in the Pro-Nicene Context of the Fourth Century," *SVTQ* 59, no. 3 (2015): 307–37.

of God from the general idea of existence, we cannot give a sound account of our faith. We must therefore confess the faith "by adding the particular to the common."[97]

Beeley argues that Basil's Trinitarianism was *homoiousian*, which affirmed a likeness of being among the *hypostases*, rather than identity of being; he was basically an antimodalist and stopped short of being a *homoousian*. He had an agnosticism about the Spirit's mode of origin, being clear only that he was not created, so Beeley considers. He adds that the main sphere of the Spirit's operation is sanctification. Basil had a generic view of the divine nature—the *ousia-hypostasis* distinction based on a distinction between the common and the particular. Nor did he have a strong view of the monarchy of the Father.[98] While this is true, Beeley may be a little harsh. Basil certainly recognized that the Spirit was one with the Father and the Son and possessed all the attributes of God. He had not worked out the full ramifications.[99]

Gregory of Nyssa (A.D. 335–95)

Basil's brother Gregory was bishop of Nyssa from 372 and present at the Council of Constantinople in 381.[100] He wrote a vast work,

97. Basil of Caesarea, *Letters*, 236.6; *PG*, 32; R. P. C. Hanson, *The Search for the Christian Doctrine of God: The Arian Controversy 318–81* (Edinburgh: T&T Clark, 1988), 691–92, 696–99; Studer, *Trinity*, 142–43; Bertrand de Margerie, *The Christian Trinity in History*, trans. Edmund J. Fortman, Studies in Historical Theology 1 (Petersham, MA: St. Bede's Publications, 1982), 99–104. For a discussion of the extent to which Basil used the idea of relations, later seen in Aquinas, with largely negative conclusions, see Xavier Morales, "Basile de Césarée est-il l'introducteur du concept de relation en théologie trinitaire?" *Revue des Études Augustiniennes* 63 (2017): 141–80.

98. Beeley, "Cappadocians," *passim*.

99. Behr presents a more evenhanded discussion of Basil. Behr, *Nicene Faith*, pt. 2, 263–324.

100. Anthony Meredith, "The Idea of God in Gregory of Nyssa," in *Studien zur Gregor von Nyssa und der Christlichen Spätantike*, ed. Hubertus R. Drobner and Christophe Klock, Supplements to Vigiliae Christianae 12 (Leiden: Brill, 1990), 127–47; G. Christopher Stead, "Why Not Three Gods? The Logic of Gregory of Nyssa's Trinitarian Doctrine," in *Studien zur Gregor von Nyssa und der Christlichen Spätantike*, ed. Hubertus R. Drobner and Christophe Klock, Supplements to Vigiliae Christianae 12 (Leiden: Brill, 1990), 149–63; Hanson, *Search*, 715–30, 784–87; J. N. D. Kelly, *Early Christian Doctrines* (London: Adam & Charles Black, 1968), 261–62; G. L. Prestige, *God in Patristic Thought* (London: SPCK, 1959), 252–55, 260; Quasten, *Patrology*, 3:254–96.

Against Eunomius, which some recent scholarship considers to have been mostly produced after Constantinople. Beeley correctly considers him to be weak on the Trinity and to have made the least contribution of the three Cappadocians.[101]

Andrew Radde-Gallwitz comments that Gregory's fundamental theme is the Spirit's inseparability from the Father and the Son.[102] Gregory's case is that the Spirit's works are the same as the Father's and the Son's and that this denotes identity of nature.[103] In terms of the manner of operation, "*all* divine activities have a triadic order and . . . the Spirit plays the role of completing or accomplishing the act."[104] In *Against the Macedonians*, Gregory has much to say about the Spirit's anointing of the Son in his incarnate ministry, which, he says, indicates that there is no gap between them. The Son is King by nature, and the dignity of kingship is the Holy Spirit.[105] For Gregory, "the Spirit's deity is shown in his activity within human lives."[106]

In *On the Holy Trinity and of the Godhead of the Holy Spirit to Eustathius*, probably written in the year before Constantinople, Gregory argues in a similar vein, saying that we know God not from his essence but from his works. The works of the three persons are one, and so we conclude that their nature is one. These works are inseparable. The Trinity is one Godhead. It follows that the Son is inseparable from the Holy Spirit.[107]

Around the same time, in *On the Holy Spirit against the Followers of Macedonius*, Gregory says that the Holy Spirit is of the same rank as the Father and the Son, exactly identical with them in status, and so equal honor with the other two persons is his due. The three are inseparable, a perfect Trinity, eternally distinct but mutually indwelling.[108]

101. Beeley, "Cappadocians," 105–8.

102. Andrew Radde-Gallwitz, *Gregory of Nyssa's Doctrinal Works: A Literary Study* (Oxford: Oxford University Press, 2018), 73.

103. Radde-Gallwitz, *Doctrinal Works*, 110.

104. Radde-Gallwitz, *Doctrinal Works*, 73.

105. Radde-Gallwitz, *Doctrinal Works*, 74, citing *Against the Macedonians*, 15–16.

106. Radde-Gallwitz, *Doctrinal Works*, 230.

107. *NPNF*[2], 5:326–30; *PG*, 46:235; *PG*, 32:683–94, where it is erroneously listed as Letter 189 of Basil.

108. *NPNF*[2], 5:315–19; *PG*, 45:1301–33.

Hence, "we are not to think of the Father as ever parted from the Son, nor to look for the Son as separate from the Holy Spirit." Again, in the same place, "the fountain of power is the Father, and the power of the Father is the Son, and the spirit of that power is the Holy Spirit; and creation entirely . . . is the finished work of that divine power . . . beginning from the Father, advancing through the Son, and completed in the Holy Spirit."[109] Consequently, "the Holy Spirit is to be apprehended as joined to the Father and Son," since "except for the distinction of order and person, no variation in any point is to be apprehended."[110] Neither here nor elsewhere does he use "*homoousios* of the Spirit" (for that matter, neither does the Council of Constantinople).[111] But he says all that needs to be said to reach that conclusion.[112]

In *Against Eunomius*, Gregory says that there is one first cause, the Father. The relations of the three he likens to a causal chain of dependence, although he qualifies this by adding that there is no interval between them, for they exist simultaneously, like the sun and a ray of light streaming from it. There is no difference between one light and the other, for both are completely perfect. Hence, there is a very clear order,[113] but one admitting no thought of discord, for the three are coeternal, mutually indwelling one another.[114] Indeed, the expressions "light from light [and] . . . true God from true God" in the creed refer to the Son's "being what the other is, except being that Father," pointing simultaneously to personal distinctions and to identity of being. Since Gregory wrote this within two years after the Council of Constantinople, it is a valuable commentary on phrases that have embedded themselves in the consciousness of the church, East and West, understanding this order (*taxis*) as fully compatible with the oneness of being of the Trinity.[115]

109. Gregory of Nyssa, *On the Holy Spirit against the Followers of Macedonius*, 15; *NPNF*², 5:319–20.

110. Gregory of Nyssa, *Against the Followers of Macedonius*, 16; *NPNF*², 5:320.

111. Hanson, *Search*, 786.

112. Studer, *Trinity*, 152; Kelly, *Doctrines*, 261–63.

113. Gregory of Nyssa, *Against Eunomius*, 1.34–36.

114. Gregory of Nyssa, *Against Eunomius*, 1.42; 2:2.

115. Gregory of Nyssa, *Against Eunomius*, 3.4. Gregory refers to a creed, citing

So much is clear too from Gregory's teaching on the full mutual relations of the Father and the Son: "Thus we conceive no gap between the anointed Christ and his anointing, . . . but as there is contemplated from all eternity in the Father the Son, . . . so there is contemplated in him the Holy Spirit. . . . For which reason we say that to the holy disciples the mystery of godliness was committed in a form expressing at once union and distinction."[116] This finds expression in worship, where the corollaries of the full mutual indwelling of the three in the one being of God are evident. When the Father is worshiped, so are the Spirit and the Son. Since the Spirit has the same status as the Father and the Son, we worship all three simultaneously. Again, in their mutual indwelling each of the three seeks the glory of the others. There is "a revolving circle of glory from like to like. The Son is glorified by the Spirit; the Father is glorified by the Son; again the Son has his glory from the Father; and the Only-begotten thus becomes the glory of the Spirit. . . . In like manner . . . faith completes the circle, and glorifies the Son by means of the Spirit, and the Father by means of the Son."[117] Worship of any of the three is worship of all three and thus worship of the one.[118]

Gregory feels obliged to defend himself against the slur of **tritheism** in his short but intriguing work *On "Not Three Gods" to Ablabius*, which G. Christopher Stead considers is written sometime after Constantinople.[119] Again he stresses one inseparable operation of the Trinity in which all three work—from the Father, through the Son, perfected in the Holy Spirit.[120] In this work Gregory responds to Ablabius's suggestion that the Trinity is comparable to three men's sharing a common human nature. This analogy follows the generic definition of *ousia* and *hypostasis* that Basil propounded and Gregory himself accepts. The problems are obvious. There are a

---

wording common to Nicaea (N) and Constantinople (C). But he omits, as C does, the phrase in N "God of God."

116. Gregory of Nyssa, *Against Eunomius*, 2.2; see also 4.8.

117. *NPNF*², 5:324.

118. On mutual indwelling, see Verna Harrison, "Perichoresis in the Greek Fathers," *SVTQ* 35, no. 1 (1991): 53–65.

119. Stead, "Three Gods?"; *NPNF*², 5:27; *PG*, 45:115–36.

120. See Swete, *Holy Spirit*, 249–50.

vast range of possible men who exist, but only three and ever three persons of the Trinity, no more, no fewer. Moreover, the Trinitarian persons indwell one another, which human beings cannot do, for they are separate and autonomous entities. The analogy points to tritheism, not the Trinity. He explains the weaknesses of the analogy further in his treatise *To the Greeks (about Common Notions)*,[121] but here he insists to Ablabius that the works of the Trinity are indivisible. None of the persons works by himself in isolation from the others. Every work of God is originated from the Father, proceeds through the Son, and is perfected in the Holy Spirit. Yet these are not three different things but one and the same work of God. Moreover, this united action precludes any possibility of referring to God in the plural. While the Father is the cause, this refers not to God's essence but rather to "the difference in manner of existence." We do not divide the essence but simply indicate that the Son exists by generation and the Father without generation. So "the idea of cause differentiates the persons of the Holy Trinity," while the divine nature (essence, being) is "unchangeable and undivided" and is to be referenced in the singular.[122]

Gregory of Nazianzus (c. A.D. 330–90)[123]

Gregory is called by the Eastern church "the theologian," a title shared with the apostle John alone. A friend of Basil, Gregory had a

121. *PG*, 45:180–81. It is effectively refuted by Gregory of Nazianzus, *Oration 31*, 15; *PG*, 36:149. There is considerable uncertainty about whether this is a genuine composition of Gregory. Radde-Gallwitz, *Doctrinal Works*, 123–28.

122. *NPNF*^{2}, 5:336, see 333–36; Studer, *Trinity*, 143–44. See also Gregory of Nyssa, *Against Eunomius*, 2.2–3; 7.4; *PG*, 32:325–40. Differing assessments of the contours of Gregory's Trinitarianism can be seen in Lucian Turcescu, *Gregory of Nyssa and the Concept of Divine Persons* (Oxford: Oxford University Press, 2005), who stresses relationality and communion in the context of perfect unity, and Radde-Gallwitz, *Doctrinal Works*, 32–163, whose approach is literary, textual, and contextual, and who considers that Gregory was more focused on the indivisible unity and **energies**.

123. For the first biography of Gregory in English, see John A. McGuckin, *St. Gregory of Nazianzus: An Intellectual Biography* (Crestwood, NY: St. Vladimir's Seminary Press, 2001). The volume contains an extensive bibliography of secondary sources. On Gregory's doctrine of the Trinity, in addition to the general works already cited, see Thomas F. Torrance, *Trinitarian Perspectives: Toward Doctrinal Agreement* (Edinburgh: T&T Clark, 1988), 21–40; Quasten, *Patrology*, 3:236–54.

wide education. Ordained in 361, he was briefly bishop of Constantinople, presiding for a while at the council. In 381 at Constantinople, he preached five sermons (the *Theological Orations*) that permanently established his reputation.[124]

The fifth and final discourse, on the Holy Spirit, is the jewel in Gregory's crown. Here the *pneumatomachii* (fighters against the Spirit) were the problem. Their tactic, common to heretics at various times, was biblical fundamentalism. The Arians, Eunomians, and **Macedonians** all appealed to Scripture, contending that the pro-Nicenes used unscriptural terms. "Time and again you repeat the argument about not being in the Bible," Gregory complains. He points out that the fathers, in their handling of the Bible, "saw inside the written text to its inner meaning."[125] Instead, the heretics' "love for the letter is a cloak for irreligion."[126] Scripture uses metaphors and figures of speech. Slavery to a literal interpretation is an erroneous exegetical and theological method.[127] In fact, the heretics' favorite terms for God, "**unbegotten**" and "unoriginated," are not in the Bible at all![128]

Gregory, in common with previous fathers, argued for the Spirit's deity from his works, specifically from **deification**. Beeley also makes this point, stating that "the knowledge of the Holy Spirit [for Gregory] derives directly from the Spirit's saving work of divinization."[129] In salvation we are made God, but if the Holy Spirit is not from eternity, how can he make me God, or join me with the Godhead?[130]

Confusion over the status of the Spirit was rife: "Among our own experts, some took the Holy Spirit as an active process, some

124. *NPNF*², 7:280.

125. Gregory of Nazianzus, *Oration 31*, 21; *PG*, 36:156–57. Citations from *Oration 31* are from Frederick Williams and Lionel Wickham, *St. Gregory of Nazianzus: On God and Christ* (Crestwood, NY: St. Vladimir's Seminary Press, 2002).

126. Gregory of Nazianzus, *Oration 31*, 3; *PG*, 36:136–37.

127. Gregory of Nazianzus, *Oration 31*, 21–24; *PG*, 36:156–60.

128. Gregory of Nazianzus, *Oration 31*, 23; *PG*, 36:157–60.

129. Christopher A. Beeley, *Gregory of Nazianzus on the Trinity and the Knowledge of God: In Your Light Shall We See Light* (Oxford: Oxford University Press, 2008), 153–86, here 176.

130. Gregory of Nazianzus, *Oration 31*, 4; *PG*, 36:137.

as a creature, some as God. Others were agnostic on the point out of reverence, as they put it, for Scripture, which has given no clear revelation either way. On these grounds they offer him neither worship nor disrespect; they take up a sort of halfway (or should I say 'a thoroughly pitiful?') position about him."[131]

His opponents had asked Gregory to make clear definitions, supposing human logic capable of unfolding the truth about God. He responded that with the procession of the Spirit, as the **begetting** of the Son, language about God cannot be understood in a **univocal** sense.[132] Consequently, we cannot define the procession of the Spirit and the generation of the Son: "What then is 'proceeding'? You explain the ingeneracy of the Father and I will give you a biological account of the Son's begetting and the Spirit's proceeding—and let us go mad, the pair of us[,] for prying into God's secrets."[133]

How, then, does the Spirit differ from the Son? Their **properties** (unbegotten, begotten, proceeding), which concern their relations, have given them their names (Father, Son, Holy Spirit) "to safeguard the distinctness of the three hypostases within the single nature of the Godhead." These properties affect their relations, not the one identical *ousia*. There are "no grounds for any deficiency, for any subordination in being."[134]

Gregory, reflecting the language of John's Gospel, here coined a new word (*procession*) for the distinctive property of the third person. "What, then? Is the Spirit God? Certainly. Is he consubstantial [*homoousios*])? Yes, if he is God."[135] Gregory had mentioned this beforehand in an early episcopal sermon,[136] and in another sermon

131. Gregory of Nazianzus, *Oration 31*, 5; *PG*, 36:137.

132. Gregory of Nazianzus, *Oration 31*, 7; *PG*, 36:140–41.

133. Gregory of Nazianzus, *Oration 31*, 8; *PG*, 36:141. Beeley considers that Gregory develops the idea of the procession of the Holy Spirit, in contrast to Basil, who professed ignorance. Beeley, *Gregory of Nazianzus*, 202. Gregory's comments here belie this claim.

134. Gregory of Nazianzus, *Oration 31*, 9; *PG*, 36:141–44; Gregory of Nazianzus, *Oration on the Holy Lights*, 39.11–13; *PG*, 36:345–49.

135. Gregory of Nazianzus, *Oration 31*, 10; *PG*, 36:144.

136. "Baptism and the anointing of the head with oil, which is perfected [completed] in the Father almighty, and the only-begotten Logos, and the Holy Spirit, who is also God." Gregory of Nazianzus, *Oration 12*, 6; *PG*, 35:849 (my translation).

preached shortly after the Council of Constantinople, he was even more emphatic.[137] Whereas Basil and his brother had a reluctance to say this openly, possibly for fear of alienating potential supporters, there is no hesitation with Gregory.[138] Gregory articulated the deity of the Holy Spirit from the start, in a Trinitarian context.[139] Unlike Basil, he never wrote of a mere "communion" in terms of the intra-Trinitarian relations.[140] These were revolutionary statements.

Appropriately, Gregory turned to consider worship. Some had questioned the Spirit's deity on the grounds that there is no record of anyone praying to the Spirit. Gregory affirms that the Spirit is the one *in whom* we worship and pray. Thus, prayer to the Spirit is, in effect, the Spirit offering prayer or adoration to himself. The adoration of the one is adoration of the three, because of the equality of honor and deity among the three.[141]

The questions of the deity of the Son and the Holy Spirit are connected—once we acknowledge the former, the other follows.[142] "We have one God because there is a single Godhead. Though there are three objects of belief, they derive from the single whole and have reference to it. They do not have degrees of being God or degrees of priority over against one another . . . but the Godhead exists undivided in beings divided [here Gregory means 'distinct']. . . . When we look at the Godhead, the primal cause, the sole sovereignty, we have a mental picture of the single whole, certainly. But when we look at the three in whom the Godhead exists . . . we have

137. "These are to be worshipped; the Father, the Son, and the Holy Spirit, one deity: God the Father, God the Son, God (unless this disturbs your stomach) the Holy Spirit, one nature in three 'properties,' understandings, perfections, distinctness, different in number but by no means in deity." Gregory of Nazianzus, *Oration 33*, 16; *PG*, 36:236 (my translation).

138. Basil was a bishop, monastic organizer, and church politician; Gregory was a scholar who, while serving for a time as a bishop, was unsuited to public life and lacked diplomatic skills. This may go some way to explaining the difference in explicit treatment of the Spirit by the two.

139. Beeley, "Cappadocians," 99–100.

140. Beeley, "Cappadocians," 100–101.

141. Gregory of Nazianzus, *Oration 31*, 12; *PG*, 36:145–48.

142. Gregory of Nazianzus, *Oration 31*, 13; *PG*, 36:148.

three objects of worship."[143] This point that no one of the three is more God than the others is vital, for Gregory undercut any idea that because the Father is the first principle, the Son or the Spirit derives his deity from the Father. He avoided the idea of a causal chain of dependence that Basil and his brother implied. The monarchy, the first cause, is the Godhead, and is one. So, as John Calvin was to point out, each is God in himself. "Each of the trinity is in entire unity, as much with himself as with the partnership, by identity of being and power."[144] As Ayres suggests, Gregory's emphasis is the harmony of unity and diversity in God.[145] As Gregory mentioned in *Oration 28*, the Godhead is "one in its distinctions and distinct in its connectedness."[146]

Gregory's reasons for the deity of the Spirit are primarily that his works prove him to be God. He shares with the Son in work of creation and resurrection, and is the author of regeneration. He deifies us in baptism.[147]

Hence, the Holy Spirit "always existed, exists, and always will exist."[148] He has no beginning or end, is everlastingly ranged with the Father and the Son, "ever being partaken but not partaking; . . . deifying, not being deified; . . . invisible, eternal, **incomprehensible**, unchangeable, . . . all-powerful . . . ; life and life-giver; . . . the Lord, . . . builder of his temple, working as he wills; . . . by whom the Father is known and the Son is glorified: and by whom *alone* he is known." Thus, "all that the Father has the Son has also, except being unbegotten; . . . all that the Son has, the Spirit has also, except the generation. And these two matters do not divide the substance, . . . but rather are divisions within the substance."[149]

Gregory ingeniously points to the progressive historical outworking of revelation to explain the comparative reticence of

143. Gregory of Nazianzus, *Oration 31*, 14; *PG*, 36:148–49.

144. Gregory of Nazianzus, *Oration 31*, 16; *PG*, 36:149–52.

145. Ayres, *Nicaea and Its Legacy*, 45–47.

146. Gregory of Nazianzus, *Oration 28*, 1.

147. Gregory of Nazianzus, *Oration 41*, 14; *NPNF*[2], 7:384, where he cites Pss. 33:6; 104:30; and Job 28:4.

148. Gregory of Nazianzus, *Oration 41*, 9; *NPNF*[2], 7:382.

149. Gregory of Nazianzus, *Oration 41*, 9; *NPNF*[2], 7:382.

Scripture on the Spirit: "The old covenant made clear proclamation of the Father, a less definite one of the Son. The new covenant made the Son manifest and gave us a glimpse of the Spirit's Godhead. At the present time, the Spirit resides amongst us, giving us a clearer manifestation of himself than before. It was dangerous for the Son to be preached openly, when the Godhead of the Father was still unacknowledged. It was dangerous, too, for the Holy Spirit to be made (and here I use a rather rash expression) an extra burden, when the Son had not been received."[150] In *Oration 41* on Pentecost, he speaks of the Holy Spirit's working on, in, and with various Old Testament figures. Then in Christ there were three distinct stages: before the passion, after the resurrection, and since the ascension. The first made him known indistinctly, the second more expressly, the third more perfectly.[151]

Returning to *Oration 31*, now, in our present era, worship and baptism establish the Spirit's deity, for we "worship the Father as God, the Son as God, the Holy Spirit as God—'three personalities, one Godhead undivided in glory, honor, substance, and sovereignty,' as one inspired saint of recent times wisely expressed it. . . . Were the Spirit not to be worshipped, how could he deify me through baptism? If he is to be worshipped, why not adored? And if to be adored, how can he fail to be God?"[152] Gregory had a clear grasp of the distinct persons while holding firmly to the unity of the indivisible Godhead. For him, the Trinity is not an abstract puzzle but the heart of the Christian faith and the center of true worship. "But when I say God, I mean Father, Son, and Holy Spirit."[153]

Constantinople I (A.D. 381)

Compared with the Creed of Nicaea (325), the declaration of the Council of Constantinople, known popularly as the Nicene Creed, is

150. Gregory of Nazianzus, *Oration 31*, 26; *PG*, 36:161.

151. Gregory of Nazianzus, *Oration 41*, 11; *NPNF*², 7:383.

152. Gregory of Nazianzus, *Oration 31*, 28; *PG*, 36:164–65.

153. Gregory of Nazianzus, *Oration on the Theophany, or Birthday of Christ*, 38.8; *PG*, 36:320.

particularly notable for additional clauses on the Holy Spirit, which we will expound in chapter 4.

> [We believe] in the Holy Spirit, the Lord and life-giver, who proceeds from the Father, who is worshipped and glorified together with the Father and the Son, who spoke by the prophets . . .

In these clauses, a number of things are asserted. The Spirit is the Lord and giver of life, sharing indivisibly with the Father and the Son in creation, providence, and grace. The Spirit proceeds from the Father and is worshiped and glorified together with the Father and the Son, affirming his deity. The Spirit spoke by the prophets. Moreover, the following section on the church and sacraments is an outflow of the comment on the Holy Spirit as the Lord and giver of life:

> And in one holy, catholic and apostolic Church;
> We confess one baptism for the forgiveness of sins;
> We wait for the resurrection of the dead and the life of the coming age. Amen.

The creed has four main sections—on the Father, the Son, the Holy Spirit, and finally the church and sacraments. It does not explicitly state that the Holy Spirit is *homoousios* with the Father and the Son. Yet it follows from everything it states about the Spirit. Moreover, the following year the Synod of Rome pronounced on the matter in its synodical letter, leaving no doubt. The Spirit is "one being, uncreated and of the identical being and eternal trinity."[154] Its series of anathemas undergird the point. These are pronounced against any who deny the eternal generation of the Son from the substance of the Father or that the Holy Spirit is also from the divine substance (*Si quis non dixerit, Spiritum Sanctum de Patre esse vere ac proprie, sicut Filium, de divina substantia et Deum verum: haereticum est*)

154. οὐσια μία ἀκτιστῷ καὶ ὁμοουσιῷ καὶ συναιδιῷ τριαδι. J. Alberigo et al., eds., *Concilium ecumenicorum decreta*, 25–30.

and against any who deny the omniscience and omnipresence of the Holy Spirit, or who say that the Spirit was created, or those who do not say that all things were made through the Son and the Spirit.[155] Again, anyone is anathematized who does not say that the Father and the Son and the Holy Spirit are one divinity (*unam divinitatem*), power, majesty, glory, and dominion, with one will; such a one *haereticus est*. This is because the Father, Son, and Holy Spirit are one divinity and power (*unam divinitatem et potentiam*), one God (*unum Deum*).[156]

Key Terms

Arians
Arius
attributes
begetting
begotten
being
creation *ex nihilo*
deification
energies
essence
Eunomius
generation
gnosticism
Heterousians
Homoians
homoousios
hypostasis
incomprehensible
Macedonians
modalism
monarchianism
monarchy
nature
ontologically
order
original cause
ousia
participation
persons
phūsis
pneumatomachii
procession
processions
properties
relations
Sabellianism
subordinationism
substance
tritheism
unbegotten
univocal

155. Peter Hünermann, *Heinrich Denzinger: Kompendium der Glaubensbekentnisse und Kirchlichen Lehrentscheidungen*, Aktualisierte Auflage 38 (Freiburg im Breisgau: Herder, 1999), 87.
156. Hünermann, *Heinrich Denzinger*, 88.

Questions for Reflection

1. Consider biblical and historical factors that led the church to consider the status of the Son before sustained attention was directed to the status of the Holy Spirit.
2. What implications can you draw from the confession that the Spirit is to be worshiped together with the Father and the Son? How does the single act of worship of the Trinity bring the three *hypostases* to distinct and indivisible expression?

2

Consolidation and Controversy

Augustine

Augustine's teaching on the Holy Spirit and the Trinity is found in a range of his works.[1] His treatise *De Trinitate* is the best known, but his *Tractates on the Gospel of John* are crucial too. While his Trinitarianism has often been contrasted with the Cappadocians', his intention was to express his agreement with the settlement they had brokered at Constantinople, not to diverge from it. Yet some features are different. The most striking nuance in Augustine is his claim that the Spirit proceeds from the Father and the Son as from a single source. Constantinople I had simply affirmed that the Spirit proceeds from the Father, without making any comment, explicit or implied, in reference to the Son. We saw that Athanasius had written that the Spirit is the image of the Son as the Son is the image of the Father. Cyril, a contemporary of Augustine, wrote that the Spirit proceeds from the Father in the Son. These two Alexandrians could be said to have held similar views to Augustine, although there is no evidence that Augustine had any contact with Cyril, nor is it certain that he was aware of his writings. Lewis Ayres and Michel Barnes comment that "at a number of points we think that Augustine's pneumatology is best understood as following to logical (if very personal) conclusions positions still emergent in the previous generation."[2]

1. See Christopher R. J. Holmes, *The Holy Spirit* (Grand Rapids: Zondervan, 2015), 45–79.

2. Lewis Ayres and Michel R. Barnes, "Conclusion," *AugStud* 39, no. 2 (2008): 235–36.

The real significance in Augustine's ideas on the internal **relations** of the Trinitarian **persons** is their impact on the following centuries and the eventual emergence of the ***filioque*** clause in the Latin church. We will discuss this question shortly. This, it has been argued, went in tandem with the development of two quite distinct doctrines of salvation; the Greek church has a **pneumatocentric** soteriology, focusing on the Spirit's transforming us, while the Latin church is strongly **Christocentric**, centered on the cross and resurrection of Christ and his work representing us. These claims can be overplayed because both East and West share commitments to both aspects, although these are definitely distinctive emphases.

Indivisibility—Inseparable Works

Perhaps the most dominant theme in Augustine's discussion of the Trinity is its indivisibility and, as a corollary, the inseparable operations. This was something held in common with the Cappadocians, although for Augustine it is particularly striking. This comes out strongly early in *De Trinitate*, where Augustine persistently asserts that the Father and the Son, while distinct, are indivisibly one and work inseparably in all of God's actions. While his attention is not oriented to the Spirit at this point, the Spirit is nevertheless included, and Augustine moves on to express this directly later.

The Holy Spirit as Love and as Gift

When he devotes attention expressly to the Spirit, Augustine presents the Spirit as love and as gift. In this he is looking for distinctive names for the Spirit that highlight the way in which the Bible presents him. This is something that Thomas Aquinas developed later.[3]

In keeping with this, insofar as love can be distinctly applied to the Spirit, Augustine sees him as the bond of love and union between the Father and the Son. This seems to imply that the Father and the Son need something or someone to unite them, as if in some way they are separable. If such were the case, however, it

3. Augustine, *De Trinitate*, 15.17.30–31.

would negate all that Augustine had affirmed about the indivisible union of the Trinity in the early chapters of *De Trinitate*. That cannot have been his intention. The construction has also been criticized as implying that the Holy Spirit is subordinate, as if his hypostatic identity were solely in relation to the other two. But the Trinity is inherently relational. The name Father entails Son, and vice versa. This in no way raises subordinationist questions, so why should such be posited of the Spirit when he is viewed in relation to the other two persons? A more plausible criticism is that love is not peculiar to the Spirit. Indeed, the Bible attributes love far more often to the Father (John 3:16; Rom. 5:8) and the Son (2 Cor. 5:14; Gal. 2:20). How, therefore, can it be used of the Spirit as a property distinctive to him?

More pertinent and applicable to the Spirit is the name "gift," since the New Testament ascribes the Spirit's coming to the church at Pentecost as a gift of the ascended Christ, and attributes the giving of the Spirit to the Father.[4] On the other hand, the New Testament also describes the Son as "gift," the Father's having given him up for us all (John 3:16; Rom. 8:32). Indeed, since in the sending of the Spirit at Pentecost all three *hypostases* are inseparably active, such that Jesus can say that he and the Father will come to the faithful disciples and make their permanent residence with them (John 14:23), might this not preclude singling out one of the *hypostases* in this manner? Moreover, this is to name a Trinitarian ***hypostasis*** in terms of the external works of God and could imply that God was being seen as dependent on creation, a limitation on his freedom and sovereignty.

In support of the twin claim, Matthew Levering points to the wide range of biblical references to the Spirit as the gift of the Father and the Son, and as the love of God poured into our hearts. He considers the propriety of using the names "gift" and "love" for the Spirit. While the Spirit is given those names in the economy of salvation, he agrees that it is more difficult to claim that the Spirit is *properly*—in himself—love and gift. Yet he concludes

4. Congar refers to Acts 2:37–38; 8:18–20; 10:44–46; 11:15–17; and Ephesians 4:7. Yves Congar, *I Believe in the Holy Spirit*, trans. David Smith (New York: Crossroad, 1997), 1:78–79.

that the repeated connection in Scripture between the Spirit and gift, love, and communion is a strong indication of the Spirit's distinctive **properties**.[5]

But some questions remain. Is it legitimate to search for additional names for the Spirit in a quest to find distinct hypostatic characteristics? Levering is aware of the dangers, singling out a range of authors who have gone overboard in this direction, effectively burying the Trinity in an avalanche of anthropomorphisms. His own case is that these names are clearly biblically authorized.

Even so, once again, is it valid to appropriate love to the Holy Spirit as a distinctive hypostatic characteristic when this is an attribute, belonging as all **attributes** to the **essence** and possessed indivisibly by all three *hypostases*? How does this impinge on the **simplicity** of God? Can love be distinct to the Spirit in a way that it is not to the Son or the Father?

Another question arises as to whether, in a commendable desire to know God, the boundaries of what is revealed are being pushed back further than they can go. Is it not better to adopt a sparser description? A more basic question than this follows from the principle that God alone has the right to name himself. Given that, to what extent has he revealed these as names that are distinctive of the Spirit rather than of the Father and the Son? How far should caution prevail or, on the other hand, to what extent may we probe further? There is no absolute answer to these questions in this context.

Holy Spirit

The two obvious names given to the Holy Spirit are "holy" and "spirit."[6] While these are common to all three persons, for God is both holy and Spirit, Yves Congar argues that because the names are common to both the Father and the Son, the Holy Spirit receives as his own names that are common to both.[7]

5. Matthew Levering, *Engaging the Doctrine of the Holy Spirit: Love and Gift in the Trinity and the Church* (Grand Rapids: Baker Academic, 2016), *passim*.

6. Augustine, *De Trinitate*, 15.19.37.

7. Congar, *Holy Spirit*, 1:78–79.

The Appearance of the Spirit as a Dove in Distinction from the Incarnation of the Son

In *Letter 169* to Bishop Evodius, Augustine discusses the uniqueness of the incarnation. The difference between the voice of the Father, the appearance of the Holy Spirit as a dove, and the incarnation of the Son is that the first two were temporary, rather than permanent, and were simply symbols, in contrast to the incarnation, in which the human nature was permanently assumed into real union. As a consequence of the incarnation, some things are said of the Son according to his human nature, and some according to his deity.[8]

In *De Trinitate,* Augustine explains this further. The Spirit did not beatify the wind, the fire, or the dove—any of the material elements in which he appeared—nor did he join them forever to himself and to his person. These physical things were themselves changed and adapted for the purpose of making him known on those particular occasions. Thus, we cannot call the Spirit both God and a fire, or God and a dove. On the other hand, we rightly call the Son both God and man. Moreover, the fire and the dove appeared simply for the purpose of signifying the Holy Spirit, then to disappear. The incarnation is both real and permanent.[9]

The Deity of the Spirit as a Basis for His Procession from the Father and the Son[10]

The Holy Spirit is God, equal, consubstantial, and coeternal with the Father and the Son. The three persons are clearly equal.[11] The Spirit is "a certain unutterable communion of the Father and the Son"[12] and "consubstantial love of the Father and the Son."[13] This full acknowledgment of the Spirit's coequal and consubstantial deity is

8. Augustine, *Letter 169*, 2.7; *NPNF*[1], 1:540–41; *PL*, 33:745.

9. Augustine, *De Trinitate*, 2.6.11; *PL*, 42:851–52.

10. Augustine, *De Trinitate*, 15.19.37.

11. Augustine, *De Trinitate*, 1.6.13; 7.3.6; *PL*, 42:827–28, 938–39; J. N. D. Kelly, *Early Christian Doctrines* (London: Adam & Charles Black, 1968), 272–73; Basil Studer, *Trinity and Incarnation: The Faith of the Early Church*, ed. Andrew Louth, trans. Matthias Westerhoff (Collegeville, MN: Liturgical Press, 1993), 174, 176.

12. Augustine, *De Trinitate*, 5.11.12; *PL*, 42:918–19.

13. Augustine, *John*, tractate 105; *NPNF*[1], 7:396; *PL*, 35:1904–8.

the basis that enables Augustine to develop his teaching on the twofold **procession** of the Spirit from the Father and the Son.[14]

> Yet there is good reason why in this trinity we call none Word of God but the Son, none Gift of God but the Holy Spirit, none of whom the Word is **begotten** and from whom the Holy Spirit originally (*principaliter*) proceeds, but God the Father. I add the word "originally," because we learn that the Holy Spirit proceeds also from the Son. But this is part of what is given by the Father to the Son, not as already existing without it, but given to him as all that the Father gives to his only-begotten Word, in the act of **begetting**. He is begotten in such a manner that the common gift proceeds from him also, and the Holy Spirit is Spirit of both.[15]

The Spirit proceeds from the Father *principaliter*, but in common from both the Father and the Son. Here are the seeds of the fateful *filioque* controversy. What exactly is Augustine saying? First, he carefully safeguards the place of the Father as the sole origin of the Holy Spirit.[16] Again, he does not assert that the Spirit proceeds from two sources as if from two parents (contrary to what Photios later alleged),[17] for the procession is from a single source. Yet the procession is not from an indistinguishable unity,[18] since the Spirit is *principaliter* from the Father. Nor does the Father give the Spirit to the Son to pass on, Augustine continues; rather, he gives his own life to the Son, which includes in it the outpouring of the Spirit. In this way, the Spirit is eternally and simultaneously given by the Father and the Son together. The Father as giver is not exhausted by being

14. Augustine, *De Trinitate*, 1.12.25; *PL*, 42:860–61.

15. Augustine, *De Trinitate*, 15.26.47. See also 15.26.45; 15.27.48; *PL*, 42:1092–96.

16. Augustine, *De Trinitate*, 4.20.29; *PL*, 42:908–10; Rowan Williams, "De Trinitate," in *Augustine through the Ages: An Encyclopedia*, ed. A. Fitzgerald (Grand Rapids: Eerdmans, 1999), 847.

17. Photios, *On the Mystagogy of the Holy Spirit by Saint Photios Patriarch of Constantinople*, trans. Holy Transfiguration Monastery (n.p.: Studion, 1983), 11–14.

18. Contra Stylianopoulos and many Eastern apologists; see Augustine, *De Trinitate*, 15.17.29; *PL*, 42:1081.

the Father of the Son, for in begetting the Son there is an excess of gift, and this excess is given to the Son to give in turn.[19]

On the other hand, Augustine's talk of the Spirit as the communion of the other two,[20] and as the mutual love uniting them,[21] has raised a question whether the Spirit is in fact subordinate. The answer must be negative. Augustine stresses the Spirit's **consubstantiality** at length and in almost the next section writes of him as the "consubstantial communion" of the Father and the Son.[22] The consistent teaching on the indivisibility of the Trinity and the inseparable operations, besides the eternal simultaneity of the relations, obviates any idea of sequence in which the **generation** of the Son might be seen as prior to the procession of the Spirit.[23] Indeed, Augustine considers that the reason why the New Testament often leaves the Holy Spirit out of formulae is that he is the bond of love between the Father and the Son and so inseparable.

The Procession of the Spirit from the Father and the Son

In *Tractate 99* on John 16:13, Augustine discusses whether the Holy Spirit proceeds from the Son as well as the Father. Three factors are involved, he suggests. First, the Holy Spirit is called the Spirit of the Son as well as the Spirit of the Father. This does not mean that there are two Spirits; he refers to Ephesians 4:4–6 ("one Lord," "one Spirit"). Rather, the Spirit is of both. Augustine mentions Romans 8:11 ("the Spirit of [the Father]") and Romans 8:9 ("the Spirit of Christ"), which, in the same context, clearly refer to the one Spirit.[24] While God is Spirit, referring to all three persons, he continues, the

19. Williams, "De Trinitate," 850. Lewis Ayres, *Augustine and the Trinity* (Cambridge: Cambridge University Press, 2010), 258–66, is a discussion that is crucial to grasp Augustine's understanding of the eternal relations.

20. Augustine, *De Trinitate*, 15.27.50; *PL*, 42:1096–97.

21. Augustine, *De Trinitate*, 15.17.27; *PL*, 42:1079–80.

22. Augustine, *De Trinitate*, 15.27.50; *PL*, 42:1096–97.

23. Ayres, *Augustine*, 263–64. For discussion of Augustine's treatment of the Spirit as the bond of love between the Father and the Son in terms of consonance, see Anne-Isabelle Bouton-Touboulic, "Consonance and Dissonance: The Unifying Action of the Holy Ghost in Saint Augustine," *StPatr* 61 (2013): 31–51.

24. Augustine, *On the Gospel of John*, 99.6; *NPNF*[1], 7:383.

Spirit is distinctly called the Holy Spirit. Why, therefore, should he not proceed from the Son?[25]

Second, after his resurrection Jesus breathed on his disciples and said, "Receive the Holy Spirit" (John 20:22). Augustine compares that comment with Luke 8:46, where Jesus remarks after healing the woman with the hemorrhage that "power is gone out from me." Elsewhere too the Spirit is called "power" (Luke 1:34–35; 6:19; 24:49; Acts 1:8), which leads to the conclusion that the Holy Spirit had "gone out" from Jesus and so to his procession from the Son.[26]

Third, in answer to the rejoinder that Jesus also says that the Holy Spirit proceeds from the Father (John 15:26), Augustine points out that Jesus attributes all that is his to the Father, such as his teaching (7:16). How much more is this so with the Holy Spirit? In John 15:26, Jesus also implies that "he proceeds also from me." Augustine concludes that "the Son has it from the Father that he is God [God of God], so he has it from him [the Father] that the Holy Spirit proceeds."[27]

Finally, Augustine addresses why the Holy Spirit proceeds and is not born. If the latter were the case, he says, he would be the Father's grandson and there would be two Sons. But that is to speak in human terms, whereas human and divine origins are distinct and different. Human origins occur at different times. Here the Holy Spirit proceeds from the Father and the Son simultaneously and eternally.[28]

The Holy Spirit Gives Faith, Life, and Understanding

Christopher Holmes draws attention to Homily 11 on the Gospel of John, where Augustine reflects on John 2:23–3:5. Here there is a stark contrast between Jesus' unwillingness to receive certain disciples because he knew what was in humanity on the one hand (2:23–25) and the work of the Spirit as he explains it to Nicodemus in the immediately following context. Nicodemus came to Jesus by

25. Augustine, *On the Gospel of John*, 99.7; *NPNF*[1], 7:383.

26. Augustine, *On the Gospel of John*, 99.7; *NPNF*[1], 7:384.

27. Augustine, *On the Gospel of John*, 99.8; *NPNF*[1], 7:384. See Congar, *Holy Spirit*, 1:78–79, on Augustine's treatment of John 15:26.

28. Augustine, *On the Gospel of John*, 99:9; *NPNF*[1], 7:384.

night (darkness was significant for John because it entailed evil and unbelief), implying that he was among those to whom Jesus could not entrust himself. Instead, Jesus stresses the need for the Spirit to move mysteriously and powerfully to effect a radical change akin to a resurrection; to receive Christ is to receive the Spirit in baptism (3:5).[29]

Augustine's Last Works

Barnes refers to *Contra Maximinius II*, written against a prominent **Homoian Arian** with whom Augustine had previously debated. In it Augustine comes to the crucial realization that the Holy Spirit is the Creator and consequently one with the Father and the Son. Augustine had maintained this earlier, but now was able to give a coherent reason for it.[30] We saw that this was an early theme in the fathers.

Cyril of Alexandria (A.D. 378–444)

A contemporary of Augustine but in the Greek-speaking church, Cyril held equally strong views of the relation between the Spirit and the Son as did his famous predecessor as bishop of Alexandria, Athanasius. Both make statements that appear little different from the later Latin doctrine. Congar lists a wide range of ways in which Cyril points to the relation between the Spirit and the Son in the eternal Trinity.[31] Although Cyril's Christology became definitive, neither he nor Athanasius features prominently in the Trinitarianism of later

29. Holmes, *Holy Spirit*, 46–55.

30. Michel René Barnes, "Augustine's Last Pneumatology," *AugStud* 39, no. 2 (2008): 223–34.

31. Congar lists the following factors in Cyril's understanding of the relation between the Spirit and the Son. The Holy Spirit belonged to the incarnate Word (*Adv. Nest.*, 4.1; *PG*, 76:173). The Spirit is proper to the Son *idiōn* (*Comm. Joel*, 35; *PG*, 71:377b), comes from—*ek*—the Son (*De recta fide ad Theod.*, 37; *PG*, 76:1189a; *de SS. Trin. dial.*, 7; *PG*, 75:1093a; *Comm. Ioan.*, 2; *PG*, 71:212b), and proceeds from the Son (*PG*, 75:585a, 608b, 612b–c, 76:1408b, 308d). Variously, the Spirit proceeds from the Son—*proeinai, prochoitoi* (*Adv. Nest.*, 4.1; *PG*, 76:173a–b), from the Father and the Son (*De recta fide*, 51; *PG*, 76:1408b; *de ador.*, 1; *PG*, 68:148a), and from the Father through the Son (*de ador.*, 1; *PG*, 68:148a; *Adv. Nest.*, 4.3; *PG*, 76:184d). The Spirit sanctifies Christ's humanity as he does ours (*Comm. Ioan.*, 11.11; *PG*, 74:557). He is the Spirit of the Son just as he is the Spirit of the Father (*Apol. contra Theod.*, *PG*, 76:433b–c) and makes us partakers of the divine nature (*Comm. Ioan.*, 2.239 on John 14:4). Congar, *Holy Spirit*, 3:35–36.

Orthodoxy. There is no evidence that Cyril influenced Augustine, even if the latter was aware of his writings, or vice versa. Congar is correct, however, that Cyril did not give close attention to the Spirit, since he was preoccupied with the **Nestorian** controversy surrounding the incarnation. He was more interested in stressing the deity of the Spirit than his relations to the other Trinitarian *hypostases*.[32] Neither was Cyril significantly influenced on the Spirit by Gregory of Nazianzus, Gregory Hillis argues against Christopher Beeley.[33]

In his celebrated commentary on the Gospel of John, Cyril writes, on John 14:14, that "we shall be orthodox in believing that the Son is naturally both of the Father and in the Father, and that the [sic] own Spirit of the Father and of the Son, that is, the Holy Spirit, is both of and in the Father. . . . Their gifts will be supplied to the worthy through the Son from the Father in the Spirit."[34] Again, "another Paraclete, however, is the name he gives to the Spirit that proceeds from the essence of God the Father and from that of himself,"[35] "for he is the Spirit both of God the Father and of the Son."[36] On John 14:16–17, he writes that the Spirit is supplied to the saints from the Father through the Son.[37] Later on, he repeats that the Spirit proceeds from the Father through the Son, and is his own, for all things are through the Son from the Father,[38] while on John 14:23 he agrees that "the same Spirit is of the Father and the Son." For no one can partake of the living God by any means other than that of the Spirit; "the inspired Paul at one time speaks of the Spirit as belonging to the Father, and at another as belonging to the Son: not by way of logical contradiction, but rather saying what is true of either, for it is so in

32. Congar, *Holy Spirit*, 3:36.

33. Gregory K. Hillis, "Pneumatology and Soteriology according to Gregory of Nazianzus and Cyril of Alexandria," *StPatr* 61 (2013): 187–97; Christopher A. Beeley, *Gregory of Nazianzus on the Trinity and the Knowledge of God: In Your Light Shall We See Light* (Oxford: Oxford University Press, 2008), 322.

34. Cyril of Alexandria, *Commentary on John*, Library of Fathers of the Holy Catholic Church 2 (London: Walter Smith, 1874/1885), 685.

35. Cyril of Alexandria, *John*, 688.

36. Cyril of Alexandria, *John*, 688–89.

37. Cyril of Alexandria, *John*, 689.

38. Cyril of Alexandria, *John*, 700.

fact. He says then to some: 'He that raised up Christ Jesus from the dead shall quicken also your mortal bodies through his Spirit that dwells in you.' Then again, 'And because you are sons, God sent forth the Spirit of his Son into your hearts, crying, Abba, Father.' Do you see that the same Spirit is of the Father and the Son?"[39] Commenting on John 20:22, he writes that the Spirit could come down to us only from the Father through the Son.[40] On the same text, Cyril compares Jesus' breathing the Holy Spirit on his disciples to God's breathing life into Adam in Genesis 2:7, entailing a new creation, reflecting the original work of the Spirit in creation.[41] We will note other contributions of Cyril when we consider the *filioque*.

John of Damascus (A.D. 675–749)

John's importance is, *inter alia*, because he distills the essence of the teaching of the orthodox consensus of the church fathers in his treatise *De Orthodoxa Fidei*. In our concern, he writes that the Holy Spirit proceeds from the Father and rests in the Son, equally glorified with the Father and the Son, since he is coessential and coeternal, proceeding from the Father and communicated through the Son, inseparable and indivisible from both, possessing all the qualities that the Father and the Son possess, except that of being begotten or born. The Father is without cause and unborn, and the Son is derived from the Father by generation, while the Spirit is derived from the Father not by generation but by procession. The generation of the Son and the procession of the Holy Spirit are simultaneous. "All then that the Son and the Spirit have is from the Father, even their very **being**."[42]

John was the first to apply the term ***perichorēsis*** to the Trinity. Previously it had been used of the natures of Christ. In this context, it refers to the three persons of the Trinity indwelling one another,

39. Cyril of Alexandria, *John*, 710.

40. Cyril of Alexandria, *John*, 928.

41. Cyril of Alexandria, *John*, 930–31.

42. John of Damascus, *On the Orthodox Faith*, 1.8; *NPNF*², 9/2:9; *PG*, 94:808–33. Cf. Gregory of Nazianzus, *Oration 25*; *PG*, 35:1193–225.

"occupying the same infinite divine space."[43] This follows from the basic axiom of the Trinity:

> For in these hypostatic or personal properties alone do the three holy subsistences (hypostases) differ from each other, being indivisibly divided not by essence but by the distinguishing mark of their proper and peculiar **subsistence**[:] . . . One simple essence existing in three perfect subsistences.[44]

The subsistences, or persons, are *in* one another,[45] so that we may not introduce a crowd and multitude of gods. Owing to the three subsistences, there is no compoundness or confusion; owing to their having the same essence and dwelling in one another, we recognize the indivisibility and unity of God.[46]

John carefully contrasts this with the faulty analogy of three men sharing human nature. The three human subsistences do not exist one within the other. Each is separate, having many points that divide it from the other—in space, time, thought, power, shape, form, habit, temperament, dignity, and pursuits, and above all, in that they do not dwell in one another but are separate. Thus we speak of two, three, or many men. In the case of the Trinity, it is the reverse. The three are coeternal, of identical essence, one in **energy**, goodness, will, power, and authority. "For each one of them is related as closely to the other as to itself: . . . the Father, the Son, and the Holy Spirit are one in all respects, save those of not being begotten, of birth and of procession." For, citing John 14:11, they dwell in one another, cleaving together. "For they are made one not so as to commingle, but so as to cleave to one another, and they have their being in each other (*perichoresin*) without any coalescence or commingling. Nor do the Son and the Spirit stand apart, nor are they sundered in essence. . . . For the Deity is undivided amongst things divided . . . and it is

43. Gerald Bray, *The Doctrine of God* (Leicester, UK: Inter-Varsity Press, 1993), 158.

44. John of Damascus, *On the Orthodox Faith*, 1.8; *NPNF*², 9/2:9–10; *PG*, 194:808–33.

45. Cf. Gregory of Nazianzus, *Oration 1*, 37; *PG*, 35:395–402; 36:279–308.

46. John of Damascus, *On the Orthodox Faith*, 1:8; *NPNF*², 9/2:10; *PG*, 94:808–33.

just like three suns cleaving to each other without separation and giving out light mingled and conjoined into one."[47]

This is an important stage in the history of Trinitarian doctrine. It had been thought that John was using here the work of the anonymous seventh-century monk Pseudo-Cyril, who purportedly countered a tritheistic outbreak associated with John Philoponos. But V. S. Conticello has demonstrated that Pseudo-Cyril is in fact the fourteenth-century Joseph the Philosopher, with the conclusion that the Damascene was the first to use the term *perichorēsis* of the mutual indwelling of the three persons. The *idea* of mutual indwelling had been present earlier in **Christology**, but John gave it a more developed treatment and applied it to the Trinity.[48]

Thus, the Spirit goes forth from the Father, "not in the manner of Sonship but of procession," in such a way that he does not change, since "a property is quite constant." We call him "the Spirit of the Father. And we do not speak of the Spirit as from the Son but yet we call him the Spirit of the Son . . . and we confess that he is manifested and imparted to us through the Son."[49] He is the Spirit of the Son not because he comes from him but because he comes through him. "But the Holy Spirit is not the Spirit of the Father but the Spirit of the Father as proceeding from the Father. For there is no impulse without Spirit. And we speak also of the Spirit of the Son, not as though proceeding from him, but as proceeding through him from the Father. For the Father alone is cause."[50]

47. John of Damascus, *On the Orthodox Faith*, 1:8; *NPNF*^{2}, 9/2:11; *PG*, 94:808–33. Congar writes of "inexistence," the three containing one another, and manifesting one another. Congar, *Holy Spirit*, 3:37.

48. Verna Harrison, "Perichoresis in the Greek Fathers," *SVTQ* 35, no. 1 (1991): 53–65; V. S. Conticello, "Pseudo-Cyril's De Sacrosancte Trinitate: A Compilation of Joseph the Philosopher," *Orientalia Christiana Periodica* 61 (1995): 117–29; Walter Kaspar, ed., *Lexicon Für Theologie und Kirche* (Freiburg: Herder, 1999), 8:707–8; Charles C. Twombly, *Perichoresis and Personhood: God, Christ, and Salvation in John of Damascus* (Eugene, OR: Pickwick, 2015).

49. John of Damascus, *On the Orthodox Faith*, 1.8; Swete, *Holy Spirit*, 281–86.

50. John of Damascus, *On the Orthodox Faith*, 1.12; *NPNF*^{2}, 9/2:15. Similar themes were present earlier in Maximus the Confessor, *Opusculum*, 10; *PG*, 91:136A–B; see Paul M. Blowers, *Maximus the Confessor: Jesus Christ and the Transfiguration of the World* (Oxford: Oxford University Press, 2016), 298.

Excursus: Grégoire on John of Damascus's Doctrine of the Procession of the Spirit

J. Grégoire indicates that John's use of *dia huiou* ("through") differs significantly from *ex huiou* ("from"). It rules out a causal explanation of the procession. Moreover, to argue for a temporal meaning of *dia* is poor linguistically and would have the sense of "following." John rules out a causal meaning, with the Father the first cause and the Son the **instrumental cause**, introduced with *dia*.[51] John also distinguishes between the procession from the Father, signified by *ekporeuesthia*, indicating a movement, not passivity, and *proievai*, which has a local meaning and means "to traverse."[52] Grégoire argues: "For if the Spirit comes from the Father by procession, and remains in him [the Son], in contrast to our breath which disappears into the air, it must be by penetrating the Son until he rests and remains in him at the same time as he does in the Father. In one word, the procession is *dia huiou* (John of Damascus) or the Spirit rests in the Son (pseudo-Cyril [sic]). *Dia huiou* is a dynamic expression—one is tempted to say 'genetic'—of the perichoresis; the compenetration of hypostases, the one in the other, is the static expression—the eternal result—of the procession *dia huiou*."[53] In short, for John—synthesizing the patristic teaching—the dynamic procession of the Spirit from the Father through the Son is the basis of the mutual indwelling or interpenetration of the three in the indivisible being of the Trinity.

Accordingly, the Damascene cites "the Johannine Pentecost," when Jesus breathed out the Spirit on his disciples (John 20:22). The sun produces both the ray and the radiance, the radiance

51. J. Grégoire, "La Relation Éternelle de l'Esprit Au Fils d'Aprés les Écrits de Jean de Damas," *Revue d'Histoire Ecclésiastique* 64, no. 3/4 (1969): 713–55, here 751.

52. Grégoire, "Jean de Damas," 752.

53. Grégoire, "Jean de Damas," 753 (my translation). "Si l'Esprit sort du Père par procession et demeure en lui, au contraire de notre souffle qui s'évanouit dans l'air, il faut bien que ce soit en «pénétrant» le Fils jusqu'à reposer et demeurer en lui en mème temps qu'en le Père. διὰ Υἱοῦ (Jean de Damas), ou que L'Esprit repose en le Fils (textes pseudo-cyrilliens). Le διὰ Υἱοῦ est l'expression dynamique—on serait tenté de dire «génétique» de la périchorèse, la compénétration et le sejour des hypostases l'une dans l'autre étant l'expression statique—le «résultat» éternel—de la procession διὰ Υἱοῦ."

being imparted through the ray.[54] Grégoire remarks that there was no open controversy over the *filioque* at the time John wrote, so while he refuted the phrase ἐξ υἱοῦ (*ex huiou*), he was not engaged in polemics.[55]

Grégoire sums up the teaching of the Damascene.[56] The Father is the sole cause of the Trinity. There is no division or **participation** in God. The category of **secondary causes** is not to be found in his writings. "Si le terme μοναρχία est rare, le Damascène affirme souvent l'unité de principe en Dieu."[57] The scheme *nous-logos-pneuma* dominates, expressing in one and the same movement that the Spirit reveals the Word and the Word reveals the Father, a pattern found in his *Dialogue contra les manichéens*.[58] He asserts that procession is not generation; the Spirit is not the Son of the Son. Rather, the Spirit rests in the Word and accompanies it, sharing indivisibly in his activity; he is the image and revelation of the Son (echoing Athanasius). In the procession, the Spirit comes out from the Father through the Son and diffuses himself in the Son. In God's works, the Son establishes the work from the Father and the Holy Spirit perfects it.

There is little that is polemical in John's discussion—perhaps some against Arianism and **Manichaeism** and possibly against Islam. But there is nothing against the *filioque* or Cyril. He is neither a filioquist nor a **monopatrist**—not a filioquist because he does not use causality, not a monopatrist because the procession presupposes the generation of the Word.[59] In all this, there is no separation between theology (God as he is in himself) and economy (God as he is toward us), for "Le Damascéne ne connaît pas cette séparation farouche entre économie et théologie qui caractérise la pensée byzantine ultérieuse."[60]

54. John of Damascus, *On the Orthodox Faith*, 1.8; *NPNF*², 9/2:11.

55. Grégoire, "Jean de Damas," 736.

56. Grégoire, "Jean de Damas," 754–55.

57. "Although the term *monarchia* is rare, the Damascene often affirms the unity of the *principium* in God." Grégoire, "Jean de Damas," 723.

58. Grégoire, "Jean de Damas," 731.

59. Grégoire, "Jean de Damas," 754–55.

60. "The Damascene knows nothing of this strange separation between economy and theology that characterizes later Byzantine thought." Grégoire, "Jean de Damas," 724.

In connection with John's doctrine of *perichorēsis*, the Word possesses the Spirit. The Spirit of God is "the companion of the Word and the revealer of His energy." The Spirit is not to be compared merely to the breath of our mouth, for he is "an essential power, existing in its own proper and peculiar subsistence, proceeding from the Father and resting in the Word, and shewing forth the Word, neither capable of disjunction from God in Whom it exists, and the Word whose companion it is, nor put forth to vanish into nothingness, but being in subsistence in the likeness of the Word, endowed with life, free volition, independent movement, energy, . . . having no beginning and no end. For never was the Father at any time lacking in the Word, nor the Word in the Spirit."[61]

Procession Compared to Generation

Thus, there is a great gulf between man's begetting and God's. Human generation is temporal, passionate, and sexual, and uses preexisting materials. In contrast, divine generation is eternal, above time, and passionless. So the Son is begotten of the Father and is ever in him, without separation, having a proper subsistence of his own. Distinct from this, the procession of the Holy Spirit from the Father is not generative in character and so is a different mode of existence, but it is still as **incomprehensible**, yet similarly involving no difference of essence. To say that the Father is the origin of the Son suggests no superiority in anything except causation. We mean that the Son is begotten by the Father and not the Father of the Son, just as light proceeds from fire, not fire from light. So in the Father's creating through the Son, the Son is not a mere instrument but the Father's subsistential force.[62]

Mutatis mutandis, to repeat our introductory comment, the Holy Spirit proceeds from the Father and rests in the Son, equally glorified with the Father and the Son, since he is coessential and coeternal, proceeding from the Father and communicated through the Son, inseparable and indivisible from both, possessing all the qualities

61. John of Damascus, *On the Orthodox Faith*, 1.7; *PG*, 194:805.
62. John of Damascus, *On the Orthodox Faith*, 1.8; *NPNF*², 9/2:6–9.

that the Father and the Son possess, except that of being begotten or born. For the Father is without cause and unborn, and the Son is derived from the Father by generation, while the Spirit is derived from the Father not by generation but by procession. The generation of the Son and the procession of the Holy Spirit are simultaneous. "All then that the Son and the Spirit have is from the Father, even their very being."[63]

The Filioque Controversy

The Niceno-Constantinopolitan Creed (C) states that the Holy Spirit "proceeds from the Father." There is no mention of his proceeding from the Son as well. But in Spain, because of the threat of a continued Arianism with its denial of the Son's deity, in localized liturgies an addition crept in—*a Patre filioque*: "from the Father *and the Son*." This addition spread and was adopted by local councils, particularly the Council of Toledo (589),[64] although there is evidence that the insertion was later, occurring at the eighth Council of Toledo in 653.[65] It was accepted by the French church in the late eighth century, but was not inserted into the creed by Rome until 1014 under Pope Benedict VIII. The fourth Lateran Council of 1215 mentioned it, and the Council of Lyons in 1274 proclaimed it as dogma. We do not intend to provide a comprehensive history of debate on this issue, since that can be found elsewhere.[66]

63. Cf. Gregory of Nazianzus, *Oration 25*; *PG*, 35:1193–1225.

64. But see R. M. Haugh, *Photius and the Carolingians: The Trinitarian Controversy* (Belmont, MA: Norland, 1975), 160–61, who questions this explanation and argues that it "first entered the Ecumenical Creed in the Latin West by a simple method of transposition and not by any willful act of interpolation in conscious violation of the Ecumenical decrees." Sergei Bulgakov rightly argues that the phrase was unnecessary, for Arianism could have been rebutted quite readily without it; "pour rejeter l'arianisme et reconnaître l'équi-divinité et la consubstantialité du Fils au Père, on n'a nul besoin de cette surérogation." Sergei Nikolaevich Bulgakov, *Le Paraclet*, trans. Constantin Andronikof (Paris: Aubier, 1946), 125.

65. Shawn C. Smith, "The Insertion of the *Filioque* into the Nicene Creed and a Letter of Isidore of Seville," *Journal of Early Christian Studies* 22, no. 2 (2014): 261–86.

66. See, for example, A. Edward Siecienski, *The Filioque: History of a Doctrinal Controversy* (Oxford: Oxford University Press, 2010); for a shorter summary, Robert Letham, *The Holy Trinity: In Scripture, History, Theology, and Worship*, rev. and expanded ed. (Phillipsburg, NJ: P&R Publishing, 2019), 229–51.

The Eastern church objects to this development on ecclesiastical grounds. Such a change (more a development, since C did not oppose the *filioque* but did not comment, because the issue had not yet arisen) should require an ecumenical council to determine the matter, it maintains. As Theodore Stylianopoulos puts it, "Can a clause deriving from one theological tradition simply be inserted in a creed deriving from another theological tradition without council?"[67]

The East also objects on theological grounds. Since it understands the Trinity from a differing perspective from the Latins, this development appears to undermine the church's teaching on the Trinity. To appreciate the significance of this question and not to dismiss it as sterile, one must, as Dietrich Ritschl observes, "let one's thought sink into the classical Trinitarian modes of argumentation."[68] Stylianopoulos comments that "at stake was not an abstract question but the truth of Christian salvation."[69] The key question is whether the clause is consistent with Scripture and C.

Biblical Teaching on the Procession of the Holy Spirit

In the *locus classicus*, John 15:26, Jesus says that he will send the Paraclete (a reference to Pentecost, the historical sending), who in turn *proceeds from* (*ekporeuetai*) the Father, denoting a continuous procession. Much modern New Testament scholarship argues that the procession here refers to economic activity only—the relations between the Father, the Son, and the Holy Spirit in human history—and not at all to eternal antecedent realities in God himself. Bertrand de Margerie rightly calls this restriction to the temporal mission "a

67. Theodore G. Stylianopoulos, *Spirit of Truth: Ecumenical Perspectives on the Holy Spirit: Papers of the Holy Spirit Consultation, October 24–25, 1985, Brookline, Massachusetts* (Brookline, MA: Holy Cross Orthodox Press, 1986), 32.

68. Dietrich Ritschl, "Historical Development and the Implications of the *filioque* Controversy," in *Spirit of God, Spirit of Christ*, ed. Lukas Vischer (London and Geneva: SPCK, 1981), 46.

69. Theodore G. Stylianopoulos, "The Biblical Background of the Article on the Holy Spirit in the Constantinopolitan Creed," in *Études Theologiques: Le Ile Concile Oecuménique* (Chambésy-Genève: Centre Orthodoxe Du Patriarcat Oecuménique, 1982), 171.

simplistic exegesis that lacks a theological background."[70] It effectively undermines the reality and truthfulness of God's revelation by positing the idea that what God does economically does not necessarily reveal who he is.

The Spirit proceeds from the Father. The question in dispute, however, concerns whether this procession is from the Son also. Jesus refers to the Father's sending the Spirit at Pentecost, in response to his request, or in his name (John 14:16, 26). But Jesus also says that he himself will send the Spirit at Pentecost (16:7), and later he breathes on the disciples and says, "Receive the Holy Spirit" (20:22). So he shares with the Father in the sending of the Spirit. Moreover, he says that he and the Father are one (10:30). So it may be asked whether the Son does not also share with the Father in spirating the Spirit in that eternal manner to which John 15:26 refers.

Overall, the Bible paints a complex picture of the relations of the Spirit to the Father and the Son. The Holy Spirit hears the Father, receives from the Father, takes from the Son and makes it known to the church, proceeds from the Father, is sent by the Father in the name of the Son, is sent by the Son from the Father, rests on the Son, speaks of the Son, and glorifies the Son. The relation between the Spirit and the Son is not one-directional but mutual and reciprocal. The Spirit plays an instrumental role in the coming of Christ and in his resurrection. The Spirit is active throughout the earthly life of the incarnate Son. So while Christ sends the Spirit, he himself lives in union with the Spirit and—as far as his incarnate existence is concerned—in dependence on the Spirit.[71] The Spirit is called the Spirit of God, referring to the Father, but he is also the Spirit of Christ, the Spirit of God's Son, and the Spirit of the Lord.

The Trinity according to the Eastern Church

The dominant influences in Eastern Trinitarianism, the Cappadocians and John of Damascus, teach that the Father is the source

70. Bertrand de Margerie, *The Christian Trinity in History*, trans. Edmund J. Fortman, Studies in Historical Theology 1 (Petersham, MA: St. Bede's Publications, 1982), 169.

71. John 14:26; 15:26; 16:7, 13–15; cf. Mark 1:10; Luke 3:22. See also Matt. 1:18–20; Luke 1:34–35; 4:1, 14; Rom. 1:3–4; 8:11.

of the personal subsistences of the Son and the Holy Spirit. Thus, the Holy Spirit proceeds from the Father. Gregory of Nazianzus corrected this emphasis with his teaching that the **monarchy** is the whole Trinity, not the Father alone, but this primary stress remains.

The Trinity according to the Western Church

Augustine has exerted an overwhelming influence on the Western church. Moreover, the continued threat of forms of Arianism led the church to lay extra stress on the consubstantiality of the Father and the Son. The *filioque* was intended to undergird this—the Holy Spirit's procession from the Father *and the Son* served, in Western eyes, to safeguard the identity of essence of the Son and the Father. In turn, following Augustine's psychological analogy, the Spirit is seen as the bond of union between the Father and the Son.[72]

The Western View according to the Eastern Apologists

Eastern objections to the *filioque* are not that it implies two separate sources for the Holy Spirit, for we saw that Augustine held that the Spirit proceeds from the Father and the Son as from a single source. Nor is it that the clause might subordinate the Holy Spirit to the Son. The main concern is that the *filioque* posits that not only the Father but also the Son is a source or origin or cause of the Holy Spirit, compromising the monarchy of the Father. The Greek fathers held that the Holy Spirit is the treasure and the Son is the treasurer—the Son receives and manifests the Spirit, but he does not cause its existence as such, since only the Father is the source or origin or cause of both the Son and the Holy Spirit through ineffably different but united acts.

Another related problem in Eastern eyes is that the clause confuses the Father and the Son. The Father is not the Son. Thus, the relation between the Spirit and the Father differs from the relation between the Spirit and the Son. Therefore, to talk of the Spirit's proceeding from the Father *and* the Son without differentiation is to confuse the two.

72. See Lukas Vischer, ed., *Spirit of God, Spirit of Christ: Ecumenical Reflections on the Filioque Controversy* (London: SPCK, 1981), 12–16, for a clear and incisive evaluation of these differences.

Augustine's teaching that the Spirit proceeds from both as from a common source avoids any suggestion that there are two separate sources of the Spirit, which would divide the Trinity, but confuses their distinctiveness.

It is clear, however, that the West has consistently affirmed that the Father is the source of the Son and the Spirit. The *filioque* was never directed against this. Stylianopoulos agrees, but adds that it appears this way from the Eastern perspective.[73] Yet the claim that the *filioque* confuses the Father and the Son is, I submit, of greater weight.

The Eastern View according to Western Apologists

According to the West, the Eastern repudiation of the *filioque* leaves no clear relation between the Son and the Holy Spirit. This is in odd contrast to the patristic teaching of *perichorēsis*, whereby the persons of the Trinity indwell and interpenetrate one another. The West holds that this exhibits subordinationist tendencies. In contrast, the *filioque* affirms the intimate relation between the Son and the Spirit. This, the West claims, has led to a gulf in the East between theology and piety. Speculative theology, grounded on the Logos, has been separated from worship, mediated by the Holy Spirit. Thus, Eastern piety, so Western observers such as Herman Bavinck claim, is unduly dominated by mysticism.[74]

Neither of these two arguments bears much scrutiny. The claim that the East, by rejecting the *filioque*, holds apart the Son and the Holy Spirit is simply wrong. Throughout, the Eastern church has accepted terminology such as "from the Father through the Son" as a valid expression of the intent of C. The East argues that the Holy Spirit rests on the Son (as at Jesus' baptism) and is received by him, and in turn is sent by the Son.[75] The relation existing in the Trinity between the Father and the Son is presupposed, for the Father is

73. Stylianopoulos, *Spirit of Truth*, 50.

74. Herman Bavinck, *The Doctrine of God*, ed., trans., and outlined by William Hendriksen (Edinburgh: Banner of Truth, 1977), 313–17.

75. Wolfhart Pannenberg, *Systematic Theology* (Grand Rapids: Eerdmans, 1991), 1:317–19.

the Father of the Son, the Son is eternally in and with the Father, and the Father is never apart from the Son.[76] The claim ignores the Cappadocian teaching on the mutual indwelling of the three, a crowning affirmation of the indivisible relations of the Son and the Holy Spirit. Besides, C affirms that the Spirit is worshiped and glorified together with the Father and the Son, and is the author and giver of life together with the Father and the Son, "by whom [the Father] made the worlds." The East affirms that the Son participates in the Holy Spirit's procession from the Father both immanently and economically.

On the second point, one of the most famous elements of Eastern piety, the Jesus prayer, is thoroughly Christocentric—"Lord Jesus Christ, Son of God, have mercy on me, a sinner" can hardly be more evangelical or Christological in tone. Furthermore, the East has no monopoly on unbridled mysticism.

Swete points to **Maximus**'s acceptance of the Western idea of the *filioque* as expressing the Greeks' terminology "from the Father through the Son." He supposed that it was intended "to emphasize the unity and unchangeableness of the divine essence." Nevertheless, he thought it posed a potential danger and preferred the Greek formula.[77] Paul Blowers agrees that this was Maximus's assessment, pointing to his firm commitment to the Father as the sole source from whom the Spirit proceeds, but recognizing that he advances (*proeivai*) through the Son.[78]

Matthew Baker discusses errors on both sides in their characterization of the East-West division over the *filioque*. He focuses on Karl Barth's defense of the clause and points to Georges Florovsky, in his opposition to Gregory Palamas and Vladimir Lossky, as being more in line with Athanasius and Cyril and so going beyond the phrase "through the Son" and stressing throughout that the Spirit

76. Jürgen Moltmann's proposal that the Spirit proceeds "from the Father of the Son" assumes that a consensus would form in the East in support; see his volume *The Trinity and the Kingdom: The Doctrine of God* (London: SCM, 1991), 185–87.

77. Henry Barclay Swete, *The Holy Spirit in the Ancient Church: A Study of the Christian Teaching in the Age of the Fathers* (London: Macmillan, 1912), 279–80.

78. Blowers, *Maximus*, 297–99.

is the Spirit of the Son, and is indivisibly one with the Son, while not prejudicing the monarchy of the Father.[79]

Pentecostal scholar Frank Macchia argues against the *filioque* on the grounds that it tends to subordinate the Holy Spirit. It also fails to adequately express the point that both the Son and the Spirit come forth from the Father. In so doing, it unduly privileges the Son.[80] This argument runs against the fact that the Spirit testifies of Christ and is invisible and anonymous. It goes against the normal *taxis*. It fits Macchia's Spirit Christology, which we will discuss in a later chapter. Still, Macchia's discussion of the importance of the baptism of Jesus as indicative of the intra-Trinitarian relations is very useful.

Recent Developments

In recent years there have been a series of ecumenical agreements, although in most cases the Augustinian position has been to a greater or lesser extent sidelined.[81] Discussions continue.[82]

The underlying issues still remain, although the heat that attended past polemics has largely been defused. There is a recognition that the two perspectives are not necessarily irreconcilable, while some have argued that both could be held together in reciprocal tension. Certainly, the Eastern churches have always been prepared to affirm that the Spirit proceeds from the Father through the Son.

The Cyrilline phrase *from the Father in the Son* seems to me to express the mutual indwelling of the three, avoids any residual subordination, and also directs us to Jesus' baptism. It also avoids a focus on the Spirit apart from Christ, for we receive the Spirit *in Christ*. The West's concern for the relation between the Son and the Spirit is maintained, and the confusion of the *filioque* avoided. Kathryn Tanner also

79. Matthew Baker, "The Eternal 'Spirit of the Son': Barth, Florovsky, and Torrance on the *Filioque*," *International Journal of Systematic Theology* 12, no. 4 (October 2010): 382–403.

80. Frank D. Macchia, "Baptized in the Spirit: A Pentecostal Reflection on the *Filioque*," in *Ecumenical Perspectives on the* Filioque *for the 21st Century*, ed. Myk Habets (London: Bloomsbury, 2014), 141–56.

81. Letham, *Holy Trinity*, 45–50.

82. See Myk Habets, ed., *Ecumenical Perspectives on the* Filioque *for the 21st Century* (London: Bloomsbury, 2014).

argues that the perichoretic relations of the three provide a solution to the impasse, going behind the clause and rendering the differences redundant, affirming the positive dimensions of both sides.[83]

Key Terms

attributes
begetting
begotten
being
Christocentric
Christology
consubstantiality
energy
essence
filioque
generation
Homoian Arian
hypostasis
incomprehensible
instrumental cause
Manichaeism
Maximus
monarchy
monopatrist
Nestorian
participation
perichorēsis
persons
pneumatocentric
procession
properties
relations
secondary causes
simplicity
subsistence

Question for Reflection

What biblical and theological arguments are advanced in support of both Western and Eastern positions on the *filioque* clause? Is it possible to reach a *lasting* resolution that would be acceptable to both sides?

83. Kathryn Tanner, "Beyond the East/West Divide," in *Ecumenical Perspectives on the* Filioque *for the 21st Century*, ed. Myk Habets (London: Bloomsbury, 2014), 198–210.

3

From Anselm to Barth

Anselm (A.D. 1033–1109)

Archbishop of Canterbury from 1093, Anselm wrote *De Fide Trinitatis et de Incarnatione Verbi* (*On Faith in the Trinity and the Incarnation of the Word*) after being wrongly accused by the monk Roscelin of teaching that the three **persons** were three "things" or that the Father and the Holy Spirit were incarnate with the Son.[1] He completed the final version in 1094. In it he proved that neither the Father nor the Spirit could have become incarnate. If the Holy Spirit had been incarnate, he would have been the son of a human being. So there would have been two sons in the Trinity: one the Son of God, the other the son of a human being.[2] Moreover, if the Father had assumed a human nature into union with his person, not only would there again be a plurality of sons, but both the Father and the Son would be grandsons. The Father would be the grandson of the virgin's parents, while the Son would be the grandson of the virgin. Therefore, "since it is impossible for there to be even any small unbefittingness in God, no person of God other than the Son ought to have been incarnate."[3] Consequently, none of the three persons of God more fittingly "emptied himself and

1. G. R. Evans, *Anselm* (London: Geoffrey Chapman, 1989), 57; Brian Davies and G. R. Evans, *Anselm of Canterbury: The Major Works* (Oxford: Oxford University Press, 1998), 237–44; Anselm, *De Incarnatione Verbi*, 1–5.

2. Anselm, *De Incarnatione Verbi*, 10; *PL*, 158:276; Davies and Evans, *Anselm*, 250.

3. Anselm, *De Incarnatione Verbi*, 10; *PL*, 158:276; Davies and Evans, *Anselm*, 251.

took on the form of a servant" than did the Son.[4] This fittingness is equivalent to necessity—not a necessity imposed on God from external sources, for this could not be, but a necessity of God's own **nature**.

From this, Anselm concludes that the three persons are distinct eternally: "He who proceeds [the Spirit] is never identical with Him from whom He proceeds. . . . Therefore, when God is **begotten** of God or when God proceeds from God, the **substance** cannot lose its singularity nor the **relations** their plurality."[5]

With that as a background, Anselm composed a treatise on the **procession** of the Holy Spirit (*De Processione Spiritu Sancto contra Graecos*) at the request of Pope Urban, addressing the Greeks in defense of the ***filioque***. It is a thorough defense of the addition, and we will not regurgitate all his points.[6] Anselm introduces an important argument for how the relations of the persons are compatible with their full equality. How can one thing exist from another without the other from which it exists somehow existing "more principally and more valuably" and without the thing that exists from this other somehow existing inferiorly and as something secondary? Anselm's reply here is that this is a unique case. We ought not to judge God's begottenness and procession after the likeness of creation. In God, "that which is begotten and that which proceeds is no other than that from which it proceeds or is begotten."[7] Since God is not greater or lesser than himself, so in the case of the three persons there is nothing greater or lesser, "and no one of them is what He is any more or any less than is another of them, even though it is true that God exists from God by proceeding and by being begotten." Yet each of the three is distinguished from the others. The Father alone exists from no one and is he from whom two others exist. The Holy Spirit exists from

4. Anselm, *De Incarnatione Verbi*, 10; *PL*, 158:277; Davies and Evans, *Anselm*, 251–52.

5. Anselm, *De Incarnatione Verbi*, 15; *PL*, 158:283–84; Davies and Evans, *Anselm*, 258.

6. Davies and Evans, *Anselm*, 390–434.

7. Anselm, *De Processione Spiritus Sancti Contra Graecos*, 8; *PL*, 158:320; Jasper Hopkins and Herbert Richardson, *Anselm of Canterbury*, vol. 3 (Toronto: Edwin Mellen Press, 1976), 224–25; Davies and Evans, *Anselm*, 413–14.

two others and is he from whom no one exists. The Son alone exists from one other and is he from whom one other exists. It is common to the three that each one stands in relation to both the others. "Thus, each [of the three persons] possesses his distinguishing **properties**"[8] without detriment to their being wholly God, for God exists from God by being begotten, and God exists from God by proceeding. Since there is not anything external to God, when God is begotten from God or when God proceeds from God, the one who proceeds or is begotten does not pass outside God but remains within God.[9] Since God has no parts but is wholly whatever he is, it follows inescapably that the Father is God as a whole, the Son is God as a whole, and the Holy Spirit is God as a whole—and they are one and the same God. When God exists from God, God is within God and there is only one God.[10] But he who exists from another cannot be one and the same as the other from whom he exists, so the three persons retain a plurality.

Thomas Aquinas (A.D. 1225–74)

Sources

Gilles Emery indicates that in his *Summa Theologia*, Thomas Aquinas considers the Spirit as God and then moves to a discussion of his work in history, whereas in his commentaries it is the other way around, for his first port of call is the biblical text. There he discusses the text in tandem with the patristic authorities and only then moves to a consideration of the immanent Trinitarian relations. In this, he is concerned to root his doctrine in the Bible and in dialogue with the patristic authors.[11] This gives a lie to claims that Aquinas capitulated to Aristotelian logic and departed from a biblically grounded theology. Most of his massive work consisted of biblical commentaries.

8. Anselm, *De Processione*, 1; *PL*, 158:323; Hopkins and Richardson, *Anselm*, 228; Davies and Evans, *Anselm*, 392–98.

9. Anselm, *De Processione*, 9–10; *PL*, 158:324; Hopkins and Richardson, *Anselm*, 229; Davies and Evans, *Anselm*, 414–20.

10. Anselm, *De Processione*, 1; *PL*, 158:325; Hopkins and Richardson, *Anselm*, 229–30; Davies and Evans, *Anselm*, 392–98.

11. Gilles Emery, *The Trinitarian Theology of St. Thomas Aquinas*, trans. Francesca Aran Murphy (Oxford: Oxford University Press, 2007), 13.

Christopher Holmes draws attention to Aquinas's commentary on John as the best way to approach his doctrine of the Trinity.[12] In particular, he refers to Aquinas's comments on John 7:37–39, 14:16–17, 15:26–27, and 16:14–15.[13] On the double procession, one of Aquinas's favorite texts is Revelation 22:1, where the Spirit is identified as "the river of the water of life, flowing from the throne of God and of the Lamb, that is, of Christ."[14]

Real Relations

Aquinas understands the *procession* of the Spirit not in physical terms but as an intelligible **emanation**, like a word proceeding from a speaker, yet remaining in him.[15] On John 14:16–17, the relations are real, distinct, and of one nature. "Another" in "another *parakletos*" opposes **Sabellianism** but does not indicate a different nature.[16] Following Augustine, the relations in God are real, not accidental.[17] They refer to what is relatively opposed, implying a real distinction, without respect to the **essence**.[18] There are only four real relations—paternity, filiation, **spiration**, and procession.[19] "It is not opposition of an essential nature but of a relational one."[20] **Relative opposition** shows that the Spirit is different from the Father or the Son, but only as the one is related to the other.[21] Hence it follows that

> Christ is called an advocate because as a human being he intercedes for us to the Father; the Holy Spirit is an advocate because he makes us ask. Again, the Holy Spirit is called a consoler

12. Christopher R. J. Holmes, *The Holy Spirit* (Grand Rapids: Zondervan, 2015), 83–122, here 83.

13. Holmes, *Holy Spirit*, 83–104.

14. Thomas Aquinas, *Commentary on the Gospel of John Chapters 9–21*, trans. Fabian R. Larcher (Lander, WY: Aquinas Institute for the Study of Sacred Doctrine, 2013), 311; Holmes, *Holy Spirit*, 85.

15. Aquinas, *ST*, 1.27.1.

16. Aquinas, *John 9–21*, 249–50; Holmes, *Holy Spirit*, 85–86.

17. Aquinas, *ST*, 1.28.1.

18. Aquinas, *ST*, 1.28.2–3.

19. Aquinas, *ST*, 1.28.4.

20. Holmes, *Holy Spirit*, 90.

21. Aquinas, *John 9–21*, 312.

> because he is formally love. But the Son is a consoler because he is the Word. The Son is a consoler in two ways: because of his teaching and because he gives the Holy Spirit and incites love in our hearts. Thus the word *another*, does not indicate a different nature in the Son and in the Holy Spirit. Rather, it indicates the different ways each is an advocate and a consoler.[22]

John 14:16–17 encourages us to consider that the Spirit and the Son have different origins with respect to the Father.[23] "The Spirit receives the Father's nature by proceeding, the Son by being begotten."[24] Since in God understanding and existence are the same, due to his absolute **simplicity**, the Word is begotten from within the same nature.[25] With both the Word and the Spirit, "all that exists in God, is God," the divine nature being communicated by every internal procession.[26] Hence, the relations are internal to God.

The Processions

Aquinas moves from the acts of the persons to the **processions**,[27] for "the shape of the Spirit's working indicates the shape of the Spirit's procession in God."[28] Relations of opposition are demonstrated in Gethsemane, indicating real plurality in God.[29] This is not opposition in the conventional sense, which implies hostility and conflict; rather, Jesus cries out to one that he is not, the Father, distinct in a relative way.[30] Furthermore, there is a distinction between the procession of love in God (the Spirit) and that of the Word, and so while the latter is **generation**, the former is spiration.[31] Here the model of Word, will, or love comes from Aquinas's reading of John 1, influenced by

22. Aquinas, *John 9–21*, 250.
23. Holmes, *Holy Spirit*, 90.
24. Holmes, *Holy Spirit*, 91.
25. Aquinas, *ST*, 2.14.4.
26. Aquinas, *ST*, 1.27.3.
27. Holmes, *Holy Spirit*, 87.
28. Holmes, *Holy Spirit*, 89.
29. Holmes, *Holy Spirit*, 101.
30. Holmes, *Holy Spirit*, 101.
31. Aquinas, *ST*, 1.27.4.

Augustine.[32] On John 15:26–27, he comments that the Spirit proceeds as love, proper to the essence of the Father and the Son;[33] as to be expected, Aquinas differs from the Greeks. "The Son is eternally begotten of the Father in the Spirit."[34] The Spirit does not receive in the same way as creatures do, for creatures receive things that are, by definition, different from themselves, whereas this is not the case with the Holy Spirit, for his relations with the Father and the Son are internal to God and so he receives from the Father, who also subsists in the one divine **being**.[35] The Trinitarian **order** is irreversible; the Spirit is from the Father and the Son.[36]

The processions should be distinguished from the **missions**. The processions are immanent in God and necessary to who he is. The missions relate to God's works in creation and redemption and are sovereign and free determinations by God. The missions mean, in God, only procession of origin, which accords with equality, not inferiority.[37] Mission and giving relate to the temporal, generation and spiration to what is eternal.[38]

Divine Persons

Aquinas follows Boethius's generic definition of *person* as "an individual substance of a rational nature." But since in the Latin West *substantia* is ambiguous and can refer to either the Greek ***hypostasis*** or ***ousia***, Aquinas prefers to use the term *subsistentia* (**subsistence**), meaning "that which exists in itself and not in another."[39] The word *persona* ("person") is appropriate to God, but it is applied to God differently than to the creatures, since his essence is perfect. We have to use extrabiblical terms, for "the urgency of confuting heretics made it necessary to find new words to express the ancient faith

32. Thomas Aquinas, *Commentary on the Gospel of St. John* (Albany, NY: Magi Books, 1980), 23ff. This covers the first eight chapters.
33. Holmes, *Holy Spirit*, 88.
34. Holmes, *Holy Spirit*, 91.
35. Holmes, *Holy Spirit*, 94–97.
36. Holmes, *Holy Spirit*, 98.
37. Aquinas, *ST*, 1.43.1.
38. Aquinas, *ST*, 1.43.2.
39. Aquinas, *ST*, 1.29.1–2.

about God." What matters is to follow "the sense of Scripture."[40] When we talk of a human person, we mean a particular individual, distinct from others. With God, however, distinction is only by relation of origin, and relation is not an **accident** (as in humans)[41] but is the divine essence itself. Therefore, "a divine person signifies a relation as subsisting" in the divine nature.[42] Aquinas here identifies the divine persons with relations, and goes on to affirm that there are three persons in God.[43] In God there is not triplicity, which denotes inequality and separation, but Trinity, which entails unity of order and essence, denoting unbreakable union.[44] We must not understand number here in the sense in which it is applied to creaturely things, as one man is simply part of a sequence of two men, and two of three, for "this does not apply to God, because the Father is of the same magnitude as the whole Trinity."[45] Aquinas is saying that the persons of the Trinity are not sequential members of a class like human individuals, for divinity cannot be exemplified by individual members of a class. He opposes here a form of "**tritheism**, according to which Father, Son, and Spirit are three individuals sharing a nature in the sense that Peter, Paul, and John are three individuals sharing a (human) nature."[46] We must avoid the error of **Arius**, and terms such as *separation* and *division*, while also steering clear of Sabellianism by refraining from words such as *confusion* and *singularity*. Thus, the Son is other than the Father as he is another person, but he is not something else, since he is of the identical essence.[47]

There is a distinction between the persons in their reciprocal relations on the one hand and in terms of relations of origin. In the former

40. Aquinas, *ST*, 1.29.3.

41. An accident in this sense is something adventitious, not intrinsic or necessary to the nature of a thing. Thus, a human male is a man of necessity, in terms of substance, but he is a husband, a father, a politician, or a schoolteacher *per accidens*.

42. Aquinas, *ST*, 1.29.4.

43. Aquinas, *ST*, 1.30.1–4.

44. Aquinas, *ST*, 1.31.1.

45. Aquinas, *ST*, 1.30.1.

46. Brian Davies, *The Thought of Thomas Aquinas* (Oxford: Clarendon Press, 1992), 187.

47. Aquinas, *ST*, 1.31.2.

sense, the Spirit is, following Augustine, the mutual love between the Father and the Son. In the latter sense, the Spirit proceeds from both as from one single principle.[48] "The *communion* of the Father and the Son and the *procession* of the Holy Spirit are so caught up with one another that the communion is inconceivable without the procession of the Holy Spirit."[49] This is comparable with Augustine and might raise similar questions whether the Spirit is somehow subordinate. Moreover, it appears to treat the Spirit as somehow less than personal. That this is not the case, however, should be clear from the overall direction of Aquinas's (and Augustine's) doctrine.

The Father

The Father is the *principle* of the Trinity. The word means only "that whence another proceeds." *Principle* must be distinguished from *cause*. It is improper to talk of the Father as cause, for that would mean diversity of substance, and the other two persons would be dependent. Neither of these problems exists with the term *principle*. Although we attribute something of authority to the Father by his being principle, "we do not attribute any kind of subjection or inferiority to the Son, or to the Holy Ghost, to avoid any occasion of error," since the word *principle* "does not signify priority but origin."[50] Here Aquinas denies that the Son and the Spirit are subordinate to the Father or dependent on him for their being. Procession neither implies nor entails dependence or subordination. Aquinas continues by saying that the Father is properly so called, since paternity distinguishes him from the other two persons.[51] As principle, he is from no one.[52]

48. Aquinas, *ST*, 1.37.1, 3; Emery, *Aquinas*, 237.

49. Emery, *Aquinas*, 241.

50. Aquinas, *ST*, 1.33.1. A reader remarked: "Surely A has priority over B if it is the origin of B. Also, how can the Father be the origin without the Son and Spirit being dependent on Him?" This would be the case if A and B were different entities. But as Aquinas has insisted, the Trinitarian relations are internal to God and simply comprise relations, not natures. The three are not distinct in an absolute sense, for if that were the case there would be three gods, but they are distinct in a relative sense. *ST*, 1.36.2, *sed contra*.

51. Aquinas, *ST*, 1.33.2.

52. Aquinas, *ST*, 1.33.4.

The Son

Thus, the Son, or Word (his proper name), is of complete identity with God.[53] He is the image of God, which is properly said of the Son, and not of the Spirit also, as the East had held.[54]

The Holy Spirit

Dominic Legge remarks that it is inconceivable for Aquinas that there be a mission of the Son without the Holy Spirit, just as it is inconceivable for there to be the Father and the Son without the Spirit, who is the mutual love that proceeds from them.[55] Because the Spirit is common to the Father and the Son, he is called by a name that is common to both. Both Father and Son are spirits, and both are holy.[56]

The Spirit Proceeds from the Father and the Son

The Spirit proceeds from the Son as well as from the Father; even the Greeks recognize that the procession of the Spirit has a connection with the Son, Aquinas remarks.[57] While it is not explicit in Scripture, "we do find it in the sense of Scripture." It is a rule of Scripture that whatever is applied to the Father applies also to the Son, except only what applies to the opposite relations.[58] We may say that the Son is everything the Father is except for being the Father and, similarly, that the Spirit is everything the Father and the Son are except for being the Father and the Son.

Aquinas continues by charging the **Nestorians** with introducing the error that the Spirit does not proceed from the Son.[59] It can be rightly said, as some in the East do, that he proceeds from the Father through the Son.[60] The Father and the Son are one principle of the

53. Aquinas, *ST*, 1.34.1–3.
54. Aquinas, *ST*, 1.35.1–2.
55. Dominic Legge, *The Trinitarian Christology of St. Thomas Aquinas* (Oxford: Oxford University Press, 2017), 17.
56. Aquinas, *ST*, 1.36.1.
57. Aquinas, *ST*, 1.36.2.
58. Aquinas, *ST*, 1.36.2.
59. Aquinas, *ST*, 1.36.2.
60. Aquinas, *ST*, 1.36.3.

Holy Spirit, since there is no relative opposition between them as the principle of the Holy Spirit—here he follows and cites Augustine.[61] In discussing John 15:26, Aquinas remarks that the Spirit could not be distinguished from the Son if he did not proceed from the Son. Only relations of origin can establish this distinction, and thus, granting the Trinity of persons, it is impossible that the Spirit could not be from the Son.[62] While John 15:26 mentions only the Father as the one from whom the Spirit proceeds, Aquinas points out that wherever the Father is mentioned, the Son is understood, and vice versa.[63] Moreover, he adds, the Spirit is also called the Spirit of the Son.[64] Commenting on John 16:14, Aquinas adds that the Son's being, with the Father, the one principle of the Holy Spirit is the reason why the Spirit's main work is to glorify the Son.[65]

Love as the Proper Name of the Spirit

Following Augustine, love is the proper name of the Spirit, and so he is the bond of love between the Father and the Son. Love in God can be taken essentially or personally. In terms of essence, love is common to all three persons, since there is one essence. But there are two processions in God—one in terms of intellect, which is the Word, and the other by will, which is the procession of love, the Spirit. The Spirit is the love of the Father for the Son. Because the Father and the Son mutually love one another, the Spirit is this mutual love proceeding from both.[66] This should be understood in connection with Aquinas's teaching that the divine **attributes** are identical to the divine essence, so that love is not reduced to an abstract, autonomous characteristic, but rather it is what God is.

Emery remarks that "as with the name *Word*, the name of Love thus primarily designates an intra-Trinitarian, person-to-person

61. Aquinas, *ST*, 1.36.4.

62. Aquinas, *John 9–21*, 311–12.

63. This is in accord with the rule of **appropriations**; otherwise, it might be held that the Father also died on the cross.

64. Aquinas, *John 9–21*, 313.

65. Aquinas, *John 9–21*, 330.

66. Aquinas, *ST*, 1.37.1.

relation: it is this eternal relation which accounts for the personality of the Holy Spirit."[67] Because this is a procession of love, God produced creatures not because he needed to do so but on account of his love.[68] Thus, creation, the gift of the Spirit to humans, and the uniting of humans to God is an outflow.[69] The creation is not the work of one person more than any other, but when created things are seen as the result of divine love, "the Holy Spirit comes to be the principle of creation."[70]

The processions are immanent, not external, actions.[71] The Spirit is love in person, an impulse toward the beloved being. What proceeds in God by way of love does not proceed as begotten, or as Son, but as Spirit, a vital movement or impulse.[72] In answer to the problem, analogous to the one above, of how the Spirit can be called love when love is a property of all three persons, Aquinas distinguishes between essential love, inherent to the one divine essence and common to all three persons, and personal love, the proper name of the Holy Spirit, seen in the affection, attraction, impulse, and movement of the Spirit in his procession within the Trinity. "There is therefore no variety of loves within God, and nor is the essential love of God compounded with the personal love."[73]

The Spirit as the Gift of the Father and the Son

The name of the Spirit is also "gift," for he is given and is the gift. Before a gift is given, it belongs only to the giver, but when it is given, it is the property of the recipient. So the Spirit is "the gift of God giving," but when he is given, he is "a gift bestowed on man."[74] Moreover, he is truly given, since he is given forever. If a gift is given to a person for a time only, it is not a true giving, since it can be withdrawn. The Spirit is with us forever, in this life

67. Emery, *Aquinas*, 243.
68. Aquinas, *ST*, 1.32.1, 3.
69. Aquinas, *Summa contra Gentiles*, 4.20.
70. Emery, *Aquinas*, 247.
71. Emery, *Aquinas*, 225.
72. Aquinas, *ST*, 1.27.4; Emery, *Aquinas*, 226.
73. Emery, *Aquinas*, 232; Aquinas, *ST*, 1.37.1.
74. Aquinas, *ST*, 1.38.2.

enlightening us and teaching us, while in the next life bringing us to see the reality.[75] In this, it is the Spirit himself and those gifts necessary for salvation, such as love, that remain in us. Other gifts of the Spirit, distributed differentially, are not necessary for salvation. But these are always present in Christ, in whom is a plenitude of power, since he alone can work miracles at any time according to his will.[76]

Emery classes Aquinas's contribution as a deepening of the tradition coming from Augustine.[77] The Holy Spirit is the gift from eternity, but he is given in time. It belongs to the Spirit to be given, and this from all eternity. But the actual donation happens only in the course of time.[78] The temporal gift exists because of the eternal relation at the heart of the Trinity.[79]

For a gift, there must also be a donor and a recipient. The first aspect directs us to the relations of origin, the latter to creatures.[80] We do receive not just the effects of the Holy Spirit, but the Holy Spirit himself.[81] This is created grace, "a gift from God which puts itself onto the **ontological** level of human nature, proportioning itself to the human in order to make it possible for men and women to be united to God from within their own human life."[82] "We receive the Holy Spirit in person because he is the gift, constituted as such through his relation to the Father and Son, who is thus given to us."[83] He is the gift because he is the person of love, in the meaning given to *love* when it refers to the personal character of the Holy Spirit.[84] He is the divine person closest to us, for through him we receive the Father and the Son.[85]

75. Aquinas, *John 9–21*, 250.
76. Aquinas, *John 9–21*, 251.
77. Emery, *Aquinas*, 249.
78. Emery, *Aquinas*, 250–51.
79. Emery, *Aquinas*, 251.
80. Emery, *Aquinas*, 251–52.
81. Emery, *Aquinas*, 252.
82. Emery, *Aquinas*, 253–54.
83. Emery, *Aquinas*, 256.
84. Emery, *Aquinas*, 257.
85. Emery, *Aquinas*, 258.

The Spirit of Truth

In John 14:16–17, the Spirit is also called "the Spirit of truth," since he proceeds from the truth and, since he is nothing else than love, speaks the truth.[86] In God, love proceeds from truth, which is the Son. In turn, it leads to knowledge of the truth.[87] He is received by those who believe, which the world does not do. Consequently, the world cannot receive him, does not desire him, and cannot know him.[88]

The Persons in Relation to the Essence

The essence is the same as the persons, due to the divine simplicity, for God cannot be apportioned into parts, yet the persons are really distinguished from one another. So the three persons are one essence. Thus, the names denoting God's essence (*God*) can be applied to the persons as well as to the essence.[89] On the other hand, abstract names (*essence*) cannot stand for the persons. The essence does not beget the essence, but the Father begets the Son. Whereas *God* signifies the divine essence in him that possesses it, the word *essence* cannot stand for the person because it signifies the essence in an abstract form.[90] While adjectival terms cannot be predicated of the essence, however, substantive terms can, owing to the real identity of essence and person. The divine essence is really the same as one person, and also as the three persons.[91] Thus, the essential attributes—power, wisdom, and so on—can be appropriated to each of the three persons.[92]

Thomas Brand argues that this distinction between essence and person is not real, such as a thing and a thing, since this would entail a quarternity, not a Trinity. On the other hand, neither is it a formal distinction, something merely conceptual, since it would then be a human mental construction in the mind of a theologian and would not correspond to anything in God. Building on Aquinas and following hints in Francis Turretin, Brand argues for a modal distinction,

86. Aquinas, *John 9–21*, 251.
87. Aquinas, *John 9–21*, 251–52.
88. Aquinas, *John 9–21*, 252.
89. Aquinas, *ST*, 1.39.1–4.
90. Aquinas, *ST*, 1.39.5.
91. Aquinas, *ST*, 1.39.6.
92. Aquinas, *ST*, 1.39.7.

referring not to **modalism** but to the distinction between a thing and the mode, or way of subsistence, of a thing, to the way that a person subsists in the divine nature.[93]

The Spirit as the Fountain of Life

On John 7:37–39, Aquinas writes that Jesus' statement "If anyone thirsts" indicates that he desires the salvation of all. The drink to which Jesus refers "is spiritual refreshment in the knowledge of divine wisdom and truth."[94] The fruit of this invitation is that "good things overflow upon others."[95] "Rivers come from fountains as their sources." There is a contrast with ordinary drinking, in which one takes only a small amount of water, "but one who drinks by believing in Christ draws in a fountain of water; and when he draws it in, his conscience, which is the heart of the inner man, begins to live and in itself becomes a fountain." Further, referring to Psalm 65:10, he states that "this fountain is the Holy Spirit." Anyone who drinks in order simply to benefit himself will not have living water flowing from his heart, whereas one who helps others and shares the gifts of grace he has received from God will have living water. "Rivers," Aquinas argues, refers to "the abundance of spiritual gifts which were promised to those who believe" (Ps. 64:10 [65:10 English]).[96] Paul "was governed by the impulsive force and fervor of the Holy Spirit" and consequently wrote that "the love of Christ spurs us on" (2 Cor. 5:14).[97] Gifts of the Spirit are living waters, since they flow directly from their source, the indwelling Holy Spirit.[98] The evangelist says that we should understand this of the Holy Spirit, since he is "the fountain and river of life" (Ps. 65:10) and is a river because "he proceeds from the Father and the Son" (Isa. 42:1; Rev. 22:1).[99]

93. Thomas Brand, "A Trinitarian Christology of the Fourth Word from the Cross: The *Communicatio Idiomatum*, the Modal Distinction, and the Forsakenness of Christ" (PhD diss., University of Durham, 2020).

94. Aquinas, *St. John*, 433 (1–8).

95. Aquinas, *St. John*, 434.

96. Aquinas, *St. John*, 434.

97. Aquinas, *St. John*, 435.

98. Aquinas, *St. John*, 435.

99. Aquinas, *St. John*, 435.

John Chrysostom had said that the words "the Holy Spirit had not yet been given"[100] meant that he had not been given to the apostles at that time. Aquinas responds that this conflicts with what the Lord said in Luke 11:19.[101] He replies, with Augustine,[102] that the apostles had the Holy Spirit before the resurrection, but that the words refer to "a more abundant giving, and one with visible signs, as the Spirit was given to them in tongues of fire after the resurrection and ascension."[103] But, he continues, if this is so, why does no one speak in the languages of all nations as then? As Augustine says, "it is not necessary," for now the church speaks the languages of all nations because of the love of God being poured into our hearts by the Holy Spirit, which makes everyone speak to everyone else. At the start, the church was small and had to speak the languages of all nations so that it could be established among them all.[104]

Summary

Aquinas points out that "spirit" and "holy" are common to all three persons so that, in Emery's words, "despite the affinity between holiness and the personality of the Spirit, and even though sanctification is the purpose of the mission upon which the Spirit is sent, one cannot set the word *Holy* on one side as designating what from all eternity distinguishes him from the Father and the Son."[105] The Spirit carries out works that are properly or formally divine, and this is why Scripture leads us to recognize him as God.[106] The word *Spirit* also means "breath" or "wind," indicating the subtle and hidden ways in which the Spirit works—impulsive force, motion, vital momentum.[107]

Emery sums up: "St. Thomas draws the whole economy together under the sign of the Holy Spirit: creation, the exercise of providence,

100. "The Spirit was not yet."
101. Aquinas, *St. John*, 435.
102. Aquinas does not specify the source from Augustine, but it is probably his *Tractate 32 on John*, found in *NPNF*[1], 7:194–95.
103. Aquinas, *St. John*, 436.
104. Aquinas, *St. John*, 436.
105. Emery, *Aquinas*, 221.
106. Emery, *Aquinas*, 221.
107. Emery, *Aquinas*, 223.

human life, human action under the motivation of the Holy Spirit, **Christology**, the sacraments, and union with God in the beatitude in which the human vocation is fulfilled."[108] The Spirit unites us to God.[109] The immanence of the three persons within one another overflows into grace by the indwelling of the Holy Spirit.[110] Indeed, "one could scarcely find a more striking formula for the divinization which the Holy Spirit brings about: presence of the Trinity in human beings and presence of human beings in the Trinity." He adds, "Being Love in person, the Holy Spirit nests human beings into friendship with God, . . . giving them . . . a 'dwelling in God.'"[111]

John Calvin (A.D. 1509–64)

The Eternal Procession of the Holy Spirit

B. B. Warfield regarded John Calvin as "pre-eminently the theologian of the Holy Spirit."[112] Calvin accepts the eternal procession of the Holy Spirit, Western style, for the Spirit comes from the Father and the Son at the same time, a teaching that he says "appears in many passages, but nowhere more clearly than in chapter 8 of Romans."[113] According to Calvin, both Christ and the Spirit are called by the same name, *paraclētos*, "comforter," for it is an office common to both to comfort, exhort, and guard us by their patronage. As long as he lived in the world, Christ was our patron. Then he committed us to the patronage of the Holy Spirit. Even so, Christ is still our patron, although no longer in a visible manner, for he guards us by his Spirit.[114] Christ sends the Spirit from the heavenly glory, and while he names the Father as the one from whom the Spirit proceeds,

108. Emery, *Aquinas*, 258.

109. Emery, *Aquinas*, 260.

110. Emery, *Aquinas*, 264.

111. Emery, *Aquinas*, 264.

112. Benjamin Breckinridge Warfield, "Calvin's Doctrine of the Knowledge of God," in *Calvin and Augustine*, ed. Samuel G. Craig (Nutley, NJ: Presbyterian and Reformed, 1974), 29–130, here 107.

113. Calvin, *Institutes*, 1.13.18.

114. John Calvin, *Calvin's Commentaries: The Gospel according to St. John 11–21 and the First Epistle of John*, ed. Thomas F. Torrance and David W. Torrance, trans. T. H. L. Parker (Grand Rapids: Eerdmans, 1959), 82; John Calvin, *In Evangelium Secundum Johannem Commentarius Pars Altera* (Genève: Librairie Droz, 1998), 147.

this is because he wants to raise our eyes to the contemplation of the Spirit's divinity, rather than to exclude himself from that role.[115] After all, commenting on John 17:21, it is Christ who communicates to us his life "by the power of His Spirit."[116]

Perichorēsis—The Mutual Indwelling of the Persons

Calvin asserted the classic doctrine that in each *hypostasis*, the whole divine nature is understood. Referring to John 14:10, he wrote that "the Father is wholly in the Son, the Son wholly in the Father."[117] He says the same in commenting on John 17:3, where Jesus ascribes eternal life to knowing himself and the Father, for "we learn that [Christ] is wholly in the Father and the Father wholly in Him. In short, whoever separates Christ from the divinity of the Father does not yet know Him who is only true God."[118] T. F. Torrance points to Calvin's use of the phrase *in solidum*, which was originally used by **Cyprian** in an ecclesiastical context, referring to the corporate interconnectedness of bishops within the one episcopate, but which Calvin adopted to attest the three persons' sharing completely and equally in the one being of God.[119] This entails their mutual indwelling or containment.[120]

Spirit and Word

Calvin asserts that faith is the principal work of the Spirit.[121] The Spirit unites us to Christ, working with the Word preached. By this

115. Calvin, *Gospel of John and 1 John*, 110; Calvin, *In Evangelium Johannem Pars Altera*, 180.

116. Calvin, *Gospel of John and 1 John*, 148; Calvin, *In Evangelium Johannem Pars Altera*, 223.

117. Calvin, *Institutes*, 1.13.19.

118. See John Calvin, *The Gospel according to St. John* on 17:3, cf. on 14:10. Cf. also Benjamin Breckinridge Warfield, "Calvin's Doctrine of the Trinity," in *Calvin and Augustine*, ed. Samuel G. Craig (Nutley, NJ: Presbyterian and Reformed, 1974), 229; Philip Walker Butin, *Revelation, Redemption, and Response: Calvin's Trinitarian Understanding of the Divine-Human Relationship* (New York: Oxford University Press, 1995), 42–43, 130.

119. Thomas F. Torrance, *The Christian Doctrine of God: One Being, Three Persons* (Edinburgh: T&T Clark, 1996), 201–2.

120. Torrance, *Christian Doctrine of God*, 194–202. See also Verna Harrison, "Perichoresis in the Greek Fathers," *SVTQ* 35, no. 1 (1991): 53–65.

121. Calvin, *Institutes*, 3.1.4.

he unites us to Christ and enables us to enter into the true knowledge of God and of ourselves. He works with the Word.[122]

The Spirit, transcending spatiotemporal realities, unites things separated by distance. This is particularly clear in Calvin's many expositions of the Lord's Supper, repeated at various times throughout his career. While Christ has ascended to the right hand of the Father and his body is in one place, ruling out transubstantiation and consubstantiation, nevertheless the faithful are enabled to feed on his flesh and blood by the Spirit in the supper.

Feeding on Christ is through the Spirit, not the letter, not in the materialistic manners claimed by Rome and Lutheranism, but through the efficacious power of the Spirit, giving faith, uniting us to Christ. He lifts us up to heaven to feed on Christ. Calvin agreed with Huldrych Zwingli on the body of Christ's being in one place, although his view of the sacrament was far stronger. He argued that the faithful feed on the body of Christ, which, although at the right hand of God, is communicated to us by the Holy Spirit, who "joins things separated by distance."[123] All this is under the authority of the Word, since Word and Spirit work together inseparably.[124] All these are works of the Spirit in the created order. Calvin does not spend much time in discussing the eternal relations, nor especially the Spirit's work in creation as such.

The Holy Spirit in Two More Recent Theologians

Matthias Scheeben (A.D. 1835–88)

One of the most interesting contributions to reflection on the Holy Spirit in the modern era was by the Roman Catholic theologian Matthias Joseph Scheeben, whose classic book *Mysterium den*

122. Calvin, *Institutes*, 1.9.3; 4.8.13.

123. John Calvin, *CO*, 6.127–28; 49.107, 487; Calvin, *Institutes*, 3.1.1; 3.2.24; 4.14.16; 4.15.15; 4.17.9–12; John Calvin, *Calvin: Theological Treatises*, trans. J. K. S. Reid (Philadelphia: Westminster Press, 1954), 137, 267–68; John Calvin, *Commentary on the First Epistle of Paul the Apostle to the Corinthians*, 246; Robert Letham, *Union with Christ: In Scripture, History, and Theology*, rev. and expanded ed. (Phillipsburg, NJ: P&R Publishing, 2011), 103–15.

124. Calvin, *Institutes*, 4.8.13.

Christentums (1865–97) has received the comment "there is no other book quite like it in the vast history of Christian literature."[125]

Scheeben wrote that the missions of the divine persons can be predicated only of those who proceed from another divine person. In this, there are two distinctions in connection with the divine persons in contrast to creatures. First, the Son and the Holy Spirit are not under the Father's authority; they proceed only on the basis of origin. Second, the one sent can never separate himself from the one who sends, since they are one in being.[126]

Scheeben unfolded the classic commitment to inseparable operations in stating that "every external operation is absolutely common to all the divine persons" and "no divine person can step into the outer world exclusively by himself." From this, "an external action can be ascribed to one person in particular only by appropriation."[127]

He continues by focusing on the missions. The real mission of the persons consists in sanctifying grace. The first kind of mission is by the impression and expression of the persons sent. A true presence of one of the persons in the creature is the result of an effect produced by that person and the other persons in common.[128]

The second kind of real mission is a living process. The divine persons become present "as object of a living, intimate procession and enjoyment."[129] Thus, in adoption "he [God] gives us himself, his own essence, as the object of our delight." The imperfect enjoyment in this life "differs from the perfect beatitude only in degree, not in kind," as the earnest or down payment (*arrha / pignus*) taught by Paul.[130] Scheeben then asks whether this is hypostatic. Are the individual persons present in the soul? He concludes positively, for

125. Cyril O. Vollert, foreword to Matthias Joseph Scheeben, *Nature and Grace* (*Natur und gnade* [1861]), trans. Cyril Vollert (St. Louis: Herder, 1954), xi.

126. Matthias Joseph Scheeben, *The Mysteries of Christianity*, trans. Cyril Vollert (orig. published 1946; New York: Crossroad, 2006), 149.

127. Scheeben, *Mysteries*, 151.

128. Scheeben, *Mysteries*, 154–58.

129. Scheeben, *Mysteries*, 158–64.

130. Scheeben, *Mysteries*, 159.

if that were not the case, the most important mark of a true possession would be lacking.[131] This appears to me to go further than is warranted and might open the doors to an equivalence with the **hypostatic union** in Christ.

Scheeben then narrows his focus further as he considers the special characteristics of this second kind of mission, the Holy Spirit and its relation to sanctification, adoption, and our union with God. This is without parallel. The Holy Spirit is sent to us, making us a temple that belongs to him and is consecrated to him—"he not only belongs to us but he himself possesses us as his property." There is a real and substantial presence of the Holy Spirit. A certain reciprocity ensues, for the Spirit is the object of our possession, and he indwells "as the proprietor of our soul and our whole being." In some sense, this is common to all the divine persons.[132] Both Scripture and the fathers affirm a possession that is "truly hypostatic." Scheeben asks, "If the Son alone takes physical possession of a created nature, why should not the Holy Spirit be able to take possession of a created being in a way proper to his own person, by means of a less perfect and purely moral possession?"[133] This would appear to suggest that possession by the Spirit is not yet at the level it will be when our salvation is complete, but that nevertheless he guides and molds our thoughts and actions.[134] Here "the two seemingly opposed aspects of the concepts of donation and possession are, in fact, related to each other," for "He takes possession of our soul as guest, but as a sweet guest, who desires to possess us only through our love[;] . . . he is seen to be not only a hypostatic gift, but also a personal gift."[135] Scheeben's language is open to misunderstanding. If by "hypostatic" he means that the Spirit personally, hypostatically, comes to us, indwells us, and pervades us, there is no problem, but at times it seems that he goes beyond this.

131. Scheeben, *Mysteries*, 160.

132. Scheeben, *Mysteries*, 165. Here there is an echo of John 14:23.

133. Scheeben, *Mysteries*, 166.

134. I am grateful to Jonathan Humphreys for this helpful observation.

135. Scheeben, *Mysteries*, 167.

Karl Barth (1886–1968)

Is Barth's Doctrine of the Trinity in CD, I/1 *Unipersonal?*

Karl Barth argues that the doctrine of the Trinity is an outflow of the proposition "God reveals himself." "God reveals himself through himself, and reveals himself."[136] Later he explains this by affirming that God reveals himself as the one he is.[137] Revelation is God's self-unveiling to human beings, who are themselves incapable of receiving God's Word because of their sinful condition. God does what man cannot do.[138] Rowan Williams points out that the idea that man is incapable of hearing the Word is nonsense, for it supposes that he knows what the Word is from which he is alienated. What Barth means, he suggests, is that "it depends entirely upon God's creative address to man, the Word spoken out of his freedom, his decision."[139] Moreover, God is concealed even in his revelation,[140] which is historical, not mythological.[141] Thus, there is a unity between the self-revealing God, his revelation and his being revealed—a union with no barriers separating the three forms of his being: subject-predicate-object. But this unity also takes the form of a differentiation, for the names *Christ* and *Holy Spirit* are inexchangeable.[142] Eberhard Jüngel observes that the doctrine of the Trinity "had to lay down the fact that God as the subject of his being is also the subject of his being known and becoming known. This is why for Barth the doctrine of the Trinity stands at the beginning of his *Dogmatics*."[143]

As a further expansion on this theme, Barth states that "God reveals himself as the Lord" is the root of the doctrine of the Trinity.[144]

136. Karl Barth, *CD*, I/1:296.

137. Barth, *CD*, I/1:396.

138. Barth, *CD*, I/1:320.

139. Rowan Williams, "Barth on the Triune God," in *Karl Barth: Essays in His Theological Method*, ed. S. W. Sykes (Oxford: Clarendon Press, 1979), 147–48.

140. Barth, *CD*, I/1:322–23.

141. Barth, *CD*, I/1:323–29.

142. Barth, *CD*, I/1:299.

143. Eberhard Jüngel, *The Doctrine of the Trinity: God's Being Is in His Becoming* (Edinburgh: T&T Clark, 1976), 42.

144. Barth, *CD*, I/1:306–7.

God's lordship is prior to his revelation, but his revelation is the root of the doctrine of the Trinity. Thus, his lordship is in some sense prior to the Trinity. His sovereignty is paramount. This will have far-reaching consequences. God "is the same in unimpaired unity and yet also the same thrice in different ways in unimpaired distinction," or "the Father, the Son and the Holy Spirit in the biblical witness to revelation are the one God in the unity of their essence, and the one God in the biblical witness to revelation is the Father, the Son and the Holy Spirit in the distinction of His persons."[145]

Immediately the question arises as to the subject of the Trinity. Barth's stress is on the oneness of God. It is "himself" that he reveals. He is God in threefold repetition. This is a strongly Western model, with obvious roots in Augustine. Alar Laats argues that it is a linear unipersonal model, and the evidence appears to support him. Laats thinks that Barth has the Father as the divine subject, although, as he points out, Jürgen Moltmann considers it to be the divine essence.[146] Williams sees it as "the order of a 'repetition' of *one* divine subject."[147]

Can Person Adequately Express the Threeness in God?

In his discussion of the concept of *person*, these questions reoccur. Barth reflects on Augustine's recognition that neither *person* nor any other term can adequately express the threeness in God.[148] Following Augustine, he states that *person* is not used to say that the three in God are persons in the same way as we are persons, but is simply a help to say that there are three in God. The modern concept of the person as a center of self-consciousness muddies the waters further, for Barth sees in this, if applied to the Trinity, a recipe for tritheism, with three separate beings, each an "I."[149] If that were true of God, there would be three "I's," which is definitely not what the classic theology meant

145. Barth, *CD*, I/1:307–8.

146. Alar Laats, *Doctrines of the Trinity in Eastern and Western Theologies: A Study with Special Reference to K. Barth and V. Lossky* (Frankfurt am Main: Peter Lang, 1999), 37.

147. Williams, "Barth," 166.

148. Barth, *CD*, I/1:355–56.

149. Barth, *CD*, I/1:359.

by *person*.[150] Therefore, "we do not use the term 'person.'" Barth's preference was for *seinsweise*, translatable into English as "mode (or way) of being." By this he hoped to express the same thing as *person*, while avoiding the problems of modern usage. The statement "God is one in three ways of being" means that "the one God . . . is what He is not just in one mode but . . . in the mode of the Father, in the mode of the Son, and in the mode of the Holy Ghost."[151] *Seinsweise* can mean "way of being" or "mode of being," but the English translator rendered it as "mode of being," conjuring up the specter of modalism for uninformed English readers. Geoffrey Bromiley, the translator, regarded such a reaction as absurd, for Barth "stays very close to the orthodox formularies," and his polemic against the term *person* "aims to defend rather than subvert the orthodox position."[152]

Indeed, on the relations of the three Barth was thoroughly orthodox,[153] as on the appropriations[154] and ***perichorēsis***, where he cites John of Damascus to the effect that "the life of God would appear to be a kind of uninterrupted cycle of the three modes of being."[155] *Perichorēsis* is, he maintains, the sum of the doctrine of *unitas in trinitate* and *trinitas in unitate*.[156] The distinctions are real. There is a certain subordination in the relations between the Father and the Son, for reconciliation is a second divine act following the first, the Son's irreversibly following the Father, not vice versa. This is emphatically not a distinction of being (essence), but one of mode of being.[157] Barth has an extensive and appreciative commentary on the clauses of the creed of Constantinople (C).[158] In passing, the Holy Spirit is not identical to the Son.[159] The Spirit guarantees us **participation** in revelation.[160] He is

150. Barth, *CD*, I/1:359; see also 350ff.
151. Barth, *CD*, I/1:359.
152. Geoffrey W. Bromiley, *An Introduction to the Theology of Karl Barth* (Grand Rapids: Eerdmans, 1979), 16, 21.
153. Barth, *CD*, I/1:363–65.
154. Barth, *CD*, I/1:373.
155. Barth, *CD*, I/1:370.
156. Barth, *CD*, I/1:370–71.
157. Barth, *CD*, I/1:413.
158. Barth, *CD*, I/1:414ff.
159. Barth, *CD*, I/1:451.
160. Barth, *CD*, I/1:453.

the communion of the Father and the Son, an obviously Augustinian comment.[161] In a similar vein, he staunchly defends the *filioque*. The Holy Spirit is not a creature but God, differentiated from the Father and the Son, although there is no possibility of our defining the distinction between generation and procession, for only God can do so.[162]

Is the Holy Spirit a Person?[163]

We indicated that, following Augustine, Barth regards the Holy Spirit as the bond of love between the Father and the Son. This at once raises the specter of a fragile unity between the Father and the Son, if it requires a third to unify them. It also has the typically Augustinian weakness of relegating the Spirit to an attribute or a quality rather than a person. It points to a duality rather than a Trinity.

Barth's consistent teaching is that the Spirit unites different entities: "The work of the Holy Spirit . . . is to bring and hold together that which is different and therefore . . . disruptive in the relationship of Jesus Christ to His community, namely, the divine working, being and action on the one side and the human on the other." "His work is to bring and to hold them together, . . . to co-ordinate them, to make them parallel, to bring them into harmony and therefore to bind them into a true unity." Thus, in the Lord's Supper, the Holy Spirit brings about the church's unity with its heavenly Lord and the receiving of his body and blood.[164] Before that, the Spirit is "the bond of peace" between the Father and the Son.[165] He unites the divine and human in the incarnate Christ,[166] and constitutes and guarantees the unity in which Christ is one with God and with the earthly body.[167] He mediates between the man Jesus and other men.[168] He brings about the existence and unity of the church, for he "constitutes and

161. Barth, *CD*, I/1:469–70.

162. Barth, *CD*, I/1:473ff.

163. For an extended comparison between Barth and Aquinas on the Holy Spirit, see Holmes, *Holy Spirit*, 133–50.

164. Barth, *CD*, IV/3:761.

165. Barth, *CD*, IV/3:760.

166. Barth, *CD*, III/2:193ff.

167. Barth, *CD*, IV/3:760–62.

168. Barth, *CD*, IV/2:343.

guarantees the unity of the *totus Christus*."[169] He unifies man as body and soul,[170] and husband and wife in marriage.[171]

All this flows from the *filioque*, for if the Spirit proceeds from the Father and the Son, his role is as a mediating force between them, and so also in creation and redemption. But this might only serve to lend credence to the idea that Barth's view of the Holy Spirit is reduced to the love between the Father and the Son, implying a distance between the Father and the Son, if a third force is needed to secure a unity that would not otherwise be there. This is also Moltmann's criticism. He states that "the Spirit is merely the common bond of love linking the Father with the Son[, so] . . . there is no need for a third person in the Trinity. . . . The Spirit is only the unity of what is separated."[172] He considers that this persistent point, handed down from Augustine, "contradicts the tradition in which the Spirit is the third person of the Trinity, not merely the correlation of the other two persons." Barth's principle "God reveals himself as the Lord" means, strictly, that the Father is the one divine personality.[173] Williams agrees, in observing that "Barth seems to be saying that, although no 'person' of the Trinity is an independent centre of consciousness in the modern sense, yet the Father and the Son more nearly approximate to it than does the Spirit," and again, "If the Spirit is the communion or love between Father and Son, the implication is that there are two subjects and one 'operation' or, perhaps, 'quality' involved." Williams concludes that for Barth, the Trinity is a society of two, not three.[174] While he admits that Barth is more pluralist in IV/1 than in I/1,[175] nevertheless "problems begin to appear in Barth's Trinitarian scheme when the controlling model of revelation or self-interpretation proves difficult to apply to a theology of the Holy Spirit." What Williams calls the "linear

169. Barth, *CD*, IV/3:760.
170. Barth, *CD*, III/2:354.
171. Barth, *CD*, IV/2:746ff.; also III/4:184.
172. Jürgen Moltmann, *The Trinity and the Kingdom: The Doctrine of God* (London: SCM, 1991), 142.
173. Moltmann, *Trinity and the Kingdom*, 143.
174. Williams, "Barth," 170–71.
175. Williams, "Barth," 175.

model," evident as early as I/1, is of no help at all. "Not very much sense can be made of 'modes' relating to each other in love." This becomes even more serious when we consider the cross.[176] If we add Barth's comparison of the Trinity as unity in distinction to man as male and female, it would be odd to consider human persons as simply "modes" of being.[177]

We will encounter some more recent and contemporary discussions in later chapters.

Key Terms

accidents
appropriations
Arius
attributes
begotten
being
Christology
Cyprian
emanation
essence
filioque
generation
hypostasis
hypostatic union
missions
modalism
nature
Nestorian
ontological
order
ousia
participation
perichorēsis
persons
procession
processions
properties
relations
relative opposition
Sabellianism
simplicity
spiration
subsistence
substance
tritheism

Questions for Reflection

1. Could the Holy Spirit have become incarnate instead of the Son?
2. Is it legitimate to consider the Spirit as love and as gift?

176. Williams, "Barth," 181.
177. Barth, *CD*, III/2:64, 246–48, 274ff.; IV/2:343.

4

Basic Axioms

The Niceno-Constantinopolitan Creed (C), composed in A.D. 381, sums up the considered biblical exegesis and doctrinal commitments of the church at the time. It has been recognized as authoritative through the centuries in both East and West.

We Believe in the Holy Spirit, the Lord and Giver of Life

Creator and Sustainer of the Universe

The Spirit, together with the Father and the Son, is confessed as the Creator of all contingent life. The one holy, catholic, and apostolic church acknowledges that the Father Almighty is the Creator of heaven and earth, that Jesus Christ is the one by whom all things were made, and that the Holy Spirit is the author and giver of life. In short, all three **persons** work together inseparably according to their distinct hypostatic particularities. In the case of the creation, the Spirit of God was hovering over the waters of creation (Gen. 1:2) and the created entities were brought forth by the breath of God's mouth (Ps. 33:6–9). This mirrors the Trinitarian structure of C, with sections devoted to each ***hypostasis***, demonstrating an awareness of their indivisibility.

This entails that the Spirit pervades the entire creation, inseparably from the Father and the Son. It demonstrates that all life is sacred insofar as it ultimately stems from God, who brought all entities other than himself into existence and continues to sustain them by his almighty power. I recall making vacation trips on a number of occasions to see family members in the USA from our home in Britain. Away for three weeks, we left in spring as the leaves were appearing on the trees and the stems were poking through the soil. What a change there was upon our return! The garden was now ablaze with color, vegetation having sprung up seemingly from nowhere. What power there was in the life force that animated each plant, shrub, and tree! It was the Holy Spirit that did it, giving vibrant life and exquisite beauty to each part, a sumptuous feast for the eyes. He also allowed a goodly number of weeds! These we were responsible to eliminate.

We cannot identify this beautiful and infinitely varied scene with the divine; that would be **pantheism**. Gustav Mahler gave a title to the first movement of his vast Third Symphony, "Pan awakes: summer marches in." While we may appreciate his love of nature, such a sentiment fails to reckon with the distinction between Creator and creature. Nor, for the same reasons, can we accept the panentheist notion that creation and Creator are mutually dependent. On the other hand, it is all too easy to assume that the created order—my garden being part of it—develops simply of itself, independent of its Creator; that is deism and, I fear, is more common than we might suppose. No, the Holy Spirit gives life to the vegetation, the trees and plants around us, and sustains it by his mighty power, in accordance with his immanent causes, such as sunshine and rainfall. This helps us to appreciate how agricultural fruitfulness was listed as one of the blessings Yahweh promised to Israel in his covenant, upon the people's faithful fulfillment of their obligations. All contingent life owes its existence to the Holy Spirit, not to innate powers of "Mother Nature." It commits us to nurture, cultivate, and preserve the environment.

> He sends the snow in winter, the warmth to swell the grain,
> The breezes and the sunshine, and soft, refreshing rain.[1]

1. From Matthias Claudius, "We Plow the Fields and Scatter" (1782), trans. Jane M. Campbell (1861).

Source of Eternal Life

This leads on to the reality that the Spirit is the source of the new creation (2 Cor. 5:17). He transforms us into the image of God (2 Cor. 3:18; 2 Peter 1:4). It was the Spirit of the Father that raised Christ, the Son, from the dead and will raise us too in union with the Son (Rom. 8:10–11; 1 Cor. 15:35–58; Phil. 3:20–21). He is the guarantee of the final renewal of the entire cosmos, concurrent with the redemption of the church (Rom. 8:18–23). In all these great works, all three Trinitarian persons work together without separation. Thus, not only is the Spirit the giver of life (Ps. 104:29–30), but behind that he is the Lord of life, since he is life itself.

Who Proceeds from the Father and the Son

Processions

The internal **relations** of the Trinity exhibit an **order**. While a range of orders are presented in the New Testament, indicating the equality of all three persons and their identical **being**, nevertheless there is a recurrent pattern throughout the Bible in creation, providence, and grace. This pattern reflects who God is in himself.

This internal order is from the Father through or in the Son and by the Holy Spirit. As Basil argued, we should not be too insistent on the prepositions, since what is most significant is what is intended. All three are one identical being, equal in status and in possession of all divine **attributes**. The order does not affect these realities, but is the way in which the three subsistent *hypostases* relate to one another. Thus, the Father generates the Son, spirates the Spirit, and is neither **begotten** nor proceeds; the Son is begotten and does not proceed; and the Spirit does not beget nor is begotten, but proceeds from the Father in and through the Son.

Missions

These **processions** are reflected in the external works of God in creation, providence, and grace. In the case of the Spirit, he proceeds from the Father in and through the Son, while in relation to the creation he is sent by the Father and the Son. We can see this at the Jordan when Jesus was baptized. There the Spirit descended from the Father, not as a dove but "like a dove" (Mark 1:10), and came to rest on the Son. That was for the purpose that the Son would bestow him on his people. This pattern is evident in the **missions** as recorded in the Bible and in the ongoing work of God thereafter. In John Owen's words, "the order of operation among the distinct persons depends on the order of their **subsistence**" in the Trinity. The missions reflect the processions. In every work of God, however, "the concluding, completing, perfecting acts are ascribed unto the Holy Ghost."[2] Or as Abraham Kuyper put it, "in every work effected by Father, Son, and Holy Ghost in common, the power *to bring forth* proceeds from the Father, the power *to arrange* from the Son; the power *to perfect* from the Holy Spirit."[3] Both echo John Calvin, who wrote that to the Father "is attributed the beginning of activity, and the fountain and wellspring of all things; to the Son, wisdom, counsel, and the ordered disposition of all things; but to the Spirit is assigned the power and efficacy of that activity."[4] Yet there is a difference. The processions are necessary acts, inherent in the **nature of God**. The missions are the consequences of his will. They might not have been, without any detriment to God's own being or to the processions themselves. Owen describes them as voluntary acts and not necessary **properties**.[5]

Who Together with the Father and the Son Is Worshiped and Adored

Given that the Spirit is one with the Father and the Son from eternity, he is to be worshiped with them in one united act of adoration. We were all baptized into the one name of the Father, the Son, and the Holy Spirit. Since God is one indivisible being, it is inconceivable that the Spirit could be anything less than the full

2. John Owen, *A Discourse concerning the Holy Spirit* (1674), in *The Works of John Owen*, ed. William H. Goold (London: Banner of Truth, 1965–68), 3:94.

3. Abraham Kuyper, *The Work of the Holy Spirit*, trans. Henri De Vries (Grand Rapids: Eerdmans, 1900), 19.

4. John Calvin, *Institutes*, 1.13.18.

5. Owen, *Holy Spirit*, in *Works*, 3:117. This is correct, as long as one understands, as Owen does, that these are not three separate wills but rather one indivisible will expressed in its hypostatic distinctions.

unqualified God and so worthy of our worship and service. The Holy Spirit is one being (***homoousios***) with the Father and the Son, one in wisdom, power, and glory.

While there are no explicit statements to this effect in the New Testament, all that the New Testament teaches demands it. In consequence, we can see the threefold patterns in the letters of Paul and Peter, the baptismal formula, the apostolic benedictions in that light.[6] While there is no express example of prayer being specifically offered to the Spirit, as there is to the Father and the Son, it is because our prayers are offered *in* the Spirit (Rom. 8:26–27; Jude 20). Moreover, since the three are indivisible, where the Father or the Son is mentioned, all three are entailed. That is why it is by the Holy Spirit that we have access through Christ, the Son, to the Father (Eph. 2:18). From this, it is clear that the Spirit is "in himself a distinct, living, powerful, intelligent divine person; for none other can be the author of those internal and external divine acts and operations which are ascribed unto him."[7]

Who Spoke by the Prophets

The Bible itself is the result of the work of the Holy Spirit. As the breath of God, he inspired the Old Testament prophets and the biblical authors. Paul teaches that "all Scripture is breathed out by God" (2 Tim. 3:16). This is a reference to the Spirit. As we will see, *pneuma* means "wind," "breath," or "spirit," according to the context. There is a frequent overlap in usage, and the Spirit is compared to the wind or the breath of God on more than one occasion (Pss. 33:6–9; 104:29–30; Ezek. 37:1–14; John 3:5–14).

Moreover, in 2 Peter 1:20–21, Peter describes the Spirit's work in the production of Scripture: "Men spoke from God as they were carried along by the Holy Spirit." The Spirit was the primary author who supervened, directing the thoughts and words of the human writers in such a way that they themselves were fully responsible and wrote according to their own particular character and inclinations.

6. Robert Letham, *The Holy Trinity: In Scripture, History, Theology, and Worship*, rev. and expanded ed. (Phillipsburg, NJ: P&R Publishing, 2019), 47–69.

7. Owen, *Holy Spirit*, in *Works*, 3:67–68.

Word and Spirit

Yves Congar considers Word and Spirit on biblical and theological foundations.[8] Of particular interest here is his discussion of the function of the Holy Spirit in the life and ministry of Jesus. He points to a general focus in the Western church on the **hypostatic union**, the assumption of humanity by the Word, as effecting and animating Jesus in his life and ministry. Congar poses the question whether Thomas Aquinas fully recognized the part played by the Holy Spirit in Jesus' conception. His theology of created grace prevented him from grasping the role of the Holy Spirit, he argues.[9] Aquinas was unsatisfactory for two reasons, Congar suggests: he gave more attention to the descent (the incarnation of the Word) than to the ascent (the work of the Holy Spirit), and his reflections on the Christological controversies, particularly the Monothelite controversy, were not completely historically oriented.[10] Luke mentions the Holy Spirit and his works in connection with Jesus many times, but Aquinas focuses on the hypostatic union, connecting the anointing at his baptism to his conception, and attributes it to the Word. Consequently, Jesus possessed everything from the start, quite apart from the anointing by the Spirit at his baptism. Congar adds that many fathers took this view.[11]

Congar, for his part, indicates that the baptism was a new act simply declaring Jesus to be the Christ.[12] He argues that consideration of a purely **ontological** structure of the incarnate Word cannot do justice to the accumulation of texts that stress the historical outworking and progression of Jesus' experience, encompassing the moments of the reception of the Spirit, the ascension, and the sending of the Spirit.[13] He is the Son by eternal **generation** (μονογενης); in terms of the economy of salvation, he became the Messiah for us as

8. Yves M. J. Congar, *The Word and the Spirit*, trans. David Smith (London: Geoffrey Chapman, 1986), 1–48.

9. Congar, *Word and Spirit*, 85.

10. Congar, *Word and Spirit*, 86–87.

11. Congar, *Word and Spirit*, 87.

12. Congar, *Word and Spirit*, 88.

13. Congar, *Word and Spirit*, 88–92.

firstborn (πρωτοτοκος).[14] In this, the Word proceeds from the Father and the Spirit *a Patre Spirituque*.[15] We might counter, however, that the New Testament is full of statements to the effect that the Father sent the Son and has none indicating that this was done by the Spirit. We are thinking here of the processions; of course, in terms of the inseparable operations of the Trinity, the Spirit is pervasively active throughout, but that is not the presenting point.

When thinking of Word and Spirit, what comes to mind is probably the Reformed interest in this relationship. In Reformed theology, this has been more in terms of the connection between the written and preached Word on the one hand and the work of the Spirit on the other. The two have typically been viewed as working in conjunction, the Spirit with the Word, *cum verbum*, in contrast to the Lutheran position, in which the Spirit is said to work through the Word, *per verbum*. The Reformed construction is held to allow for the freedom of the Spirit, whereas the Lutheran idea appears to tie the Spirit to the Word or even to equate the two. While the context is different from the area considered by Congar, the principles remain the same. The two are distinct but inseparable. They are indivisible but are not to be equated. In the Trinity, the eternal Word and the Spirit are distinct but indivisibly one being with the Father. In the preaching of the gospel, the Spirit works inseparably from the written Word he inspired, but is not to be equated with it, nor is it proper to propose constructions that would diminish his freedom. Analogously, the Spirit pervasively and inseparably accompanies the incarnate Christ, strengthens him in his humanity, and enables him, but this does not reflect on the action of the Word in assuming his humanity into union in the indissoluble hypostatic union. We will reflect on this topic in chapter 6.

Spirit Christologies in the Light of the Church's Witness

In the middle part of the last century, the argument arose that the Holy Spirit had been neglected in theology and the life of the

14. Congar, *Word and Spirit*, 92.
15. Congar, *Word and Spirit*, 93.

church. This claim more or less coincided with the emergence of the charismatic movement. The assumption gained ground that this neglect had spawned a massive gap between the institutional practice of the Christian faith and the living empowerment attested in the New Testament and experienced in varying ways in church history and contemporary movements. It is, of course, quite right that a careful evaluation of the biblical record of the Spirit and his work should proceed. Imbalances do occur over time and need to be corrected. It is a perennial task to retrieve and refine our inherited understanding of key elements of revelation. Regardless of the position one might take on this question, however, it cannot be classed as a "basic axiom," since it is a novel proposal that has generated a lot of criticism.

Indeed, as a consequence of this development, there have been calls for the doctrine of the Trinity to be revised in order to properly account for the place of the Spirit. In turn, it is suggested that this will have repercussions throughout the theological spectrum. It will impact our view of creation, the ministry of Christ, the process of salvation, the doctrine of the church, and the Christian life as a whole. It will bring a needed correction to our grasp of the balance of the gospel, turning from a preoccupation with Christ, his death, and his resurrection to the life-giving work of the Spirit as the climax and ultimate purpose of God's revelation.

Attention has subsequently been directed to the many places in the Bible, especially the New Testament, where the Spirit is highlighted in connection with his part in the life of the incarnate Christ. This, it is said, should reorient our thinking away from traditional patterns of thought to new ones in which the Spirit is seen to be the primary focus. In short, such a change would revitalize our understanding of the Bible and our exegetical practices and also effect a sea change in our whole theology. This would renew the church and, by a new stress on the Spirit as Creator, encourage a more integrated view of revelation, the environment, and the cosmos. This sounds all very well, as long as it is kept within the bounds of the church's historic doctrine, but has this been the case? Indeed, is the entire project fraught with danger?

Kyle Claunch[16] surveys what he terms "non-Trinitarian Spirit Christologies," which are not developed from a foundation in classic Trinitarian theology, and finds them to be resurrecting the early heresy of **adoptionism**. In such proposals, Jesus is not preexistent Son of God, but he began to be at conception and was merely a man, totally dependent on the Holy Spirit. He was exalted to divine status at his resurrection. Among modern exponents, Claunch lists James D. G. Dunn, Geoffrey Lampe, and Roger Haight. Trinitarian Spirit Christologies, operating expressly within the bounds of the historic Christian faith, he divides into two groups. Some are mainly exegetical in their approach, especially those of Gerald Hawthorne, Bruce Ware, and Thomas Oden. Those with a more historical and theological bent include contributions by David Coffey, Congar, Myk Habets, John Zizioulas, Gary Badcock, Clark Pinnock, and Amos Yong.

Non-Trinitarian Spirit Christologies

Lampe identifies God as Spirit. This does not mean the Holy Spirit as an eternally distinct *hypostasis* in the Trinity, but rather is a descriptor for God active in the world in a **unitarian** manner. Lampe alleges that the New Testament writers, Paul in particular, missed this insight. They overlooked the point that the term "Spirit" expresses the totality of God in his creativity. They were unable to do this because they insisted on the personal preexistence of Christ and his "post-existence" after his resurrection.[17] Jesus Christ's alleged human nature "corresponds to nothing in the actual concrete world; Jesus Christ has not, after all, really 'come in the flesh.'"[18] On the other hand, the creative purposes of God's Spirit may be realized here on earth in a human community.[19] Lampe's theology is unitarian, is effectively humanistic, and stems from the total eclipse of anything resembling

16. Kyle Claunch, "The Son and the Spirit: The Promise and Peril of Spirit Christology," *Southern Baptist Journal of Theology* 19, no. 1 (2015): 91–112.

17. G. W. H. Lampe, *God as Spirit: The Bampton Lectures, 1976* (Oxford: Clarendon Press, 1977), 118–19.

18. Lampe, *God as Spirit*, 144.

19. Lampe, *God as Spirit*, 174.

a biblical **Christology** by a thoroughgoing focus on "spirit."[20] Jesus was a mere man, God is a unitary spirit, the human community is the focus. This has barely a passing resemblance to the Christian faith.

Dunn's focus on the Spirit led him to an adoptionist Christology. As he expresses it in his book *Jesus and the Spirit* it is hardly surprising, in view of his focus on experience. "The core of religion is religious experience" is his first sentence.[21] This was the major theme of the theology of Friedrich Schleiermacher (1768–1834), and while Dunn distances himself from Schleiermacher, Adolf von Harnack, and the nineteenth-century liberal theology, the premise is very close to theirs and equally mistaken. Dunn then immediately cites Rudolf Bultmann in support of his paradigmatic claim to the effect that true faith does not consist in believing as such, since for the Christian, *"faith can be only the recognition of the reality of God in his own life."*[22] Substantive truth is not the point; it is subjective experience that defines the Christian religion. Jesus then becomes merely an outstanding example of experiencing God, little different from what Schleiermacher argued, with his stress on absolute dependence. This is a lesson that a focus on the Holy Spirit can easily sideline Christology and replace confession of doctrine with a priority for experience, which, in the absence of doctrinal boundary markers, opens the door to unbridled subjectivism.

Trinitarian Spirit Christologies

Perhaps the most graphic attempt to construct a Spirit Christology in relation to Trinitarianism is that of Jürgen Moltmann. Moltmann begins with a full-blooded assault on the received doctrine of the Western church and the Reformed paradigm of Word and Spirit. Instead, in contrast to the ministries of the church, the Word and sacraments, experience is determinative of Christian doctrine, with

20. Nevertheless, we can be thankful for his great work on the *Patristic Greek Lexicon*.

21. James D. G. Dunn, *Jesus and the Spirit: A Study of the Religious and Charismatic Experience of Jesus and the First Christians as Reflected in the New Testament* (London: SCM, 1975), 1.

22. Dunn, *Jesus and the Spirit*, 1, citing Rudolf Bultmann, *Jesus and the World* (London: Fontana, 1958), 113f. (Dunn's italics).

priority given to individual experience.[23] Experience is as necessary as revelation.[24] Moltmann states that he is attempting to develop a Trinitarian pneumatology out of the experience and theology of the Holy Spirit.[25] This, as we have said, is to put the cart before the horse.

Moltmann views the Spirit as life force connecting the experience of the community to the liberation of life in political and ecological dimensions. Moltmann's universalist tendencies are evident in the prominence he gives to the Spirit in creation and on environmental concerns.[26] Moreover, Moltmann's focus on the Holy Spirit is in line with his pronounced **social Trinitarianism**, which verges on **tritheism**. Paul Molnar cites a number of scholars who accuse Moltmann of tritheism, including George Hunsinger, who responds to Moltmann's claim that there has never been a Christian tritheist by saying that "one can only conclude that Moltmann is vying to be the first. . . . *The Trinity and the Kingdom* is about the closest thing to tritheism that any of us are ever likely to see."[27] Moltmann considers that the unity of the Trinity consists in the community of the three persons, for "the essential nature of the triune God is this community."[28] His trilogy of books on Trinitarianism began with *The Trinity and the Kingdom*, which occasioned Hunsinger's criticism. In this he argued that the Trinity is akin to a human community. In *God and Creation*, his **panentheism** was to the fore in his consideration of the Spirit as the life of creation. Effectively, God and the universe are codependent. In *The Spirit of Life*, he takes this a stage further. The eternal processions no longer have any meaning, since they "are seen and contemplated in their eternal **perichoresis** and their eternal simultaneity. Through their reciprocal relationships they indwell one

23. Jürgen Moltmann, *The Spirit of Life: A Universal Affirmation* (Minneapolis: Fortress Press, 1992), 1–3.

24. Moltmann, *Spirit of Life*, 5–8.

25. Moltmann, *Spirit of Life*, 14.

26. See, e.g., Moltmann, *Spirit of Life*, 56–57.

27. George Hunsinger, Review of Jürgen Moltmann, *The Trinity and the Kingdom*, *Thomist* 47, no. 1 (1983): 129–39, here 131, quoted in Paul D. Molnar, *Divine Freedom and the Doctrine of the Immanent Trinity: In Dialogue with Karl Barth and Contemporary Theology* (London: T&T Clark, 2002), 201–2.

28. Moltmann, *Spirit of Life*, 309.

another, forming their unity through their unique community, no longer through their unilinear movement. Their unity is constituted by their 'togetherness' . . . [and] the original hypostatic differentiations are ended and consummated in the eternal perichoresis."[29] Elsewhere I have subjected Moltmann's treatment of the Trinity to trenchant criticism.[30] Another example of an attempt to construct a Spirit Christology in harmony with the Councils of Constantinople and Chalcedon, by Roger Haight, moves in a different direction, with Haight's constantly referring to "God as Spirit," creating the impression that the Spirit is less than a distinct personal subsistence.[31]

Evaluation

Christopher Holmes writes that highlighting the active work of the Holy Spirit is laudable, but to argue as Myk Habets does that in the economy the Spirit is prior to the Son goes against the order of redemptive action from the Father, whereby the Father sends the Son and, together with the Son, sends the Spirit. Moreover, for Habets the Spirit comes through the Son—the argument for Spirit Christology goes in reverse.[32] In contrast, Holmes cites Bruce Marshall, who states that the temporal pattern teaches us about the irreversible eternal processions.[33] Furthermore, Holmes adds, the Spirit teaches us not about the Spirit but about Christ.[34] Nor does the Son proceed from the Spirit.[35] Holmes is critical of Thomas Weinandy and, more so, of Habets.[36] Max Turner has similar concerns, pointing to the risen Christ's demonstrating his lordship over the Spirit and concurrently providing a basis for a Trinitarian account

29. Moltmann, *Spirit of Life*, 308.

30. Letham, *Holy Trinity*, 363–78.

31. Roger Haight, "The Case for Spirit Christology," *Theological Studies* 53, no. 2 (1992): 257–87.

32. Christopher R. J. Holmes, *The Holy Spirit* (Grand Rapids: Zondervan, 2015), 127; Myk Habets, *Anointed Son: Toward a Trinitarian Spirit Christology* (Eugene, OR: Pickwick, 2010).

33. Holmes, *Holy Spirit*, 128.

34. Holmes, *Holy Spirit*, 128.

35. Holmes, *Holy Spirit*, 129.

36. Thomas G. Weinandy, *The Father's Spirit of Sonship: Reconceiving the Trinity* (London: T&T Clark, 1995); Habets, *Anointed Son*.

of God. The problem with Spirit Christologies, as Turner says, is that they reverse this pattern and absorb Christology.[37]

Claunch tries to be evenhanded. He explores possible benefits of Spirit Christology. It corrects a perceived neglect of the Holy Spirit in Western Trinitarian theology. It highlights the humanity of Christ in his dependence on the Spirit, in contrast to an implicit **Docetism**. In doing so, it makes sense of the concept of the imitation of Christ, since he is seen as one of us. It can also shed light on a number of biblical passages. Yet it appears to suggest that the humanity of Christ is somehow set apart from the Son, who assumed it into union, requiring the Spirit to empower it. The danger of an incipient **Nestorianism** potentially looms—a danger, not necessarily a reality.[38] To my mind, many deviant theologies can produce some side benefits here and there in the midst of a mound of dross, but that this may occasionally be so cannot of itself ameliorate their negative force.

But Claunch also notes some dangers. We have already seen the tendency toward adoptionism; the stress on the humanity of Christ and the eclipse of reference to the eternal Son as one with the Father create pressure to see Jesus as a mere man who became elevated to divine status at his resurrection. Additionally, Spirit Christology entails a rejection of the conceptual framework of classic Trinitarianism, with a different view of the eternal processions. This flies in the face of two millennia of Christian biblical exegesis. Very serious is the neglect of the person of Christ. Christ becomes subordinate to the Spirit, the work of Christ in his death, resurrection, and ascension a prelude to the Spirit's activities. It also overemphasizes the possibility of the ecumenical dialogue for which it hopes.[39]

37. Max Turner, *The Holy Spirit and Spiritual Gifts* (Carlisle, UK: Paternoster, 1996), 169–76.

38. Tony Lane points out that Cyril of Alexandria, with his unitive Christology that became the standard and touchstone of the later ecumenical councils, was able to agree that Jesus' works were effected by the Holy Spirit and that the Son does everything by the Spirit, since the Spirit was and is his. Anthony N. S. Lane, "Cyril of Alexandria and the Incarnation," in *The Spirit and Christ in the New Testament and Christian Theology: Essays in Honor of Max Turner*, ed. I. Howard Marshall, Volker Rabens, and Cornelis Bennema (Grand Rapids: Eerdmans, 2012), 285–302, here 299.

39. Claunch, "Spirit Christology," *passim*.

I concur with these criticisms. There are considerable perils in this move. Even in the case of John Owen—which we will consider later—there are definite dangers. Owen argued that Jesus Christ was, according to his humanity, dependent on the Spirit. We will partially agree with this in chapter 6.[40] It is part of what it means to be human, living in obedience to God. But if this is made the main or sole vehicle of support for the assumed humanity, rather than the person of the Son himself supporting and enabling his own humanity, the door is open to Nestorianism. It would suggest a division between the Son and his humanity such that the Spirit was needed to act in this way. The inseparable works of the Trinity instead underline the point that all three persons work together in all of God's activities, and so, in the case of the incarnate Christ, the Spirit is clearly active, as the biblical evidence demonstrates, but this is not to displace or supplant the Son without jeopardizing the personal union.[41] Owen, however, has a looser view of the incarnational union. This was present in the Reformed church earlier, in its determination to preserve the integrity of the assumed humanity, as it emerged at the time of the disputes over the Lord's Supper and was exemplified in some alarming statements of Calvin, to which I have directed attention elsewhere.[42]

This development is of benefit in pointing to neglected treatment of the work of the Spirit in and upon the incarnate Christ. Taken beyond that, however, it can come close to a subtle assault on the authority and sovereignty of Christ. This it does if and when it goes against the grain of the biblical testimony that the chief ministry of the Holy Spirit is to point to and glorify Christ, for then it fosters

40. Owen, *Holy Spirit*, in *Works*, 3:168–76.

41. See the discussion in Leopoldo A. Sánchez M., *T&T Clark Introduction to Spirit Christology* (London: T&T Clark, 2022), 121–41.

42. Calvin, *Institutes*, 2.14.3; John Calvin, *Calvin's Commentaries: The First Epistle of Paul to the Corinthians*, ed. Thomas F. Torrance and David W. Torrance, trans. John W. Fraser (Grand Rapids: Eerdmans, 1960), 327; Robert Letham, "The Person of Christ," in *Reformation Theology: A Systematic Summary*, ed. Matthew Barrett (Wheaton, IL: Crossway, 2017), 313–45; Robert Letham, *Systematic Theology* (Wheaton, IL: Crossway, 2019), 517–18.

an effective subversion of the church's historic testimony to the intra-Trinitarian hypostatic order.[43]

Key Terms

adoptionism
attributes
begotten
being
Christology
Docetism
generation
homoousios
hypostasis
hypostatic union
missions
nature of God
Nestorianism
ontological
order
panentheism
pantheism
perichorēsis
persons
processions
properties
relations
social Trinitarianism
subsistence
tritheism
unitarian

43. Note the comments of Steve M. Studebaker, who, in pursuit of an appropriate pneumatological reading of the Trinity, does so "in place of traditional Trinitarianism's tendency to treat pneumatology as a derivative doctrine of the theology of the Father and the Son." Steve M. Studebaker, "The Spirit and the Fellowship of the Triune God," in *The Routledge Handbook of Pentecostal Theology*, ed. Wolfgang Vondey (London: Routledge, 2020), 185–94, here 191. He views the church doctrine of the processions as "skewed and inadequate" because they do not reflect the Spirit's work in redemption (192), treating the Spirit as passive, but he ignores the biblical point that the Father sends the Son and that the Father and the Son send the Spirit, but the Spirit sends neither.

Leopoldo Sánchez, in a broad survey of a range of Spirit Christologies, classifies various proposals as they relate to Nicene Trinitarianism and Chalcedonian Christology. He identifies Nicene Spirit Christology, pre-Nicene Spirit Christology, and post-Nicene Spirit Christology. Nicene Spirit Christology, within which Sánchez operates, affirms the conclusions of the ecumenical councils as the governing base. The pre-Nicene version, seen in Ignatius and Tertullian, identifies the Spirit with the divine nature rather than as a distinct *hypostasis*. Post-Nicene Spirit Christology, as Sánchez presents it in the case of Roger Haight, identifies God as Spirit and sees the incarnation as the presence of Spirit in Jesus. Sánchez subjects these views to sharp criticism of the kind I have mentioned and points to Haight's having been prohibited from teaching Catholic theology by the Vatican's Congregation for the Doctrine of Faith. Sánchez provides a clear and effective attempt to keep within Nicene and Chalcedonian boundaries. See Sánchez, *Spirit Christology*, 1–17, here 16.

Questions for Reflection

1. Carefully evaluate how the clauses in the Nicene Creed relating to the Holy Spirit should impact the faith and worship of the church.
2. Consider how Word and Spirit are related in Scripture.

For Further Reading for Part 1: Chapters 1–4

Primary Sources

DelCogliano, Mark, Andrew Radde-Gallwitz, and Lewis Ayres. *Works on the Spirit: Athanasius the Great and Didymus the Blind*. Yonkers, NY: St. Vladimir's Seminary Press, 2011.

Williams, Frederick, and Lionel Wickham. *St. Gregory of Nazianzus: On God and Christ*. Crestwood, NY: St. Vladimir's Seminary Press, 2002.

Secondary Sources

Ayres, Lewis. *Augustine and the Trinity*. Cambridge: Cambridge University Press, 2010.

———. *Nicaea and Its Legacy*. Oxford: Oxford University Press, 2004.

Behr, John. *The Formation of Christian Theology*. Vol. 2, *The Nicene Faith*. Pt. 2, *One of the Holy Trinity*. Crestwood, NY: St. Vladimir's Seminary Press, 2004.

Habets, Myk, ed. *Ecumenical Perspectives on the* Filioque *for the 21st Century*. London: Bloomsbury, 2014.

Letham, Robert. *The Holy Trinity: In Scripture, History, Theology, and Worship*. Rev. and expanded ed. Phillipsburg, NJ: P&R Publishing, 2019.

Levering, Matthew. *Engaging the Doctrine of the Holy Spirit: Love and Gift in the Trinity and the Church*. Grand Rapids: Baker Academic, 2016.

Sánchez M., Leopoldo A. *T&T Clark Introduction to Spirit Christology*. London: T&T Clark, 2022.

Siecienski, A. Edward. *The Filioque: History of a Doctrinal Controversy*. Oxford: Oxford University Press, 2010.

Part 2

The Holy Spirit in the Bible

In this section, we will consider the overall teaching of Scripture about the Holy Spirit, from the Old and New Testaments. Starting with the Old Testament, the Spirit is seen as the Creator and then as the presence of Yahweh with his covenant people. The focus of the Old Testament is more on the covenant community than with individuals, but there is enough to demonstrate that the Spirit was operative in all the ways evidenced later in the New Testament.

We then consider the work of the Spirit in the life and ministry of the incarnate Son before tracing his work at Pentecost and its ensuing development through the apostles and in the church.

5

The Old Testament

The Meanings of *Ruach*

The word *ruach* means "spirit," "wind," or "breath," depending on context. It occurs 387 times in the Old Testament, with three broad meanings in generally equal numbers: (1) wind or breath, (2) a force that unifies humans, (3) the life of God. It does not refer to spirit as opposed to body in some dualist sense that demeans the body, but rather refers to living and generating **substance**, "subtle corporeality," animating the body. While it is opposed to "flesh," *nephesh*, flesh is not identical to body, but as Yves Congar points out, it expresses the weakness and fragility of earthly reality.[1]

It is extremely important to distinguish between references to a human disposition, as in statements about someone's spirit being revived or a particular mental attitude such as team spirit, and on the other hand those that denote the Spirit of God, since the same word is used for both. Moreover, as Anthony Thiselton remarks, this must be clearly differentiated from contemporary discussions of "spirituality," which imply some innate human capacity. In contrast, the pervasive stress in the Bible is on what stems from God, not from humanity.[2] Thiselton refers to 1 Corinthians 2:6–16. At the same time, it is also important to note that differing ascriptions are given in the

1. Yves M. J. Congar, *I Believe in the Holy Spirit: The Complete Three Volume Work in One Volume*, trans. David Smith (New York: Crossroad, 1997), 1:3.

2. Anthony C. Thiselton, *The Holy Spirit—In Biblical Teaching, through the Centuries, and Today* (London: SPCK, 2013), 6.

Old Testament to the Spirit—"Spirit of God," "my Spirit," and the like—which nevertheless all refer to the one Holy Spirit.

B. B. Warfield points to the relatively limited attention to the Spirit of God in the Old Testament. It is found as often in Paul as in the whole Old Testament. It occurs in only about half the Old Testament books. But there is no huge difference between the Old Testament and the New Testament in their respective presentations of the Holy Spirit. The New Testament writers identify the Holy Spirit with "the Spirit of God" of the Old Testament.[3] The Spirit of God is called *Holy* because it is from God and "its reality belongs to the sphere of God's existence."[4] The action of the breath of God is vividly seen in Numbers 24:2ff. and 1 Samuel 10:6f. and 19:20–24, "rushing" in turn on Balaam and Saul with dynamic power.[5]

Breath or Wind, Clearly Not the Spirit of God

Ruach can mean "wind," as in the account of the flood when, after the rain had stopped, "God made a wind blow over the earth" and the floodwaters began to recede (Gen. 8:1). Similarly, in Psalms 18:10 and 104:3, God is said to ride "on the wings of the wind."

Again, the word can also denote breath, as in Job 7:7, where the clause "my life is a breath" refers to the fragility and fleetingness of human existence. Something similar is found in Psalm 39:5, while even more clearly in Psalm 144:4 we read that "man is like a breath; his days are like a passing shadow." Psalm 150:6 refers to "everything that has breath," presumably including all animate creatures in its reach.

The Human Spirit

When *ruach* does mean "spirit," it may refer not to the Spirit of God but to the human spirit or to some principle that may animate a person.[6] The author of Ecclesiastes writes of the spirit, at death,

3. Benjamin Breckinridge Warfield, "The Spirit of God in the Old Testament," in *Biblical and Theological Studies*, ed. Samuel G. Craig (Philadelphia: Presbyterian and Reformed, 1952), 127–56, here 127–30.

4. Congar, *Holy Spirit*, 1:4.

5. Congar, *Holy Spirit*, 1:4.

6. The Christian school that my children attended in Delaware held an annual

returning to God who gave it (Eccl. 12:7). The psalmist talks of "my spirit" (Ps. 31:5), and Isaiah of God's giving "breath" to the people of the earth (Isa. 42:5). Proverbs 16:2 may come into this category too. Besides this, there are plenty of references to a spirit of this or that, to revived spirits, broken spirits, and the like.

Harmful Spirits

There are also nasty spirits. On one occasion, a harmful spirit from the Lord tormented Saul (1 Sam. 16:14–23). It appears to have influenced him spasmodically, was assuaged by music, and consequently departed. While evil spirits are ranged against God, they are under his sovereign rule and can act only with his permission. Such is the case with the evil spirit from Yahweh that came upon the false prophets of the northern kingdom to entice Ahab to battle and to his downfall (1 Kings 22:19–23).

The Spirit of God

Genesis 1:2 contains the phrase *ruach elohim*, "the Spirit of God." While the full revelation of creation awaited the New Testament, it is clear that it was the work of the indivisible Trinity, since all that God does is the work of all three **persons**. Therefore, the whole work of creation is attributable to the Spirit of God as it is inseparably to the Father and the Son. This is why the Niceno-Constantinopolitan Creed describes the Holy Spirit as "the author and giver of life." Here in Genesis 1, the Spirit of God is brooding over the waters. These are later pushed back to accommodate life on earth. The implication is that the Spirit gives life to all creatures, and ultimately to humans. Hence, in Genesis 2:7, God breathed the breath of life into Adam, although in this case *ruach* is not used.[7] Again, in the

---

"Spirit Week." In my naiveté, I imagined that this was concerned with the work of the Holy Spirit. This understanding could hardly have been further from the truth. As far as I was capable of comprehending it, the week was devoted to building up something like "team spirit" or "esprit de corps."

7. On the work of the Spirit in the creation and formation of humanity, see John Owen, *A Discourse concerning the Holy Spirit* (1674), in *The Works of John Owen*, ed. William H. Goold (London: Banner of Truth, 1965–68), 3:99–101. See also Abraham Kuyper, *The Work of the Holy Spirit*, trans. Henri De Vries (Grand Rapids: Eerdmans, 1900), 30–31.

Psalms, the Spirit is described as Creator ("by the breath of his mouth," Ps. 33:6–9), the giver of life, and preserver and governor of the universe (104:27–30).[8]

This theme underlies much of the Old Testament. In Genesis 6:3 ("my Spirit"—*ruach*), the Spirit of God is seen no more to preserve the lives of the human race for such long times as before, limiting its duration to 120 years. At the same time, the Spirit of God is clearly understood to be the one who provides and oversees life, in this case limiting it in judgment. In Ezekiel 37:5–9, *ruach* is translated "breath" in the ESV, but the context points to the Spirit of God who gives life to the dead bones in Ezekiel's vision.

According to Psalm 51:11, it might appear that the Spirit of God was with his people on an intermittent basis. But this is not the case; David, in his confession of sin, realizes that continued impenitence is incompatible with the presence of the Holy Spirit. We will soon note a comment from John Goldingay that the confession of Yahweh was as much dependent on the Holy Spirit as Paul writes of the confession of Jesus as Lord (1 Cor. 12:3). God's Spirit instructed Israel in the exodus and wilderness (Neh. 9:20), but was grieved by the rebellious Israelites (Isa. 63:7–10). Above all, the future realization of the kingdom of God in the coming of the Messiah was to be the result of an outpouring of the Spirit of God (Isa. 42:1f.; 61:1f.; Joel 2:28–32; Zech. 4:6).

The Spirit of God and Action

The Spirit of God is sometimes equated with the breath of God, indicating action that effects dramatic change. In 1 Samuel 10:5–6, Samuel informs Saul that the Spirit of the Lord will rush upon him, with the result that he would start to prophesy and be turned into another man. God gave him another heart (v. 9), the Spirit of God rushed upon him, and he prophesied, to everyone's astonishment, so much so that their comments ("Is Saul also among the prophets?") became a permanent epigram (vv. 10–12). Later, Saul's having sent

8. Elihu's speech in Job 33:4 indicates that it was widely recognized in the ancient Near East that the Spirit of God was the Creator and the giver of contingent, creaturely life.

messengers to capture David, the Spirit of God comes upon them and they join the company of the prophets in prophesying (19:18–20). After dispatching two further groups in succession with the same intention and identical results (v. 21), Saul comes in person, "and the Spirit of God came upon him also, and as he went he prophesied. . . . And he too stripped off his clothes, and he too prophesied before Samuel and lay naked all that day and all that night" (vv. 22–24).

The Spirit is depicted in 1 Samuel 16 in a series of dramatic actions. In verse 13, "the Spirit of the LORD rushed upon David from that day forward," in association with his being anointed with oil as king by Samuel, while in verse 14 the Spirit departed from Saul. Earlier, in 1 Samuel 10:6–10, the Spirit of the Lord had rushed upon Saul following his anointing. The idea is of a sudden, overwhelmingly powerful impulse enabling the recipient to undertake actions that would have otherwise been beyond him, an impulse that was not necessarily an abiding or permanent endowment. It could also happen regardless of the individual's own personal condition; God eventually rejected Saul as king. These impulses are evident earlier in the judges Jephthah (Judg. 11:29–33) and Samson (13:25; 14:19).

In a dramatic scenario, Elisha requests a double portion of Elijah's spirit, the portion of the firstborn (2 Kings 2:9f.). Elisha sees him depart (the condition for reception), with the results that follow, twice as many recorded miracles as his master had performed. The wider context indicates that the Spirit of God was the **efficient cause** of Elijah's (and therefore Elisha's) miracles and that Elisha's request was not for the transfer of Elijah's personal, human spirit but rather for the endowment of the Spirit that had worked such signs.

In keeping with the semantic range of *ruach*, the Spirit of God is often compared to the wind; we see the Spirit from his effects, as we see the wind from the swaying of the crops or the trees.[9] In line with this, Warfield describes the Spirit in the Old Testament as "the executive of the Godhead[,] . . . the divine principle of activity."[10] Warfield considers that the Old Testament discussion of the Spirit

9. Thiselton, *Holy Spirit*, 4, 20–21.
10. Warfield, "Spirit of God," 131.

of God is divided into two broad categories. On the one hand is the work of the Spirit in the world and on the other his work in God's people. The latter is in turn divisible into the Spirit's work in the theocracy and in the individual soul.[11]

Yet did Warfield go far enough? The Spirit is not merely God at work in the world, but is the presence of God himself. Thiselton remarks: "The Spirit who reveals and inspires does so because he is often understood as more than the Agent of God; *he represents God's presence*. It would be anachronistic to suggest that Old Testament writers consciously anticipated the later doctrine of the Holy Trinity; but they certainly laid the groundwork for such a doctrine by associating God's Spirit with God himself."[12] Warfield's comment, *only insofar as it concerns the Old Testament*, is little different from the Socinian notion that the Holy Spirit is simply the power of God. While it may be stretching a point to say that the Old Testament writers viewed the Spirit in a distinctly personal sense, there is more to it than that. In terms of the synonymous parallelism of Hebrew poetry, the Spirit of God is presented in parallel with the presence of God or with God himself (Pss. 51:11; 104:29–30; 139:7; Ezek. 36:23–33; Hag. 2:4–5).[13]

The Holy Spirit and the Creation

Warfield argues that the Spirit is regarded as the source of order, life, and light. Genesis 1:2 is crucial.[14] The Spirit of God is seen here as like a mother bird hovering or brooding over the creation. In all that follows, the production of light, dry land, vegetation, creatures in the sea, air, and land, and ultimately humanity itself, we should understand that the Spirit of God is comprehensively engaged. This work entails making the earth—originally empty, formless, dark, and wet—into a place fit for humans to live, flourish, and exercise jurisdiction on behalf of God. This has obvious application to the environment today; since it belongs to the Trinity, caring for it is a

11. Warfield, "Spirit of God," 132–56.
12. Thiselton, *Holy Spirit*, 4.
13. Thiselton, *Holy Spirit*, 13–14.
14. Warfield, "Spirit of God," 133.

task of the whole human race, including the covenant people. Nevertheless, it is striking that the fathers rarely used this chapter for the work of the Spirit in creation—Psalm 33:6 was their common base.

In particular, as we noted above, the Spirit was fully engaged in the creation of humanity. The plural in Genesis 1:26–27—"let us make man in our image"—entails what Abraham Kuyper called a "conference" within the divine **being.**[15] All three persons of the Trinity were involved, each performing a distinct part of the work and each working together inseparably. The Spirit's involvement is underlined in the next chapter, where the inbreathing of God constitutes Adam "a living soul" (2:7 KJV).

The Spirit pervades the created order, maintaining it and granting life to his creatures (Job 26:13; 27:3; 32:8; 33:4; 34:14–15; Ps. 104:29–30; Isa. 40:7; 59:19). Thiselton comments that it is strange that the Spirit is often associated "with chaos or lack of order, when from the first the Spirit is associated with order; and strange that 'peace' often obscures creativity." The picture in Isaiah 63:11–14, he says, "is that of a dynamic, powerful, creative agent of God," if anything more than that, for "he represents God's presence."[16]

As the living God, the Spirit is the source of all life. He gives life to dead bones (Ezek. 37:5–14) and to all living creatures (Job 33:4; Ps. 104:27–30; Isa. 42:5).[17] He is omnipresent, inescapable (Ps. 139:7), identified with God rather than created beings (Isa. 40:12–13), the breath of the Almighty that gives humans understanding (Job 32:8) and that sustains or withers contingent entities (Isa. 40:7). In addition to working in, through, and with regular created patterns, he also operates in ways that surpass our own ability to comprehend (1 Kings 18:12; 2 Kings 2:16; 19:7; Isa. 37:7).

In line with this, Robin Routledge points to the connections between *ruach* in Genesis 1:2 and its use in Genesis 6:3. In both contexts, the reference is to the Spirit of God, "my spirit" or "my breath" in chapter 6 expressing the same idea. In Genesis 1, the Spirit is presiding over the creation. In Genesis 6, there has been a

15. Kuyper, *Holy Spirit*, 36.
16. Thiselton, *Holy Spirit*, 4.
17. Thiselton, *Holy Spirit*, 4–5.

presumptuous revolt by the human race, possibly involving illicit relations with fallen angels, which often take human form in Genesis. It foreshadows the flood and the destruction of everything that has "the breath of life." In Genesis 6:3, "my Spirit" clearly belongs to God. The Spirit is seen to have cosmological authority, separating the waters in creation on the one hand, withdrawing, in judgment, and allowing the waters to return on the other. It has an echo in Psalm 104:29–30, where the withdrawal of the Creator Spirit effects the disintegration of created life. These connections indicate the total dependence of creation, and therefore all humanity, on God.[18]

Kuyper draws attention to the widest context for the work of the Spirit, adumbrated in the Old Testament, which is to bring the whole created order to the destiny that God has appointed for it, which above all is the glory of God.[19]

> Let us not be understood to say that God comes into contact with the creature only in the regeneration of his children, which would be untrue. To the Gentiles at Athens, Paul says, "In him we live and move and have our being." And again: "For of his offspring we are." To say nothing of plant or animal, there is on earth no life, energy, law, or element but the almighty and omnipresent God quickens and supports that life from moment to moment, causes that energy to work, and enforces that law. . . . The energy that proceeds from God must therefore touch the creature in the very center of its being, whence, its whole existence must spring. Hence there is no sun, moon, nor star, no material, plant, or animal and, in much higher sense, no man, skill, gift, or talent unless God touch and support them all.[20]

Usually, the focus on the activity of the Spirit has been in relation to the church and the individual. This cosmic purpose has been missed. In fact, this is the context in which the Spirit's redemptive work takes place. It displays the grand overall design of God. It

18. Robin Routledge, "'My Spirit' in Genesis 6:4," *JPT* 20, no. 2 (2011): 232–51.
19. Kuyper, *Holy Spirit*, 22.
20. Kuyper, *Holy Spirit*, 44.

renders attempts to construct a sacred-secular division out of court. Especially in these days, when the state of the environment is a major concern, the church must recognize that the world around us is not ours but belongs to God, with Jesus Christ its Ruler and the Holy Spirit the animator, both working inseparably with the Father in the unity of the Trinity to bring the creation to its perfected goal, the redeemed humanity to participate in its administration.

The Spirit of God and the People of God

While we note the previous discussion and associated caveats, Warfield is on the right lines when he writes that the Spirit of God is described in the Old Testament as the "executive of the Godhead within the sacred nation."[21] He "represents the presence of God with his people."[22] Indeed, the Spirit gives life that the community could not possibly possess of itself (Ezek. 37:1f.). Thiselton opposes this to the illusions of much contemporary religious thought. He writes: "One of the popular misconceptions of today is that 'spiritual' or 'spirituality' denotes a religious human aspiration or capacity. If the term denotes, in a biblical sense, 'what is of the Spirit' (as it usually does in Paul), nothing could be further from the truth. . . . The adjective 'spiritual' . . . denotes precisely what issues from God, not from humankind."[23]

The Spirit Gives Endowment for Office

Deuteronomy 34:9 records that Joshua was full of the Spirit of wisdom. This is related to Moses' having laid his hands on him. Here there is a direct connection between ordination and the gift of the Spirit.[24] Similarly, Samuel anoints Saul (1 Sam. 10:1), stating that the Lord has anointed him. The human action of pouring a flask of oil on Saul's head is conjoint with the Lord's anointing. The purpose of the anointing is that Saul be king over the people of the Lord. This

21. Warfield, "Spirit of God," 142.

22. Warfield, "Spirit of God," 143.

23. Thiselton, *Holy Spirit*, 6.

24. See Max Turner, "Levison's *Filled with the Spirit*: A Brief Appreciation and Response," *JPT* 20, no. 2 (2011): 193–200, here 195.

is followed by three signs that establish this reality (vv. 1–8). Later, in 1 Samuel 16:13, Samuel anoints David as king in place of Saul. At that point, "the Spirit of the Lord rushed upon David." In Numbers 11:16–25, the Lord takes some of the Spirit that is on Moses and puts it on the seventy elders so that they prophesy and bear the burden of the people. This, as Max Turner remarks, is a charismatic endowment.[25]

The Spirit Gives Knowledge and Insight

The Spirit of God is said to give Joseph unsurpassed discernment and wisdom, in interpreting Pharaoh's dream, in an age when such abilities were greatly prized and led to major advancement. The account indicates that revelation through dreams was in accord with contemporary norms (Gen. 41:38). The Spirit also equipped the seventy elders of Israel for the task of sharing administrative duties with Moses (Num. 11:16f., 25). Immediately the Spirit rested on them and they prophesied, although only on that occasion. A similar ordination took place some time afterward, when Moses commissioned Joshua, although there is no evidence that he prophesied (Num. 27:18–20).[26] The Spirit gave Ezekiel insight into the task to which Yahweh had called him (Ezek. 3:12–24), provided him with knowledge of the contemporary abominations committed in the Jerusalem temple (8:3f.; 11:1, 5), and returned him to his fellow exiles in Chaldea (11:24). The Spirit of the Lord also gave Ezekiel the vision of the valley of dry bones, with the promise of a renewing of Israel to come (37:1).

The Spirit Rushes on the Judges

The Spirit "comes" on the judges or on the prophets. Repeatedly, the positive actions of the various judges are attributed to the Spirit of God's coming or "rushing" upon them and changing them, whether Othniel, Gideon, Jephthah, Samson, or Saul. This is irrespective of the personal character of the particular judges, few of whom were especially examples to follow (Judg. 3:10; 6:11–18;

25. Turner, "Levison's *Filled with the Spirit*," 195.
26. Congar, *Holy Spirit*, 1:5.

11:29; 13:25; 14:6, 19; 1 Sam. 10:6–13; 11:6; 16:13). Congar remarks on the Spirit's effects on people and, referring to the events in 1 Samuel connected with Saul and his messengers, states that "God . . . never seizes hold of man without involving him completely." Meanwhile, he continues, with David "something quite definitive" occurred.[27] These comings are intermittent and not the possession of the human instruments, clearly demonstrating that the Spirit cannot be under their control or act at their behest. It is a divine gift *from God* (Isa. 11:1–5; 42:1f.; 61:1f.), ultimately to be poured out on the Messiah.[28] Eventually, with the promised Messiah, the ultimate Ruler and Judge, the Spirit was to come and rest upon him for righteous rule (11:1–4).

The Spirit Is the Source of Prophecy

The Niceno-Constantinopolitan Creed states that the Holy Spirit spoke through the prophets. In this the various prophets acted and spoke under the direction of the Spirit. This may have occasionally come in ecstatic ways, as with Saul and others (1 Sam. 10:6), but this was an exception rather than a rule. The writing prophets were hardly taken up into another realm in a trancelike state; their faculties were fully engaged in crafting their writing. On some occasions, particularly in connection with the predictive element of prophecy, the Spirit would have put in the minds of the prophets statements that could never have come from their own resources. In the majority of cases, however, when the word of the Lord was engaged in applying the covenantal requirements to the contemporary situation, there was more a confluence of direct inspiration from the Spirit and receptive activity on the human level in crafting the utterance. Hence, the distinctive contributions of the human authors are preserved; we can readily distinguish between the characteristic styles of Isaiah and Amos, even in those passages in which they cite directly the words of the Lord.

It is noteworthy that the Spirit gave rise to prophetic speech among some persons who were not part of the covenant community,

27. Congar, *Holy Spirit*, 1:6.
28. Warfield, "Spirit of God," 143–44.

such as Balaam (Num. 24:2), or who were clearly acting in a rebellious and faithless manner, such as Saul (1 Sam. 10:16). That the capacity to prophesy came from God, the Spirit's giving utterance to the prophet, and not from inherent human qualities is clear in the record in Numbers 11:16–25, where the Lord takes some of the Spirit that is on Moses and puts it on the seventy elders so that they prophesy and bear the burden of the people.[29] This is confirmed, as Congar points out, by the presence of *ruach* about fifty times in Isaiah and forty-six times in Ezekiel (Isa. 48:16; 61:1; Ezek. 2:2; 11:5). He comments that it is God who communicates life (2 Chron. 15:1; 20:14; 24:20; Zech. 7:12).[30]

From this we can conclude, with Paul and others, that the Spirit of God inspired or, better, breathed out the Scriptures of the Old Testament in all the various ways in which they were produced. This includes not only utterances specifically attributed to the Lord, but also the narratives, the historical archival records, and the Wisdom Literature. Throughout the history of the people of God in the Old Testament, the Spirit was at work in producing a written record of the great redemptive acts of God. Furthermore, the Spirit's voice was and is living and dynamic, for the author of Hebrews attests that he still speaks (present tense) through the Old Testament text he inspired, specifically Psalm 95 (Heb. 3:7).

The Spirit Is Shared Out among the Leaders of Israel

The Lord took some of the Spirit that was on Moses and placed it on the seventy elders, who then prophesied (Num. 11:25). Again, Moses laid hands on Joshua, who was to succeed him and bring the people into the land of promise, with the result that he was filled with the Spirit of wisdom (Deut. 34:9). Later, Elisha received a double portion of the Spirit from Elijah (2 Kings 2:5–14).[31] Each of these events underlines the point that the Spirit of God is not a

29. See also the cases of David (1 Sam. 16:13), Azariah (2 Chron. 15:1), Jahaziel (2 Chron. 20:14), Zechariah (2 Chron. 24:20), and the whole body of the prophets (Neh. 9:20–30; Hag. 2:5; Zech. 7:12; 4:6).

30. Congar, *Holy Spirit*, 1:7.

31. Thiselton, *Holy Spirit*, 5.

possession of any individual, however significant the person may be. The Spirit comes on individuals in the Old Testament, but for the good of the community of God's people.[32]

Nor is the fact of the Spirit's coming on a person to be identified with some ecstatic experience. This is clear in the case of Bezalel, the craftsman selected by God to produce the furniture for the tabernacle (Ex. 31:1–5), who had been filled by the Spirit of God for this express purpose. It follows that throughout Bezalel's life, the Spirit had guided and equipped him to develop the skills and craftsmanship requisite for the task to which God was to call him. This could be only through the superintendence of his work, encompassing a lifetime of patient learning and development. The providential guidance and government of God is included.[33]

In this context, Warfield writes that the Spirit of God has an official character as the "executive of the Godhead within the sacred nation." God is in and among his people through inspired instruments in supernatural leading and teaching (Hag. 2:5; Zech. 4:6). The Spirit represents the presence of God with his people. The intermittent nature of his evident operations points to the fact that he is not the possession of his instruments. The Spirit is a divine gift—*from God* (Isa. 11:1f.).[34] It is impossible to explain the history of salvation, the production of the Scriptures of the Old Testament, and the expressions of Israel's worship apart from the Spirit.[35]

In all this, the Spirit works in a range of ways. At times, in the case of prophecies of future events, in great and astounding miracles, and in the breathing out of Scripture, his actions through his human agents far exceed human ability. Who among us can accurately predict events centuries in the future? How many of us can raise the dead or part a great river with a word of command? Yet on the other hand, the Spirit employs the dedicated labors of a lifetime of craftsmanship, overseeing every stage from apprenticeship to fully

32. Thiselton, *Holy Spirit*, 9.

33. Warfield, "Spirit of God," 138.

34. Warfield, "Spirit of God," 142–44.

35. John Goldingay, "The Holy Spirit and the Psalms," *JPT* 27, no. 1 (2018): 1–13, here 13.

matured skill. Whether a Moses and an Elijah, or a Bezalel and an Oholiab, the Spirit of God works how he pleases, suddenly or, more often, patiently over many years.[36]

The Spirit of God and the Individual

Warfield asserts that in the Old Testament we find "the indwelling Spirit of holiness in the hearts of God's children."[37] He points to "the revolutionary ethical consequences"[38] that follow, with conviction of sin, changes in lives, and protection from the nation's enemies (1 Sam. 10:6; Pss. 51:11; 143:10–11; Isa. 63:10–14). Particularly in Psalm 51, it is clear that he is the Spirit of holiness, before whom sin is abhorrent. Congar points to the Spirit-breath of God purifying hearts (Neh. 9:20; Isa. 44:3–5; 63:11–14; Jer. 31:31–34; Hag. 2:5; Zech. 4:6), while in the Wisdom Literature Wisdom and the Spirit are "almost identified, at least if they are viewed in their action."[39] Goldingay affirms the point that the Spirit filled the people of God in the Old Testament, enabling them to confess what was at the time contrary to the prevailing cultures when they asserted the lordship of Yahweh. He remarks that "it requires God to do something supernatural to enable people to declare that Yahweh is Lord."[40] He continues by asserting that "the praying in the Psalms is done by people who are assured by the Spirit that God is their Father and who are sure of the confidence that they can have in approaching their Father in order to . . . do something about intolerable situations."[41] In the same way as Paul writes in Ephesians 2:18, they were praying in the Spirit to the Father.[42] The anger that is often expressed in the Psalms, directed toward God from a condition of helplessness in the face of injustice and threat, can also be seen as a consequence of the Spirit's work.[43] In reality,

36. See Owen, *Holy Spirit*, in *Works*, 3:126–50.
37. Warfield, "Spirit of God," 146.
38. Warfield, "Spirit of God," 147.
39. Congar, *Holy Spirit*, 1:9.
40. Goldingay, "The Holy Spirit and the Psalms," 2.
41. Goldingay, "The Holy Spirit and the Psalms," 3.
42. Goldingay, "The Holy Spirit and the Psalms," 4.
43. Goldingay, "The Holy Spirit and the Psalms," 5.

it is God speaking to God in and through the anguished sighs of his suffering people.[44]

John (Jack) R. Levison argues that all people are indwelt by the Holy Spirit, and this also applied in the Old Testament. This is because the Spirit is the author and giver of life.[45] While there is an obvious case to be made that since the Spirit is the Creator, the whole creation in some sense participates in the activity and movement of the Spirit (Psalm 139:7 is a case in point), nevertheless, as Turner argues, this is contrary to the teaching of Scripture in general and the New Testament in particular. The New Testament "did not think of the s/Spirit as the breath of life/understanding given to all," for "those who have not received the gift of the Spirit simply do not have God's Spirit *at all*, according to Luke-Acts." For Paul and John, there are only two types of people: those in the flesh or darkness, and those in the Spirit or the light.[46] Similarly, Jenny Meyer Everts points out that Levison misses the point that there was "a decisively different understanding of the Spirit" with the death and resurrection of Christ and the inauguration of the new covenant.[47] Levison, Everts, and others seem to regard Christianity as something that began in only the first century, regarding it as separate from the Old Testament from the very first, an extreme example of discontinuity. Moreover, while Levison's book *Filled with the Spirit* has been called a magnificent contribution,[48] its universalizing tendency places extrabiblical literature effectively on a par with Scripture and approaches the biblical canon in a highly fragmented manner, claiming that 1 John is a radical call for an end to teaching.[49] Levison asks whether future

44. Goldingay, "The Holy Spirit and the Psalms," 8.

45. John R. Levison, *Filled with the Spirit* (Grand Rapids: Eerdmans, 2009). See also John R. Levison, *The Holy Spirit before Christianity* (Waco, TX: Baylor University Press, 2019).

46. Turner, "Levison's *Filled with the Spirit*," 193–200, here 198–99 (Turner's italics).

47. Janet (Jenny) Meyer Everts, "Filled with the Spirit from the Old Testament to the Apostle Paul," *Pneuma* 33, no. 1 (2011): 63–68.

48. Turner, "Levison's *Filled with the Spirit*," 193. The book has aroused both praise and censure; see John R. (Jack) Levison, "*Filled with the Spirit*: A Conversation with Pentecostal and Charismatic Scholars," *JPT* 20, no. 2 (2011): 213–31.

49. Levison, *Filled with the Spirit*, 109–221, 415–21, 427.

discussions will adequately account for the Spirit's working in all people from birth to death, and will incorporate the indispensable extrabiblical sources from Jewish and Greco-Roman contexts. He insists that "correspondences [with such sources] should not be hamstrung by a particular hermeneutical grid or assumption about the superiority of Christianity."[50]

The Spirit of God and the Messiah

The Old Testament looks forward to the coming of Yahweh to deliver his people definitively in the future, in the day of the Lord. At that time the Spirit of God will be poured out on the Anointed One, the Messiah, who will receive the Spirit permanently (Isa. 11:1–10; 32:15–18). Repeatedly, it is stressed that the Messiah will be characterized by the Spirit of God's coming on him and resting on him for his work (42:1f.; 61:1f.), poured out in abundant measure. This particularly relates to prophecies about the future (32:15; 34:16; 44:3f.).[51] In that day, the Spirit will be poured out on all flesh (Joel 2:28–32).

Similar effusion is seen in David's anointing in the midst of his brothers, for the Spirit rushed upon him from that day on, in contrast to Saul (1 Sam. 16:13). The New Testament presents Jesus as anointed above his brothers (Heb. 1:8–9, quoting Ps. 45:6–7).[52]

Redemptive-Historical Development

Warfield stresses that the principle of progressive revelation is assumed by the Scriptures in the case of the Spirit.[53] The Old Testament was "a time of preparation yet there was 'a deep and thorough grasp upon his individual work.'"[54] Congar stresses **eschatology** and progressive revelation in this connection. He comments that "in the Jewish Bible, the Breath-Spirit of God is the action of God." God reveals himself as active in giving life at the natural level, leads

50. John R. (Jack) Levison, "Recommendations for the Future of Pneumatology," *Pneuma* 33, no. 1 (2011): 79–93, here 90.

51. Warfield, "Spirit of God," 145–48.

52. Warfield, "Spirit of God," 149.

53. Warfield, "Spirit of God," 130–31.

54. Warfield, "Spirit of God," 150.

his people, raising up heroes and leaders. The Messiah brings all these functions together. Congar continues that "the 'economy' or God's plan . . . moves forward in the direction of greater and deeper interiority."[55] Progress is clear in the Old Testament and reaches its conclusion in the New.

Warfield adds that "the foundational unity of the conception [of the Spirit of God in the Old Testament] with that of the Holy Ghost of the New Testament grows ever more obvious the more attentively it is considered." The reason for this is that "the Spirit of God of the Old Testament performs all the functions which are ascribed to the Holy Ghost of the New Testament, and bears all the same characteristics."[56]

Congar remarks that in the later theology of the Holy Spirit in the Old Testament, two things are to be noted. "The Spirit is to some extent personalized" in terms of wisdom in Proverbs. Wisdom—and the Spirit—is also "characterized by its subtlety and purity, which enable it to enter everything and everyone and, while remaining unique, to be in everything and everyone as the principle of life, newness, and holy conduct."[57] This does not mean that the Holy Spirit was conceived as a distinct ***hypostasis*** in the divine **nature**. He was seen as personal as God was, but not as if the one personal God were embracing in his unity hypostatic distinctions.[58] Can we see the Holy Spirit of the Old Testament as the personal Holy Spirit of the New Testament? Yes. Are there hints of the hypostatic Spirit of the New Testament? Yes. Do these hints reveal this doctrine? No. There is a tendency toward hypostasizing,[59] but the focus is on the unity of God.[60] The Old Testament has a preparatory nature, "to prepare for the outpouring of the Spirit upon all flesh."[61] According to Warfield, the work of the Holy Spirit in the New Testament is no

55. Congar, *Holy Spirit*, 1:12.

56. Warfield, "Spirit of God," 151.

57. Congar, *Holy Spirit*, 1:11, where he cites in support Basil of Caesarea, *On the Holy Spirit*, 9, and also refers to Gregory of Nazianzus, *Oration 31*, 29; *PG*, 36:165.

58. Warfield, "Spirit of God," 151.

59. Warfield, "Spirit of God," 152.

60. Warfield, "Spirit of God," 153.

61. Warfield, "Spirit of God," 154.

more real than in the Old Testament. It is not merely that it is universal, but that it is directed to a different end. In the Old Testament, it is focused on the preservation of the covenant seed, whereas in the New Testament, it is directed to "the perfecting of the fruitage and the gathering of the harvest."[62]

Key Terms

being
efficient cause
eschatology
hypostasis
nature
persons
substance

Questions for Reflection

1. Noting the wide range of ways in which the Spirit of God is said to have acted in the Old Testament, consider how far this may or may not differ, whether in degree or kind, from the ways in which he is seen to operate in the New Testament.
2. How far do the varying stages of the history of redemption have a part to play in these similarities and differences?

62. Warfield, "Spirit of God," 156.

6

The Life and Ministry of Jesus

Because of the Holy Spirit's invisibility and anonymity, his presence is not always noted, even though it may be known that he is present. His presence is known by what he does. Even so, there is a vast increase in references to the Holy Spirit in the New Testament compared with the Old Testament. The Holy Spirit is mentioned more times by Paul alone than in the entire Old Testament. The New Testament, while never explicitly calling the Holy Spirit God, ascribes to him divine characteristics. Among other things, fellowship with one another, and with the Father and the Son, is by the Holy Spirit, and the Spirit sanctifies, gives joy in sufferings, opens people's minds to believe, enables us to worship, and brings about union with Christ.

While the New Testament portrays the Holy Spirit as active at every stage of redemption, this is especially so in the life and ministry of Jesus Christ from conception to ascension.[1] Jesus is conceived by the Holy Spirit. An angel of the Lord tells Joseph that the shocking news of Mary's pregnancy is a result of the work of the Spirit (Matt. 1:20).

1. On the Holy Spirit in the New Testament, see Donald Guthrie, *New Testament Theology* (Leicester, UK: Inter-Varsity Press, 1981), 510–72; Jules Lebreton, *History of the Dogma of the Trinity: From Its Origins to the Council of Nicæa*, trans. Algar Thorold, 8th ed. (London: Burns, Oates & Washbourne, 1939), 252–58, 280–84, 314–31, 352–54, 398–407; Arthur Wainwright, *The Trinity in the New Testament* (London: SPCK, 1963), 199–234; Peter Toon, *Our Triune God: A Biblical Portrayal of the Trinity* (Wheaton, IL: Bridgepoint, 1996), 175–94; Boris Bobrinskoy, *The Mystery of the Trinity: Trinitarian Experience and Vision in the Biblical and Patristic Tradition*, trans. Anthony P. Gythiel (St. Vladimir's Seminary Press, 1999), 95–136.

More expansively, Gabriel informs Mary that "the Holy Spirit will come upon you, and the power of the Most High will overshadow you; therefore the child to be born will be called holy—the Son of God" (Luke 1:35). The angel here compares the Spirit's role in Jesus' conception with his work in creation, where he brooded over the primeval waters (Gen. 1:2). Jesus was to be the author of a new creation, begun as the first through the overshadowing action of the Spirit of God. In turn, the holiness of the child is the result of his conception by the Holy Spirit.

In this, we agree with James D. G. Dunn, who stresses that throughout Scripture the Spirit is associated with life, "not just about life as a context for other things, as the background for other activities, but life as vitality, life as expressing that divine breath, life as gifted and manifesting the divine character of that life."[2] He draws the conclusion that there can be no artificial distinctions between particular manifestations of the Spirit, since in each case it is the same Spirit who is in view, manifesting and giving life.

Conception

Matthew and Luke approach the conception and birth of Jesus from different perspectives, Matthew from that of Joseph, Luke from Mary. In both cases, the Holy Spirit is seen as directly involved in the new life (Matt. 1:18–21; Luke 1:34–35). Joseph is not only alarmed by the news of Mary's pregnancy but determined to divorce her. This was the right thing to do in the circumstances. Since he was a good man, however, he opted for a discreet process (Matt. 1:18–19). Only the intervention of an angel in a dream, conveying the news that the pregnancy was due to the Holy Spirit, forestalled this plan. In Mary's case, the angel Gabriel informed her of the imminent pregnancy directly. Evidently, this announcement preceded the one to Joseph by several months. Mary was already noticeably pregnant when Joseph was informed, and additionally, he had time to have

2. James D. G. Dunn, "'The Lord, the Giver of Life': The Gift of the Spirit as Both Life-Giving and Empowering," in *The Spirit and Christ in the New Testament and Christian Theology: Essays in Honor of Max Turner*, ed. I. Howard Marshall, Volker Rabens, and Cornelis Bennema (Grand Rapids: Eerdmans, 2012), 1–17, here 6.

hatched his plan before the angel appeared to him. Mary had probably not informed him of the angelic visitation she had received. Alternatively, if she had done so, Joseph may not have believed her tale, coming from her own lips.

The content of these messages is very familiar. Both Joseph and Mary are informed that the child will be called Jesus ("Yahweh saves," Savior), since he will save his people from their sins (Matt. 1:21; Luke 1:31).[3] Since salvation is seen in the Old Testament as a work of Yahweh, it entails a status of identity with God by the child. This is reinforced by the revelation to Mary that the child "will be called the Son of the Most High," an expression often used for God. Moreover, he will inherit the promises of the Davidic covenant, reigning over the house of Jacob forever (Luke 1:32–33). Even more astonishing was the fact of Mary's virginity, clearly evident in her reply (v. 34). As Joel Green remarks, "her question plays a vital theological role, for it accents the fact that she is still a virgin."[4] So Gabriel explains:

> The Holy Spirit will come upon you,
> and the power of the Most High will overshadow you. (Luke 1:35)

The poetic explanation evokes its mysterious nature; it is incapable of adequate expression in ordinary language. Both Mary and Joseph are told that this is to be the result of the work of the Holy Spirit, a divine intervention reminiscent of the creation, when "the Spirit of God was hovering over the face of the waters" like a mother bird (Gen. 1:2). It was to be a creative act of God, the beginning of a new creation brought about by the direct action of the Spirit.[5] The fulcrum of redemptive history—of world history—was imminent. To underline

3. On the meaning, see Joseph A. Fitzmyer, *The Gospel according to Luke (I–IX)*, Anchor Bible 28 (New York: Doubleday, 1970), 347.

4. Joel B. Green, *The Gospel of Luke* (Grand Rapids: Eerdmans, 1997), 89.

5. Most commentators draw attention to a kindred phrase in Acts 1:8, to manifestations of the glory of God in the exodus and wilderness period or to the transfiguration, but miss this point. Green is right, however, in that "these parallel affirmations do not suggest sexual activity, but do connote divine agency." Green, *Luke*, 90. But what element of divine agency is more compelling in this case than creation? Karl Barth expresses it well when he describes the virgin birth as "a creative act of divine omnipotence." Karl Barth, *CD*, IV/1:207.

that this is a sovereign, creative act of God, we now know that parthenogenesis (virginal conception) can produce only a female, since, without the participation of a male, the Y chromosome is missing.

The result of the Spirit's action in conceiving the child is that he set the child Jesus apart from any involvement in the corruption inherited by humans from the sin of Adam, constituting him the head of the new humanity as the Son of God (Luke 1:35). Mary is his mother; the Spirit conceives him. The process of gestation and birth is normal; the conception is an act of the Spirit. Hence, the church confesses that Mary is *theotokos* ("God-bearer"), expressing in one word the personal identity of the child and the reality of his humanity.[6]

Gabriel gives Mary further reassurance. Among other things, the angel points to the invincible power of God's Word (Luke 1:37). He fulfills what he says he will do. As in the original creation, when God spoke and it was done (Gen. 1:1–5), he brought into existence what had no prior existence. The Word and the Spirit work together.

The virginal conception stands at the start of the Gospels with the resurrection at the climax, like bookends framing the whole, pointing to the mighty acts of God, effected by the Spirit, constituting and establishing the entire drama of salvation.[7]

Moreover, this is a striking example of the inseparable works of the Trinity, for the Spirit is acting in harmony with the Father and the Son in indivisible union. Elsewhere and later, Jesus consistently refers to himself as the Son sent by the Father. Thus, the conception of Jesus results from the Father's sending and is accomplished by the Spirit's sovereign creativity.[8]

Birth and Infancy Narratives

In Luke's account, the Holy Spirit surrounds the events at the nativity pervasively. Boris Bobrinskoy writes of "an exceptional

6. See here Green, *Luke*, 91.

7. The finest exposition of the doctrine of the virgin birth is Thomas F. Torrance, *Incarnation: The Person and Life of Christ* (Milton Keynes, UK: Paternoster, 2008), 94–104. See also Barth, *CD*, I/2:138–41.

8. See John Owen, *A Discourse concerning the Holy Spirit* (1674), in *The Works of John Owen*, ed. William H. Goold (London: Banner of Truth, 1965–68), 3:162–67.

convergence between the outpouring of the Spirit and the birth of Christ," so much so that he describes the Holy Spirit as "the Spirit of the incarnation, the One in whom and through whom the Word of God breaks into history."[9] Elizabeth's husband, Zechariah, is filled with the Holy Spirit when he prophesies concerning his son, John the Baptist (Luke 1:67ff.). When Mary visits her cousin, Elizabeth is filled with the Holy Spirit, and her baby leaps for joy in her womb (vv. 41–44). After Jesus' birth, when his parents take him to the temple for the ritual of purification, Simeon receives them. The Holy Spirit's being upon him, Simeon had been informed in advance by the Spirit that he would see the Christ in person, and on that day, he entered the temple "in the Spirit" (2:25–28). The implication of the account of the prophetess Anna reinforces this (vv. 36–38). While there is no explicit reference to the Spirit, it is clear that when she encountered the baby Jesus, her utterance, in thanksgiving to God and speaking of him to all who were waiting for the redemption of Jerusalem, was under the Spirit's direction.

The concise accounts of Jesus' childhood and growth that follow present a record of his development on a range of levels—physical, intellectual, social, and in relation to God. In each case, the text presents a narrative of harmony with God and creation. Among other features, his discussions in the temple with the rabbis at the age of twelve disclose a growing awareness of his relation to the Father, indicated by his reference to "the things/business of my Father" (Luke 2:49 [my translation]). This relational name entails his being the Son and implies, in the wider canonical context, that this relation is sustained by the Spirit.

Baptism and Public Ministry

Baptism

We saw in chapter 1 how Irenaeus understood the Trinity to be preeminently revealed at the Jordan, when Jesus was baptized by John. Indeed, at the outset of Jesus' public ministry, the Holy Spirit pervades all that happens. John the Baptist's ministry includes,

9. Bobrinskoy, *Mystery*, 87.

inter alia, announcing that the one who was to come would baptize "with the Holy Spirit and fire" (Luke 3:16). At Jesus' baptism, the Spirit descends on him in the form of a dove (Luke 3:22 and parallels; John 1:32–33). Bobrinskoy calls this "a revelation of the eternal movement of the Spirit of the Father who remains in the Son from all eternity," the Savior's entire being defined "in a constant, existential relation with the Father in the Spirit."[10] It manifests the eternal resting of the Spirit on the Son.[11]

John contrasts his baptism with the baptism that Jesus was to employ. John's was with water, "a baptism of repentance for the forgiveness of sins" (Luke 3:3). In contrast, the one mightier than he was to baptize with the Holy Spirit and with fire (v. 16). From this has arisen a common distinction between water baptism and Spirit baptism. It is carried over into Christian baptism, which, so it is claimed, is purely with water, whereas baptism proper is baptism with, by, or in the Holy Spirit. Such a distinction is untenable, resting as it does on a dualistic **ontology** and epistemology. Indeed, it supposes that Christian baptism is no more efficacious than the baptism of John, which in effect denies the efficacy of the work of Christ. Moreover, the context here is the difference between John and Jesus, and this between John's baptism, with water only, and Jesus' baptism, which is not only with water but also with the Holy Spirit.[12]

As John insisted, Jesus did not need to be baptized on his own account. Since he had no sin, it was unnecessary to undergo the baptism of repentance. He did so in his representative capacity, to fulfill all righteousness. Ultimately, his baptism was completed at the cross (Luke 12:49–50). For our purposes, what happened immediately after the baptism is the important point. As he came up out of the water, Jesus heard a voice from heaven intoning, "This is my beloved Son, with whom I am well pleased" (Matt. 3:17), a conflation of Isaiah 42:1 and Psalm 2:7, both of which refer to the anointed Son

10. Bobrinskoy, *Mystery*, 88, 91.

11. Bobrinskoy, *Mystery*, 94, 99.

12. Sarah Hinlicky Wilson, "Water Baptism and Spirit Baptism in Luke-Acts: Another Reading of the Evidence," *Pneuma* 38, no. 4 (2016): 476–501. We will explore this in more detail in chapter 7.

and Messiah.[13] At the same time, the Holy Spirit descended on him, not as a dove but in a form resembling a dove. We note the difference between the appearance of the Son and the appearance of the Spirit. The Son became incarnate in an indestructible personal union and remained so, whereas the manifestation of the Spirit like a dove was temporary and fleeting. The appearance of the Spirit was a type of **theophany**; it was not another incarnation, nor was it in human form. This was more a fulfillment of the Old Testament expectation of the anointed Messiah on whom Yahweh was to put his Spirit. It was the anointing for ministry, the outset of Jesus' public ministry in Israel as the Christ, the Anointed One.[14]

Anthony Thiselton stresses that the Synoptic Gospels agree that Jesus' ministry from his baptism to the cross occurred in the power of the Holy Spirit.[15] Jesus returns from the Jordan "full of the Holy Spirit," and in turn he is led by the Spirit into the wilderness to be tempted by the devil (Luke 4:1). After this great ordeal, which nevertheless was self-evidently under the direction of the Spirit of God, Jesus returns to the public sphere, to Galilee, "in the power of the Spirit" (v. 14). There in the synagogue he reads from the prophet Isaiah, where he refers to the Spirit of the Lord resting on the Messiah for his work (v. 17ff.), declaring that this is now fulfilled in himself. And so on and so forth—in all this, Luke is telling his readers that Jesus himself was governed and directed by the Holy Spirit in all that he did. His ministry as the Christ, the Anointed One, was empowered by the Spirit. Behind that, Jesus from his earliest days was in all his human development (cf. 2:40–52) under the immediate leading of the Spirit. Everything that follows in Luke's Gospel is to be read along those lines, which have been repeatedly stressed. That includes the clinching, climactic events

13. It is more than interesting that the Father's use of his own Word in Scripture treats that Word as a unity, bringing together statements and contexts from more than one document. Moreover, the Father—like the Son himself (Luke 24:25–27, 44–47)—understood his own Word, given by the Holy Spirit to focus throughout on his incarnate Son.

14. Anthony C. Thiselton, *The Holy Spirit—In Biblical Teaching, through the Centuries, and Today* (London: SPCK, 2013), 34–35.

15. Thiselton, *Holy Spirit*, 33.

of the cross, resurrection, and ascension, to which we will attend in the next chapter.

Temptation

Luke notes that after his baptism, Jesus was "full of the Holy Spirit" and entered the desert, where he was tempted for forty days and nights. This he undertook "in the Spirit" (Luke 4:1–2 [my translation]). Moreover, after the ordeal was over, he returned to Galilee "in the power of the Spirit" (v. 14). We should conclude that throughout the onslaught he faced from the devil, he was upheld and strengthened by the Holy Spirit, since these comments come as frames around a picture, descriptive of the events there portrayed.

Thiselton notes that the temptations of Jesus were not confined to the events that followed immediately from the baptism (Luke 4:13), since the devil left him until an opportune time.[16] He refers to "Luke's special interest in the Holy Spirit."[17] In this light he considers the exorcisms as the inbreaking of the kingdom of God, connected with the self-effacing nature of the Holy Spirit.[18]

Thiselton refers to J. A. T. Robinson's suggestion that since Jesus was fully human and every human depends on the Holy Spirit for communion with God, therefore Jesus lived in dependence on the Holy Spirit.[19] Moreover, as the church fathers acknowledged, wherever the Father and the Son are active, the Holy Spirit is present as well.[20] The author of Hebrews writes that Jesus learned obedience. He did so in conjunction with the things he suffered (Heb. 5:8). Evidently his human learning was enabled by the Spirit.

John Owen advanced this claim. He was followed later by Edward Irving, although Bruce McCormack argues correctly that this is typical of Reformed theology in contrast to the fathers.[21] The fathers generally considered that Jesus was sustained in his

16. Thiselton, *Holy Spirit*, 37.
17. Thiselton, *Holy Spirit*, 39.
18. Thiselton, *Holy Spirit*, 40, 44–45.
19. Thiselton, *Holy Spirit*, 42.
20. See chapters 1–4 *passim*.
21. Bruce L. McCormack, *For Us and Our Salvation: Incarnation and Atonement in*

humanity and preserved from sin by the indissoluble **hypostatic union**, his humanity being suffused by divine qualities flowing from his divine person. Owen, on the other hand, sought to do justice to the reality of the incarnation. In this he argued that humans are dependent on the Holy Spirit for their relationship with God. Since the eternal Son took into union a human nature and lived as man, so in his incarnate state he too lived in dependence on the Spirit. This was necessary in order to restore the image of God in man that had been lost at the fall; first it had to be renewed in the incarnate Christ. What the Holy Spirit does in the mystical body of Christ, the church, he did first in his natural body.[22] I have written of this elsewhere.[23]

This claim has the advantage that it provides a paradigm for our own experience and finds biblical support in the portrayal of Christ's humanity in Hebrews (Heb. 2:10–11; 5:7–9). It also demonstrates that the Spirit was and is active in these ways and so, again, all Trinitarian **persons** act together inseparably. But it is not a case of two opposed realities. The very fact that the humanity assumed into union in the incarnation is the human nature of the eternal Son of the Father should be enough to establish that these things took place within the indivisible person of the incarnate Son. United to the Son by the Spirit by whom he was conceived, his human nature developed under the direction of the Spirit and was progressively deified in union with the Son by the same Spirit and so grew in his relation to the Father.[24] If it were to be held that the Spirit empowered the incarnate Christ while the Son who had taken his humanity into union was passive, an incipient **Nestorianism** would result, a division in the person of Christ; it would then appear that the Spirit was needed to effect the union that would otherwise not have occurred. This is a criticism leveled at Owen.[25] Owen argues that

---

the Reformed Tradition, Studies in Reformed Theology and History 1, no. 2 (Princeton, NJ: Princeton Theological Seminary, 1993), 17–22.

22. Owen, *Holy Spirit*, in *Works*, 3:168–76.

23. Robert Letham, *The Work of Christ* (Leicester, UK: Inter-Varsity Press, 1993), 114–15.

24. See Robert Letham, *Systematic Theology* (Wheaton, IL: Crossway, 2019), 500–503.

25. Oliver D. Crisp, *Revisioning Christology: Theology in the Reformed Tradition*

whatever the Son did according to his human nature was by the enabling power of the Holy Spirit.[26] At first sight, this sounds a bit like a form of Nestorianism, but Owen qualifies it by reference to the inseparable operations of the Trinity, ensuring that it is understood to be inseparable from the action of the Son himself.

Again, Abraham Kuyper is helpful. In the incarnation there was an extraordinary operation of the Spirit, enabling the Son to take our nature without being defiled by sin, Kuyper argues. The incarnate Son was not born a human *person* but assumed into union with his own person a human *nature*, so that there could be no possibility of his turning away from conformity to God. The weaknesses of humanity that he assumed could not be sinful weaknesses, since he was the eternal Son of the Father. The sanctifying work of the Spirit ensured that. What he needed was "the gifts of the Holy Spirit to enable his weakened nature . . . to be his instrument in the working out of his holy design" and to transform his humanity into a glorious nature—not by regeneration, as is necessary in our case, but by resurrection.[27] Thus, in his humanity, he was sealed by the Spirit beyond measure (John 3:34).[28] This has the support of Paul's important statement in Romans 1:4 that Jesus, the Son of God, entered into a new stage of his mediatorial work at the resurrection, that of "Son of God with power according to the Spirit of holiness."[29] One caveat might be that, for our part, we need transformation *both* by regeneration and then, as its climax, *also* by resurrection.

Public Ministry

Forewarning about future persecution, Jesus promises that the Holy Spirit was to give guidance to the disciples in crisis conditions

---

(Farnham, UK: Ashgate, 2011), cited by Leopoldo A. Sánchez M., *T&T Clark Introduction to Spirit Christology* (London: T&T Clark, 2022), 138–39.

26. Owen, *Holy Spirit*, in *Works*, 3:161–62.

27. Abraham Kuyper, *The Work of the Holy Spirit*, trans. Henri De Vries (Grand Rapids: Eerdmans, 1900), 88–92.

28. Kuyper, *Holy Spirit*, 94.

29. See John Murray, *The Epistle to the Romans* (Grand Rapids: Eerdmans, 1965), 5–12; C. E. B. Cranfield, *A Critical and Exegetical Commentary on the Epistle to the Romans* (Edinburgh: T&T Clark, 1979), 57–64.

(Matt. 10:19–20; Mark 13:11; Luke 12:12; cf. 21:14–15), "one of the few references genuinely to link the Holy Spirit with 'spontaneity.'"[30]

Famously, Jesus warns about the sin of blasphemy against the Holy Spirit, which is unforgivable (Matt. 12:31–32). This worries many recent converts, who think they may have committed it themselves. The point that it is unforgivable, however, indicates that it is a type of sin by which a person places himself or herself beyond the possibility of repentance. Since God promises forgiveness to all who repent (1 John 1:7–9), the unforgivable nature of the sin establishes that it is one from which a person will never repent. Therefore, it is a settled, determined, and final repudiation of the grace of God. In particular, it is a decisive, rancorous insult to the Holy Spirit, who powerfully conveys the message of the gospel as it centers in Jesus Christ. The author of Hebrews states that those who have done this have "outraged the Spirit of grace" (Heb. 10:29). It is not a sin ever committed by any who have a deep concern about it.

Jesus speaks of the Father's gift of the Holy Spirit to those who ask (Matt. 7:7–11; Luke 11:1–13). Thiselton remarks that there was a relative restraint in the Synoptic Gospels about the Spirit, for which he provides a range of possible reasons: the self-effacement of the Spirit, the focus on the cross, and the later occurrence of Pentecost.[31]

Jesus and Covenant Fulfillment

John 3

Jesus, in his conversation with Nicodemus, emphasizes that the Holy Spirit gives birth from above. Nicodemus, a member of the Sanhedrin, should have realized this. Was Nicodemus, at this stage, one of those to whom Jesus would not commit himself (John 2:23–25)? The fact that he came to Jesus at night—remembering that John wrote of darkness as indicative of evil and unbelief—suggests that. If that were so, it would reinforce the point that he would have needed a work of the Spirit "from above" to change him (3:3 [my translation]). Jesus compares the Spirit to the wind, in its incomprehensibility and

30. Thiselton, *Holy Spirit*, 44.
31. Thiselton, *Holy Spirit*, 47.

power (v. 8). John presents a play on words: πνεῦμα (*pneuma*) means both "wind" and "spirit" and ἄνωθεν (*anōthen*) means "from above" as well as "again." The sense of "again" is present in verses 3–6, where Nicodemus understands Jesus to be talking of some form of rebirth, while there is a shift to "from above" in verses 8–19, where Jesus refers to his ascension and his coming into the world. Jesus is pointing to the sovereign and mysterious action of God, which is not under human control. In both senses, entry into the kingdom is by neither natural birth nor privileged status but by the Spirit.

In John 3:5, Jesus states to Nicodemus that "unless one is born of water and the Spirit, he cannot enter the kingdom of God." Discussion has surrounded this phrase, γεννηθῇ ἐξ ὕδατος καὶ πνεύματος, "born of water and spirit." The clear majority interpretation is that "water" refers to baptism, entry into the kingdom being by baptism and the Spirit, the baptism of Jesus accompanied by the renewing power of the Spirit. Others think it is effectively a hendiadys, in which two or more terms express the same thing, with "water" indicating the regenerating work of the Spirit, which would appear to fit the immediate context of Jesus' stressing the necessity of new birth.[32] Some point to the cleansing by water foreshadowed in Ezekiel 36:25.

Aside from the point that baptism is frequently connected with resurrection, renewal, and new creation, effected by the Spirit, and would by no means be inappropriate to the context, a range of factors support the reference to baptism. The strong language that Jesus uses about the sharp transition to entry into the kingdom fits baptism and its identification with Christ in his death and resurrection. The accompanying themes of judgment and new creation do so also, as does the focus on the ascension that follows. Moreover, Jesus corrects Nicodemus's assumption that *anōthen* means "to be born again" by turning to the alternative rendering "from above" and focusing on the mysterious work of the Spirit and the mysteries of the incarnation and ascension. Baptism is connected with the washing away of sins (Acts 2:38–39; 22:16; 1 Cor. 6:11), with the concomitant cleansing,

32. John Murray, *Select Lectures in Systematic Theology*, vol. 2 of *Collected Writings of John Murray* (Edinburgh: Banner of Truth, 1977), 181.

and is said to save us through the resurrection of Christ, just as Noah was delivered by water (1 Peter 3:18–22). Baptism itself does not save us, but it is the Spirit working in and with baptism that effects this great change. We will discuss this further in chapter 7.

John 4:21–24; 7:37–39

In chapter 1, we saw the patristic discussion of John 4:21–24 in connection with true worship as Trinitarian.[33] Here, the earlier reference in the chapter to "living water" (v. 10) that Jesus would provide to those who thirst is clearly to the Holy Spirit. John records Jesus, after his resurrection, breathing out the Spirit on his disciples (John 20:21–22) and so having authority to send the Spirit, as he mentions in the Upper Room Discourse (14:16, 26; 15:26; 16:7). In this light, Jesus' announcement that for whoever believes in him rivers of living water will flow from him is fulfilled after his ascension when he poured out the Spirit (7:37–39, fulfilling Isaiah 55:1f.).[34] Believers in Jesus were to become sources and fountains of life from the Holy Spirit in terms of both the presence he would maintain in them and the gifts he would disburse to them. Statements like these should be viewed in connection with Jesus' overall teaching, which provides their context. Hence, his announcement that he is the source of everlasting life, received by faith and by eating his flesh and drinking his blood, is found in the context of his eucharistic discourse (John 6:63).[35]

Atonement

At the final point in the crucifixion narrative, Mark records that Jesus "breathed his last" (*exepneusen*), and Luke translates it the same (Mark 15:37; Luke 23:46). The sense of εκπνευω is "to breathe out, to

33. See also Robert Letham, *The Holy Trinity: In Scripture, History, Theology, and Worship*, rev. and expanded ed. (Phillipsburg, NJ: P&R Publishing, 2019), xxxv, 67, 150, 159, 502–3.

34. Thomas Aquinas, *Commentary on the Gospel of St. John* (Albany, NY: Magi Books, 1980), 433–36.

35. Robert Letham, *The Lord's Supper: Eternal Word in Broken Bread* (Phillipsburg, NJ: P&R Publishing, 2001); Letham, *Systematic Theology*, 753–57.

breathe one's last," as a circumlocution for "to die."[36] Matthew writes that Jesus "yielded up his spirit" (*apheken to pneuma*, Matt. 27:50). This is normally taken to mean that Jesus committed his own spirit or soul to the Father. In support of this, Stephen prays in identical fashion as he is being stoned. Yet it is more than possible, perhaps probable, that Jesus is referring to the Holy Spirit. There are good reasons why this may be so.

Theologically, we have repeatedly seen that in all of God's actions, all three persons are inseparably involved. One of the Trinity died according to the flesh. There can be no separation within the Trinity. The Spirit upheld the Son, but in accord with the eternal decree of the undivided Trinity, the Son was left to die defenseless according to his assumed humanity. I will be discussing this at greater length in a subsequent book on the eternal Son.[37]

Moreover, Paul describes the Spirit as "the Spirit of the Son" or "the Spirit of Christ." He so closely associates the Spirit with Christ that at times he appears to identify them (2 Cor. 3:16–17). We saw how the Spirit upheld him in his human weakness and so cannot possibly have been distanced from him at any time.

In terms of biblical exegesis, Jesus the Son offered himself on the cross to the Father as the definitive sacrifice for human sin, and he did so "through the eternal Spirit" (Heb. 9:14). This can hardly be a reference to the human spirit or to some abstract quality or virtue. The author of Hebrews was not under the influence of Platonic philosophy or the exegetical methods of Philo of Alexandria, as some once posited.[38] That the offering was directed to the Father entails

36. *BAGD*; *LN*.

37. See Thomas Brand, "A Trinitarian Christology of the Fourth Word from the Cross: The *Communicatio Idiomatum*, the Modal Distinction, and the Forsakenness of Christ" (PhD diss., University of Durham, 2020), which builds on Cyril of Alexandria, Thomas Aquinas, and Francis Turretin to construct an important proposal that maintains Trinitarian and Christological orthodoxy and provides a theologically convincing framework for understanding the full ramifications of the fourth word.

38. See Ronald Williamson, *Philo and the Epistle to the Hebrews* (Leiden: Brill, 1970), 509, 576–79, who concludes that it is doubtful whether the anonymous author of Hebrews had ever read Philo; cited by Philip Edgcumbe Hughes, *A Commentary on the Epistle to the Hebrews* (Grand Rapids: Eerdmans, 1977), 29, 83n60, 293–95.

that it was in or by the Son. This puts the comment in a Trinitarian context that in turn requires the reference to be to the Holy Spirit. The atonement was an event that integrally involved all three persons of the Trinity.[39]

Burial

Owen discusses this question in his great treatise on the Holy Spirit. It is not a subject commonly aired, yet the burial of Jesus is integral to the gospel (1 Cor. 15:4). Death disrupts the human being, forcing soul and body apart (2 Cor. 5:8–9). But Jesus' body was preserved from decay (Ps. 16:10; Acts 2:31) "without those **accidents** of change that affect other dead bodies." Angels guarded the tomb from any threat of human violence (Matt. 28:1–4; John 20:12), while the Spirit kept the body from decay. The union of the incarnate person was preserved.[40]

Key Terms

accidents
hypostatic union
Nestorianism
ontology
persons
theophany

Question for Reflection

Read the first four chapters of Luke and note how the Spirit is connected to the events there, particularly the conception, birth, and life of Jesus. What does this imply for the rest of Jesus' earthly life and ministry?

39. See also Owen, *Holy Spirit*, in *Works*, 3:176–80.
40. See Owen, *Holy Spirit*, in *Works*, 3:180–81.

7

Resurrection, Ascension, and Pentecost

The Resurrection

Jesus makes explicit this indivisibility of the Spirit with the Father and the Son in his final instructions to the apostles before his ascension (Matt. 28:18–20). He outlines that baptism in particular, and the ministry of the church in general, is to be integral to the spread of the kingdom of God in the ages to follow. Thus, the church is to make the nations to be disciples, beginning with baptism. This baptism is to be into "the name of the Father and of the Son and of the Holy Spirit." Behind this lies the fact that at every stage of the outworking of God's covenant, he names himself. In the Abrahamic covenant, he names himself "El Shaddai," God Almighty (Gen. 17:1). In the Mosaic covenant, he reveals his name "Ehyeh," I will be who I will be (Ex. 6:3). Matthew has shown how Jesus fulfills all the successive covenants God made. He has now brought into effect the new covenant promised through the prophets (Matt. 26:27–29), in which not only Israel but all nations participate through faith (cf. 8:11–12). Hence, in this ultimate climactic revelation of the new covenant in Christ, God reveals his covenant name in its fullness, the *one* name of the Father, the Son, and the Holy Spirit. The Spirit is on an equality with the Father and the Son. Moreover, the Spirit subsists in the one **being** of God. The Spirit is not only equal to but indissolubly one with the Father and the Son.

Paul expounds the work of the Spirit in resurrection (Rom. 8:10–11). The Father raised Christ the Son from the dead by his Spirit. At an undisclosed date in the future, he will also raise us from the dead in union with Christ by his Spirit. Meanwhile, the same Spirit who raises the dead lives in us. From this we gather that in the time between the resurrection of Christ and our resurrection, the Holy Spirit is dominantly active. This is not, of course, in any way separable from the engagement of the Father and the Son, but just as the work of the indivisible Trinity is seen at the cross, while the particular work itself terminates on the Son, so here the particular work of the Spirit is inseparable from the operations of the whole Trinity. We will consider this later in chapter 10, on the Holy Spirit and the last things.

Accordingly, there are two great realms or aeons, one according to the flesh and the other according to the Spirit (1 Cor. 15:35–58). The first is in Adam and applies to all descended from him by natural generation. It also includes Jesus Christ in his incarnate lowliness, since he took Adam's place living in our nature in a fallen world, distorted by sin (Rom. 1:3–4). It consists of the provisional nature of the cosmos, declared to be very good but itself awaiting fulfillment (8:23–25). The second realm is governed by the risen Christ, and here the Holy Spirit directs it, bringing it to its destined fulfillment at the return of Christ when the church and the whole creation will be transformed.[1]

The Ascension

The Ascension and the Holy Spirit

Luke records the details of the ascension from the perspective of the apostles (Luke 24:50–51; Acts 1:9–11), but there are important references to it throughout the New Testament. When Jesus was taken up into heaven, the disciples looked on. This connects the event with the ascension of Elijah in 2 Kings 2 (Acts 1:8–9). There

1. See Geerhardus Vos, *The Pauline Eschatology* (Grand Rapids: Eerdmans, 1972). See also the older essay by Vos, "The Eschatological Aspect of the Pauline Conception of the Spirit," in *Biblical and Theological Studies*, ed. by the members of the faculty of Princeton Theological Seminary (New York: Charles Scribner's Sons, 1912), 209–59.

Elijah warned Elisha that he was going to be taken from him. Elisha asked, in view of the impending absence of his leader, that he receive a double portion of Elijah's spirit, the portion appropriate to the firstborn son (2 Kings 2:9). Elijah replied that this was a hard thing for which to ask, but that his request would be granted if he saw Elijah depart (v. 10). The fact that the disciples watch as Jesus ascends is to be seen in this light, particularly so because, at the same time, Jesus affirmed that they would receive the promised Holy Spirit (Acts 1:4–5, 8). Some might point to a difference between Elijah's human spirit that Elisha received and the Holy Spirit, who was to come on the disciples, disbarring this connection. But the idea that the passage in 2 Kings refers to the human spirit of Elijah is mistaken. It was not by Elijah's own capacities that he performed the miracles he did. These were acts of a prophet invested with the power of God, giving life to the dead.

Elisha's request was granted on his observation of Elijah's ascension, the ensuing record listing twice as many miracles to his account as to his predecessor. Similarly, the rest of the book of Acts enumerates the mighty works of God done by the Holy Spirit through the ministry of the apostles. Luke describes, by implication, this second volume of his works as the continuation of all that Jesus did and taught (Acts 1:1), this time through the apostles. The apostles of themselves, however, did not have the abilities to perform such works or to teach what they did. Their works followed their investiture with the Holy Spirit. At first they were sequestered away in an upper room (vv. 12–26). When the Spirit came, they proclaimed the Word of God with boldness, resisted all pressure to the contrary, performed acts of power, and saw huge crowds come to faith (e.g., 2:1–4:31). Luke's Gospel led up to the ascension; Luke's record in Acts is grounded on the ascension and the sending of the Spirit. All that follows is the account of the works performed by the Spirit through the ministry of selected apostles, mainly but not exclusively Peter and Paul. All this follows on from the ascension (cf. John 20:17–22) and the glorification of Jesus as the Christ (7:37–39).

The action of the Spirit in the ascension and consequent to it is seen in a number of ways. The apostles' last glimpse of Jesus is of his hands raised in priestly benediction. It is to be characteristic of his ongoing ministry, in and through the Holy Spirit, who was to be poured out a few days later at Pentecost.

The parting of Jesus from the disciples distinguishes the ascension from the resurrection appearances. Then Jesus disappeared, only to reappear later; this is permanent. The direct person-to-person contact of the past has ended. It is an ongoing departure. But this has to be weighed against his presence by the Holy Spirit. Jesus is absent in one sense, present in another (Matt. 28:20; John 14:16–18). This presence is grounded in the fact that all three ***hypostases*** are inseparable in the indivisible Trinity, as expressed in the baptismal formula.

Jesus is passive; the Father takes him up to heaven, to his right hand. The movement originates from God. Jesus in his incarnate state lived in dependence on the Spirit and obeyed the Father's will. The ascension mirrors the virginal conception (Luke 1:26–38); the Spirit takes the initiative in both. The Spirit brings about the conception of the incarnate Son; just as the Father raised Jesus from the dead by the power of the Spirit, so the Spirit takes him to the realm of the Father.

The Holy Spirit is directly related to the high priestly ministry of the ascended Christ. The blessing poured out on his church, recorded throughout Acts and experienced in the midst of persecution, comes from the Spirit. The author of Hebrews records the pattern: ascension ("passed through the heavens"), access ("let us . . . draw near"), and grace ("find grace to help") (Heb. 4:14–16).

Douglas Farrow's comment on the centrality of the ascension to Luke-Acts is important. He argues that it is the climax toward which the Gospel heads and the starting point for the accounts of the expansion of the church in Acts. Peter's sermon at Pentecost (Acts 2:14–36) is about Jesus' ascension to the Father, from where he sends the Spirit.[2] Again, all three **persons** of the Trinity work together inseparably. The ascension of Christ and his high priestly ministry is integrally related to the sending of the Spirit at Pentecost.

2. Douglas Farrow, *Ascension and Ecclesia: On the Significance of the Ascension for Ecclesiology and Christian Cosmology* (Edinburgh: T&T Clark, 1999), 16.

The Ascension, the Holy Spirit, and the Lord's Supper

The relationship between the Spirit and the ascension was prominent in the debates surrounding the Lord's Supper at the time of the Reformation. This came to a head at the Colloquy of Marburg in 1529, when Martin Luther and Huldrych Zwingli crossed swords. Luther held to the ubiquity of the humanity of Christ, since he thought that divine **attributes** were communicated to the humanity in the incarnation. Zwingli, on the other hand, maintained that the body of the ascended Christ was in one place, at the right hand of God, and so could not be present simultaneously in a variety of places. Luther countered with the argument that the right hand of God is everywhere.[3] John Calvin, who appeared on the scene some years later, agreed with Zwingli on the body of Christ's being in one place, although his view of the sacrament was stronger. He argued that the faithful feed on the body of Christ, which, although at the right hand of God, is communicated to us by the Holy Spirit, who "joins things separated by distance."[4] Calvin's riposte to Luther and Lutheranism included the point that in that view, justice had not been done to the reality of the ascension and consequently to the work of the Spirit. We will consider the relationship of the Spirit to the sacraments in more detail in chapters 8 and 10.

The Holy Spirit and Truth—The Apostolic Preaching and Writing

We noted that the Spirit's divine status is clear from Jesus' teaching in John 14–16 on his coming at Pentecost. Here he calls the Spirit "another *paraclētos* [paraclete]" (John 14:16), another like himself. The word παράκλητος (*paraclētos*) has often been translated as "Comforter"

3. B. J. Kidd, *Documents Illustrative of the Continental Reformation* (Oxford: Clarendon Press, 1911; repr., 1967), 247–54.

4. John Calvin, *CO*, 6.127–28; 49.107, 487; John Calvin, *Institutes*, 3.1.1; 3.2.24; 4.14.16; 4.15.15; 4.17.9–12; John Calvin, *Calvin: Theological Treatises*, trans. J. K. S. Reid (Philadelphia: Westminster Press, 1954), 137, 267–68; John Calvin, *Commentary on the First Epistle of Paul the Apostle to the Corinthians*, 246; Robert Letham, *Union with Christ: In Scripture, History, and Theology*, rev. and expanded ed. (Phillipsburg, NJ: P&R Publishing, 2011), 103–15.

or "Counselor" (the ESV prefers "Helper"), but no one word in English accurately captures its meaning. It is most akin to "defense attorney," one who speaks on our behalf in opposition to an accuser, represented by the *diabolos* ("devil").[5] Jesus' comments here bring the Spirit into the closest possible union with the Father and the Son. The Father will send the Spirit in response to the Son's request (vv. 16, 26). Jesus identifies the Spirit's coming with his, for it is as if Jesus himself were to come in person (v. 18). This reminds us of John's earlier comment that the Spirit could come only when Jesus had been glorified (7:37–39; cf. 16:7). When the Spirit comes, he will enable the disciples to know and recognize the mutual indwelling of the Father and the Son (14:20). The Spirit's coming to those who love Jesus is the equivalent of the Father's and the Son's coming, with the Spirit's taking up residence in them as in a permanent home (vv. 21, 23). The Holy Spirit will bring to the disciples' minds all that Jesus had said to them (v. 26). So close is the union that Jesus can say that the presence and work of the Spirit is interchangeable with that of the Father and the Son.

This interchangeability is also evident when Jesus says that it is he who sends the Holy Spirit from the Father (John 15:26; cf. 16:7), whereas he had earlier spoken of the Father's sending the Spirit in response to his request (14:16, 26). Jesus also refers to the Spirit as proceeding from the Father. This is a continuous **procession** (present tense), implying that the procession is eternal, in distinction from his future sending at Pentecost. Later, Jesus will breathe the Spirit on his disciples, commissioning them to go into the world as the Father had sent him into the world (20:21–23).

In view of this inseparable union, one of the tasks that the Spirit will perform after Pentecost is to convince the world of sin, righteousness, and judgment (John 16:8–11). Each of these results is seen in unbreakable connection with the Father and the Son. The Spirit convicts the world of sin because it does not believe in the Son. His ministry is to speak of the Son and, in so doing, to expose resistance and opposition where it occurs, thus displaying the nature of sin as

5. Bertrand de Margerie, *The Christian Trinity in History*, trans. Edmund J. Fortman, Studies in Historical Theology 1 (Petersham, MA: St. Bede's Publications, 1982), 32–34.

unbelief in the Son of God. He also convicts the world of righteousness, seen in the Son's going to the Father. This refers to the resurrection, ascension, and glorification of Jesus Christ the Son, and the correlative approval and vindication given him by the Father. Only one who is of identical status as the Father and the Son could ever effect this. Finally, the judgment facing the world following the judgment of the ruler of the world cannot be detached from the Father or the Son. John has already spoken of the prince of this world as having been cast out in connection with the cross of Jesus (12:31–32). The ruler of this world, the world in rebellion against God, the world that refused to receive the Word made flesh (1:9–14), the world for which the Father gave his only-**begotten** Son (3:16), has been dethroned. Jesus the Son has done it by his cross. God the Father has shown his immeasurable love for this wicked world by giving his Son. Yet the world faces judgment itself if it continues impenitent. And of this the Holy Spirit convicts it. In each case, the Trinitarian work is obvious.

He is thus "the Spirit of truth" (John 16:12–15). He was to guide the apostles into all truth. This is directed to the apostles and their subsequent task rather than as a blanket statement for all believers indiscriminately. He was to teach them what Jesus could not teach, since they were as yet unable to understand. Their teaching would be equivalent to his. Evidently the Holy Spirit would not only disclose the reality of redemption, but also enable the apostles to understand what would have otherwise been beyond them. It was to be a case of revelation plus illumination. The Spirit's work in both capacities is in tandem with the Word. As Richard Gaffin remarks, "to look for some word other than this Word, now inscripturated for the church, is to seek some spirit other than the Holy Spirit."[6]

In this, the Holy Spirit was to teach not his own things but those he heard from the Father, concerning the Son: "He will glorify me, for he will take what is mine and declare it to you. All that the Father has is mine; therefore I said that he will take what is mine and declare it to you" (John 16:14–15). The Spirit's teaching, given to the apostles,

6. Richard B. Gaffin Jr., *Perspectives on Pentecost: Studies in New Testament Teaching on the Gifts of the Holy Spirit* (Phillipsburg, NJ: Presbyterian and Reformed, 1979), 34.

was to center on Christ the Son, not on himself. There was to be a basic anonymity and self-effacement about the Spirit's ministry; he and his work were to be the field and the medium through which the Father would lead his people to his Son. Along these lines, we can recognize the Spirit's work after the resurrection when the disciples remembered sayings of Jesus, their significance not recognized when he uttered them and only then coming to light (2:16–17, 22). As the Spirit brought these things to their recollection, they believed the Scriptures, the Spirit working with the Word that he had originally uttered (v. 22).

From this we can see the source of some of the emphases of other New Testament writers, such as Paul and Peter. Paul writes that the revelation of God appears foolish to those who do not believe (1 Cor. 1:18–2:16), for it is only through the Spirit that the truth is disclosed and so discerned. Enlightenment, illumination, is needed, for "the natural person does not accept the things of the Spirit of God, for they are folly to him, and he is not able to understand them because they are spiritually discerned" (2:14). The Spirit is the ultimate author of Scripture (2 Tim. 3:16; Heb. 3:7; 2 Peter 1:20–21), and consequently his help is required to understand it.

Pentecost

> For when God designed the great and glorious work of recovering fallen man and the saving of sinners, to the praise of the glory of his grace, he appointed, in his infinite wisdom, two great means thereof. The one was *the giving of his Son for them*, and the other was *the giving of his Spirit unto them*. And hereby was made for the manifestation of the glory of the whole blessed Trinity; which is the utmost end of all the works of God. . . . To these heads may all the promises of God be reduced. . . . Hence, the Holy Ghost, the doctrine concerning his person, his work, his grace, is the most peculiar and principal subject of the Scriptures of the New Testament, and a most eminent immediate object of the faith of those that do believe.[7]

7. John Owen, *A Discourse concerning the Holy Spirit* (1674), in *The Works of John Owen*, ed. William H. Goold (London: Banner of Truth, 1965–68), 3:23.

Christ and the Spirit[8]

"Jesus said to them again, 'Peace be with you. As the Father has sent me, even so I am sending you.' And when he had said this, he breathed on them and said to them, 'Receive the Holy Spirit'" (John 20:21–22). This is known as "the Johannine Pentecost" because it appears to parallel, or to foreshadow, Luke's account of the day of Pentecost in Acts 2. Here Jesus' breath is the occasion for the sending of the Spirit (breath).

There are a wide range of views on the relationship of this statement in John 20:22 to Acts 2. Behind the account in John lies not only the Old Testament, but earlier events and comments in the Gospel itself. In particular there is the statement in John 7:37–39 that "the Spirit was not yet because Jesus had not yet been glorified" (my translation). This poses questions not only of the relationship between Jesus' resurrection and ascension and the giving of the Spirit on the one hand, but also of the status of the apostles and all others before these great events took place.

First, it would seem that the giving of the Spirit in John 7:37–39, who at that time was "not yet" (my translation), is to be found in John 20:22, when Jesus breathes out the Spirit, rather than in Acts, since this is in the same book and by the same author. In short, there is a giving of the Spirit in its own right that, at least chronologically, is distinct from Acts 2. It remains to ask what the nature of Jesus' breathing out of the Spirit there may be.

Second, Jesus' comment in John 16:7 is also relevant. There, talking of the sending of the *paraclētos*, he remarks that "if I do not depart, the *paraclētos* will not come to you, but when I go, I will send him to you" (my translation). Therefore, this sending is either concurrent with or consequent on Jesus' own departure, which he proceeds to identify with his going to the Father at his ascension (v. 10; cf. 20:17). This strongly suggests that the incident in John 20:22 is preliminary and subordinate to Pentecost.

Third, the expression "the Spirit was not yet" cannot mean that the Spirit did not yet exist, which would mean that he was a creature,

8. On this, see Yves M. J. Congar, *I Believe in the Holy Spirit: The Complete Three Volume Work in One Volume*, trans. David Smith (New York: Crossroad, 1997), 1:37–39.

nor that he was not yet operative, for John was heir to the Scriptures in which the Spirit of God is said to be breathed out. Furthermore, the Spirit brooded over the original creation and thus shared in it. There are many other kindred comments to which we referred in chapter 5. Rather, this statement has to be taken in a comparative sense in relation to the nature and consequences of his being given or breathed out as recorded later on in the Gospel.

The main views on the relation between John 7:37–39, 16:7, and 20:22 on the one hand and Acts 2 on the other are as follows. Some understand there to have been two different events, with the Spirit being breathed out as *paraclētos* (John 20) and separately at Pentecost for empowerment in witness. This is very much a minority view and appears to be overly analytical. There is one Holy Spirit, operating inseparably with the Father and the Son, and there is one movement of God's grace in redemption. The majority view is that this is one event, fulfilled when the precondition of Jesus' glorification takes place. The account in Acts, where the disciples were self-consciously awaiting the gift of the Spirit (Acts 1:4–5, 8), suggests that they did not regard the Johannine Pentecost as the decisive moment. Cornelis Bennema considers that it is one event occurring in stages, in step with the process of Jesus' glorification, from the cross to the resurrection to the ascension. At the cross he returns the life-giving Spirit to the Father (John 19:30), at the resurrection he gives the Spirit to the disciples (20:22), while at the completion of his glorification he sends the Spirit to empower his church. Bennema insists that these stages are not paradigmatic for today.[9] While such a theory cannot be conclusive, it has the merit of being in harmony with the overall already/not yet feature of biblical eschatology.[10] Yet it must be weighed against the mass of evidence that Pentecost was the decisive moment. As James D. G. Dunn states, it is best to view

9. Cornelis Bennema, "The Giving of the Spirit in John 19–20: Another Round," in *The Spirit and Christ in the New Testament and Christian Theology: Essays in Honor of Max Turner*, ed. I. Howard Marshall, Volker Rabens, and Cornelis Bennema (Grand Rapids: Eerdmans, 2012), 86–104.

10. This is the pervasive stress that the kingdom of God has already come in the presence of Jesus and the outpouring of the Spirit, but that its full realization awaits the return of Christ and the ultimate completion of salvation.

the Paraclete promises in relation not to John 20:22 but to Pentecost and the continuity between the ministry of Jesus and the Paraclete.[11] Underlying this is the point that "the coming of the Son from the Father to dwell among men in human flesh was something which had never happened before and which has never happened since. Similarly the relation of Jesus' disciples to him in the period before Pentecost was one which simply cannot be known again."[12] Consequently, it cannot be a pattern for experience today.[13]

Acts 2

On the occasion of the day of Pentecost, not surprisingly, all the disciples were gathered together in one place (Acts 2:1). They were anticipating the realization of the prior promise of the Father (Joel 2:28–32), communicated and explained by Jesus (Luke 24:49), and reiterated before his ascension (Acts 1:4).

The Sound

As Acts 2:2 tells us, this loud sound came suddenly "from heaven." It was not a normal sound, nor could it be described as a meteorological event, such as a whirlwind, tornado, or thunderstorm. It defied explanation in purely immanent categories. It was supernatural. It came from God, since "heaven" is God's place. It was powerful and dynamic, "like a mighty rushing wind." It had certain similarities to a powerful wind, but it was different. It was *like* a wind. That was the nearest intelligible comparison that could be made, but one that was merely approximate. "It filled the entire house"; it was all-encompassing, inescapable. No one in the house could evade it. It was not a private matter, heard by certain individuals in the gathering but not by all, but it was public and corporate.[14]

11. James D. G. Dunn, *Baptism in the Holy Spirit: A Re-Examination of the New Testament Teaching on the Gift of the Holy Spirit in Relation to Pentecostalism Today* (London: SCM, 1970), 175–77.

12. Dunn, *Baptism in the Holy Spirit*, 178.

13. Dunn, *Baptism in the Holy Spirit*, 181–82.

14. See Tom Holland, *Contours of Pauline Theology: A Radical New Survey of the Influences on Paul's Biblical Writings* (Fearn, Scotland: Mentor, 2004), 141–56. Anthony Thiselton regards this as "a decisive rejection of the classical Pentecostal view of

The Appearance

"Divided tongues as of fire appeared to them" (Acts 2:3). Again the powers of human observation and description were incapable of expressing adequately what was observed. This was the nearest comparison that could be made. There was something *like* fire, not exactly fire but akin to it. It was divided into segments. It was *like* tongues, presumably a reference to the shape and contours of the appearance of the firelike sight. Here "tongues" refers to a visual event rather than to any human speech. Moreover, once again these "tongues [that appeared like] fire" "rested on each one of them." This was no private or individual matter, something experienced by select individuals from which others were excluded. It included everyone present. This appearance and the resting, the fire, was a corporate reality.

Furthermore, it was not something that was anticipated in the manner in which it was experienced, nor was it an event that could be earned by prior virtues of those who experienced it. It was not an immanent matter that arose from within the church. It came from above, from God, suddenly, unexpectedly.

All Were Filled with the Holy Spirit

This, once more, was not an individual but a corporate and universal reality (Acts 2:4). It was not dependent on the state or condition of those present in the house. It happened regardless of that. It happened to them all. *It was an objective, corporate event, not a subjective, individual experience.* Since so many claims are based on the Pentecost event, with suggestions that this is a repeatable phenomenon, these factors must be fully taken into consideration. Pentecost has no connection with individually based experiences.[15]

---

an individualist and 'single event' character of 'baptism in the Spirit.'" Anthony C. Thiselton, *The Holy Spirit—In Biblical Teaching, through the Centuries, and Today* (London: SPCK, 2013), 467.

15. Arie Zwiep focuses on the corporate nature of baptism with the Spirit, Pentecost as the anticipation of **eschatological** promises. Arie W. Zwiep, *Christ, the Spirit and the Community of God: Essays on the Acts of the Apostles* (Tübingen: Mohr Siebeck, 2010), 108–9.

The range of languages, apparently unknown to the speakers, is described later on (Acts 2:5–12). The audience was predominantly Diaspora Jewish, most probably gathered in Jerusalem for Pentecost. The range was "from every nation under heaven." This may well be hyperbole. The list in verses 9–11 is wide-ranging, but refers to those from which pilgrims might be expected to have come.

Theologically, it represents a reversal of the judgment of Babel. The list of representative nations here is similar to the table of the nations in Genesis 10 that precedes the account of Babel. There the judgment on humanity for its godless, hubristic boasting was a proliferation of languages, with the resulting breakdown of communication. Here at Pentecost is the restoration of communication in the universal comprehension of the mighty acts of God in redemption. At the back of this is Jesus' command to the church that "repentance and forgiveness of sins should be proclaimed in his [Christ's] name to all nations" (Luke 24:47), with the commission that "you will be my witnesses . . . to the end of the earth," having received "power when the Holy Spirit has come upon you" (Acts 1:8). The signs were audible and also visible.[16]

A Miracle of Hearing?

It has been suggested that the miracle of Pentecost was that while the disciples all spoke in their native tongue, the crowds heard the speech of the disciples in their own language. Some of the fathers thought this was the case, but as Thiselton points out, it begs the question whether the hearing of the crowd in their own languages was based on a prior reality in the speech of the disciples.[17] It was, so this proposal claims, a miracle that enabled hearing in a diverse range of languages even though the utterances were made in the native tongue of the speakers or, possibly, in unintelligible ecstatic form.

This argument cannot be sustained. If it were so, the event would have primarily involved the hearers rather than the disciples. The meaning of all the passages cited by Peter in his sermon, and

16. Thiselton, *Holy Spirit*, 52.
17. Thiselton, *Holy Spirit*, 53.

the contexts from which they come, is that the Spirit would descend on the apostles and the church (Acts 2:14–21, citing Joel 2:28–32). If this were a miracle of hearing, the features described in Acts 2:1–4 would be virtually irrelevant. The tongues that were heard by the "devout men from every nation" (v. 5) were spoken by those who were in the house (v. 4). The suggestions from the crowd that drunkenness was involved establish the fact that what was at stake was the speech, not the hearing (v. 13). The decisive thing was not ordinary speech from which supernaturally empowered hearing resulted, but supernaturally empowered speech, from which the hearing naturally followed.[18]

The Focus of Peter's Speech

Peter's speech to the crowds that had gathered points to these events as the fulfillment of God's covenant. The outpouring of the Spirit had been foretold by Joel (Acts 2:17–21) and was to be universal in extent, to "all flesh" (v. 17), so that "everyone who calls upon the name of the Lord shall be saved" (v. 21). This outpouring would be indiscriminate, on male and female, old and young, rich and poor, including slaves. Moreover, it would be accompanied by convulsive signs of judgment. Since the language of Joel has similarities with Isaiah 13:8–16, where the overthrow of Babylon is foretold, there is a probable reference to impending judgment on Israel.

This covenant fulfillment reaches its apex, Peter continues, in the life, ministry, death, resurrection, and enthronement of Jesus of Nazareth, "a man attested . . . by God" (Acts 2:22), raised from the dead (vv. 24–32), and exalted at the right hand of God. He it is who received the Holy Spirit from the Father and poured him out (v. 33). This is effectively an announcement that the Jesus whom the people had killed was in reality one with Yahweh, since he had

18. Thiselton remarks that "the understanding of tongues-speech is now a moving and varied set of beliefs" and cites Max Turner, who writes that Luke "would hardly be inclined to suggest that the apostolic band merely . . . babbled ecstatically and incomprehensibly." Thiselton, *Holy Spirit*, 58–59, quoting Max Turner, "Early Christian Experience and Theology of Tongues," in *Speaking in Tongues: Multi-Disciplinary Perspectives*, ed. Mark J. Cartledge (Milton Keynes, UK: Paternoster, 2006), 5.

the authority to dispense the Spirit of God. This Peter affirms by quoting Psalm 110 in calling him "Lord" (Acts 2:34–35) and declaring that God has appointed him Lord and the Christ, long promised and keenly anticipated (v. 36).

In short, the Spirit directs Peter to proclaim Jesus as the Christ, risen, ascended, exalted, one with Yahweh, and that he had now sent the Holy Spirit to his people in fulfilling the covenant of God. Here is a clear demonstration of Jesus' teaching that the Spirit would not bear self-witness but would direct attention to Jesus as the Christ.

Integrally bound up with Peter's speech is his exhortation to baptism, repentance, and faith—the four spiritual doors, as Tony Lane calls them: repentance, baptism, faith, and reception of the Holy Spirit.[19]

Its Theological Significance

Baptism with the Holy Spirit was foretold by John the Baptist (Matt. 3:11–12; Mark 1:7–8; Luke 3:16–17; John 1:29–34) and reinforced immediately before the ascension by Jesus (Acts 1:4–5). Clear in this account is that Word and Spirit were linked closely together. As Frederick Dale Bruner remarks, the focus of attention was Peter's sermon, not any supposed spiritual ecstasy of which there is none, since the tongues consisted of a clear and intelligible account of "the mighty works of God."[20]

There is also a conjunction here of the outpouring of the Spirit with baptism. The two go together, although as we will see later, there is no invariable temporal order between them.

A Unique Event or a Paradigm for Continued Experience?

These events are to be seen as an integral part of the complex: death-burial-resurrection-ascension-enthronement-Pentecost. Since

19. Tony Lane, *Sin and Grace: Evangelical Soteriology in Historical Perspective* (London: Apollos, 2020), 93-103.

20. Frederick Dale Bruner, *A Theology of the Holy Spirit: The Pentecostal Experience and the New Testament Witness* (Grand Rapids: Eerdmans, 1970), 165. This is contrary to John R. Levison, *Filled with the Spirit* (Grand Rapids: Eerdmans, 2009), 325–65, who argues that the disciples were in an ecstatic state over which they had

that is so, Pentecost is nonrepeatable in its theological meaning and significance. The death, resurrection, and ascension of Jesus Christ cannot be repeated, for they are once-for-all events, inextricably bound together. Not only do biblical statements join them together, but each is inexplicable in isolation. Each is part of the one movement of God toward us in grace in Jesus Christ. Without the resurrection, the death of Christ would be a meaningless charade (1 Cor. 15:12–19). Resurrection presupposes a prior death. Jesus' resurrection is the prelude to his ascension to the right hand of the Father and his glorification. The sending of the Spirit follows his ascension and glorification (John 7:37–39; 16:7–11; Acts 2:29–36). To extract Pentecost from this nexus is to tear it from the context that God has given it. To argue that it is repeatable is to empty it of its meaning.

The Pentecostal and charismatic claim that it is a paradigm for ongoing Christian experience places an onus on individuals to seek a comparable experience themselves and creates an elite level of believers who claim to have received such an experience. Yet apart from the three events below relating to the entry of the gospel to Samaria and the Gentiles, together with an unusual situation at Ephesus involving disciples of John the Baptist, the New Testament contains no evidence that the church was expected to seek a repeat, still less seek it for particular individuals. Here the corporate reality of Pentecost is key. It was decidedly not an individualistic matter. Moreover, its unique redemptive-historical location must be at the forefront of our thinking; Pentecost is no more repeatable than is the death, resurrection, and ascension of Christ. Finally, we noted above that Pentecost is an objective event, not a subjective experience.

Gaffin also draws attention to the New Testament portrayal of Pentecost as inseparably connected with the death, resurrection, and ascension of Christ. He compares John the Baptist's baptism and Jesus' baptism with the Holy Spirit. The descent of the Spirit at Jesus' baptism at the hands of John had a reference to judgment.

---

no control (329). This would have been opposite to the fact, revealed by the Spirit himself, that he produces self-control (Gal. 5:22–23; 2 Tim. 1:7).

Jesus was to fulfill all righteousness in being baptized, connecting it with his suffering judgment in and at the cross (Matt. 3:13–15; Luke 12:49–51), so that his people might receive the blessings of the baptism of the Holy Spirit. Hence Pentecost—the reference of the baptism with the Holy Spirit—as it is connected with the death, resurrection, and ascension, is a once-for-all event, unique, and relates to the church, the corporate dimension, rather than the individual.[21] Thus, Gaffin argues, "Pentecost is nothing less than the establishment of the church as the new covenant people of God, as the body of Christ."[22] This is echoed by Dunn, who also views Pentecost together with the death, resurrection, ascension, and exaltation of Christ as a theological unity.[23]

Acts 8

Three further events in Acts are relevant here—the sudden and dramatic reception of the gospel in Samaria (Acts 8:17), the conversion of Cornelius and his friends (10:44–46), and the coming of the Spirit on the newly baptized former disciples of John the Baptist at Ephesus (19:6–7). Thiselton asks whether these were exceptions or, as Pentecostals and charismatics claim, norms. In Acts 8, Luke seems to imply that there are some who are to be regarded as Christians who

21. Gaffin, *Perspectives*, 13–41. Interestingly, Frank Macchia draws the same connections between the baptism of Jesus, the cross, and baptism with the Holy Spirit as Gaffin does, but he comes to very different conclusions, largely because he inverts the biblical and theological **order** of the Trinity in his Spirit **Christology**. Frank D. Macchia, *Jesus the Spirit Baptizer: Christology in the Light of Pentecost* (Grand Rapids: Eerdmans, 2018), *passim*. One might conceivably argue, against Gaffin, that the obedience of Christ leading to the death of the cross is regarded as a paradigm for our discipleship (Matt. 20:20–28; John 15:12; Phil. 2:5–7; 1 Peter 2:21–25) despite being once-for-all, unrepeatable, and one with Pentecost, and so therefore Pentecost should also be paradigmatic. But the references above are from the incarnate Christ, who shares our nature. Pentecost is an act of God's utter sovereignty, which, by definition, is inimitable.

22. Gaffin, *Perspectives*, 21.

23. Dunn, *Baptism in the Holy Spirit*, 173–74; James D. G. Dunn, "'The Lord, the Giver of Life': The Gift of the Spirit as Both Life-Giving and Empowering," in *The Spirit and Christ in the New Testament and Christian Theology: Essays in Honor of Max Turner*, ed. I. Howard Marshall, Volker Rabens, and Cornelis Bennema (Grand Rapids: Eerdmans, 2012), 13.

have not yet received the Holy Spirit (vv. 14, 16).[24] They had believed in Jesus Christ but required the apostles to travel from Jerusalem to lay hands on them so that they could receive the Spirit. This, as Thiselton goes on to explain, was a unique situation. The triumph of the gospel in Samaria was a turning point in the missionary expansion of the church. Furthermore, the intense historical animosity between the Jews and the Samaritans was a pervasive feature of life in Palestine. The apostolic message needed confirmation there.[25] The visit of Peter and John was a visible and tangible act signifying the unity of the church and the solidarity of the apostles with Samaria.[26]

Acts 10

Similar features apply to the situation surrounding Cornelius. Here was a gathering exclusively composed of Gentiles, with whom Jews were forbidden to associate. Thiselton argues that the faith status of the group involved both the Word of God and the Holy Spirit. Both the Word and the Spirit were conjointly involved. Reporting this event to the Council of Jerusalem, Peter represents these aspects, their cleansing, their coming to faith, and the reception of the Holy Spirit, as a single event (Acts 15:7–8).[27] Only convincing confirmation could persuade the leaders of the church in Jerusalem that Peter was right to associate with Gentiles and that they had exhibited genuine faith. Each of these vital new steps required authentication by the Spirit. Peter himself could be persuaded to travel to Cornelius's house only by a three-times-repeated vision accompanied by a verbal declaration from the Lord (10:19, 44; 11:12, 18). How much more, we might ask, would this be the case for those who had not been afforded this special revelatory intervention? Thiselton argues that "it is crucial that each radical new step in the expansion of the church to all the world is perceived as expressly initiated by the Holy Spirit as the Spirit of Jesus Christ."[28]

24. Thiselton, *Holy Spirit*, 63.
25. Thiselton, *Holy Spirit*, 64.
26. Thiselton, *Holy Spirit*, 65.
27. Thiselton, *Holy Spirit*, 65.
28. Thiselton, *Holy Spirit*, 65.

Acts 19

Here we encounter "certain disciples" (my translation), a small group of about twelve men. As Conrad Gempf argues, these are not treated as twelve individuals but as a distinct people group. It becomes apparent that they were disciples of John the Baptist. They had not heard of the Holy Spirit. The probable cause of this lack of knowledge, Gempf proposes, lies with their focus on the ethical brunt of the Baptist's ministry, as Luke recorded (Luke 3:3–14). Moreover, like their mentor, their thinking about the Coming One may have been eclipsed or muddled (cf. 7:18–30).[29] Clearly, they were lacking in their understanding of who Jesus was and is, and the impact of his ministry, since it was corrected by Paul's announcement that the Baptist's message had been fulfilled by Jesus. Thus, they could not be considered Christian at the point of encounter with Paul; this had to be corrected. Consequently, they were baptized in the name of the Lord Jesus, and in consequence received the Holy Spirit with its immediate evidence in speaking in tongues and prophecy (Acts 19:4–7). As with the reception of the gospel in Samaria, here was the reception of a distinct group rather than the conversion of disparate individuals. It also highlights the difference between John's baptism with water and Jesus' baptism with the Holy Spirit and fire, a baptism that was a mere rite and symbol on the one hand and Christian baptism that is in the Holy Spirit and power on the other.

Baptism of/with/in the Holy Spirit

Following on from the above, we need to draw attention to the contrast that Dunn and others make between what they term "water-baptism" and "Spirit-baptism."[30] This has developed to the

29. Conrad Gempf, "Apollos and the Ephesian Disciples: Befores and Afters (Acts 18:24–19:7)," in *The Spirit and Christ in the New Testament and Christian Theology: Essays in Honor of Max Turner*, ed. I. Howard Marshall, Volker Rabens, and Cornelis Bennema (Grand Rapids: Eerdmans, 2012), 119–37.

30. See Anthony R. Cross, "Baptism in the Theology of John Calvin and Karl Barth," in *Calvin, Barth and Reformed Theology*, ed. Neil B. MacDonald (Eugene, OR: Wipf & Stock, 2008), 57–87. We will discuss this matter further in chapter 8.

stage at which it is widely accepted, almost as a truism. Bruner attacks the distinction. Since his book was published in the same year as Dunn's first major work on the Spirit, he does not refer to him. Bruner argues that baptism is an integral part of the conversion process and that material elements cannot be excluded.[31]

Four problems are evident in the proposals of Dunn and his friends, at least three of which are consequences of Kantian post-Enlightenment thought. The first such problem is individualism, whereby the baptism with the Holy Spirit is seen as related to the individual believer rather than the church. Second, there is a lack of attention to redemptive history, from which baptism with the Holy Spirit is considered to be an ongoing phenomenon instead of part of the unique complex of events relating to Christ. The third problem is **ontological dualism**, by which the material and spiritual are held apart, thus inhibiting material elements from playing a part in the transmission of spiritual grace. In this, the work of the Spirit becomes detached from the sacraments, with the latter reduced to rites of a purely human and symbolic character. A fourth complication is analytic thinking whereby realities are broken down into constituent parts. Consequently, the theological connections that bind various elements together are missed. In the present case, baptism with the Holy Spirit is considered to be separate from baptism with water, the reality consisting in the former, while the latter is at the most a symbol.

In contrast to this common dualism, in which "water baptism" is viewed simply as a human rite, Sarah Hinlicky Wilson, in a crucial article, argues that the contrast in Luke-Acts is not between "water baptism" and "Spirit baptism" but between the water baptism of John the Baptist without the Holy Spirit, and the water baptism of the apostles with the Spirit.[32] She argues that Luke-Acts does not intend to provide a template for individual

31. See Bruner, *Theology of the Holy Spirit*, 165–71; Robert Letham, *Systematic Theology* (Wheaton, IL: Crossway, 2019), 634–47, 716–18; Sarah Hinlicky Wilson, "Water Baptism and Spirit Baptism in Luke-Acts: Another Reading of the Evidence," *Pneuma* 38, no. 4 (2016): 476–501.

32. Wilson, "Spirit Baptism in Luke-Acts," 476–501.

spiritual experience but instead highlights the contrast between John the Baptist and Jesus. There is evidence in the New Testament that many in Jewish circles were followers of the Baptist. Acts contains a persistent stress on the difference between his ministry and that of Jesus and, with it, its insufficiency.

Wilson remarks on Luke's lack of interest on the precise time when people were "converted." There is nothing to mark the precise time when this happened to the disciples or even to Paul. Rather, the focus is on the gathering of communities to discipleship—Jews, Samaritans, Gentiles—with any experiences illustrative, not normative.[33]

Wilson argues that where baptism and the Holy Spirit are mentioned, there is a contrast to the baptism of John. John started baptism with water and, uniquely, administered it to people other than himself. To be baptized by John was to identify with repentant Israel, but there is no mention of the forgiveness of sins. John merely called people to repentance. Forgiveness is effected only by Jesus. In contrast, with Jesus' baptism the Holy Spirit descends, marking the start of his ministry—this did not happen with any others baptized by John.[34]

Evidently, the two baptisms were alike in an outward sense. But with Jesus' baptism, three new things occur—forgiveness of sins, the gift of the Spirit, and the extension of the kingdom beyond Israel—together with the promise of baptism with the Spirit and empowerment for mission.[35] Baptism and the Spirit are repeatedly connected.[36] In the case of Samaria, there was a time lapse allowing for authentication in the case of a new, despised people group. The unusual nature of this episode merely establishes the point that the connection between baptism and the Spirit was firmly in place, settled in the mind of the church.[37] This connection is clear in the case of Paul in Acts 9 and the Gentiles in Acts 10. Peter's account in Acts 11 supports this, containing again a strong contrast with the

33. Wilson, "Spirit Baptism in Luke-Acts," 479.
34. Wilson, "Spirit Baptism in Luke-Acts," 479–82.
35. Wilson, "Spirit Baptism in Luke-Acts," 483.
36. Wilson, "Spirit Baptism in Luke-Acts," 484.
37. Wilson, "Spirit Baptism in Luke-Acts," 485–87.

baptism of John.[38] Paul also stresses this contrast in Acts 13:24–25—John's was a baptism of repentance, with no mention of forgiveness of sins—but later in verse 38, forgiveness is in the name of Jesus.[39]

The case of Apollos in Acts 18:24–28 shows how long the confusion between the two baptisms lasted. Here was a prominent preacher who needed instruction.[40] The group at Ephesus in Acts 19 knew nothing about the Spirit, since they had been baptized into John's baptism. There is nothing here about forgiveness in connection with John's baptism. Their baptism in the name of Jesus was not rebaptism, since John's baptism was not Christian baptism.[41] Wilson concludes that "the discussion ends here. Jews, Samaritans, proselytes, Gentiles, disciples of John the Baptist have all received Christian baptism and the gift of the Holy Spirit."[42] "The job has been done; all the estranged groups (if not all their members) have been claimed."[43]

Wilson argues that Pentecostals have conflated the missionary intent of Luke-Acts and the gift of the Holy Spirit and then reified it as a repeatable "experience." They consider John's contrast between baptism with water and baptism with the Holy Spirit in Luke 3:16, repeated in Acts 1:5, as referring to two separate events rather than a contrast between John and Jesus and their different baptisms.[44] Consequently, "a distinct, missional empowering experience going by the name of 'baptism in the Holy Spirit' cannot be sustained from the text of Acts."[45] She concludes that Pentecostal experience is "an experience in search of a name and a justification."[46] There are plenty of events in Acts in which the Spirit is powerfully at work—it is "unfortunate that all these correct interpretations of the Spirit in Luke-Acts became linked to the term 'baptism.'"[47] Baptism in the

38. Wilson, "Spirit Baptism in Luke-Acts," 488–90.
39. Wilson, "Spirit Baptism in Luke-Acts," 490.
40. Wilson, "Spirit Baptism in Luke-Acts," 491.
41. Wilson, "Spirit Baptism in Luke-Acts," 492–93.
42. Wilson, "Spirit Baptism in Luke-Acts," 493.
43. Wilson, "Spirit Baptism in Luke-Acts," 501.
44. Wilson, "Spirit Baptism in Luke-Acts," 497.
45. Wilson, "Spirit Baptism in Luke-Acts," 497.
46. Wilson, "Spirit Baptism in Luke-Acts," 498.
47. Wilson, "Spirit Baptism in Luke-Acts," 498–99.

name of Jesus is not merely a rite or a human act of testimony. But neither is it the end, for we pray for more of the Holy Spirit. Indeed, the absence of an unvarying sequence points to the sovereign freedom of the Spirit. "God cannot be cornered" because salvation is his work.[48] We, on our part, should note that this claimed division between water baptism and Spirit baptism implies that the work of Christ is ineffective and accomplishes nothing more than John the Baptist did.

This paradigm affects biblical exegesis. In this way of thinking, when Jesus, in his interview with Nicodemus, mentions being born of water and the Spirit, the water is customarily referred to cleansing, not to baptism, since the assumption is that something material like baptism cannot convey the grace of the Holy Spirit. Hence, in the immediately ensuing contrast between birth according to the flesh and birth according to the Spirit, the latter must be seen in nonmaterial terms (John 3:5–6). When Paul writes of believers' being saved by "the washing of regeneration," the involvement of baptism is ruled out (Titus 3:5). Similarly, the implied reference to baptism in the radical transition from an ungodly life that some at Corinth had undergone is understood to be metaphorical when Paul says that they had been washed "in the name of the Lord Jesus Christ and by the Spirit of our God [the Father]" (1 Cor. 6:11).

This pattern of thought flies in the face of the insistence of the gospel on the goodness of the material creation, the reality of the incarnation, and the vital importance of the *bodily* resurrection. It requires a form of intellectual gymnastics to circumvent Ananias's command to Paul to "rise and be baptized and wash away your sins" (Acts 22:16) and Peter's comment that "baptism . . . now saves you" (1 Peter 3:21). No, we must insist that the Spirit works in and with the material world that he made, not apart from it. The powerful work of the Holy Spirit is deeply related to, and inseparable from, the baptism with water that all believers have had, and it is to be regarded as one reality.

48. Wilson, "Spirit Baptism in Luke-Acts," 500.

Excursus: Frank Macchia on Jesus the Spirit Baptizer[49]

Frank D. Macchia argues that everything in Jesus' life and ministry, and his death, resurrection, and ascension, is directed toward and fulfilled by his pouring out the Holy Spirit on all flesh. Pentecost is the goal. This is in contrast to the usual traditional Western model in which the death of Christ—the atonement, together with the resurrection—is the hub and Pentecost is a consequence. Macchia's argument makes the Spirit, or rather Jesus as the Spirit baptizer, the magnetic center of the gospel rather than the cross and resurrection, for Macchia sees the Spirit's work not in isolation but as the goal of the work of Christ.

What is the answer to this? I suggest that it depends on the theological context. In juridical and representational terms, it is clear that atonement and justification are the crux. This is argued by Paul in 1 Corinthians 15:3–4, where he states that the gospel he preached is that "Christ died for our sins in accordance with the Scriptures, that he was buried, [and] that he was raised on the third day in accordance with the Scriptures." Again, in Romans 4:25, he declares that Jesus our Lord "was delivered up for our trespasses and raised for our justification." This transpired when Jesus the Son "through the eternal Spirit offered himself without blemish to [the Father]" (Heb. 9:14).

But in terms of transformation by the Holy Spirit sent from the Father and the Son, Pentecost and all that follows is the locus in which we are being transformed into the image of Christ "from one degree of glory to another. For this comes from the Lord [the risen Son] who is the Spirit" (2 Cor. 3:18). This is the goal to which redemption leads, for when Christ returns "we shall be like him, because we shall see him as he is" (1 John 3:2).

Atonement and justification are the vital and indispensable entry points, transformation the ultimate destination. In short, these are not, or should not be, competing elements, for the Son and the Spirit work inseparably with the Father from beginning to end. In Macchia's case, while he makes a valiant attempt to tie all this together,

49. Macchia, *Jesus the Spirit Baptizer*.

he does so at the expense of a robust doctrine of justification and with a cursory doctrine of atonement. We will see later that he sets aside the Protestant doctrine of justification and disavows being called a Protestant. While elements of his argument are well taken—it is vital to hold together the work of the Spirit with that of Christ—his overall drift is away from this healthy biblical and theological unity. In effect, for Macchia the work of Christ serves the ministry of the Spirit, which is the reverse of the Spirit's biblically declared operations. It contrasts too with the church's commitment at Nicaea and Constantinople. In the end, it leaves us with a **pneumatocentric** rather than a **Christocentric** doctrine of salvation. In contrast to Macchia, Yves Congar rightly argues that both the New Testament and patristic theology trace the saving activity of Christ back to the incarnational union of the Logos with the assumed humanity rather than to the anointing of the Spirit.[50]

Key Terms

attributes
begotten
being
Christocentric
Christology
dualism
eschatological
hypostases
ontological
order
persons
pneumatocentric
procession

Questions for Reflection

1. How, in the Bible, is the inseparable activity of the Trinity seen in the crucial events of Jesus' resurrection, his ascension, and Pentecost?
2. Consider how Jesus' death, burial, resurrection, and ascension and Pentecost are once-for-all events. To what extent are they connected? How far are they to be understood as corporate events?

50. Congar, *Holy Spirit*, 1:21–22.

8

The Apostolic Ministry

Lexicography

Anthony Thiselton opposes the prevalence of interpretations that refer "spirit" and "spiritual" to some human capacity:

> It is crystal clear, and impossible to deny, that when Paul uses the Greek word *pneumatikos*, "spiritual," he is alluding specifically to the agency, work, and effects of *the Holy Spirit*, for whom the lordship of *Jesus Christ* has become the supreme criterion (1 Cor. 12:3). When in 1 Corinthians he uses *pneumatikos* ("spiritual person"), Paul is referring to those whose life and thought are characterized by the Holy Spirit. When he uses *pneumatika* ("spiritual things"), Paul is referring to spiritual truths which the Holy Spirit reveals and imparts. He is not using either term in some quasi-Gnostic or **anthropological** sense, to mean "appertaining to the human spirit."

This would imply a view of humankind that Paul does not hold and, as Thiselton rightly insists, is "wholly unbiblical, and does not reflect Paul's own use of the vocabulary."[1] **Eschatologically,** "spiritual body" refers to a body under the complete direction of the Holy Spirit and thus dynamic and ever-progressing. This is in stark contrast to the anthropological idea of a disembodied existence.[2]

1. Anthony C. Thiselton, *The Holy Spirit—In Biblical Teaching, through the Centuries, and Today* (London: SPCK, 2013), 471 (Thiselton's italics).
2. Thiselton, *Holy Spirit*, 471–72.

The plural "spirits"—*pneumata*—refers to unfallen angels (Heb. 1:14) or demons (1 Peter 3:19) or to the prophets (Rev. 22:6), created spirits rather than the Holy Spirit. In Hebrews 9:14, however, the reference of *pneuma* is to the Holy Spirit. There, *theos* ("God") has the customary use for the Father, and it is Christ who offers himself. Hence, "eternal spirit" means the Holy Spirit. It is highly unlikely that the author would speak of an abstract principle in this connection. We mentioned this in the section on the atonement.

The Holy Spirit in the Evangelistic Sermons

Tony Lane uses the expression "the four spiritual doors" to refer to the content of the apostolic gospel expressed in the exhortations at the climaxes of the evangelistic sermons recorded in Acts.[3] These "doors" are repentance, faith, baptism, and the gift of the Holy Spirit. Not all occur explicitly in each sermon, but cumulatively their presence is inescapable.

The following are the relevant parts of these sermons, with the elements mentioned in the call of the gospel:

- Acts 2:38 (repentance, baptism): forgiveness of sins, the gift of the Holy Spirit.
- Acts 3:19 (repentance): forgiveness of sins.
- Acts 5:31–32 (repentance): forgiveness of sins, the Holy Spirit given to all who obey him.
- Acts 8:9–17 (faith, baptism): the Holy Spirit.
- Acts 8:26–39 (baptism).
- Acts 9:17–18 (baptism): the Holy Spirit (cf. 22:16 [baptism]: forgiveness of sins).
- Acts 10:42–48 (faith, baptism): forgiveness of sins, the Holy Spirit.
- Acts 13:38–39 (faith): forgiveness of sins.
- Acts 16:30–33 (faith, baptism).
- Acts 17:30–31 (repentance).
- Acts 22:16 (baptism): forgiveness of sins.

3. Tony Lane, *Sin and Grace: Evangelical Soteriology in Historical Perspective* (London: Apollos, 2020), 93–103.

- Acts 26:17–18, 20 (repentance): forgiveness of sins.

Additionally, Paul, in his defense before the rioting crowd in Jerusalem, recalls the visit of Ananias when he was in Damascus, with his exhortation, "Rise and be baptized and wash away your sins, calling on his name" (Acts 22:16). The earlier record has Ananias reporting that God has sent him to Saul (as he then was) in order for him to regain his sight and "be filled with the Holy Spirit" (Acts 9:17). All four features are present: rise and call on his name (repentance and faith), be baptized, wash away your sins, be filled with the Holy Spirit. Reception of the Spirit, together with baptism, was part of the gospel call.

Along similar lines, James D. G. Dunn identifies three or four elements—baptism, faith and repentance, the reception of the Holy Spirit.[4] Baptism, he remarks, "is for the New Testament essentially the act of faith and repentance . . . without which, usually, commitment to Jesus as Lord does not come to its necessary expression. As the Spirit is the vehicle of saving grace, so baptism is the vehicle of saving faith."[5] The New Testament never says that baptism effects what it signifies; it is distinct, the divine instrument.[6] No Christian was unbaptized, but not all baptized persons were Christians. No Christian lacked the Holy Spirit, since only those who received the Holy Spirit were Christians. "Faith demands baptism as its expression; baptism demands faith for its validation; the gift of the Holy Spirit presupposes faith as its condition; faith is shown to be genuine only by the gift of the Holy Spirit."[7]

Thus, the gospel is called by Paul "the ministry of the Spirit" (2 Cor. 3:8), since, as John Owen remarks, "take away the Spirit from the gospel and you render it a dead letter."[8] There is no efficacy

4. James D. G. Dunn, *Baptism in the Holy Spirit: A Re-Examination of the New Testament Teaching on the Gift of the Holy Spirit in Relation to Pentecostalism Today* (London: SCM, 1970), 224–28.

5. Dunn, *Baptism in the Holy Spirit*, 227.

6. Dunn, *Baptism in the Holy Spirit*, 227–28.

7. Dunn, *Baptism in the Holy Spirit*, 228.

8. John Owen, *A Discourse concerning the Holy Spirit* (1674), in *The Works of John Owen*, ed. William H. Goold (London: Banner of Truth, 1965–68), 3:26.

resident in human efforts; all is dependent on the Spirit. Owen alludes to the point that the only unforgivable sin is what is directed specifically against the Holy Spirit.[9]

The Holy Spirit Directs the Church

Throughout Acts, it is clear that the actions of the apostles and the church as a whole are under the sovereign direction of the Holy Spirit. The Spirit selects Saul and Barnabas for the work to which he himself had called them (Acts 13:1–7). This came while the prophets and teachers in the church at Antioch were ministering to the Lord, evidently while worshiping and in prayer. It came in the form of a speech-act of some kind.[10] One may conjecture about the nature of the speech, but the evidence of the rest of the book would point to a conjunction with some action of the church leaders. This might have been the climax of a series of discussions and deliberations about future strategy. But it is directly attributable to the Holy Spirit.

After the Spirit's declaration to the prophets and teachers about the ministry of Saul and Barnabas, they laid hands on the two of them and sent them out on their mission (Acts 13:3). Luke then records that they were "sent out by the Holy Spirit" (v. 4). The actions of the prophets and teachers were also the act of the Holy Spirit. This reinforces the point that the initial declaration about the calling of Saul and Barnabas was most likely through a speech-act of the Spirit that he made through the collective body of the prophets and teachers. The actions of the Spirit were synchronous with those of the church. Earlier, in Acts 5, Ananias and Sapphira had lied to the church about the value of the property they had sold and then given to the church. They claimed to have given all the proceeds, whereas the sale price was significantly greater than their bequest. Peter declares that they had lied not merely to the church but to God (v. 4). In the same comment, he equated this with lying to the Holy

9. Owen, *Holy Spirit*, in *Works*, 3:27.

10. Speech-act theory is derived from the work of J. L. Austin and John R. Searle, who built on the work of Ludwig Wittgenstein and others. It analyzes speech utterances between locutions (a word or group of words), illocutions (what is intended by the words, such as statements, promises, warnings, and the like), and perlocutions (what the speech-act accomplishes).

Spirit (v. 3) and later, in confronting Sapphira, with testing the Spirit of the Lord (v. 9). Lying to the church was tantamount to lying to the Spirit, who is God.

Later in Paul's career, traveling to Jerusalem, the Spirit warns him of trouble ahead. This came "in every city" he had recently visited (Acts 20:22–24), presumably through a series of prophetic messages. When he reached Tyre, getting close to Jerusalem, the disciples warned him not to go there (21:4); in this case, it is unclear whether this came by way of prophecy or whether it was simply commonsense advice in view of current circumstances. At Caesarea, however, the prophet Agabus came down from Judea and gave a more detailed warning (vv. 10–14). While it is possible that Agabus spoke in the light of his knowledge of the situation in Jerusalem, the text connects his warning with his being a prophet, having already referred to his effective prediction of a serious famine (11:27–28). These were all warnings, not instructions. Everyone urged Paul to abandon his plans; Paul disregarded the entreaties. We will discuss these events later when we consider prophecy in the New Testament.

The Holy Spirit Directs the Apostles

The Spirit, on occasion, prevented certain proposed ministry (Acts 16:6–7). How did this happen? We are not specifically informed. But there seems to be a distinction between the two sets of circumstances recorded here. In the first instance, the Spirit forbade the apostles to speak the Word in Asia. This was a particular obstacle rather than a permanent one. Jesus had commanded the church to take the gospel to all nations, which entails that it was a required task to include Asia. Consequently, the prohibition must have related to speaking the Word in Asia at that particular time, the Spirit's having other purposes in mind for Paul and his team.

The second occurrence is reported in this way: "they attempted to go into Bithynia, but the Spirit of Jesus did not allow them" (Acts 16:7). In this case, there was a definite attempt by Paul, Silas, and Timothy to enter Bithynia to preach the gospel. Somehow the Spirit prevented them from entering. It was likely that some providential hindrance occurred, the Spirit's using it to bring about a divergent itinerary. It happened after the trio had purposefully headed off in that direction. In the earlier event, it seems that they had very seriously considered going to Asia, but that the Spirit intervened and prevented them from even beginning the journey. In view of the Spirit's announcement that brought about Paul's first missionary journey (13:1–7), this may well have come in the form of a prophetic message. Yet we cannot exclude the possibility that it was as the result of a deliberative process by Paul's team in which they may have weighed the prospects for a variety of courses of action, the Spirit's indicating through their discussion that at that time neither Asia nor Bithynia was the most propitious place to go.

This chain of events, which may have been more than a little discouraging, was ended by Paul's vision of the man of Macedonia requesting them to cross the Aegean to help them (Acts 16:9–10). From this, they all concluded that God was calling them to preach the gospel there. The traveling evangelists reached these decisions by a chain of reasoning, informed by their theological background. They concluded that God was calling them to go to Macedonia on the basis of the Holy Spirit's sovereign direction over the details of everyday life, his revelation through a vision, and his superintendence over their own deliberations and thought processes.[11]

Action by the Church Is Conjointly Action by the Holy Spirit

We have already noted the conjoint sending of Saul and Barnabas by the Holy Spirit and the church (Acts 13:1–5). The church's action was initiated by, and in harmonious conjunction with, the Spirit. Similarly, the decrees of the Council of Jerusalem were in accord with the mind of the Holy Spirit. These came at the end of lengthy deliberation over a crucial theological and practical matter relating to the Gentiles and their relationship to the Mosaic law. Various reports were given, comments made, the mind of the Spirit in Scripture expounded, and conclusions reached on that basis. James, referring to Amos, had intervened to establish the point that the inclusion of the Gentiles had been

11. Yet one cannot rule out direct intervention by vision or prophecy in any of these incidents. I am thankful to Jonathan Humphreys for this observation.

foretold as an integral part of redemptive history. The council reached conclusions on the basis of Scripture, reports of the extension of the kingdom to the nations, and careful argument and discussion. Rational argument is not divorced from the work of the Spirit—rather, the reverse.[12] There are occasions in Acts when the Holy Spirit's direction is very clear (26:16–18). Sometimes it arrives through discussion and deliberation, sometimes through providential circumstances. In this case, the council agreed to send a letter to the Gentile churches: "it has seemed good to the Holy Spirit and to us" (15:28). The connection between the sovereignty of God and human agency is very evident.

This statement has to be seen in context. It can hardly be a blank check for assuming that any decision of the church is in accord with the Spirit's will. History shows that many decisions made by the church and churches may diverge from Scripture and so cannot be claimed as demonstrating the will of the Holy Spirit. Here in Acts is a council that included the apostles and the elders of the church at Jerusalem. Today we do not have apostles in our presence. There is a connection with the relationship between the Holy Spirit and preaching. Chapter 1 of the Second Helvetic Confession states that when preachers *of the Word* lawfully called declare the Word of God, the Word of God is heard.[13] Karl Barth writes of proclamation as the Word of God.[14] There is a biblical case for this in Romans 10:14 and Ephesians 2:17, among other places.[15] When actions or words conform to the voice of the Holy Spirit recorded in Scripture, we can say that "it has seemed good to the Holy Spirit and to us," but we can do so in only a tentative manner, realizing that it is possible that we are mistaken.

The Holy Spirit and Human Agency

From this it is apparent that the Spirit works in conjunction with human actions, leading and directing them, superintending the acts and the outcomes in ways that are in keeping with the natures

12. See Thiselton, *Holy Spirit*, 68.

13. In Philip Schaff, *The Creeds of Christendom* (Grand Rapids: Baker, 1966), 3:237, 872.

14. Karl Barth, *CD*, I/1:88–99; I/2:743–58.

15. Robert Letham, *Systematic Theology* (Wheaton, IL: Crossway, 2019), 623–34.

of the particular human agents. As the Westminster Confession of Faith puts it (WCF 5.2–3):

> Although, in relation to the foreknowledge and decrees of God, the first cause, all things come to pass immutably, and infallibly; yet, by the same providence, he ordereth them to fall out, according to the nature of second causes, either necessarily, freely, or contingently.
>
> God, in his ordinary providence, maketh use of means, yet is free to work without, above, and against them, at his pleasure.

Kathryn Tanner discusses two main tendencies in modern thinking.[16] One line of thought is that the Holy Spirit works immediately and directly without mediation, a view held by various groups from the Ranters of the seventeenth century onward. The second position is that the Spirit works through normal human processes. She points to a comparable division between views on the relationship between faith and reason.[17]

The first group encourages appeals to the Spirit that can bypass immanent processes. The claim that "God spoke to me" is difficult to contradict.[18] The appeal to direct working by the Spirit "presupposes a more thoroughgoing attack on the usual sources of religious authority [the church and Scripture] themselves across the board. . . . [It] amounts to a fundamental questioning of all of them."[19] Tanner cites three Richards—Baxter, Sibbes, and Hooker—in support of the second view.[20]

Tanner proceeds to appeal to the relation between divine and human action in **Christology**. The first view, that the Spirit works directly, is influenced by empirical philosophy and the scientific

16. Kathryn Tanner, *Christ the Key* (Cambridge: Cambridge University Press, 2010), 274–301.

17. Tanner, *Christ the Key*, 264–76.

18. Tanner, *Christ the Key*, 277.

19. Tanner, *Christ the Key*, 288.

20. Tanner, *Christ the Key*, 278–79.

methods of the early modern era, an "experiential approach," with a reliance on personal experience.[21] Today, revivalists and pietists of various kinds focus on the experiential; this can be strongly criticized as an anthropocentric distortion, given turbocharged impetus by the eighteenth-century revivals, and at root is mystical.

For the second view, Tanner writes that "the Spirit works in much the same way God works in Christ. Christ becomes the key to it." In Christ God does not evacuate the human or push it aside. Humanity and divinity are present together in Christ.[22] She refers to T. F. Torrance's argument that humans are completed beyond themselves in Christ, and established as human minds and wills. The incarnation effects the presence of man in his completeness in God. God's presence "is creative[;] instead of excluding or overwhelming what is human, it posits it, upholds and renews it. Elevated beyond the humanity through **participation** in divinity, the humanity nevertheless remains itself."[23] She continues, "God works in Christ as the Spirit works in us: in and through the humanity. . . . The Spirit directs our lives as we attempt to direct our own, in and through our efforts, together with us."[24] This needs some qualification, one suggests, in order to avoid **semi-Pelagianism**.

Thus, Christ's divinity was hidden, which is mirrored in the hiddenness of the Spirit in the human.[25] Again, while such a connection appears fruitful, a caveat is required or it could be extended to a form of **universalism**. For her part, and correctly, Tanner argues that this prompts us neither to despair of our failings nor to try to flee our humanity,[26] for the Spirit doesn't act "when human processes vacate [the scene] but appears in and through them."[27] As a consequence, our lives gain a whole new character in the Spirit.[28] Yet, we must add, Christ was not entirely incognito in the incarnation,

21. Tanner, *Christ the Key*, 294.
22. Tanner, *Christ the Key*, 296.
23. Tanner, *Christ the Key*, 297.
24. Tanner, *Christ the Key*, 297.
25. Tanner, *Christ the Key*, 298.
26. Tanner, *Christ the Key*, 299.
27. Tanner, *Christ the Key*, 300–301.
28. Tanner, *Christ the Key*, 301.

for there were occasions when he performed astonishing miracles and when revelatory scenes were given, such as the transfiguration. Similar episodes are occasionally present in Acts too. As a general rule, however, it has validity.

The Holy Spirit and Salvation

The Holy Spirit and the Formation of the Church

The church is produced by the Holy Spirit, who is sent by the Father and the Son. Acts is a record of this. While the Old Testament exhibits the same lineaments, in the New Testament the Spirit is more plenteously dispensed. No one in the Old Testament could believe and follow faithfully apart from the working of the Spirit. The depravity inherited from Adam was the same as now. The built-in aversion to the living God occasioned by sin was present then as we now know it. Only the Spirit could overcome this ingrained unbelief.

In 1 Corinthians 12:13, where Paul writes that we all were baptized into Christ by the Spirit and were given the Spirit to drink, he affirms that when we believed in Christ, we were simultaneously made part of his body, the church. This "all" refers to all without exception, all to whom Paul wrote, not only the self-styled spiritual elite. The metaphor of the body of Christ in 1 Corinthians 12 and 14 develops this point. As a body is a living organism, joined to and directed by a head, so the church is indissolubly joined to Christ, animated by the Holy Spirit. From one angle, it is a human institution, yet it is much more than that; it is the dwelling place of God in and by the Spirit, with all three Trinitarian ***hypostases*** inseparably active and all its members integral to the whole, whatever their backgrounds, education, social status, or personal capabilities may be.

It follows that the church precedes the individual members. These individuals are added to the body. There is but one holy, catholic, and apostolic church, and those who are saved are saved in no other way than as part of this one body of Christ and are added to the body by the Spirit.

In connection with this, Paul teaches that the Spirit gives gifts to the church from the ascended Christ (Eph. 4:7–11). Particular gifts are given to each member (v. 7), but the focus here in Ephesians 4 is on people: apostles and prophets, evangelists, pastors, and teachers. We will develop this perspective more fully in chapter 9.

The Holy Spirit and Scripture

Literally hundreds of times in the Old Testament, the prophets would preface their remarks with "thus says the Lord" or "the word of the Lord came to me." Their words were not simply uttered at one point, then to fall away into the ether. The author of Hebrews states that the Holy Spirit continues to speak to this day whenever the words he inspired are uttered (Heb. 3:7, in connection with Psalm 95).

This reality lies behind Paul's comment that all Scripture was breathed out by God (2 Tim. 3:16). He has in view what we now know as the Old Testament, although he was also aware that new Scripture was being added by the Spirit in connection with the fullness of revelation in Christ, when he refers to the Gospel of Luke as Scripture (1 Tim. 5:17–18). The breathing out (*theopneustos*) signifies its origin as from the Spirit, a play on the word *pneuma* as breath. Similarly, Peter acknowledges that the prophets and other human authors of Scripture "spoke from God as they were carried along by the Holy Spirit" (2 Peter 1:20–21).

As we mentioned, Paul considers the writings of Luke to be part of Scripture, as Peter does the letters of Paul (1 Tim. 5:18; 2 Peter 3:15–16). This recognition, in the first-century context when the composition of what are now the New Testament documents was still in process, is founded on Jesus' own comments to his apostles, as recorded in John 16:12–15. There Jesus indicates that when the Spirit was to come at Pentecost, he would guide the apostles into all truth. By this he meant that they would continue and complete the teaching that Jesus would have given himself if the disciples had been equipped to receive it:

> I still have many things to say to you, but you cannot bear them now. When the Spirit of truth comes, he will guide you into all the truth, for he will not speak on his own authority, but whatever he hears he will speak, and he will declare to you the things that

> are to come. He will glorify me, for he will take what is mine and declare it to you. All that the Father has is mine; therefore I said that he will take what is mine and declare it to you.

The Spirit receives from the Father and the Son. He takes what relates to the Son and illuminates the minds of the apostles so that they are enabled to pass these things on to the church. Since he takes and communicates what is the Son's, so the Son does with the Father, since, as John has established throughout his Gospel, the Son is one with the Father.

This raises the question of the relationship between the church and Scripture. Some have argued that Scripture derives its authority from the church, while it has been common among Protestants to assert that the church is dependent on the preaching of the gospel and therefore on Scripture. It is evident, however, that both the church and the Scriptures derive their authority from the Holy Spirit, sent by the Father and the Son.[29] Scripture is the supreme authority, which is nothing less than the voice of the Holy Spirit (WCF 1.10), and as such is over the church, whose task is to receive and obey the Spirit as he speaks in Scripture. Both Scripture and the church, however, flow from and depend on the Holy Spirit, who is their author. Scripture is witness to God's revelation while being one with it. The revelation precedes Scripture and so is distinct, yet the inscripturation is "the same" as the revelation (WCF 1.1). Again, the central focus of Scripture is Christ, while the principal ministry of the Spirit is also to testify of Christ, and in turn Scripture is breathed out by the Spirit. Where do we expect to hear the word of the Spirit? In the Word that he himself has breathed out so that we may be complete, fully equipped for every good work (2 Tim. 3:17).

The Holy Spirit, Regeneration, and Faith

In John 16:8–11, Jesus indicates what the principal work of the Spirit was to be after Pentecost. He would "convict the world concerning sin and righteousness and judgment." Each of these elements

29. See my discussion of this point in Letham, *Systematic Theology*, 239–40.

is to be seen in relation to Jesus himself. Conviction of sin was to be on the basis that people did not believe in him, of righteousness because of his vindication and exaltation, and of judgment since he was to judge the world.

These operations are seen as preparatory to regeneration. Conviction of sin is essentially conviction of unbelief in Jesus Christ. Behind it lies rebellion against God, who is life itself, and it is ultimately evidenced in the world's murderous assault on the one who gave it life (John 1:3–5). This conviction entails an awareness of the reality of its unbelief, of Jesus' exaltation and his impending judgment. With it comes an impression of the urgency of the gospel. This is clearly not the same as a person's feeling worthless. In existential terms, not everyone has a deep, profound sense of sin. Moreover, there are no prior qualifications for faith. As the hymn-writer penned, "all the fitness he requireth is to feel your need of him."[30] If that were not so and lacerating agonizing was required, the gospel would be submerged into a morass of legalism. Pietism is a dangerous threat. Moreover, Jesus says that *the Spirit* will convict the world. It is his work, not ours.

The coming of the Spirit at Pentecost was the equivalent of Jesus' remaining. The Spirit is "another *paraclētos*" (John 14:16). Jesus goes; the Spirit comes. Bearing in mind the inseparability of the Trinity, the Spirit proceeds from the Father (15:26), is sent by the Father (John 14:16) upon request of the Son following his ascension (v. 16), and is sent by the Son from the Father (15:26; 16:7).

The focus throughout is on faith in Christ, on the basis of the promise of the gospel: "Believe in God; believe also in me," Jesus said (John 14:1). The evangelistic sermons call on people not to be regenerated—a task that none of us can do—but to repent and believe, and to be baptized. Regeneration is out of our hands. In order to believe in Christ and the gospel promise, however, it is necessary to be changed by the Holy Spirit. All people since the fall are averse to God and biased toward unbelief and rebellion. They are covenantally dead (Eph. 2:1), unable to believe (John 6:64–65).

30. Joseph Hart, "Come, Ye Sinners, Poor and Wretched" (1759).

Saving faith and repentance are likened to a resurrection, a new creation (Ezek. 37:1f.; John 3:1–14; Rom. 6:1–9; 2 Cor. 5:17; Eph. 2:1–10). Regeneration precedes faith. When regeneration occurs, a person willingly believes and repents, and follows Jesus. This is because the orientation of the person's will has been decisively changed. The crux is the relationship between regeneration and saving faith. Regeneration comes first; faith follows.

John Owen recognizes that the Spirit directs all preparatory elements, such as they may be. Additionally, there is a direct work of the Spirit in the mind, creating, giving life, forming and giving a new heart. Paul compares this to the Spirit's work in raising and exalting Christ from the dead to the right hand of the Father (Eph. 1:18–20). It is infallible, always efficacious, and according to our particular natures and persons. This is because "he doth not act in them otherwise than they themselves are meet to be moved and move, to be acted and act, according to their own nature, power, and ability." Nor does he "possess the mind with any enthusiastical prophetical inspirations."[31] In short, the Spirit does not do violence to the human will but works with it. One wonders here whether Owen is self-contradictory. If the Spirit operates in accord with our own personalities, which seems to be a reasonable and sustainable argument, then would he not operate in more "enthusiastical" ways with those of a comparable temperament? This is a question, not an answer.

At any rate, following Augustine and the Augustinian tradition, Owen affirms that the human will is initially passive, the Spirit's acting on it to change it, but then the will acts in believing, while yet the act of faith itself, and indeed the whole transition, is a work of the Spirit. Hence, the Spirit "offers no violence or compulsion unto the will," preserving the liberty of the human agent while working infallibly and efficaciously.[32]

While this is a personal work of the Holy Spirit, it is, of course, a work of the whole Trinity, specifically referred to the Spirit. This

31. Owen, *Holy Spirit*, in *Works*, 3:317–18.
32. Owen, *Holy Spirit*, in *Works*, 3:19–324, here 319.

is how it appears explicitly in John 14:23. There, Jesus states that he and the Father will together come and take up permanent residence with the one who loves and obeys him. This occurs as the climax to the initial description of the Spirit's post-Pentecost work in the Upper Room Discourse. The Father and the Son take up residence in and with the Spirit, whose action it personally, hypostatically, is. The Spirit is the principal **efficient cause** of regeneration.[33]

Meanwhile, the **instrumental cause** of regeneration is the Word and prayer. This applies to everyone who believes. If someone is regenerated, it brings about faith in Jesus Christ and the gospel. Christ is revealed in the Word of God. No one—literally and absolutely no one in human history—is ever regenerated independently of the Word. Someone, perhaps on a beach in Cyprus, may shoot like an Exocet to his keyboard to point to "elect infants, dying in infancy," or "other elect persons uncapable of being called by the outward preaching of the Word" (WCF 10.3). Yes, of course. But even for those infants or the intellectually challenged, their salvation, in the eternal good pleasure of God, is grounded on the work of Jesus Christ, applied by the Holy Spirit and revealed in his Word. Even if that Word is never preached to them, or if they are incapable of understanding it when it is preached, it can be only on the basis of that Word that they are regenerated and saved.

This should lay to rest the mystical notion that the Spirit operates independently of the Word. This may occasionally be true in an existential sense, in terms of the chronological sequence of our lives, but in reality the two go together, are inseparable, and it is on the basis of that unbreakable union that such rare exceptions may happen.

Normally, attendance on the ministry of the Word is necessary. This may be in the form of regular preaching in a church service, it may be through a similar but occasional event, it could be through reading the Bible or a book, or it might be in the context of personal discussion in which Christ is presented. It often happens through pondering such events at a later time. Luke Short, a New England

33. Owen, *Holy Spirit*, in *Works*, 3:208–9. See also Abraham Kuyper, *The Work of the Holy Spirit*, trans. Henri De Vries (Grand Rapids: Eerdmans, 1900), 298–99.

farmer, came to saving faith at the age of one hundred while reflecting on a sermon he had heard in Devon preached by John Flavel eighty-five years earlier.[34] I have heard of people regenerated in their sleep: they went to bed as unbelievers; they woke up regenerate. With C. S. Lewis, it happened in an ordinary, uneventful bus journey. God works in mysterious ways and operates generally in accordance with our personal characters and dispositions; after all, he made us, each one, and knows us thoroughly (Ps. 139:1–6). The Spirit is mysterious, and so is his work, like the wind, not under our control but sovereign and beyond our powers of analysis. In reality, it is the same for all, from dramatic transformations like Saul of Tarsus to the quiet and unremarkable with C. S. Lewis. One cannot be more or less regenerate than others. In every case, the Spirit regenerates, whether it was the apostle Paul or the converted heroin addict who was lying in the gutter.

The Holy Spirit and Justification

The work of the Spirit in regeneration encompasses his work in justification. We are made righteous in the sight of God on the basis of the obedience of Jesus Christ, with whom the Spirit unites us. Justification itself, being a strictly legal and forensic reality relating to our status, cannot be based on anything we do or on anything in us, since we by nature were covenantally dead, having sinned both in Adam and on our own behalf. Only by participating in the righteousness of Christ, joined to him by the Holy Spirit and sharing in all that he is and has done, can this be established on a valid ground. Moreover, it is not on the ground of the Spirit's work uniting us to Christ, nor on the basis of what he does in and with us, that we have this status. It is through faith alone, whereby we renounce reliance on ourselves and trust exclusively in Christ. Nor is it something that faith achieves, for it is only through what faith receives. The Spirit's work in changing the bias of our minds, enabling us to trust Christ alone, brings us there.

34. John Flavel, *The Mystery of Providence* (1678; repr., London: Banner of Truth, 1963), 11.

Indwelling

The term *indwelling* can sound like liquid poured into a bucket. It is based on biblical language. Jesus speaks of the Father's and his making believers their permanent residence (John 14:23), and Paul speaks of the love of God being "poured into our hearts through the Spirit" (Rom. 5:5). Another metaphor to describe it could be *saturation* or *pervasion*, both indicating that the Spirit is present thoroughly and comprehensively in every facet of our being.

Abraham Kuyper distinguishes between pervasion and indwelling. The Spirit pervaded Adam, he says, but did not indwell him. *Pervasion*, for Kuyper, is equivalent to inspiring one's being, whereas *indwelling* conveys the idea of permanence.[35] I agree with Kuyper on the substance of his argument but differ in the words to express it. I am using *pervasion* as a synonym for *indwelling* in order to underline the point that the Spirit, in regeneration and his subsequent work, affects every nook and cranny of the regenerate human being (1 Thess. 5:23). As depravity is total, impacting every faculty, so does the Spirit pervade our entire being, overcoming the impact of sin, not all at once but gradually throughout our life until at the eschaton we will be entirely and visibly transformed. Not long before I wrote this, I had a nasty fall, thankfully with no broken bones but with dislocations, cuts, swellings, and heavy bruising. The bruises were deep purple and very extensive, but gradually they dispersed as the body's recuperative powers got to work. Before long, they had gone. Even so, the Spirit bit by bit clears up the mess of our broken lives, the inheritance of Adam's sin and our participation in it, until the time when we will be like the glorified Christ. This is the basis of progressive sanctification (see later) and transformation (to be considered in chapter 10). The Greek and Russian churches consider these together as one vast process of *theosis*.

The Holy Spirit and Baptism

Some might think that we will devote disproportionate space to the sacraments in what follows. In many respects, this is necessary,

35. Kuyper, *Holy Spirit*, 35.

since the sacraments have been neglected in recent generations under the influence of post-Enlightenment individualism. Much of this has been fueled by a concern at being identified in any way with Rome. In these trends, there has been a tectonic shift away from classic Reformed and Puritan theology, to say nothing of the New Testament.

We saw how in Peter's sermon at Pentecost and elsewhere in Acts reception of the Holy Spirit is integral to the gospel message; it is one of the four spiritual doors. Paul, in 1 Corinthians 12:13, writes that we all have been baptized into Christ by the Spirit. This is common to all. Each member of the church received the sacrament of baptism, undergoing its cleansing washing. All were baptized into Christ and his body, the church. It was a corporate event, it was efficacious, it was inseparably related to union with Christ, and it was integral to the formation and growth of the church. It was not a private or individualized experience. It should be obvious that this does not rule out individuals, since people are baptized one at a time and the body of Christ consists of individual members. Nevertheless, it strongly placards the reality that redemption is something not for individuals as such but for individuals as part of the community, the body of Christ. Without the written revelation of God, human societies veer either to corporate suppression of the individual, as in Marxism, or else toward a state of almost unbridled license. In both cases, individual and community are set apart. Paul demonstrates that in the purposes of God, the individual and the community are not in competition, still less in conflict. God's redemptive purpose brings harmony, that of a body and its members. It is the Spirit who effects this in, through, and by baptism.

In Romans 6, Paul writes that we were baptized into Christ in his death, burial, and resurrection. In baptism we were incorporated not only into Christ's death but also into his resurrection, so that we now live in newness of life. Peter follows the same train of thought. He writes that we were born again through the resurrection of Jesus Christ from the dead (1 Peter 1:3). Later, he records that "baptism . . . now saves you . . . through the resurrection of Jesus Christ" (3:21). Regeneration comes through the resurrection of Christ, in baptism.

In baptism we are raised to new life, reborn, regenerated, through Christ's own resurrection.

Moreover, resurrection is effected by the Holy Spirit. This is true for both Christ's resurrection and ours (Rom. 8:10–11), since they are effectively the same reality (1 Cor. 15:20–23). Thus, we conclude that the Holy Spirit is powerfully at work in baptism. That is why the Reformed confessions speak of the efficacy of baptism.[36] The WCF expresses it well:

> 28.1. Baptism is a sacrament of the new testament, ordained by Jesus Christ, not only for the solemn admission of the party baptized into the visible Church; but also, to be unto him a sign and seal of the covenant of grace, of his ingrafting into Christ, of regeneration, of remission of sins.
>
> 28.6. The efficacy of baptism is not tied to that moment of time wherein it is administered; yet, notwithstanding, by the right use of this ordinance, the grace promised is not only offered, but really exhibited, and conferred, by the Holy Ghost, to such (whether of age or infants) as that grace belongeth unto, according to the counsel of God's own will, in his appointed time.

As T. F. Torrance has argued, we are baptized *into Christ*. Christ himself was baptized; his baptism by John prospectively foreshadowed his ultimate baptism on the cross. It is into the one baptism of Christ, into participation in his death and resurrection, that the Holy Spirit baptizes us, into covenantal union with Christ. This is a reality that took place historically in the death and resurrection of Christ himself, when his covenant people underwent this ordeal and deliverance in union with him. With this, because of the inseparability of spirit and matter, of

36. Catechism of the Church of Geneva 324–27; French Confession 28, 34–38; Belgic Confession 33–34; Scots Confession 21; Heidelberg Catechism 69–74; Thirty-Nine Articles 25–27; WCF 28.1, 6; WLC 161–67; Johannes Polyander, *Synopsis Purioris Theologiae, Disputationibus Quinquaginta Duabus Comprehensa* (Leiden: Ex officina Elzeverianus, 1625), 644–54. See esp. Lyle D. Bierma, *Font of Pardon and New Life: John Calvin and the Efficacy of Baptism* (New York: Oxford University Press, 2021), 175–240.

sign and reality, baptism by water is indivisibly related. These are not separable realities—they are joined together, distinct but inseparable.[37]

For this it is important to see the sacramental connection between the sign and the reality throughout the history of redemption. In each case, the sign is not the reality, but it is appropriate to it. The tree of life signified everlasting life (Gen. 3:22). The rainbow is appropriate to God's promise never again to flood the whole earth (9:14). The Passover lamb was connected to the angel's "passing over" the people of God through a substitutionary sacrifice. Moreover, the sign is related to the reality, as a road sign to the destination, and by using the sign, as well as traveling the road, one will reach the intended goal. Furthermore, the sacraments are primarily signs for God (vv. 13–14). Underlying all this is that God keeps his appointments; Jesus was born "when the fullness of time had come" (Gal. 4:4); Jesus died as the Passover Lamb on the exact day (1 Cor. 5:7); the Spirit came precisely on the day of Pentecost (Acts 2:1f.).

We must stress this even more. "In the beginning, God created the heavens and the earth" (Gen. 1:1). Spirit and matter—both are created and owned by him. He can, and does, use matter as a vehicle for his grace. Creation, the incarnation, the resurrection *of the body*—these are central to the faith. By disparaging matter, the road to **gnosticism** has been taken.

On this point, Tom Holland makes an unfortunate disjunction between "water baptism" and corporate baptism into Christ. In his discussion of Ephesians 4:6, he asserts: "To put water baptism into a statement which is to do with the great foundational realities that the confession declares is obviously misplaced. It cannot be claimed to have the sort of significance possessed by the eternal truths Paul has listed. If, however, the one baptism is not a reference to water, but to the one great event in which the Spirit made the Lord one with his

37. Thomas F. Torrance, "The One Baptism Common to Christ and His Church," in *Theology in Reconciliation: Essays towards Evangelical and Catholic Unity in East and West* (Grand Rapids: Eerdmans, 1975), 82–105. This was originally a lecture delivered to the *Académie Internationale des Sciences Religieuses*. Here Torrance brings together in a masterly way the complex relationship between Christ's baptism at the Jordan, the cross, the Spirit's baptizing us into Christ, and the sacrament.

people in the event of his vicarious atoning death, then it fits logically and naturally."[38] The nature-grace, spirit-matter **dualism** here is clear. The disjunction between baptism and union with Christ is also present.[39] But these cannot be either-or matters. Jesus' parting words to the church are enough to resolve the question; the building and nurturing of his church throughout the age is to be achieved first by baptism—and it is indisputable that by this he means the sacrament—and then by comprehensive teaching. The God who created heaven and earth uses material means in his saving purposes. We recall the striking article by Sarah Hinlicky Wilson, to which we referred in the previous chapter. There Wilson indicates that Luke's argument surrounds a contrast not between two separate events—a claimed distinction between "water baptism" and "Spirit baptism"—but between the powerless baptism of John and the baptism of Jesus, efficacious by the Spirit.[40] This division between water baptism and Spirit baptism implies that the work of Christ is ineffective and accomplishes nothing more than John the Baptist did.

The clearest and most obvious reference in these passages is to the sacrament of baptism, common to all the people of God, of which they all were aware. Not surprisingly, this has been recognized down through the centuries. Yet this baptism in the life experience of the members of the church is indissolubly related to the reality that occurred in the death and resurrection of Christ, in whom all are together and corporately united. Our baptism is a participation in Christ's baptism effected by the Holy Spirit, and for that reason, it saves us.[41]

38. Tom Holland, *Contours of Pauline Theology: A Radical New Survey of the Influences on Paul's Biblical Writings* (Fearn, Scotland: Mentor, 2004), 148.

39. See Letham, *Systematic Theology*, 716–18.

40. Sarah Hinlicky Wilson, "Water Baptism and Spirit Baptism in Luke-Acts: Another Reading of the Evidence," *Pneuma* 38, no. 4 (2016): 476–501.

41. See the connection between the redemptive-historical and the personal-existential elements of union with Christ in Romans 6 drawn by John Murray, "Definitive Sanctification," *Calvin Theological Journal* 2, no. 1 (1967): 5–21, here 19. Murray states in his inimitable way, "The sustained introduction of the once-for-all past historical in a context that clearly deals with what occurs actually and practically in the life-history of individuals makes inevitable the interpretation that the past historical conditions the continuously existential, not simply as laying the basis for it and as providing the

The material and spiritual are admirably tied together by Paul in 1 Corinthians 12:13. Faced with a church influenced by a culture that despised the body and all things material—hence their questions over the resurrection (1 Cor. 15:1–58)—Paul stresses the material means God uses to dispense his grace. Moreover, to a church riven by factions (1:10–17), he makes the point that *they all* were baptized into *one body* by the *one Spirit*, whether Jew or Greek, slave or free, and were given *one Spirit* to drink. The obvious reference is the baptism that *all* would have seen and experienced—the baptism to which Paul refers in 1:13–17, where, denying that they were baptized into the name of Paul, he implies that they were all baptized into the name of the Trinity (cf. Matt. 28:19) or the Lord Jesus Christ (Acts 2:38; 22:16). This same baptism is probably in view in 1 Corinthians 6:11, where he refers to their being "washed . . . in the name of the Lord Jesus Christ and the Spirit of our God" at the same point as their being justified and sanctified. It is baptism into Moses in the cloud and the sea that he comments on in 10:1ff., where he urges his readers to be on their guard against temptation; they have all been baptized, but so were all the Israelites, and they fell into sin. So the evidence is overwhelming that the Corinthians would have understood Paul to mean that they all had been baptized into the one body of Christ, and that this was done by the Holy Spirit. The Spirit, the water, and the blood go together. The Baptist theologian G. R. Beasley-Murray affirmed that here "we meet an explicit declaration that baptism leads into the Church" with the result of "the incorporation of the baptized through the Spirit into the Body of Christ."[42] As Paul could write to Titus, the saving mercy of God appeared through "the washing of regeneration and renewal of the Holy Spirit" (Titus 3:5). On this Beasley-Murray affirms that "no statement of the New Testament,

---

analogy in the realm of the past historical for what continues to occur in the realm of our experience, but conditions the latter for the reason that something occurred in the past historical which makes necessary what is realized and exemplified in the actual life history of these same persons." See also Herman N. Ridderbos, *Paul: An Outline of His Theology* (Grand Rapids: Eerdmans, 1975), 406–10; Richard B. Gaffin Jr., *The Centrality of the Resurrection: A Study in Paul's Soteriology* (Grand Rapids: Baker, 1978), 53–58.

42. G. R. Beasley-Murray, *Baptism in the New Testament* (Exeter, UK: Paternoster Press, 1972), 169–70.

not even John 3:5, more unambiguously represents the power of baptism to lie in the operation of the Holy Spirit."[43]

In summary, Paul argues that we are the body of Christ, and each a member of it, through the work of the Spirit. This the Spirit effects in and through baptism and all it signifies. Moreover, we are thenceforth given the Spirit to drink (1 Cor. 12:13)—a possible allusion to the Eucharist.[44]

We mentioned that the sacraments are primarily signs for God (Gen. 9:13–17), God's working to confirm his promises and to grant grace. God keeps his appointments.[45] That this pattern is present with baptism is supported by the strong language that the New Testament uses of it. As with the tree of life, the rainbow, circumcision, and the Passover, baptism signifies, seals, and exhibits the grace of God, while the Holy Spirit powerfully confers that grace of union with Christ.

This does not mean that God's grace in baptism is given automatically. In contrast to Rome, this grace is received through faith. The Spirit is sovereign and is not tied to the act of baptism. We are neither made a member of Christ nor regenerated *because* we have been baptized. Grace is not given to a baptized person on the grounds of baptism; rather, it is due to the electing grace of God in Christ. That grace is given in baptism "to those to whom it belongs."[46] Not all who are baptized will be saved. Saving faith is necessary. At Pentecost, Peter, alongside his requirement of baptism,

43. Beasley-Murray, *Baptism in the New Testament*, 215. John Stott supports this claim: "*Washing* (*loutron*) is almost certainly a reference to water baptism. All the early church fathers took it this way." John R. W. Stott, *The Message of 1 Timothy and Titus: The Life of the Local Church* (Leicester, UK: Inter-Varsity Press, 1996), 204. In footnote 20, Stott points to 1 Corinthians 6:11 and Ephesians 5:26 in support. See also John Calvin's comment: "I have no doubt that there is at least an allusion here to baptism and, I have no objection to the explanation of the whole passage in terms of baptism." John Calvin, *Calvin's Commentaries: The Second Epistle of Paul to the Corinthians and the Epistles to Timothy, Titus, and Philemon*, ed. David W. Torrance and Thomas F. Torrance, trans. T. A. Smail (Grand Rapids: Eerdmans, 1964), 382. I am grateful to the Rev. Todd Matocha for pointing me to the latter two references.

44. See, for further reading, Torrance, "The One Baptism Common to Christ and His Church," 82–105.

45. Letham, *Systematic Theology*, 634–47.

46. WCF 28.6.

coupled the demand for repentance. Repentance and faith are gifts from the Holy Spirit. Notwithstanding all this, the grace of union with Christ, signified, sealed, and exhibited in baptism, is conferred by the Holy Spirit. This is due to the Spirit alone, yet it does not occur independently of baptism, but rather in and through it. The Spirit is the efficient cause of regeneration, election is the **original cause**, the Word is the instrumental cause, and baptism is the **accompanying cause** or co-instrumental cause.[47] The sign and the reality are fully appropriate and compatible.[48]

At a time known only to God, the Spirit regenerates a person. This, the New Testament asserts, is connected to the preaching of the Word (Rom. 10:14–17; James 1:18; 1 Peter 1:23); it is not tied to the Word, but neither is it separated from it. It happens *with* the Word preached. But regeneration is also connected to baptism. Regeneration may be at the instant of baptism, possibly many years afterward, or it may happen earlier, even from the womb, as with John the Baptist. The connection between baptism and regeneration is not automatic, or temporal, or logical, but *theological*.

This theological relationship needs explanation. It is grounded on the connection between baptism into union with Christ in his death and resurrection, and the unbreakable link between resurrection, renewal, new creation, and regeneration. This unbreakable complex has to be grasped in order to get to the root of what Paul and the other apostles assert.

On different levels, both regeneration and baptism occur at the very start of the Christian life.

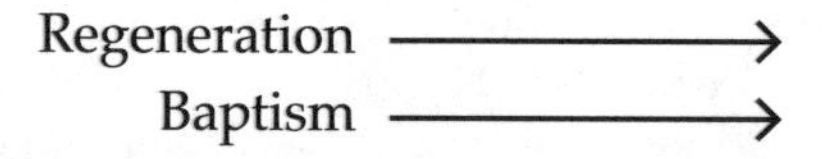

47. This is my own adaptation—some might say mangling—of Aristotelian causality.

48. God's covenant contains promised blessings but also warnings to those who do not believe or live in disobedience. Baptism, as a sacrament of the new covenant, also conveys a curse as well as blessing. This is clear in 1 Corinthians 10:1ff. While unbelief and its consequences occur, however, they are not germane to the purpose of the sacrament but are incidental to it.

Furthermore, regeneration is a resurrection (1 Peter 1:3). We have been "born [or **begotten**] again . . . through the resurrection of Jesus Christ from the dead," united to Christ in his resurrection as in his death and burial. This union takes effect as the Holy Spirit enables us to share in Christ's resurrection in our regeneration. Paul refers to our being united with Christ in his resurrection, and thus renewed to newness of life (Rom. 6:1ff.). In Ephesians, the resurrection motif is again present, when Paul affirms that we have been made alive together with Christ. The allied concept of a new creation is present in 2 Corinthians 5:17. This epochal moment is marked by baptism. Baptism is into union with Christ in his death and resurrection, and since we are regenerated in union with Christ's resurrection, our baptism and regeneration are inseparably connected theologically. The Spirit effects this.[49] As Sinclair Ferguson remarks, "It is not only *because of Christ* that we come to know the Spirit more fully, but actually *in Christ*. . . . He declines to disclose himself in any other way."[50]

The Holy Spirit and the Knowledge of God

Calvin famously wrote that the principal work of the Holy Spirit is faith. By this he unites us to Christ and enables us to enter into the true knowledge of God and of ourselves.[51] This is foundational to the entire Christian life. Referring to William of Thierry (d. 1148), Rik Van Nieuwenhove comments that unless we have faith and love, we cannot relate to the triune God, since both these qualities are a participation of the Holy Spirit within us. The Spirit is the common

49. The Reformed confessions are clear on the connection between baptism and regeneration. They consistently oppose the Roman Catholic doctrine of *ex opere operato*, but are equally severe on those who would reduce baptism to a mere symbol. See the Tetrapolitan Confession (1530); the First Helvetic Confession (1536); the French Confession (1559), 34–38; the Heidelberg Catechism (1563), QQ. 69–73; the Belgic Confession (1561), 33–34; the Scots Confession (1560), 21; the Thirty-Nine Articles of the Church of England (1563, 1571), arts. 25–27; the Second Helvetic Confession (1566), XXX. See also the landmark work the Leiden Synopsis (1625); Polyander, *Synopsis Purioris Theologiae*, 644–54.

50. Sinclair B. Ferguson, *The Holy Spirit* (Leicester, UK: Inter-Varsity Press, 1996), 30.

51. John Calvin, *Institutes*, 3.1.1; 3.1.4.

bond between the Father and the Son, and consequently, unless we participate in the Holy Spirit, we cannot know and love the Trinity. This knowledge and love come only from the Spirit.[52]

The Holy Spirit and Adoption

I have written elsewhere about the centrality of union with Christ in salvation.[53] It encompasses the entire panorama from election to the consummation when Christ returns. By taking our nature in his incarnation, Christ united himself to us; the Holy Spirit unites us to Christ through faith. The Spirit is the bond of union. As such, it is he who effects our salvation, in unbreakable union with the Father and the Son.

Nowhere is this more vividly evident than in adoption. The Father, in the fullness of time, sent his Son, born of the virgin, and then he sent the Spirit of his Son, by whom we recognize and confess that we have received sonship and so share by grace the relation that the Son has, by nature, to the Father (Gal. 4:4–6). This is true, whoever we are, for the Jews cry "Abba!" and the Greeks "Pater!," both meaning the same thing—"Father!" Therefore, by the Spirit, both Jew and Gentile have access through Christ the Son to the Father (Eph. 2:18). Consequently, we are coheirs with Christ! All that is his is ours (Rom. 8:15–17)! See what kind of love the Father has given us (1 John 3:1). It underlies the comment of Peter that we have been made "partakers of the divine **nature**" (2 Peter 1:4).

This also has a redemptive-historical dimension. The people of God before the incarnation and Pentecost were, comparatively speaking, like minor children, under the charge of a guardian. In contrast, we are now adult, the status of the church secured by the **missions** of the Son and the Spirit (Gal. 3:23–4:6). Nevertheless, there is also continuity, since it is the people of God who are in view, who share the faith of Abraham.

52. William of Thierry, *The Mirror of Faith*, trans. Thomas Davis (Kalamazoo, MI: Cistercian Publications, 1979), no. 31, 75–76, cited in Rik Van Nieuwenhove, *An Introduction to Medieval Theology* (Cambridge: Cambridge University Press, 2012), 118.

53. Robert Letham, *Union with Christ: In Scripture, History, and Theology*, rev. and expanded ed. (Phillipsburg, NJ: P&R Publishing, 2011).

Strictly, the sonship belongs to the church, since it flows from Christ, the eternal Son; because it relates to the church as such, it is possessed by all its members in union with Christ. It is the Spirit who has brought this about. This is a reason why assurance of salvation is experienced; the Spirit capacitates us to realize that the status that he, together with the Father and the Son, has effected is ours. Indeed, even when we pass through difficult times in this world, the same Spirit intercedes for us as we share the intense labor pains of the pregnant creation as it awaits with existential ferment the birth of the consummate order (Rom. 8:18–27). This strongly anticipates our discussion of our expectations for the future in chapter 10.

The Holy Spirit and Sanctification

John Owen's definition of sanctification takes some beating:

> Sanctification . . . *is the immediate work of God by his Spirit upon our whole natures, proceeding from the peace made for us by Jesus Christ, whereby, being changed into his likeness, we are kept entirely in peace with God, and are preserved unblamable, or in a state of gracious acceptation with him, according to the terms of the covenant, unto the end.*[54]

Paul understands there to be two realms, the flesh and the spirit. This has a twofold application. Flesh stands, on the one hand, for the weakness and fragility of humanity in its natural state, in contrast to the realm of the Spirit, which is under the direction of the Holy Spirit. Paul elaborates on this in 1 Corinthians 15 and makes a clear allusion to it in Romans 1:3–4. The state of flesh entails weakness, mortality, and their corollaries, whereas the realm of spirit is life, power, and immortality. Since the Spirit is the author and giver of life, he gives life to the point of resurrection.

There is also an ethical contrast. The condition of the flesh is bound up with Adam and the fall. The consequences of Adam's sin were guilt and corruption, resulting in death. While those in Christ have been delivered from this dire condition, its impact remains as

54. Owen, *Holy Spirit*, in *Works*, 3:369 (Owen's italics).

long as we are alive in this fallen world. In Galatians 5:22f., Paul draws attention to an ongoing conflict between the flesh and the Spirit. The flesh is marked by a range of works, the plurality hinting at division, fragmentation, and discord. In contrast, the fruit of the Spirit is singular, since all the features described there come not from disparate sources but from the one Holy Spirit. It is by the Holy Spirit that we are enabled to put to death the deeds of the flesh and so live, because the Spirit is the Spirit of life that overcomes death. Thus, we are to work out our salvation with fear and trembling, since it is God the Spirit who is at work in us (Phil. 2:13). In the light of this, Paul urges us not to grieve or quench the Spirit (Eph. 4:30; 1 Thess. 5:19). This entails the Holy Spirit's being a (divine) person.

Paul writes that being in the Spirit is life, in contrast to death, which inevitably accompanies living according to the flesh. So he urges his readers that "if by the Spirit you put to death the deeds of the body, you will live" (Rom. 8:13–14). There is clear personal responsibility: "you put to death the deeds of the body," the "body" here an effective synonym for the "flesh" in the ethical sense. Notwithstanding, we cannot do it of ourselves, for it is the Spirit who brings it to pass. In Philippians 2:12–13, Paul says the same thing in different words: "work out your own salvation with fear and trembling"—there's the personal responsibility again—"for it is God who works in you [by the Spirit]."

The Holy Spirit, Prayer, and Worship

Access to the Father is secure through Christ the Son and is effected by the Holy Spirit (Eph. 2:18). The way is open, and we can draw near (Heb. 10:19–25). Prayer and worship are inherently and pervasively Trinitarian. We noted this pattern in discussing the Trinity in chapter 1. Prayer is in response to the action of God, from the Father, through the Son, by the Holy Spirit. It entails that every aspect of prayer and worship is undertaken in a Trinitarian context. This does not mean that we know how to pray or can ever become experts in it. Paul recognizes this great need, that "we do not know what to pray for as we ought" (Rom. 8:26–27). Since he includes himself in this category, we can hardly exclude ourselves.

Donkey's years ago, at a summer Bible school in the congregation in which I was then the minister, the organizers had this ditty sung by the assembled children:

> Abraham was a friend of God,
> and he really knew how to pray.[55]

My counter to that was that Abraham was certainly a friend of God, but he did *not* know how to pray! That, I think, is very reassuring for the vast majority of us—Paul would say for all of us.

There is a solution. Paul goes on to say that the Spirit helps us in our weakness, with inexpressible groans. Debate has surrounded whether the groans and sighs are ones that we emit or whether they are utterances of the Spirit himself. If the latter, some think that this is a reference to the tongues that were spoken in the primitive church and are claimed to be present today; we will consider this subject later. For now, the statement in Romans would suggest that it is the Spirit who utters these groanings and that for that reason they are unutterable for us. It is the Spirit who intercedes and the Spirit who searches the heart, and so it is the Spirit who groans (Rom. 8:26–27). This is an immense encouragement for us, for when we are weak, the Holy Spirit is strong and comes to our aid.

The Holy Spirit and the Lord's Supper

The Spirit unites us to Christ and enables us to feed on him by faith in the Eucharist. This is a deduction from the holistic biblical witness to the works of God, the nature of the sacraments, and the Lord's Supper in particular.

As is well known, Rome holds that the Spirit is at work in the Eucharist in transforming the bread and wine into the **substance** of the body and blood of Christ, while the **accidents** of the bread and wine remain. In this the focal point is the eating of the transformed sacramental elements. At the other end of the spectrum, the majority position of contemporary Protestant evangelicalism is that the

55. Author and date unknown.

supper is purely symbolic and that it does not convey grace to, or effect any change in, those who receive it.

Contrary to both these positions, the Reformed churches have affirmed that in the supper the faithful "receive and feed on Christ" (WCF 29.7). As we wrote in connection with baptism, there is here a distinction between the sign and the reality, but at the same time the sign is appropriate to the reality. Feeding on Christ is through the Spirit, not the letter, through the Spirit's efficacious power, in giving faith and uniting us to Christ. Christ does not come down to us in his body and blood, as Rome teaches, but the Spirit lifts us up to him. Christ has ascended; we are enabled to rise to him and partake of his body and blood. We have come to Mount Zion and to the blood that speaks better things than the blood of Abel (Heb. 12:18–24).

Consequently, we are lifted up by the Spirit to feed on Christ in the Spirit. This is real and true, for it is communion with the Son in the Holy Spirit and thus entails personal access to the Father. We are given to share in the life of the Trinity. Since he is God, the Spirit joins things separated by distance, as Calvin said.[56] The Spirit and the Son are indivisible with the Father in the unity of the Holy Trinity. Moreover, the Spirit's distinctive work is to glorify Christ and lead his people to him through the faith he gives them and thus to the Father (Eph. 2:18). Indeed, Paul regards the Spirit as so close to the risen Christ that he can call him "the Spirit of the Lord" and "the Lord[,] the Spirit" (2 Cor. 3:17).

Excursus: Max Turner on the Work of the Spirit in the Church[57]

While it was written some time ago, Max Turner's book on spiritual gifts is still important, marked throughout, as one would expect, by thorough and careful scholarship. Turner attempts to provide a conciliatory statement that will bridge the gap between conservative evangelicalism on the one hand and Pentecostal and

56. Calvin, *Institutes*, 4:17:10.

57. Max Turner, *The Holy Spirit and Spiritual Gifts* (Carlisle, UK: Paternoster, 1996).

charismatic theology on the other. This reflects something of Turner's own background as a leading evangelical New Testament scholar with connections to the renewal movement. It is worth pointing out some criticisms of an otherwise splendid book. These criticisms here concern Turner's discussion of the work of the Spirit in the church in general rather than spiritual gifts as such.

Turner argues against treating Luke, John, and Paul with reference to one another; rather, he advocates viewing them each as separate, or else one would not hear the distinctive voices of any of them. In contrast, Thiselton writes, "Are we claiming that the difference between Luke and Paul gives adequate grounds for a fundamentally different understanding of the Holy Spirit, and fundamentally different Church practices?" Again, "can we really imagine that this 'Luke,' the traveling companion of Paul, declined to discuss the Spirit with him . . . ? . . . To overpress a radically sharp contrast between them seems implausible."[58]

Yet at the same time, Turner's thesis is based in large part on intertestamental Judaism and its view of "the Spirit of prophecy" and an assumption that this was incorporated into the New Testament writings. On what basis can this be? Why should the writings of those who were enemies of the church and the apostolic message be given priority, putative priority even over those of fellow apostles? Is it even conceivable that the apostles would have used such writings? How, amid the greatly variegated nature of intertestamental Judaism, are we to discern which source is applicable? Would the apostles even have known about them? This is especially the case with Luke, who did not have a rabbinical education but was a Gentile doctor!

Furthermore, Turner attempts a systematic theological description of the Spirit and spiritual gifts without any reference to Augustine, Aquinas, Calvin, or Barth, to any Eastern theologian or contemporary Orthodox writer, or to the ***filioque*** or the Nicene Creed.[59] This is akin to the case of my attending to such a question from the New Testament without mentioning Turner!

58. Turner, *Holy Spirit*, 133; Thiselton, *Holy Spirit*, 493–94.
59. Turner, *Holy Spirit*, 133–65.

Turner has a caricature of orthodox views of the work of the Spirit in the church by restricting it simply to divine immanence and thereby effectively equating the Spirit with human institutional practices. This may be true of liberal ideas, in which "Spirit" was identified as the human spirit or perhaps in certain respects of Rome and its view of the church as itself the sacramental bearer of grace. It may have some credence with the view that seeped into conservative circles in the last century, with Jesus' statement that true worship is "in spirit and truth" (John 4:23–24) taken to refer to the attitude of the worshiper. But it cannot be squared with the confessions of the churches, whether Rome, Orthodox, or Protestant.

Turner misses the point that even in Rome this is not the case.[60] Moreover, he dismisses any connection with the sacraments without any serious attempt to understand them. For example, the classic Reformed view expressed in the Leiden Synopsis and the Westminster Confession of Faith is not even mentioned.[61] Any of these would have disabused Turner of the idea that this entails nothing related to the work of the Spirit. The Reformed confessions see a strong connection between the Spirit and the sacraments, while seeking to hold on to the freedom of the Spirit to work when and how he wills.

Key Terms

accidents
accompanying cause
anthropological
begotten
Christology
dualism
efficient cause
eschatologically
filioque
gnosticism
hypostases
instrumental cause
missions
nature
original cause
participation

60. Turner, *Holy Spirit*, 156–58; *Catechism of the Catholic Church* (London: Geoffrey Chapman, 1994), 685–90, 797–801.

61. Turner, *Holy Spirit*, 160. See my discussion in Robert Letham, *The Westminster Assembly: Reading Its Theology in Historical Context* (Phillipsburg, NJ: P&R Publishing, 2009), 332–47; Letham, *Systematic Theology*, 644–45; Polyander, *Synopsis Purioris Theologiae*, 644–54; WCF 28.1–6.

semi-Pelagianism
universalism
substance

Questions for Reflection

1. Evaluate the extent to which divine and human action cohere in the record of the apostolic ministry. To what extent can this be said to be applicable now? Why cannot it be a blank check, allowing us to project divine status to any churchly decision?
2. Consider carefully and cautiously the work of the Holy Spirit in and with the preaching of the Word, and also the sacraments.

9

New Testament Gifts

Contextual Comments

In this chapter, we will consider the gifts of the Holy Spirit as recorded in the New Testament. We will not venture into the question whether these have resurfaced in the last few decades. That will occupy us in the appendix. What we will discover here is a great deal of scholarly uncertainty and disagreement about what many of these gifts actually were. Some readers might wish for clear explanations, asserting confident conclusions, but in some cases to do so would come at the expense of ignoring part of the evidence. Quentin Skinner warns of the dangers of what he terms the "mythology of coherence," whereby contemporary writers seek to impose an order on classic texts in answer to questions of which the classic thinkers could not have been aware.[1] Something rather similar can be at stake in investigations such as this.

Richard Gaffin distinguishes between the *gift* of the Holy Spirit and the *gifts* of the Holy Spirit. He writes: "The work of the Spirit (the gift), experienced by all in the church, the Spirit given on the principle of 'universal donation,' is to be distinguished from those workings of the Spirit given on the principle of 'differential distribution.' Both these principles are clearly expressed in 1 Corinthians 12, the former

1. Quentin Skinner, "Meaning and Understanding in the History of Ideas," in *Visions of Politics*, vol. 1, *Regarding Method* (Cambridge: Cambridge University Press, 2002), 59–97.

in verse 13 . . . , the latter in verses 29, 30."[2] The point here is that the Spirit is given to the church, to all believers, but that his particular gifts differ widely, whether in number, degree, or kind.

Moreover, it is important to repeat something we mentioned in chapter 8. Not only does it bear repetition, but it is as integral to our current question as it was to the discussion of the ministry of the apostles. According to Gaffin, revelation is both covenantal and redemptive-historical. All of God's purposes of redeeming grace are expressed in terms of covenant, whereby he commits himself to an everlasting relationship with a people he redeems from sin and death. Moreover, he enacts and reveals his covenant progressively through the course of history, from promise to deliverance to fulfillment.[3] Since his covenant is enacted with a people—"I will be your God, and you will be my people" is the central promise, repeated at each stage of the history of redemption (Gen. 17:7–8; Jer. 11:1–5; 24:7; 30:22; 31:33; 32:38; Ezek. 37:23–28; Rev. 21:1–3)—"Scripture leaves no place for privatized, localized revelations for specific individual needs and circumstances."[4] This does not mean that the individual is excluded or neglected; it simply refers to the fact that individuals are saved in the context of the community of God's people.

In the first century, the canon of Scripture was incomplete. There was yet no New Testament as we have it. This was even more significant when we remember the overwhelmingly portentous events of the death and resurrection of Christ, which was the historical focus of all of God's redemptive covenants. When Jesus was to depart from personal interaction with his disciples by his ascension, he conferred on them his own authority and promised the gift of the Holy Spirit to enable them to be his witnesses.[5] In this connection, the apostolate was the foundation of the church appointed by Christ.[6] The gifts

2. Richard B. Gaffin Jr., *Perspectives on Pentecost: Studies in New Testament Teaching on the Gifts of the Holy Spirit* (Phillipsburg, NJ: Presbyterian and Reformed, 1979), 43–44.

3. Gaffin, *Perspectives*, 97.

4. Gaffin, *Perspectives*, 98.

5. Gaffin, *Perspectives*, 100.

6. Gaffin, *Perspectives*, 101.

of the Spirit for this time flowed out of the apostolic ministry that Christ himself had appointed. In this, he conferred his own authority on them in their teaching (John 16:12–15). Paul reinforces the point (2 Cor. 12:12; Eph. 2:19–22; 4:7–16). These gifts Paul describes as "signs of a true apostle" (2 Cor. 12:12).

Anthony Thiselton makes a brilliant comment on the disproportionate attention given to the gifts of the Spirit in comparison with love, contrary to Paul's intention throughout 1 Corinthians 12–14. Having remarked that Paul's discussion of gifts moves swiftly to the paramount need for love, he writes: "Paul would not have been unduly surprised that so much more debate and striving, and many more books are devoted to 'spiritual gifts' than to learning to love. He would simply recall Corinth, and reflect 'Nothing has changed!'"[7] Indeed, the gifts of the Spirit feature very little in the rest of the New Testament.[8] That we will devote so much attention to this matter is due to its having been a matter of contention in recent decades.

Thiselton strongly opposes ideas that the Holy Spirit and human spontaneity are to be assumed to go together. In particular, he argues that when Paul mentions prophecy, there is no evidence that he is referring to spontaneous utterances, even less ecstatic ones; rather, Thiselton considers that careful preparation and reasoned discourse are in view. In the Old Testament, Bezalel is said to have been filled with the Spirit of God for the task of constructing the tabernacle. This was hardly a spontaneous event; rather, it embraced a whole lifetime of disciplined craftsmanship (Ex. 31:1–5). We can add that behind this is the reality that spontaneity bypasses the exercise of the human intellect. This is out of keeping with the way in which God normally works and the way in which the apostles functioned. God requires that we love him with all our mind. The gospel addresses the understanding. Paul on his missionary journeys sought to convince and persuade his hearers. He used reasoned argumentation (Acts 9:29; 14:1; 17:2, 17f.;

7. Anthony C. Thiselton, *The Holy Spirit—In Biblical Teaching, through the Centuries, and Today* (London: SPCK, 2013), 94.

8. Thiselton, *Holy Spirit*, 85.

18:4, 19; 19:8–9; 24:25; 28:23–24). He himself remarks that spiritual warfare consists primarily in persuasion, in the subverting of godless arguments (2 Cor. 10:1–6); it begins in the library.

The New Testament teaches that the Spirit, sent by the ascended Christ, gives gifts to his church. These consist of persons (Eph. 4:11–14) whom he equips to lead and teach his church. Paul had written in 1 Corinthians 3:5–10 that he and Apollos were servants, the Holy Spirit's apportioning them as gifts for service.[9] The Spirit's gifts also include a wide range of charisms distributed differentially among all members of the church, covering a huge variety of capabilities, all given for the common good: the advancement and strengthening of the church and the extension of Christ's kingdom. The lists that Paul gives in 1 Corinthians 12 and Romans 12 are hardly comprehensive. They are more a sample that he highlighted for the respective contexts. Max Turner agrees, arguing that the gifts of the Spirit are much broader than is often thought. They are most appropriately used in the service of the spiritual transformation envisaged in Ephesians 4, which entails a corporate and cosmic reconciliation in Christ, rather than for the enhancement of individual life.[10]

Commenting on 1 Corinthians 12:1, Thiselton remarks that the meaning of *ton pnematikon* ("spiritual") is uncertain. The masculine and neuter genitive plurals share the same Greek ending and can refer to spiritual persons (masculine) or spiritual gifts (neuter). The majority prefer the latter, pointing to the parallel with *charismata* and also the occurrence in 14:1, where "gifts" is clearly the meaning. Thiselton cites C. K. Barrett, who states that many consider that it is "impossible to find objective ground for a decision between the two possibilities, and little difference in sense is involved—spiritual persons are those who have spiritual gifts."[11] Charles Hodge, and

9. Anthony C. Thiselton, *The First Epistle to the Corinthians: A Commentary on the Greek Text* (Grand Rapids: Eerdmans, 2000), 931–32.

10. Max Turner, "Spiritual Gifts and Spiritual Transformation in 1 Corinthians and Ephesians," *JPT* 22, no. 2 (2013): 187–205, here 205.

11. C. K. Barrett, *A Commentary on the First Epistle to the Corinthians* (London: Adam & Charles Black, 1968), 278.

later Archibald Robertson and Alfred Plummer, considered that the context refers to gifts rather than persons;[12] the personal conflicts at Corinth, however, lie behind the need to consider the gifts.[13] Thiselton thinks both are applicable in this context and support Paul's asking what criteria are there to apply to either specific people or specific gifts for them to be considered genuinely of the Holy Spirit.[14]

Certainly, this supports a rejection of all humanly constructed religious "spiritualities," notions that have proliferated in recent decades. For Paul, being spiritual means being dependent on the Holy Spirit.[15] It is clear that Paul's stress is that "spirituality," if we want to use that term, is centered on Christ. John records Jesus as stating that when the Spirit came, he would testify not of himself but of Christ. Paul reiterates this by his comment that when the Spirit turns a person from idolatry to the truth, he elicits the confession "Jesus is Lord" (1 Cor. 12:3). The humblest and most insignificant Christian is directed by the Holy Spirit; therefore, those who had received special gifts must not regard other people as lacking.[16]

Moreover, the Spirit brings us into a thoroughly Trinitarian ethos. Baptized into the one name of the Father, the Son, and the Holy Spirit (Matt. 28:19–20), washed "in the name of the Lord Jesus Christ and by the Spirit of our God [the Father]" (1 Cor. 6:11), the Spirit gives us all access, Jew and Gentile, whoever we may be, "through [Jesus Christ] . . . to the Father" (Eph. 2:18).

Paul's stress to the Corinthians, torn into factions as they were, is on unity rather than diversity—"the cohesive bestowal of gifts

12. Charles Hodge, *A Commentary on the First Epistle to the Corinthians* (London: Banner of Truth, 1958), 239; Archibald Robertson and Alfred Plummer, *A Critical and Exegetical Commentary on the First Epistle of St Paul to the Corinthians* (Edinburgh: T&T Clark, 1999), 259.

13. Gordon Fee considers the matter uncertain, whereas Roy Ciampa and Brian Rosner, preferring a focus on gifts, do not rule out the alternative. Gordon D. Fee, *The First Epistle to the Corinthians* (Grand Rapids: Eerdmans, 1987), 575; Roy E. Ciampa and Brian S. Rosner, *The First Letter to the Corinthians* (Grand Rapids: Eerdmans, 2010), 561–62.

14. Thiselton, *First Corinthians*, 909.

15. Thiselton, *First Corinthians*, 913–14.

16. Robertson and Plummer, *First Corinthians*, 261–62.

ensures their fundamental unity" (1 Cor. 12:1–4).[17] The change of term from *pneumatika* to *charismata* in 1 Corinthians "calls attention to God's generous act of *freely* apportioning different gifts to different recipients," as "freely bestowed . . . expressions of the divine favor."[18] The focus is on God's freely giving—note the repetition of "the same" in verses 4–7, which directs attention to the gifts' origin and their purpose.[19] They were given not for individual gratification but freely, gratuitously, for the common good of the church (v. 7).[20] Love is the key, for without this all is lost (13:1–14:1).

As we consider the various gifts that Paul mentions, we would do well to heed this wise comment of Thiselton: "It is almost universally agreed that reference to modern Pentecostal and charismatic phenomena cannot be used as an exegetical tool for proposed interpretations of Paul and Corinth. This would be to presuppose the validity of one specific tradition of interpretation in a circular fashion."[21] It would assume that current phenomena are identical to those in the New Testament, without clear evidence of what those New Testament phenomena actually were. Moreover, even if the two *were* identical, it would exclude, *a priori*, any consideration of the unique redemptive-historical place and function of the apostolic witness, which renders the contemporary situation principially different from the apostolic.

The Pentecostal scholar Gordon Fee acknowledges that contemporary phenomena cannot be equated with those in Corinth, since there is no way of knowing whether they do in fact replicate them. Referring to tongues, he comments that "whether the 'speaking in tongues' in contemporary Pentecostal and charismatic communities is the same in kind as that in the Pauline churches is moot—and probably irrelevant. There is simply no way to know."[22] In other

17. Thiselton, *First Corinthians*, 928.

18. Thiselton, *First Corinthians*, 929; Fee, *First Corinthians*, 586–87.

19. Thiselton, *First Corinthians*, 930–31.

20. Thiselton, *First Corinthians*, 936; Hodge, *First Corinthians*, 243–44.

21. Thiselton, *First Corinthians*, 979.

22. Gordon D. Fee, *Paul, the Spirit and the People of God* (London: Hodder and Stoughton, 1996), 169.

words, it is an assumption that has no evident basis in reality. Fee in the passage above, however, mentions tongues in the Pauline *churches*, whereas we have evidence that it occurred in only one church, at Corinth.

In what follows we will follow the order of gifts in 1 Corinthians 12:8–10, bearing in mind that this list is highly selective.

Word of Wisdom

Logos refers to more than simply a word, more an articulate utterance. *Sophia* was a term in vogue at Corinth, judging by the frequency with which Paul uses it. This *logos* could be an utterance derived from the wisdom of God (subjective genitive) or an utterance about God's wisdom (objective genitive). Paul's discussion of word and wisdom in 1 Corinthians 1:18–4:21 suggests wisdom as an intelligible evaluation of this or that in the light of God's grace in Jesus Christ. It is wisdom hidden from the world and foolishness to the natural person. There is no firm evidence to suggest that this included inspired messages for particular individuals.[23] Fee, a Pentecostal, agrees that it is unlikely that Paul had anything like this in mind, whether in this term or the one that follows. Instead, he writes, it concerns "spiritual utterances that proclaim Christ crucified."[24]

Word of Knowledge

There exists no agreement among scholars on the nature of the word of knowledge. "Knowledge" was also a Corinthian catchphrase, and some in the church there prided themselves on having it. It seems most probable that Paul intended a discourse relating to the knowledge of God in Christ.[25] How the knowledge signified here is to be distinguished from "wisdom" in the previous gift is, writes Fee, "perhaps forever lost to us."[26] Ciampa and Rosner hit the nail on the head when they observe that underlying the supposition that

23. Thiselton, *First Corinthians*, 938–40.
24. Fee, *First Corinthians*, 592.
25. Thiselton, *First Corinthians*, 941.
26. Fee, *First Corinthians*, 593.

these gifts must consist in the revelation of information or advice beyond our human capacities is an assumption that "what is truly spiritual must be completely distinct from our human abilities," thus resting on a nature-grace **dualism**, a devaluation of creation and reason.[27]

Faith

There is widespread agreement that "faith" here is not the same as saving faith, since it is a gift given to some rather than others, whereas saving faith is obviously possessed by all believers. It is possibly a special endowment of faith in particular circumstances. Jesus talks of faith that removes mountains (Matt. 17:20; cf. 1 Cor. 13:2).[28] It would be a mistake to speak in terms of a supernatural ability because categories of natural and supernatural were unknown to Paul, arising much later after the rise of deism, and rest on dualistic assumptions. Rather, the biblical teaching is that God is the Creator of all entities other than himself and is sovereign over all that he has made, in whatever realm it may be.

Various Kinds of Healings

The phrase "gifts of healing" entails that these were gifts of more than one kind. Such diversity may point to sudden or gradual physical or psychological healings, whether direct or through means, a sheer gift of God, "not a stereotypical ministry performed by a permanently endowed 'healer.'"[29] Fee considers that it may be based on each healing's being a distinct gift in its own right.[30]

Physical or psychological healing in this present life is not promised unconditionally. In plenty of biblical examples, no healing was given (1 Cor. 2:3–5; 4:8–13; 2 Cor. 12:8; Gal. 4:15). Timothy was urged to use means to ameliorate his digestive problems (1 Tim. 5:23), Paul left Trophimus sick and did not heal him (2 Tim. 4:20), and Epaphroditus at one point was so ill, he nearly died (Phil. 2:27). The lame man at

27. Ciampa and Rosner, *First Corinthians*, 576–77.
28. Thiselton, *First Corinthians*, 943–46.
29. Thiselton, *First Corinthians*, 946–49, here 949.
30. Fee, *First Corinthians*, 594.

the temple, healed by Peter and John, had been a presence there for years (Acts 3:1–10); Jesus had not healed him throughout the time of his visits to the temple. At the pool of Bethesda, Jesus healed one man and left the rest crippled and diseased (John 5:2–9). This is to say nothing of the legion of believers who had died of various ailments. Thiselton remarks that reconciliation and justification are promised to all who have faith in Christ, but that "no such universal promise relates to various kinds of healings."[31] Turner accepts the continuation of healing gifts but is cautious and also considers evidence from the New Testament of sicknesses, deaths, and suffering to counterbalance it.[32] He notes the reference by Paul to his thorn in the flesh in 2 Corinthians 12 that the believer's experience is as much dying with Jesus as it is rising with him.[33]

In this instance, we are thinking of deliverance from ailments that allows a person to continue living and flourishing in this life; certainly death and the eventual resurrection will bring permanent healing to all believers, since it will release us permanently from the sphere affected by sin, with all its concomitant challenges. Everything is under the sovereign will and gift of God.

Thiselton makes some important observations on healing, particularly in connection with claims that a prerequisite for healing is faith that it will occur; he points to how this can increase the suffering if healing does not happen, since its lack can then be attributed to a deficiency of faith on the part of the sufferer. Moreover, he adds, Paul is not necessarily excluding healing by medical means; Thiselton refers to the Pentecostal scholar Donald Gee, besides a wide range of others, in support. He also stresses the corporate nature of faith and draws attention to the widespread lack of focus on this.[34] It is worth remarking that the healing of the paralytic lowered from the roof occurred through the faith of those who brought him (Matt. 9:1–2; Mark 2:3–5; Luke 5:18–20), while the healing of the sick mentioned

31. Thiselton, *First Corinthians*, 950.

32. Max Turner, *The Holy Spirit and Spiritual Gifts* (Carlisle, UK: Paternoster, 1996), 235–54.

33. Turner, *Holy Spirit*, 253–54.

34. Thiselton, *Holy Spirit*, 102.

in James happens in connection with the prayer of faith by the elders (James 5:14–15).[35]

Deeds of Power

These appear to be particular actions, effective deeds, whether rational or suprarational, to overcome spiritual or earthly forces of opposition.[36] A number of exorcisms are recorded in Acts, as well as the striking dead of Ananias and Sapphira, the raising of the dead, and the infliction of blindness on Elymas (Acts 5:1–11; 9:36–43; 13:8–11; 19:11–17; 20:7–12).[37]

Prophecy

Essence and Purpose

Thiselton comments that "a number of specialist writers on 'prophecy' conclude after many pages of discussion that (a) we cannot be entirely certain of its scope; and (b) we have no hermeneutical entitlement simply to read *into* the use of the term in Corinth and by Paul modes of popular understanding of the term today."[38]

35. See Kimberly E. Alexander, *Pentecostal Healing: Models in Theology and Practice*, Journal of Pentecostal Theology Supplement 29 (Blandford Forum, UK: Deo, 2006); Frederick J. Gaiser, *Healing in the Bible: Theological Insight for Christian Ministry* (Grand Rapids: Baker Academic, 2010). Gaiser's relating illness to the demonic has been controversial. John Christopher Thomas, "Frederick J. Gaiser, *Healing in the Bible: Theological Insight for Christian Ministry* (Grand Rapids: Baker Academic, 2010)—An Appreciative Engagement," *JPT* 21, no. 1 (2012): 16–26, points out that the New Testament does not support this. The closest connection is Paul's thorn in the flesh (2 Cor. 12), which he describes as a messenger of Satan; Thomas here assumes that the "thorn" was an illness. The Gospels only occasionally link an illness to a demon, Thomas indicates, and they clearly distinguish the two throughout. At the same time, the connection between sin and sickness is not noted by Gaiser, while it is fairly clear in James 5 and 1 Corinthians 11, and there is a discussion about a possible connection in John 9, which Jesus averts.

36. Thiselton, *First Corinthians*, 955–56.

37. Hodge, *First Corinthians*, 247.

38. Thiselton, *First Corinthians*, 901. Among major discussions of prophecy in the New Testament are David Hill, *New Testament Prophecy* (London: Marshall, 1979); David E. Aune, *Prophecy in Early Christianity and the Ancient Mediterranean World* (Grand Rapids: Eerdmans, 1983); Thomas W. Gillespie, *The First Theologians: A Study in Early Christian Prophecy* (Grand Rapids: Eerdmans, 1994); Gordon D. Fee, *God's Empowering Presence: The Holy Spirit in the Letters of Paul* (Carlisle, UK: Paternoster,

Hodge was more sure. He thought it meant "occasional inspiration and revelations . . . either in some new communications relating to faith or duty, or simply an immediate impulse and aid from the Holy Spirit, in presenting truth already known." Whereas the apostles were permanently inspired, their teaching infallible, the prophets were occasionally infallible, and ordinary teachers uninspired.[39] Robertson and Plummer thought it was "preaching the word with power," implying special insight into revealed truths.[40]

Yves Congar comments that the Old Testament prophets spoke in the name of the living God. Only occasionally were they predictive, although we might add that the tests for true and false prophets in Deuteronomy include one for predictive accuracy (Deut. 13:1–5). Overall, however, Congar is correct that "the one who prophesies expresses what God wants to communicate."[41] In the New Testament, Congar distinguishes prophets from apostles, since the prophets gave an "inspired explanation of the Scriptures" focusing on Christ.[42] He cites selected fathers, who wrote that prophets were needed at the start of the church but that prophecy had now ceased.[43] For Congar, New Testament prophecy was an understanding of the depth of Scripture and the divine mysteries.

Turner understands the essence of New Testament prophecy to consist in the declaration of a revelation imparted by God or Jesus in the Spirit.[44] This need not be ecstatic and in the vast majority of cases clearly was not. At Corinth, the revelation was "distinct and compelling," but the one prophesying was aware of the surroundings so

---

1994). For a recent assessment, see Richard M. Blaylock, "Towards a Definition of New Testament Prophecy," *Them* 44, no. 1 (2019): 41–60, who considers that none of the main attempts to identify New Testament prophecy are convincing, for "each of these proposals is ultimately found wanting" (41).

39. Hodge, *First Corinthians*, 247.

40. Robertson and Plummer, *First Corinthians*, 266.

41. Yves M. J. Congar, *The Word and the Spirit*, trans. David Smith (London: Geoffrey Chapman, 1986), 62–63.

42. Congar, *Word and Spirit*, 65.

43. Congar, *Word and Spirit*, 65–67. He cites Justin, who called Polycarp a prophet (*Martyrdom of Polycarp*, 16:2; *Dialog.*, 82.1; cf. 39.2), Irenaeus (*Adversus Haereses*, 5.6.1; see also 2.30.4), and Origen, *Contra Celsum*, 7.11; *PG*, 11:1456–57.

44. Turner, *Holy Spirit*, 196.

that he or she could stop if a revelation was given to someone else (1 Cor. 14:30). Turner argues that those asked to give way received their revelation before coming to the meeting, although it would seem to me that Paul allows for this happening in the meeting itself. While a trancelike state may be evident in Acts 10:45–46 and 19:6, there is no reason to think that this was the norm or that even in these instances anyone lost control of their senses.[45] Indeed, the strength of the revelation could vary from powerful visions to a gradually dawning conviction (Phil. 3:15).[46]

Turner considers that the content of New Testament prophecy was wide-ranging. It could relate to directions to churches,[47] solutions to disputes, assurance to missionaries, or warnings of famine or arrest. These were specifically detailed in content, not vague general principles. But, Turner continues, prophecy also went beyond these matters to "the revelation of theological mysteries" (1 Cor. 13:2), or else, he asks, why would Paul list prophets next to apostles and before pastors and teachers?[48] He cites the work of David Aune, who lists fifty-nine prophecies mentioned in the New Testament. These are extremely varied, but among them are included doctrinal matters. Aune's conclusion was that "the distinctive feature of prophetic speech was not so much its content or form, but its (direct) supernatural origin."[49]

Prophecy and Preaching

Is there a relationship between New Testament prophecy and preaching in the contemporary context? Some argue for an identity

45. Turner, *Holy Spirit*, 199.

46. Turner, *Holy Spirit*, 200.

47. Not guidance on how to get to a church, although that might be possible! It would have come in handy to me on one occasion when I took a wrong turn on the way to a preaching engagement!

48. Turner, *Holy Spirit*, 200.

49. These cover assurance (Acts 18:9; 23:11; 27:23–24; 2 Cor. 12:9), prescriptive matters (Acts 13:2; 21:4; Gal. 5:21; 2 Thess. 3:6), announcements of salvation (Rev. 14:13; 19:9), announcements of judgment (Acts 13:9–11; 1 Cor. 14:37–38; Gal. 1:8–9), legitimization oracles (1 Cor. 12:3; Rev. 1:8, 17), and eschatological **theophany** oracles (Rom. 11:25–26; 1 Cor. 15:51–52; 1 Thess. 4:16–17). Cited from Aune, *Prophecy in Early Christianity*, 247–48, 317–18, 338, 441, in Turner, *Holy Spirit*, 201.

between preaching and prophecy, since both declare the Word of God. Nevertheless, Thiselton thinks that there is little evidence to establish that prophecy was a twenty- to thirty-minute monologue. All agree that prophecy addressed "issues of the moment." All agree with Gillespie that it contained (1) reinterpretation of a tradition, (2) continuity with prophetic declaration and argument in the Old Testament, (3) intelligibility, and (4) edification, exhortation, and encouragement.[50] Still, we might ask, how does this differ from biblical preaching in any era? It seems ironic that later, on 1 Corinthians 14:1, Thiselton writes that "we shall argue . . . that here prophecy amounts to healthy preaching, proclamation, or teaching which is pastorally applied for the appropriation of gospel truth and gospel promise, in their own context or situation, to help others."[51] This seems to be a description of Christian preaching. Fee regards prophecy as "spontaneous, Spirit-inspired, intelligible messages, orally delivered in the gathered assembly, intended for the edification or encouragement of the people," and definitely *not* a previously prepared sermon.[52] Thiselton, on the other hand, is correct in arguing that it *can* include prepared messages—"why must revelation be instantaneous?" he asks.[53] The example of the Old Testament writing prophets would seem to support this case, although it would not restrict prophecy to such forms.

As we gather, Thiselton is strongly critical of the idea that prophecy is spontaneous and entails direct revelation from God, as espoused by Turner, Dunn, and others. David Hill in *New Testament Prophecy* is alone, with Thiselton, in indicating that Paul is steering the Corinthians away from short, disconnected "revelations" toward something more coherent, akin to pastoral preaching. Paul's statement in 1 Corinthians 14:30, about the need for critical reflection, supports that idea. Thiselton concludes that "nothing

50. Gillespie, *First Theologians*, 130–50, cited in Thiselton, *First Corinthians*, 960–61.

51. Thiselton, *First Corinthians*, 1084.

52. Fee, *First Corinthians*, 595.

53. Thiselton, *First Corinthians*, 962.

remains of the 'spontaneity' argument except assumption and conjecture."[54] He considers that in Paul's theology, "prophecy" refers to "intelligible, articulate, communicative speech-acts, the operative currency of which depends on the active agency of the Holy Spirit mediated through human minds and lives to build up, to encourage, to judge, to exhort, and to comfort others in the context of interpersonal relations."[55] It seems to me, with Thiselton, that to connect faith with spontaneity is a fallacy. God is a planner and has given us minds to think, reflect, and make considered and wise decisions. Congar remarks that Paul was a prophet, yet he communicated the gospel by rational, reflective argument rather than "thus says the Lord," persuading and convincing people. The work of the Spirit is joined with considered argument.[56]

Turner considers that charismatic exegesis, preaching, and teaching had characteristics of prophecy, but questions whether that is *meant* by preaching, exegesis, or teaching. He argues strongly against Earl E. Ellis, Thomas Gillespie, and others that prophecy is not to be equated with preaching. If that were the case, he indicates, prophecies like those of Agabus would be ruled out.[57] That may be an argument against identifying the two, but it does not follow that there is no overlap or that preaching is not a form of prophecy. Certainly the words of a preacher cannot be directly equated with the words of the Spirit, but if done appropriately, they are an explanation and application of those words.[58] Gaffin sums up the difference well when, identifying the issue in terms of the origin of the respective utterances, he writes that "the prophet reveals the Word of God, the preacher expounds that Word."[59]

54. Thiselton, *First Corinthians*, 1091–93, here 1093; Thiselton, *Holy Spirit*, 109f., 489.

55. Thiselton, *First Corinthians*, 1094.

56. Congar, *Word and Spirit*, 67–68.

57. Turner, *Holy Spirit*, 202–7.

58. Second Helvetic Confession 1, in Philip Schaff, *The Creeds of Christendom* (Grand Rapids: Baker, 1966), 3:237, 872; Robert Letham, *Systematic Theology* (Wheaton, IL: Crossway, 2019), 623–34.

59. Gaffin, *Perspectives*, 72.

Not all were prophets (1 Cor. 12:29), although Paul appears to have encouraged all to seek the gift (14:1, 5, 39).[60] But how far was that a rhetorical attempt on his part to divert the Corinthians from their obsessive preoccupation with tongues, rather than a prescriptive call?

Wayne Grudem's Theory

Wayne Grudem argues that there are three strands of prophecy in the Bible. The first two are commonly recognized. False prophecy, which encourages worship of pagan deities or is shown to be spurious by its predictive element failing, is strenuously condemned in the Bible (Deut. 13:1–5). True prophecy, in which the prophet speaks under the direction of God, is borne out by events or by faithful application of the law.[61]

What is distinctive about Grudem's proposal, however, is his third category. This concerns speech inspired by the Spirit, conveying advice that need not be accepted. In these cases, the language might be imprecise. Often such prophecies were given to specific people in particular situations. They are not infallible, inerrant, or canonical, and the receiver could follow the advice or ignore it at his or her discretion. Among a range of arguments, he presents in support the warnings of Agabus to Paul in Acts 21:10–14.[62] In the account in Acts, Agabus bound his own hands and feet with Paul's belt and declared, "Thus says the Holy Spirit, 'This is how the Jews at Jerusalem will bind the man who owns this belt and deliver him into the hands of the Gentiles.'" Despite this warning and the entreaties of his friends, Paul was not to be diverted from his plan to go to Jerusalem. It was a message from the Holy Spirit to Paul that he did not consider to be binding.

Grudem argues that the prophecy was not accurately fulfilled. Paul was not taken prisoner by the Jews and handed over to the Roman authorities; instead, he was about to be lynched by the Jews,

60. Turner, *Holy Spirit*, 207–8.

61. Wayne A. Grudem, *The Gift of Prophecy in the New Testament and Today* (Westchester, IL: Crossway, 1988); Wayne A. Grudem, *Systematic Theology* (Grand Rapids: Zondervan, 1994), 1049–61.

62. Grudem, *Systematic Theology*, 1052–55.

was rescued by the Romans, and was taken into protective custody. The Romans, not the Jews, bound him. This, Grudem thinks, would have been sufficient for the prophecy to be condemned in the Old Testament. Moreover, Paul disregarded the prophecy and went to Jerusalem regardless. Evidently, he felt free to set aside a warning delivered in the name of the Holy Spirit. This was a prophecy from the Spirit that was wrong in its details and could legitimately be disregarded.[63] Grudem thinks that mistakes can be made, since prophecies must be weighed and tested.[64]

Grudem was well answered by Edmund Clowney.[65] Only a pedant would say that the prophecy was inaccurate. Moreover, it is a challengeable assumption that the Spirit was requesting Paul to abandon his journey. It is more than likely that the Spirit was simply warning him of the danger to which he was heading and the eventual outcome. It is reminiscent of Jesus' repeated warnings to his disciples that he would be arrested in Jerusalem and put to death.

Thiselton remarks in connection with Grudem's idea of different levels of prophecy that his definition is very broad and could include "any kind of speech activity which would be helpful to the hearers."[66] Moreover, this does not require ecstatic utterances.

Turner is also skeptical. Prophecies were falling into disrepute at Thessalonica (1 Thess. 5:20). He relates that fact to the need at Corinth for prophecies to be tested by other prophets, implying that some were of questionable validity (1 Cor. 14:29–33). In connection with Grudem's sharp distinction between apostolic prophecy and prophecies of lesser weight, based on the latter's alleged inaccuracy, Turner comments that "semantically it is not the surface structure of the *wording* of a communication that is of primary significance, but rather the *semantic structure of the propositions* it contains and entails that is of first importance."[67] At first sight, Turner might

63. Grudem, *Systematic Theology*, 1052–53.

64. Thiselton, *First Corinthians*, 963–65.

65. Edmund P. Clowney, *The Church* (Downers Grove, IL: InterVarsity Press, 1995), 255–68, dealt with this matter in a way similar to the argument that follows.

66. Grudem, *Gift of Prophecy*, 229.

67. Turner, *Holy Spirit*, 210.

appear to be supporting Grudem's thesis, whereas he is pointing to the question of a prophecy's validity, not to the threefold structure that Grudem proposes.

Prophecy and Theology

It is unclear what contribution prophecy made to New Testament theology. Was it foundational only, as Gaffin claims, appealing to Ephesians 2:20 and 3:5?[68] For Gaffin, "Scripture leaves no place for privatized, localized revelations for specific individual needs and circumstances."[69] He bases his case on the sufficiency of Scripture (2 Tim. 3:16–17). He argues that Agabus's prophecy of a general famine had a crucial role for the church, cementing Jew-Gentile unity at Antioch (Acts 11:28).[70] Turner considers that there is nothing to suggest that. But in support of Gaffin, the whole context of Acts 11 relates to Jew-Gentile relations in the church!

On Agabus's other prophecy in Acts 21:10–11, Gaffin naturally rejects an individualized interpretation[71] and Turner disagrees, on the grounds that it does not involve any significant theology but is a personal prophecy.[72] But given the presentation in Acts of Paul's apostolic office and all that it entailed for the church—and it was precisely in Jew-Gentile relations that his trip to Jerusalem consisted—Turner is wrong again. Overall, Turner is dismissive of Gaffin, but he lacks the covenantal and redemptive-historical framework, so that he never deals effectively with the underlying basis of Gaffin's argument, which is precisely there.[73]

Turner concludes that there is little evidence that prophecy played a role in the development of New Testament theology. It was more directed to the pastoral oversight of congregations. Paul subordinates the authority of the prophets to his own (1 Cor. 14:37); he did not let them set the agenda, and required their prophecies to

68. Gaffin, *Perspectives*, 213.
69. Gaffin, *Perspectives*, 97–98.
70. Gaffin, *Perspectives*, 95.
71. Gaffin, *Perspectives*, 65–66, 95.
72. Turner, *Holy Spirit*, 210–14.
73. Turner, *Holy Spirit*, 214.

be sifted and tested.[74] Yet Turner's argument has to be qualified. Paul also allowed his own apostolic preaching and teaching to be sifted and tested by members of his newly founded churches (Acts 17:11), and Luke commends them for doing so, for he considered that the Scriptures were foundational, and consequently, it was a responsible action to test teaching on that basis from whatever source it came.

Thiselton argues that it goes beyond the biblical text to say that prophecy is a permanent gift to particular individuals, like an office. But he also considers that the text of 1 Corinthians gives no support to the idea that it was to cease before the parousia, still less to link it with "trivial" messages to individuals.[75]

In the end, we are left with the conclusion that prophecy is "a direct message from God."[76] Even this has to be qualified. Some prophecies clearly are simply informative and do not require action on the part of the recipients. Jesus' warnings of his impending death and Agabus's message to Paul come into this category. The bulk of the Old Testament prophets' activity was to press the requirements of the covenant on Israel and to call for repentance, something very close to contemporary preaching. There were also writing prophets. In many cases, there was no evidence of immediate revelation, but rather a considered exposition and application of already-received covenantal terms. For the most part, however, discussion has surrounded the immediate message, "thus says the Lord," or "the word of the Lord came to me."

Discernment of Spirits

The plural has sometimes been interpreted as a reference to an ability to distinguish between angels and fallen angels. The opposition of truth and error is quite widespread in the intertestamental literature and the Jewish pseudepigrapha and also surfaces in the New Testament, where John mentions different spirits in connection with true and false teaching, specifically relating to **Christology**

74. Turner, *Holy Spirit*, 215.

75. Thiselton, *First Corinthians*, 1060–66.

76. I am thankful to Keith Underhill for this statement, which cuts through much of the ambiguity and verbiage. But a lot of questions still remain unanswered.

(1 John 4:1–6).[77] Thiselton considers discernment of spirits to be a critical capacity to distinguish the transcendent activity of the Spirit from human attempts to replicate it, or to be pastoral discernment of the ways in which the Holy Spirit is working.[78] This may be so, but it seems to me that, if this were the case, it would be subordinate to, and dependent on, the primary base of knowing and understanding the voice of the Holy Spirit revealed in Scripture as he focuses on Jesus Christ. Fee considers that it refers to discerning of prophetic utterances, in an analogous way to the connection between tongues and interpretation of tongues; Ciampa and Rosner agree.[79] In chapter 11, we will consider various attempts to understand the phrase in the writings of contemporary Pentecostal and charismatic theologians.[80]

Various Kinds of Tongues

The main suggestions concerning the identity of New Testament tongues are that they are either foreign languages, unknown to the speaker and hearers (**xenolalia**), or ecstatic prearticulate speech (**glossolalia**).[81] As we observed in chapter 7, the evidence from Acts clearly supports tongues as other languages. Questions surround the identity of the tongues described in 1 Corinthians. Turner recognizes that the phenomenon in Acts 2 was xenolalia. He suggests that in Acts 10:46 and 19:6, at least in part, there is glossolalia.[82] But it seems to me that when Peter visited Jerusalem, the council recognized that the Gentiles had received the Spirit in the same way as they themselves had, as recorded in Acts 2 (Acts 11:17). This points strongly to xenolalia.

There are few references to tongues in the New Testament. Only in Acts and 1 Corinthians do we read of it, in the writings of Paul and his friend Luke. Moreover, as Turner points out, apart from Acts 8

77. Paul does not use *pneuma* or the plural *pneumata* to refer to evil spirits, although Peter probably does in his reference to "the spirits in prison" in 1 Peter 3:19—but I'll leave that comment for another day!

78. Thiselton, *First Corinthians*, 966–67. Thus, with minor nuances, Hodge, *First Corinthians*, 248; Robertson and Plummer, *First Corinthians*, 267.

79. Fee, *First Corinthians*, 596–97; Ciampa and Rosner, *First Corinthians*, 582.

80. See Thiselton, *Holy Spirit*, 113–14.

81. See the discussion in chapter 11.

82. Turner, *Holy Spirit*, 217–18.

(Samaria), Acts 10 (the Gentiles), and Acts 19 (disciples of John the Baptist), in no other record of conversion are tongues involved.[83] Moreover, on these occasions did all speak in tongues? The overall records in Acts do not require that everyone spoke in tongues or even had initial evidence of some kind of having received the Holy Spirit. Turner comments that "Luke considered invasive charismatic praise . . . occasionally to mark conversional Spirit-reception." Furthermore, there is no evidence in Acts that either glossolalia or xenolalia played any part in evangelism.[84]

Turner considers that Paul viewed tongues as foreign languages, not ecstatic shouts or precognitive mumblings. It is the normal meaning of *glossa*. Contrary to Thiselton, he argues for "translate" rather than "put into speech" as the meaning of *hermēneuein*.[85] Paul appeals to the parallel between *glossais lalein* ("to speak in tongues") and the *heteroglossoi* ("foreign languages") of Isaiah 28, which he quotes in 1 Corinthians 14:21. Turner states, "We conclude that Paul probably thought of tongues-speech as *xenolalia* and (possibly) heavenly languages."[86]

The phrase "various kinds of tongues" in 1 Corinthians 12:10 should be given its due. It is followed by the gift of intelligible articulation of tongues-speech. Thiselton asks that "kinds" should be taken seriously. It points to the tongues as covering a variety of forms. In the papyri,[87] *genos* means "species," as in species of plants.[88] He argues that whereas prophecies are speech-acts from God to the community, tongues are seen here in 1 Corinthians 12–14 as from believers to God. Is it transparently clear, however, that the "various kinds of tongues"

83. Turner, *Holy Spirit*, 220.

84. Turner, *Holy Spirit*, 221.

85. The verb *hermēneuein* can mean "to translate from one language to another" or "to interpret," depending on context. *LN*, 1:405. See also *BAGD*, 309–10.

86. Turner, *Holy Spirit*, 223–24.

87. This refers to the vast number of papyrus manuscipts covering a wide range of matters, often regular letters or records of business transactions, dating from around the time of the New Testament writings.

88. Thiselton, *First Corinthians*, 970. Vern Poythress recognizes "that we do not know exactly what happened at Corinth." Vern S. Poythress, "The Boundaries of the Gift of Tongues: With Implications for Cessationism and Continuationism," *Them* 44, no. 1 (2019): 61–69, here 63.

are directed primarily to God? In Acts 2, they were directed in praise to God but were also heard by other people in their own languages; the latter was the dominant theme. The same applied in the conversion of Cornelius and his friends; although the details are not so accessible in that event, Peter later reported it as the same thing that had occurred in Acts 2 (Acts 11:15–17). At the very least, humans were a prominent part of the receptor community. The hearing in both cases followed the speaking, and the speaking was a declaration of the mighty acts of God. The grounds for distancing the phenomena at Corinth from those in Acts are not clear-cut. The literature on this is vast, not only from biblical and theological angles, but also from psychological investigations. We cannot address it here, nor does a theologian have the competence to evaluate investigations of ecstatic speech, if that was what was involved.[89]

Tongues as Signs

In 1 Corinthians 14, Paul says that tongues were a sign of judgment, with Isaiah 28 as the background. Gaffin argues that tongues were a sign of judgment against Israel.[90] Turner disagrees, since the context in Corinth is Gentile, and any unbelievers would almost certainly be Gentile.[91] Notwithstanding Turner's comments, in Luke's account of the founding of the church at Corinth in Acts 18, Paul went first to the synagogue, following which there was a riot instigated by Jewish sources. There were many Jews in Corinth, and they were notable for persecuting Paul. It is by no means to be discounted that this was Paul's meaning.

The question remains as to the nature of the sign. Was it for building up the church? Turner asks. This could have been so only if tongues were interpreted or translated, since, Paul says, intelligible speech is far superior.[92] Therefore, we may conclude that tongues as such, apart from being put into intelligible speech, could not have been a sign peculiarly for the church.

89. See Thiselton, *Holy Spirit*, 116–20.
90. Gaffin, *Perspectives*, 102–9.
91. Turner, *Holy Spirit*, 224–26.
92. Turner, *Holy Spirit*, 226–27.

The majority view is that tongues at Corinth were given as an aid to private devotion.[93] Turner adds that "Paul saw a variety of functions to be fulfilled by tongues-speech, including a doxological and simultaneously revelatory role to the congregation (when accompanied by revelation), but he possibly saw its *major* role to be a private one."[94] One may well ask how this highly individualistic view fits the predominantly corporate model of both Old and New Testaments. Is it not a reflection of the individualism, catalyzed by the printing press, that became characteristic of the post-Enlightenment West? Moreover, evidence for the difference of the features mentioned in 1 Corinthians from those in Acts is at best inconclusive and generally unconvincing.

Clearly, Paul did not expect all to speak in tongues (1 Cor. 12:30).[95] Nor did tongues arise from Hellenistic sources, for "Christian *glossolalia* was . . . something of a religious *novum*."[96] Turner agrees with the important point that "we do not know much about the psychological state of New Testament tongues-speech" and so cannot determine whether tongues-speech was ecstatic or not, whatever *ecstatic* may mean. Most modern tongues-speech is not ecstatic, Turner reports.[97] Paul thinks it's no more or less ecstatic than prophecy, which is usually nonecstatic (1 Cor. 14:28).[98] Both prophets and tongues-speakers were able to remain silent when needed (vv. 26–31).

Both Luke and Paul regarded tongues as "invasive charismatic praise in languages unknown to the speaker," Turner argues. This was not an evangelistic sign-miracle. It was a sign of judgment only if it was not interpreted / translated. Nor is there any evidence that it was seen as a sign to corroborate apostolic authority. In Acts 2, it was an **eschatological** sign marking God's renewing presence.[99] But it seems to me that tongues in Acts 2 was declaratory, and directed to the crowds that were present, for they all heard the exposition

93. Turner, *Holy Spirit*, 227.
94. Turner, *Holy Spirit*, 229.
95. Turner, *Holy Spirit*, 229–30.
96. Turner, *Holy Spirit*, 232.
97. Turner, *Holy Spirit*, 232–33.
98. Turner, *Holy Spirit*, 233.
99. Turner, *Holy Spirit*, 233.

of the mighty works of God in their own languages. The resulting speech by Peter clearly refers to judgment on Israel. Peter's allusion in verse 20 to Isaiah 13:10, an oracle on the overthrow of Babylon, is a probable reference to the impending demise of Jerusalem and the temple. It is followed by an urgent call to repentance for the forgiveness of sins in the context of "this crooked generation" (Acts 2:40). It is hard to detach such statements from the idea of judgment.

Turner argues that "there is no indication that he [Paul] thought that any of these functions of tongues would be eclipsed by (e.g.) the establishment of something like a canon of Scripture . . . or that God would remove them before the Parousia."[100] Here Turner chooses to ignore what Paul wrote in 2 Timothy 3:16–17 about the sufficiency of Scripture; coming in the last letter that Paul wrote, it reflects strongly on a situation later than the Corinthian correspondence.

Tongues as Distinct from Prophecy

Thiselton argues that "a cluster of generic characteristics mark off tongues from prophecy."[101] Prophecy consists of articulate sounds, whereas tongues are inarticulate sounds. Tongues, Thiselton continues, are addressed to God, whereas prophecy is addressed to human persons. Prophecy is in the ordinary public domain, whereas tongues are angelic utterance. Tongues make some believers feel like strangers and repel unbelievers, while benefiting the tongues-speaker. In short, tongues are no easier to define than is prophecy.[102] Yet Thiselton has no difficulty in distinguishing them!

This can be challenged. Thiselton's case rests on tongues' being ecstatic utterance, addressed to God, nonintelligible unless put into intelligible speech. That there is the possibility of translation or interpretation does mean that the tongues as such are unintelligible. Their lack of intelligibility, however, may depend on the inability of the audience to understand them, rather than any necessarily inherent quality. Languages unintelligible to speaker and hearers alike come into this category. The kinds of tongues to which Paul

100. Turner, *Holy Spirit*, 231–32.
101. Thiselton, *First Corinthians*, 971.
102. Thiselton, *First Corinthians*, 971.

refers could come into either of these categories. Ecstatic utterance, while possible, is not demanded.

Thiselton himself recognizes that the many instances of ecstatic frenzy recorded in Greco-Roman texts should not be the model for understanding Paul in 1 Corinthians 12–14, while the lexicographical background is inconclusive, whether from the LXX, the New Testament, the Greco-Roman world, Qumran, or the post–New Testament period.[103]

Tongues as Angelic Speech?

Fee tentatively opts for angelic speech, but agrees that the precise identity of the phenomenon is irrelevant, since the tongues were unintelligible, whatever their actual nature might have been.[104] In contrast, Thiselton considers but dismisses the case for tongues as angelic speech, which could be based on Paul's reference to "the tongues . . . of angels" (1 Cor. 13:1). An obvious point is that angelic tongues will hardly pass away at the parousia, whereas these tongues will do so at some unspecified time (v. 8).[105] Since prophecies will be rendered redundant when the final judgment comes, for they will be overtaken by the fullness of knowledge, the same applies to tongues (v. 8). The future middle, *pausontai,* means "to stop." This undermines the idea that tongues are the language of heaven. Additionally, Thiselton argues, it overthrows the idea that they express "exalted intimacy with God." If that is what they did, we would expect them to continue at the eschaton. It points to the idea that tongues express unconscious, inarticulate longings and praise, raw and in need of intelligible articulation (Rom. 8:26). At the resurrection there will be no need for them to be brought to an end because they will vanish, since the reality so deeply anticipated will have dawned. Precisely when tongues cease is not the theme of this verse; that matter has to be decided on other grounds.[106] Thiselton comments that Hodge, Thomas Aquinas, John Calvin, and B. B. Warfield do

103. Thiselton, *First Corinthians,* 971–72.
104. Fee, *First Corinthians,* 598.
105. Thiselton, *First Corinthians,* 973.
106. Thiselton, *First Corinthians,* 1061–62.

not use this passage to support their cessationist views. Indeed, he adds, "these verses should not be used as a polemic for either side in the debate."[107] As Barth says, love is the one form of Christian action that does not require transformation into another higher form.[108] Thiselton is correct that 1 Corinthians 13 is indeterminate as to when tongues will cease, and it is doubtful whether a purely exegetical case can be pressed either way. We will discuss this further in chapter 11.

Tongues as Miraculous Power to Speak Languages Not Known to the Speaker

Thiselton dismisses this on a number of grounds, including the point that it has apparently been withheld from foreign missionaries and seminary students learning Greek and Hebrew![109] Additionally, Paul writes of tongues' being unintelligible, which was not the case at Pentecost.[110] As we noted in the previous chapter, however, these were unintelligible to the speakers at Pentecost but not to the hearers, and they were intelligible at Corinth if an interpreter or translator was present. It is interesting, possibly corroborating the idea that tongues were unknown but real human languages, that there have been reported instances of people who have suffered strokes, or certain types of brain damage, suddenly speaking languages, such as Swedish, of which they had no prior knowledge. An early exponent of this position was Gregory of Nazianzus, who writes of Pentecost as a reversal of the judgment of the Tower of Babel and refers to the apostles as speaking "with strange tongues."[111]

Tongues as Ecstatic Speech

Thiselton argues:

> Where the boundaries lie between the species of Paul's own gift (14:18), a *glossolalia* which seems controlled (14:28), and that

107. Thiselton, *First Corinthians*, 1063–64.
108. Karl Barth, *CD*, IV/2:837, cited by Thiselton, *First Corinthians*, 1064.
109. Perhaps they should pray for the gift.
110. Thiselton, *First Corinthians*, 974–78.
111. Gregory of Nazianzus, *Oration 41*, 15–16; *NPNF*², 7:383–84.

> which brings confusion, repugnance, and divisive status division, is hidden within the phrase "species of tongues," in which one aspect shades off into another in which the positive and negative, grace and sin, may become mixed, like every other phenomenon in the life of the Christian church which still sins but is *in process* of being saved.[112]

This follows from Thiselton's commitment to the various kinds of tongues' being ecstatic speech of some kind. Yet to assert that tongues at Corinth were ecstatic requires a commitment against their being foreign languages. In the face of the description in Acts 2, this appears contrary to the evidence elsewhere.

It has been suggested that tongues may have been a psychological release, perhaps a subconscious yearning—in the words of Gerd Theissen, "the language of the unconscious which becomes capable of consciousness through interpretation."[113] This idea has not been widely developed, although this has recently changed with the proposals of Frank Macchia in reference to Romans 8:26–27.[114] Thus, it would indicate subconscious languages released in "sighs too deep for words," an eschatological yearning for the completion of redemption, prompted by the Spirit through Christ to the Father.[115] Earlier, Robertson and Plummer suggested that "the soul was undergoing experiences which ordinary language could not express, but the Spirit which caused the experiences supplied also a language in which to express them. This ecstatic language was a blissful outlet of blissful emotions, but was of no service to any one but the speaker and those who had the gift of interpretation."[116] Krister Stendahl writes that while it may be wise for the inarticulate to have the opportunity for praise to gush out, "few human beings

112. Thiselton, *First Corinthians*, 984.

113. Gerd Theissen, *Psychological Aspects of Pauline Theology*, trans. John P. Galvin (Edinburgh: T&T Clark, 1987), 79, cited in Thiselton, *First Corinthians*, 984.

114. But see Frank D. Macchia, "Groans Too Deep for Words: Towards a Theology of Tongues as Initial Evidence," *Asian Journal of Pentecostal Studies* 1, no. 2 (1998): 149–73.

115. Thiselton, *First Corinthians*, 985; Thiselton, *Holy Spirit*, 118–20.

116. Robertson and Plummer, *First Corinthians*, 267–68.

can live healthily with high-voltage religious experience over a long period of time."[117]

Paul writes that tongues have a value, but he is uneasy, since they were individually oriented, while everything should be done for the good of the church. Tongues used in public gatherings of the church can be divisive. They can become specific to a certain group within the church, can create a syndrome of dependency on a particular leader, and may have gained popularity due to the socioeconomic divisions at Corinth—the rich and articulate appealing to Scripture, the poor in understandable reaction reveling in tongues.[118] On this basis, Thiselton argues that Paul prays that the tongues-speaker would be given the gift of articulate speech, bringing it up from the unconscious to cognitive consciousness, from "a more primitive level of speaking" to openly accessible and intelligible speech.[119] While we agree that the evidence for such divisions is clear, these conclusions are somewhat speculative and should be received with caution. Whatever conclusions one draws, Thiselton is on sound ground in writing that "assumptions of a one to one match between ancient and modern phenomena remain speculative."[120]

Gaffin comments that "the view that holds that tongues are given primarily for the personal prayer life of the believer and not for public exercise in the congregation, along with interpretation, can be said only to have completely inverted Paul's outlook in 1 Corinthians 14."[121] This view has an impressive pedigree. Aquinas references John Chrysostom, who had said that the clause "as yet the Spirit had not been given" in John 7:37–39 meant that he had not been given to the apostles at that time. This, Aquinas counters, conflicts with what the Lord said in Luke 11:19.[122] He agrees with

117. Krister Stendahl, *Paul among Jews and Gentiles* (London: SCM, 1977), 123, cited by Thiselton, *First Corinthians*, 986.

118. Thiselton, *First Corinthians*, 987.

119. Thiselton, *First Corinthians*, 988.

120. Thiselton, *First Corinthians*, 988.

121. Gaffin, *Perspectives*, 83.

122. Thomas Aquinas, *Commentary on the Gospel of St. John* (Albany, NY: Magi Books, 1980), 435.

Augustine that the apostles had the Holy Spirit before the resurrection. The words refer to "a more abundant giving, and one with visible signs, as the Spirit was given to them in tongues of fire after the resurrection and ascension."[123] But if this is so, Aquinas asks, why does no one speak in the languages of all nations as then? He cites Augustine, who says that "it is not necessary," for now the church speaks the languages of all nations because the love of God has been poured into our hearts by the Holy Spirit, which makes everyone speak to everyone else. At the start, tongues were needed, since the church was small and limited to one nation, but it had to speak the languages of all nations so that it could be established among them all.[124]

A Cautionary Comment

John-Christian Eurell argues that references to tongues occur exclusively in the writings of Luke and Paul and that Corinth is the only church in the whole New Testament where the practice was demonstrably present. He concludes that 1 Corinthians is the sole source of direct information, accounts in Acts and later in Irenaeus all being derived from Paul in some way.[125] Moreover, he considers that "there is no reason to believe that glossolalia as practised in Corinth was an expression of incomprehensible, ecstatic speech. On the contrary, Paul clearly views glossolalia as divinely inspired speech in a foreign language."[126] Nor, we add, is there a requirement anywhere in Scripture that it be practiced; there is not a trace of evidence that the apostles demanded it. Whatever its nature may have been, it was a marginal practice. As Ciampa and Rosner indicate, since the tongues were unintelligible it is probable that none at Corinth, not even Paul, knew precisely what they were.[127] It seems to me that whether they were foreign languages unknown to the speaker and

123. Aquinas, *St. John*, 436.

124. Aquinas, *St. John*, 436.

125. John-Christian Eurell, "The Nature of Pauline Glossolalia and Its Early Reception," *SJT* 72, no. 2 (2019): 182–90.

126. Eurell, "Nature of Pauline Glossolalia," 189.

127. Ciampa and Rosner, *First Corinthians*, 586.

hearers, or alternatively inarticulate sounds, none could have known their identity, or else the tongues would not need interpretation or translation. If that was the case, it follows that neither can we in the twenty-first century know for sure what they were. That, bearing in mind the probability that xenolalia is intended in Acts, is my own conclusion about the situation in Corinth. It may be to some extent probable that the same phenomenon is in view there as in Acts, but full confidence is lacking.

Interpretation/Translation of Tongues

Thiselton has some sane comments here. On 1 Corinthians 14:5, he writes that interpretation of tongues is commonly understood to refer to a person other than the tongues-speaker. Thiselton argues that this is a disastrous interpretation. The one who speaks remains the subject—it means "to put into words," "to render in articulate intelligible speech." The tongues-speaker should pray for the ability to produce articulate speech.[128] The common view has inserted "someone" into the text, governed by its own assumptions.[129] It is the tongues-speaker who is to render the tongue into language intelligible to the other people present. But how can translation be required if tongues are addressed to God, as Thiselton thinks, rather than as a message to be decoded?

Ultimately, as Hodge remarks, the nature of this gift will be viewed on the basis of one's position on the nature of the tongues to be interpreted or translated.[130] That interpretation of some sort is needed if tongues are to be intelligibly articulated in church worship would tend to undermine the idea that they were simply sighs and groans as expressed in Romans 8:26–27.[131] Gaffin agrees, since the Spirit intercedes for all the saints, whereas tongues were given only to some, and tongues could be translated, whereas the Spirit's groans are inexpressible.[132] Moreover, these are the Spirit's groans, not ours.

128. Thiselton, *First Corinthians*, 1098.
129. Thiselton, *First Corinthians*, 1100.
130. Hodge, *First Corinthians*, 252.
131. See Ciampa and Rosner, *First Corinthians*, 588.
132. Gaffin, *Perspectives*, 84–85.

Apostles, Prophets, Teachers

In 1 Corinthians 12:28, Paul lists more gifts. The first three—apostles, prophets, teachers—are clearly persons whom God has put into the church to lead it strategically. In Ephesians 4:8–10, he explains that these people are gifted and called by the ascended Christ by his Spirit. There he describes God's purpose to bring the church to maturity, growing into union with Christ, on the basis of sound teaching. It is by the ministry of these gifts that the church flourishes or not. This is the strategic basis of the church so that the whole body grows in unity and develops to maturity. Turner considers teaching to be even more significant than prophecy; Paul did not prophesy to the churches but wrote teaching letters.[133]

The apostles were appointed by Christ, witnesses of his resurrection, invested with his authority, foundational to the church (John 16:12–15; Acts 1:21–26). The prophets declared the word of God and related it to the contemporary situation of the church and its members. The teachers handed down the faith once for all delivered in unbroken succession, unimpaired (2 Tim. 1:12, 14; 2:2). Ephesians 4:11–16 lays out three consequences of their work. They were given to equip the saints, for the work of ministry, and for building up the body of Christ. All this is the work of the Holy Spirit, sent by the ascended Christ from the Father. There has been considerable disagreement on the syntax at this point, and there are at least five major proposals. These differences have implications for how the ministry of the church is to be construed.

The older view was that the three prepositional phrases in Ephesians 4:12 ("to equip the saints," "for the work of ministry," "for building up the body of Christ") denote ways in which the ministry of pastors and teachers is to be implemented. In other words, in English there would be commas separating the clauses. These persons are the strategic gifts for the development of the church. These persons equip the saints, undertake the work of the ministry, and build up the body of Christ by their faithful teaching. This is the position of Calvin and Hodge.[134]

133. Turner, "Spiritual Gifts and Spiritual Transformation," 196.

134. John Calvin, *Calvin's Commentaries: The Epistles of Paul the Apostle to the Galatians, Ephesians, Philippians and Colossians*, ed. Thomas F. Torrance and David W.

In recent years, the idea has gained ground that Paul is saying that the task of the apostles, prophets, pastors, and teachers was and is primarily to prepare the members of the church to do the work of ministry and to build up the body of Christ. There could be no commas separating the clauses in English, or perhaps one comma distinguishing the second and third clauses. Thus, these offices were intended to facilitate believers, and it is believers in general who build up the body of Christ. The pastors and teachers simply equip the saints to do the ministry of the church.[135] The idea has some validity and appeal in the sense that Paul goes on to describe the body of Christ as harmoniously growing, all its parts contributing to the well-being and maturing of the whole. That may be true in itself, but both the syntax and the argument point elsewhere.

The focus of the context is the strategic gifts that Christ has given the church, which are the pastors and teachers themselves. It is most natural to see the three prepositional phrases as coordinate. The apostles, pastors, and teachers have been provided by the ascended Christ (1) to equip the saints, (2) to perform the work of ministry, and (3) to build up the body of Christ. The manner by which this is to be done is through "the unity of the faith and of the knowledge of the Son of God" (Eph. 4:13), in order that there will be doctrinal stability "so that we may no longer be children, tossed to and fro . . . by every wind of doctrine" (v. 14). It is through faith, knowledge, and clear and faithful doctrinal teaching, grounded on the Word of God, that the church of Jesus Christ will progress to maturity. These were tasks of the apostles and prophets, and now are the responsibility of the pastors and teachers. These persons are gifts of Christ, donated by the Holy Spirit, and from the wider context, the Spirit builds up the church through these means so that each member is enabled to use his or her particular gifts for its development.

Torrance, trans. T. H. L. Parker (Grand Rapids: Eerdmans, 1965), 180–84; John Calvin, *Commentarii in Pauli Epistolas*, Ioannis Calvini Opera Omnia (Genève: Librairie Droz, 1992), 231–36; Charles Hodge, *A Commentary on the Epistle to the Ephesians* (London: Banner of Truth, 1964), 222–38.

135. An example of this claim, with extensive discussion of grammar, syntax, and contextual factors, is Markus Barth, *Ephesians: Translation and Commentary on Chapters 4–6*, Anchor Bible 34A (New York: Doubleday, 1974), 477–97.

Helps (Service)

This also is a gift of the Spirit, listed in 1 Corinthians 12:28. It does not receive much attention. Nevertheless, it is the quintessential gift. It is most likely care for the poor and those in need, close to what the office of deacon was intended to perform. All believers are called to be servants for the very good reason that their Lord came to serve not himself but others (Matt. 20:28; Mark 10:45; Phil. 2:5–7). Among all the machinery and apparatus of church organization, in the midst of all the wisdom and knowledge that the Spirit may give, this is the oxygen that the church must breathe, this is the power that will cause it to advance. As Paul writes in 1 Corinthians 12–14, without love we are nothing. Love is exemplified in works of service, serving others, especially those who are despised and marginalized. I will develop this theme in the final chapter.

Administration or Government

Paul mentions a range of other gifts in Romans 12 and 1 Corinthians 12:28. This demonstrates that these lists cannot be comprehensive. Rather, Paul highlights gifts that may be pertinent in the contexts to which he writes. In reality, the Spirit gives a multitudinous range of gifts and abilities to the church. In Romans 12:6–8, Paul lists prophecy again (evidently of prime importance), exhortation, giving, and acts of mercy (presumably practical good works). Noticeably absent is tongues. Among these gifts is governing, ruling, or administration (*proistamenos*).

This is not a featured item on the front page of revivalist material, but it is, of course, vital. All human organizations of whatever kind require leadership. Here we have a gift dispersed by God widely and indiscriminately throughout the human race, but here enhanced and adapted by the Spirit for the leading of the church of Jesus Christ. It comes to particular expression in the office of elder. Classic Reformed church documents refer to Romans 12:8 and 1 Corinthians 12:28 in support of the ruling elder.[136] It is noteworthy that, contrary to the

136. Church of Scotland, *The Form of Presbyterial Church-Government*, in *The Confession of Faith, the Larger and Shorter Catechisms with the Scripture Proofs at Large, Together with The Sum of Saving Knowledge* (Applecross: Publications Committee

high status they had among sections of the church in Corinth, healing and tongues in that particular place rub shoulders "with works of mercy and church finance" at Rome.[137]

This gift demonstrates the wide variety of charisms that the Spirit gives. Some may be given from outside and not native to the one to whom they are given, whereas in many other instances—probably the greatest majority—it takes the form of enhancement and sanctification of natural gifts. Besides, the distinction between natural and spiritual, nature and supernature, is foreign to the biblical authors, for whom God is sovereign over all he has created.

Order in Church Worship

Paul's main practical concern in 1 Corinthians 14 is order in the worship of the church. Evidently a situation close to chaos reigned at Corinth, largely because of a lack of love arising from socioeconomic differences that had been allowed to fester and create serious division. Some prided themselves on their knowledge and their ability to articulate the faith. Others, not so blessed, perhaps not so well educated, reveled in tongues-speech, leaving those who did not speak in tongues feeling like outsiders. Paul insists that Christians should not be made to feel alien in their own meetings as if they were unbelievers.[138] The context is the regulation of worship.[139] Gaffin comments that "the one and same Spirit is the Spirit of both ardor and order."[140] He rejects the alleged distinction between the supposed spontaneity of the Spirit and structured, bureaucratic order in the church, a distinction that he argues is a consequence of a Kantian dichotomy.

From 1 Corinthians 14:21–25, it is clear that prophecy, as intelligible discourse, was intended for unbelievers as well as believers.[141] On the other hand, in verses 6–11 it is clear that the sounds generated

---

of the Free Presbyterian Church of Scotland, 1970), 402, in which elders are called "other church-governors."

137. R. A. Knox, *Enthusiasm* (Oxford: Oxford University Press, 1950), 22, quoted in Thiselton, *First Corinthians*, 1096.

138. Thiselton, *Holy Spirit*, 119.

139. Thiselton, *First Corinthians*, 1109.

140. Gaffin, *Perspectives*, 51.

141. Thiselton, *First Corinthians*, 1093.

by tongues are unintelligible. Thiselton states that they are neither music nor speech but simply noise, the product of the release of inhibitions by the Holy Spirit and the production of inarticulate groans and sighs. It is not a heavenly language, since it is not a language at all.[142] This rests on his assumption that they are forms of ecstatic speech directed to God. He writes of the disastrous idea of equating "my spirit" with the Holy Spirit and thus "associating the operation of the Holy Spirit more closely with non-cognitive 'spontaneous' phenomena than with a self-critical reflection on the word of God as that which addresses the understanding and thereby transforms the heart." For Paul, being "spiritual" occurs when the Holy Spirit controls *both* the spirit *and* the mind.[143]

There have been many different proposals for 1 Corinthians 14:21–22. The quotation from Isaiah 28 (neither exactly from LXX nor from the Hebrew) indicates the impending judgment of God on Judah, through the Babylonians, because of their unbelief and rebellion. In that case, the foreign tongues of the Babylonians were a sign of judgment. In the Corinthian context of worship, tongues made many in the church feel alienated as if they were unbelievers. That should not happen in church worship. In contrast, prophetic speech conveys the gospel and so will convict the unbeliever, whereas he or she, upon hearing the inarticulate sound of tongues, will think that the church is mad, "raving and out of your mind."[144] Tongues, given as a means of blessing, had become a curse by their misuse, a sign of judgment rather than grace, since unbelievers upon hearing them would pronounce the church mad and continue on a trajectory for judgment, whereas prophetic speech, on the contrary, proclaims grace.[145] Tongues would identify the church as an emotionally self-indulgent cult.[146] On the other hand, with coherent and intelligible speech an unbeliever may be convicted and worship God.[147]

142. Thiselton, *First Corinthians*, 1108.
143. Thiselton, *First Corinthians*, 1112–13.
144. Thiselton, *First Corinthians*, 1120–26, here 1126.
145. Hodge, *First Corinthians*, 293; Fee, *First Corinthians*, 681–83.
146. Thiselton, *First Corinthians*, 1127.
147. Thiselton, *First Corinthians*, 1127–30.

Thiselton interprets revelation, tongues, and interpretation as referring to the same speaker in particular speech-acts. An analogy is our waking from a dream and piecing everything together or from a subdued state, a scrambled dream, when meaning emerges.[148] In short, while they were by no means to be despised, since these gifts were each given to some, not to all, they were not means of grace that are indispensable for growth in union with Christ. Rather, this belongs to the ministry of the Word, the sacraments, and prayer.[149]

Key Terms

Christology
dualism
eschatological
glossolalia
theophany
xenolalia

Questions for Reflection

1. There is much debate and disagreement on the precise nature of many of the gifts given by the Spirit in the New Testament. Does it create a problem?
2. Given that Paul provides differing lists of spiritual gifts in different letters, how far might these lists be directed toward particular circumstances in the churches to which he was writing?

148. Thiselton, *First Corinthians*, 1145–46.
149. Gaffin, *Perspectives*, 87.

10

The Future

The Holy Spirit and Proclamation of the Gospel

I have written elsewhere about the future prospects for the church and the spread of the gospel throughout the world.[1] Christ has been given plenipotentiary authority as our Savior and Mediator for the very purpose of bringing the nations to discipleship (Matt. 28:19–20). He reigns, seated at the right hand of the Father, until all his enemies are subjugated (1 Cor. 15:20–26). Whatever adverse circumstances the church may face in this place or that, at this time or another, in the larger context the picture is one of progress and conquest in the midst of suffering and difficulty. Any other reading implies that God's eternal purposes can be thwarted by human hostility and unbelief. This cannot be so and is counteracted by Jesus' affirmation that the gates of hell cannot prevail against his redemptive plans in and through his church (Matt. 16:17–18).

This overall scenario is borne out by the worldwide spread of the gospel, particularly in its dramatic growth in the last hundred years or so. Immediately after Jesus' ascension, his disciples gathered in the upper room in Jerusalem, numbering around 120, all of them Jewish. Today there are billions, from the overwhelming majority of the nations of the world. The story continues. As in the book of Acts, the Holy Spirit—not without difficulties, setbacks, and disappointments—empowers the preaching of the gospel, renews

1. Robert Letham, *Systematic Theology* (Wheaton, IL: Crossway, 2019), 817–41.

the minds and hearts of those to whom it is brought, and secures the establishment and growth of the church.

In this situation, we need to reflect on the overthrow of "the lawless one" mentioned by Paul in 2 Thessalonians 2:8. This figure, if indeed it is an individual, is destroyed by Christ by "the spirit of his mouth [ὃν ὁ κύριος Ἰησοῦς ἀνελεῖ τῷ πνεύματι τοῦ στόματος αὐτοῦ]." *Pneuma* here is best translated "breath." There is most probably an allusion to the Holy Spirit, particularly in view of the inseparable works of God.

The reference to "the lawless one" is uncertain, especially in view of Paul's remark in 2 Thessalonians 2:5 that the readers would know what he was writing about from the private teaching he had given them on his visit to Thessalonica. We do not have access to that teaching and can only try to infer what it might have been from those comments to which we do have access. Many have thought that he referred to a figure who would appear shortly before the parousia and launch a fierce and unprecedented attack on the church. But this would have had little resonance with the Thessalonians, since it would make sense only centuries, millennia, later. Most likely, the comments related to persons or events in the first century, in the not-too-distant future. This lawless one was to set himself up in the temple and proclaim that he was God. A succession of Roman emperors in the first century claimed divine honors for themselves. A future emperor, Titus Vespasian, led the Roman army that besieged and entered Jerusalem at the climax of the Jewish revolt, desecrating and destroying the temple.

That still leaves a lack of clarity about what Paul meant by the Lord Jesus' slaying the lawless one by the breath of his mouth. It may mean through the Holy Spirit's empowerment of the preaching of the gospel, which in due time conquered the same empire over which these hideous figures then presided. It could refer to the Spirit's exacting God's judgment. We cannot know for sure. Indeed, the reference may not be confined to that or any other particular situation, but might also encompass other circumstances, including a final display of triumphant vindication at the parousia.

In 1 Thessalonians, Paul writes that when Christ returns, we will meet him in the air. This is unlikely to mean some sort of mass levitation. Rather, the air was considered to be the abode of evil spirits, as in Ephesians where the devil is described as "the prince of the power of the air" (Eph. 2:1–2). Thus, at his return Christ will publicly and universally demonstrate his overthrow of the forces of darkness, and his people, resurrected, will be associated with that victorious parade. Consequently, in our passage in 2 Thessalonians, Paul may be looking forward to the final overthrow and judgment of the forces of oppression, which will include the putative figure about which he is writing. The point for us here and now is that this will be by his Spirit, who will evidently, with the Father and the Son, be integrally participating in that denouement.[2]

It is clear from all this that the church from Pentecost on is suffused by, and in the process of transformation by, the Holy Spirit in union with Christ the Son. As Sinclair Ferguson remarks, "the central role of the Spirit is to reveal Christ and to unite us to him and to all those who participate in his body."[3] On the one hand the events at Pentecost were unique and nonrepeatable. But for us to conclude that the Spirit has somehow retracted his operations is contrary to the entire witness of the New Testament and the prospective prophecies of the Old. Christ is absent from us physically, but he is present by the Spirit ("I am with you all the days until the consummation of the age," Matt. 28:20 [my translation]). Pentecost was the harbinger of the new age it inaugurated. It is in the last days, begun at Pentecost but not limited to it, that the Lord pours out his Spirit on all flesh. In that sense, we are all Pentecostals and charismatics.

The Holy Spirit and Transformation

In his teaching about the coming of the Spirit at Pentecost, Jesus states that both he and the Father, together with the Spirit, would take up permanent residence (*mone*) with his disciples (John 14:23). On the basis of the inseparable operations of the Trinity, the Spirit's

2. See Revelation 13:15, where *pneuma* here means "life." The beast from the earth (the false prophet) is empowered to give life to the image of the beast. Life of a perverted kind is in view, not the Holy Spirit.

3. Sinclair B. Ferguson, *The Holy Spirit* (Leicester, UK: Inter-Varsity Press, 1996), 100.

coming and indwelling entails the presence of the indivisible Trinity. The Spirit came to indwell the church and its members and to effect a change. This was foretold by Ezekiel (Ezek. 36:23–36). Speaking of the covenant community in its then rebellion but its future transformation, the Lord talks of replacing the heart of stone with a heart of flesh, promising that "I will put my Spirit within you, and cause you to walk in my statutes and be careful to obey my rules" (v. 27).

The work of the Spirit promotes the glory of Christ in keeping with Jesus' own words in John 14–16. Paul remarks, in 2 Corinthians 3:18, that we are being transformed into the glory of God by the Holy Spirit as we focus on the risen Christ. The Spirit of the Lord transforms us from one degree of glory to another. This occurs as the focus is "the glory of the Lord," seen through a mirror but with unveiled face, in contrast to Moses. Paul is arguing for the superiority of his ministry of the new covenant to Moses and the Mosaic covenant. At the root of that superiority is the Holy Spirit, who transforms us, which the law given through Moses was powerless to do.

The same idea is present in 1 John 3:1–2, where John indicates that when Christ returns in his full glory, we will share in that glory. We will be like the glorified Christ, for we will see him as he is. Peter too states that even now we have been given to be participants in the divine **nature** (2 Peter 1:4). This is effected by the Holy Spirit, who dwells within us. In each of these contexts, from Paul, John, and Peter, the focus of the Spirit's work is to transform us into the image of the risen and glorified Christ, "who is the image of the invisible God" (Col. 1:15 [my translation]).[4]

Paul writes about the Spirit's enabling us to put to death the deeds of the flesh (Rom. 8:13–14), a process he sees as ongoing throughout life, in tandem with this transformation. Since "glory" in the Old Testament is directly connected with God, expressing what is distinctive about God,[5] Paul implies that this transformation is into the likeness of God. This fulfills the purpose for which God

4. Note John Owen's treatment of this theme: John Owen, *A Discourse concerning the Holy Spirit* (1674), in *The Works of John Owen*, ed. William H. Goold (London: Banner of Truth, 1965–68), 3:374–76.

5. Ferguson, *Holy Spirit*, 139–40.

created humanity in his image (Gen. 1:26–27). Moreover, it comes to complete expression in Jesus Christ, God incarnate, who is the second Adam, "the image of the invisible God" (Col. 1:15), "the express images of [the Father's] **being**" (Heb. 1:3). Consequently, it consists in progressive conformity to the image of Christ, who is "the firstborn among many brothers" (Rom. 8:29), so that when he returns, in the full glory of God, "we shall be like him, because we shall see him as he is" (1 John 3:1–2).

This is evidently the context for Peter's remark that we have been made "partakers of the divine nature" (2 Peter 1:4). As I have written elsewhere, this does not mean that we lose our humanity and are somehow absorbed into God.[6] Rather, it entails that our humanity is enhanced. In being partakers of the divine nature, we participate in God; we do not become God. When Athanasius made his famous comment, following Irenaeus, that the Son became man that we might become God,[7] he no more meant that our **deification** means abandoning our humanity and creatureliness than he meant that the Son ceased to be God in becoming man. He is renowned for his defense of the deity of Christ; deification in the sense he intended entails our continued humanity. Such an idea in no way involves a blurring of the Creator-creature distinction, foundational to the whole of biblical revelation. It cannot mean being changed into the **essence** of God. That would be a contradiction of the Christian faith. It would negate the classic teaching of the church on the person of Christ, in which Eutyches was rejected as a heretic for submerging Christ's humanity. Athanasius constantly referred to the Son as being "proper" (*idios*) to the Father's being, but when he wrote of our deification, he spoke of our being "participants" (*metochoi*).[8]

6. Robert Letham, *Union with Christ: In Scripture, History, and Theology*, rev. and expanded ed. (Phillipsburg, NJ: P&R Publishing, 2011), 88–128; Letham, *Systematic Theology*, 768–88.

7. Athanasius, *On the Incarnation*, 54; *PG*, 25:192.

8. Athanasius, *Letters to Serapion on the Holy Spirit*, 1.23–25; *PG*, 26:584–89; Mark DelCogliano, Andrew Radde-Gallwitz, and Lewis Ayres, *Works on the Spirit: Athanasius the Great and Didymus the Blind* (Yonkers, NY: St. Vladimir's Seminary Press, 2011), 89–93; Norman Russell, *The Doctrine of Deification in the Greek Patristic Tradition* (Oxford: Oxford University Press, 2004), 176–78.

Christ's very nature is deity; we are given to partake in a finite and creaturely way in union with God in Jesus Christ. We are to be enabled to fulfill all that God intended for us. This is to take place in union with Christ, effected by the Spirit. Peter describes this in ethical terms in 2 Peter 1. This, we must stress, is God's ultimate goal, fulfilled at the return of Christ, and consists in the reality that "we shall be like him" (1 John 3:2), like Christ in glory.

God made us for himself. The incarnation establishes it. There the eternal Son, one of the Trinity, lived and lives as man, one coherent and fulfilled person. The indwelling of the Holy Spirit brings it toward its great purpose. Again, one of the Trinity has been sent to saturate us, to shape the whole orientation of our beings and direct us into conformity to the incarnate Son.

This is not **pantheism**, a breakdown of the Creator-creature distinction. Nor is it some mixture of the divine and human, as advocated by some Eastern religions, in which both are like ingredients merged into an **ontological** soup. Rather, our humanity is not only preserved but enhanced. As Christ's humanity was not absorbed in the incarnation but retained its distinct integrity, so we remain human. Christ is the eternal Son, one with the Father and the Holy Spirit, by nature; we are sons by grace. Thus, even our bodies are temples of the Holy Spirit (1 Cor. 6:19). This transformation by the Spirit occurs in union with Christ.

This transformation is *cultivated by the Word and sacraments*. Elsewhere I have indicated how John 6 portrays the reality of union with Christ in a sacramental context.[9] Those who have eternal life eat and drink Christ's flesh and blood. This occurs by the Holy Spirit (John 6:63) through faith (v. 47). Robert Bruce argued that there is nothing in the Lord's Supper that is not available in the Word (the sacrament depends on the Word to be a sacrament), but that in the Lord's Supper we "get Christ better."[10] As Augustine described it, it is "a

9. Robert Letham, *The Lord's Supper: Eternal Word in Broken Bread* (Phillipsburg, NJ: P&R Publishing, 2001); Letham, *Systematic Theology*, 751–89.

10. Robert Bruce, *The Mystery of the Lord's Supper: Sermons on the Sacrament Preached in the Kirk of Edinburgh in A.D. 1589*, ed. and trans. Thomas F. Torrance (London: James Clarke, 1958), 56.

kind of visible word of God."[11] It is the point of union covenantally and personally between Christ and his people. Even those who do not accept a sacramental interpretation of the chapter agree that it finds its truest fulfillment in the Lord's Supper.[12]

In the words of Nicholas Cabasilas (1322–?), this union with Christ by the Holy Spirit "is closer than any other union which man can possibly imagine and does not lend itself to any exact comparisons." The martyrs laid down their heads and limbs with exultation and could not be separated from Christ even so far as to be out of earshot of his voice. In short, this union is closer than what joins a man to himself.[13]

As surely as we eat the bread and drink the wine, so Christ enters our souls.[14] As WCF 29.7 says, the faithful receive and feed on Christ in the Lord's Supper really and truly. No amount of stress on the spiritual aspect of the supper, which is, of course, a correct stress, can ever be used to diminish the real and true feeding that takes place there. As Jesus said, "my flesh is true food, and my blood is true drink" (John 6:51–58). Or as Paul notes, in union with Christ we are given one Spirit to drink (1 Cor. 12:13).

We taste thee, O thou living bread,
and long to feast upon thee still;
we drink of thee, the fountainhead,
and thirst our souls from thee to fill.[15]

11. Augustine, *On the Gospel of John*, 80.3; *NPNF*[1], 7:344.

12. G. R. Beasley-Murray, *John*, Word Biblical Commentary 36 (Waco, TX: Word, 1987), 94–95; D. Carson, *The Gospel according to St John* (Leicester, UK: Inter-Varsity Press, 1991), 288–98.

13. Nicholas Cabasilas, *Life in Christ*, trans. Margaret I. Lisney (London: Janus, 1995), 5–6.

14. "I call them signs because they have the Body and Blood of Christ conjoined with them. Indeed, so truly is the Body of Christ conjoined with the bread, and the Blood of Christ conjoined with the wine, that as soon as you receive the bread in your mouth (if you are a faithful man or woman) you receive the Body of Christ in your soul, and that by faith. And as soon as you receive the wine in your mouth, you receive the Blood of Christ in your soul, and that by faith. It is chiefly because of this function that they are instruments to deliver and exhibit the things that they signify. . . . [For] the Sacrament exhibits and delivers the thing that it signifies to the soul and heart, as soon as the sign is delivered to the mouth." Bruce, *Mystery*, 44.

15. Bernard of Clairvaux, "Jesus, Thou Joy of Loving Hearts" (c. 1150).

The reality, extent, and far-reaching effect of this union immeasurably exceed the merely symbolic. Even if we were to suppose it to be purely symbolic, the symbols symbolize *something*. For our present purposes, we note that it is the Spirit who, as John Calvin wrote, "joins things separated by distance" who effects and cultivates this union in the supper.[16]

The Spirit does not unite us **hypostatically** to the Son. There is only one such union—the incarnate Christ, who remains so forever and ever. The indwelling of the Trinity through the Holy Spirit (John 14:23) is different. Whereas in the incarnation the Son has indissolubly united himself to a human nature in one person, the Spirit indwells countless human persons. What he does is to enhance our humanity to be what God eternally intended it to be.

Jesus Christ is the archetype and exemplar. As man, he was led by the Spirit at all times. He is the author, pioneer, and perfecter of our salvation in his incarnate life and work, sharing our faith, our very nature of flesh and blood, our temptations, our sufferings, our death and burial (Heb. 2:5–18), besides our resurrection (Rom. 8:10–11; 1 Cor. 15:35–50).

It is union with *Christ, with his person*. The indwelling of the Holy Spirit in the church and its members, as explained by Jesus in John 14 and expanded by Paul in Romans 8 and Galatians 4, effects and cultivates this union. It is grounded in his incarnation—he united himself to humanity forever; the Spirit unites us to him in a spiritual union forever.

The consequence is that we have more than fellowship with Christ. Fellowship takes place between separate persons by means of presence, recognition, conversation, shared interests, and the like. Adam had fellowship with God before the fall. Redemption has not simply restored us to that condition. The incarnation has happened; the Son of God is forever human. The outpouring and indwelling of the Spirit has occurred and endures; the Spirit of God has taken up permanent residence in and with those who love Christ, and in so

16. John Calvin, *CO*, 6.127–28, 487; John Calvin, *Institutes*, 3.1.1; 3.2.24; 4.14.16; 4.15.15; 4.17.9–12; John Calvin, *Calvin: Theological Treatises*, trans. J. K. S. Reid (Philadelphia: Westminster Press, 1954), 137, 267–68; Letham, *Union with Christ*, 88–128.

doing the Holy Trinity now lives in us. It goes beyond communion. It entails union.

It is more than **participation** in the communicable **attributes** of God, as some have suggested. It is not to be restricted to union with righteousness, goodness, holiness, or truth; neither is it union with the benefits of Christ, as if it were union with the doctrine of sanctification. It is union with *Christ*.

It is effected and developed by the Holy Spirit through faith, in and through the means of grace: the ministry of the Word, the sacraments, and prayer (WSC 88). It is churchly, not individualistic. It is not a private experience to be developed in isolation from life in the church. It occurs in the humdrum everyday experience of the means God has appointed rather than in superficially exciting or dramatic events.

It is not automatic; it is through faith. There is a certain responsibility on our part to cultivate our union with Christ. Participation in the means of grace is essential, for it is there that God has undertaken to meet with us. At the same time, it is not an immanent process under our control; it is initiated and developed by the Holy Spirit. It transcends our capacity to explain. But we can expect the Spirit to work with and through the means that he himself has appointed for that purpose.

It will eventually lead to our being "like [Christ]" (1 John 3:1–2; see also Rom. 8:29–30; 2 Cor. 3:18), for "it is the intention of the gospel to make us sooner or later like God."[17] For the present, we are "partakers of the divine nature," having escaped the corruption that is in the world by lust (2 Peter 1:4). When Christ appears at his parousia, however, we will see him as he is, in his glorified humanity, and we will be finally and climactically transformed to be like him, our present lowly bodies changed to be like his glorious body (Phil. 3:20–21).

17. Calvin, *Calvin's Commentaries: The Epistle of Paul the Apostle to the Hebrews and the First and Second Epistles of St Peter*, ed. Thomas F. Torrance and David W. Torrance, trans. William B. Johnston (Grand Rapids: Eerdmans, 1963), 330; John Calvin, *Commentarii in Epistolas Canonicas*, Ioannis Calvini Opera Omnia (Genève: Librairie Droz, 2009), 327–28.

Our proper place is to share God's glory. By sin we fell short and failed to participate in his glory, but in and through Christ we are restored to the glory of God in presently unimaginable ways as our ultimate destiny. Glory is what belongs distinctively and peculiarly to God. We are called to partake of what God is. This is more than mere fellowship. Fellowship entails intimate interaction but no participation in the nature of the one with whom such interaction takes place. Peter's language means that this goes far beyond external relations. It stops short of sharing in the being of God. There is an actual participation in the divine nature.

Cyril of Alexandria wrote:

> For God the Father, at the beginning, by his own Word, took of the dust of the ground, as is written, and fashioned the animal, that is man, and endowed him with a soul, according to his will, and illuminated him with a share of his own Spirit; for he breathed into his nostrils the breath of life, as is written. And when it came to pass that through disobedience man fell under the power of death, and lost his ancient honour, God the Father built him up and restored him to newness of life, through the Son, as at the beginning. And how did the Son restore him? By the death of his own flesh he slew death, and brought the race of man back again into incorruption; for Christ rose again for us. In order, then, that we might learn that he it was who at the beginning created our nature, and sealed us with the Holy Spirit, our Saviour again grants the Spirit, through the outward sign of his Breath, to the holy disciples, as being the firstfruits of renewed nature. For Moses writes concerning our creation of old, that God breathed into man's nostrils the breath of life. As, then, at the beginning, man was formed and came into being, so likewise is he renewed; and as he was then formed in the image of his creator, so likewise now, by participation in the Spirit, is he transformed into the likeness of his maker. For that the Spirit impresses the Saviour's image on the hearts of those who receive him surely does not admit of question; for Paul plainly exhorteth those who had fallen through weakness into observance of the

> Law, in the words: "My little children, of whom I am again in travail until Christ be formed in you." For he says that Christ will not be formed in them save by partaking of the Holy Spirit, and living according to the law of the gospel. Therefore, as in the firstfruits of creation, which is made regenerate into incorruption and glory and into the image of God, Christ establishes anew his own Spirit in his disciples. For it was necessary that we should also perceive this truth, namely, that he brings down and grants the Spirit unto us. Therefore, also, he said: All things, whatsoever the Father hath, are mine. And as the Father hath, of himself and in himself, his own Spirit, so also the Son hath the Spirit in himself, because he is consubstantial with him, and essentially proceeded from him, having by nature in himself all the attributes of his Father.[18]

The Spirit and Anticipation of the Eschaton

We have discussed the Holy Spirit as the *arrabōn*, the guarantee, of our full and completed salvation at the eschaton (2 Cor. 1:22; Eph. 1:13–14).[19] He is the pledge given by God, the deposit ensuring to us the full payment in due course. Concurrent with this is the fact that the Spirit assures us of our future destination and produces in us an eager expectation for it. This is because the ultimate realization of God's saving purposes will be in the realm in which the Spirit is the ruling factor. The deposit is of the same kind as the full payment, just as the firstfruits are of the same kind as the full harvest. Hence, the verbs Paul uses in 2 Corinthians 5:1–5 are highly emotional, conveying longing, powerful and intense striving toward the prize. The creation itself exhibits the same deep, profound turmoil, like that of a woman in labor, as it awaits its liberation and ours (Rom. 8:23–25).

The Holy Spirit and Assurance

The Holy Spirit instills assurance of our ultimate salvation. Paul writes that the Spirit grants us knowledge that we are the children

18. Cyril of Alexandria, *Commentary on John*, Library of Fathers of the Holy Catholic Church 2 (London: Walter Smith, 1874/1885), 930–31.

19. See *BAGD*, 109; *LN*, 2:577.

of God (Rom. 8:15–16). The filial cry "Father!" is the same whether it is made in Aramaic (*Abba*) or Greek (*Pater*) or any other language on the face of the earth. This was part of God's eternal plan, as much as the sending of his Son (Gal. 4:4–6).

John wrote his first letter to combat false teaching that stemmed from a rejection of the incarnation (1 John 4:1–6). It had a wide impact and was a form of perfectionism (1:6–2:2). It claimed a special form of knowledge that was denied to the ordinary Christians. John countered it by asserting that believers know that they belong to Christ. In five short chapters, he writes "we know" fifty-five times. We know that we have passed from death to life because we love the brothers (3:14). We know that we belong to Christ because we believe the teachings of the gospel (4:1–6). We know this because God has given us the Holy Spirit (3:24; 4:13). We know, we know, we know.

Along similar lines, Paul writes of the Spirit as the "earnest" of our inheritance. The word *arrabōn* denotes the guarantee of a future possession. The gift of the Spirit is the down payment by God on the fulfillment of his promised redemption. If we want to be seriously anachronistic—who doesn't from time to time?—in modern Greek, the word means "engagement ring." The meaning is very close. God, having given us the deposit, will pay the rest in due time, for he is faithful. We can reflect on what Paul writes elsewhere that Christ's resurrection is the "firstfruits" of the full harvest (1 Cor. 15:20, 23), the first payment, and one that is of the same kind as the rest. The firstfruits of the apple harvest are apples; the deposit of our inheritance is the Holy Spirit, who governs the sphere of life in the coming age. Indeed, the Spirit of the Father raised Jesus the Son from the dead, and the same Spirit will raise us in union with the Son at the last day; he it is who now indwells us as the gift of the Father (Rom. 8:10–11). The Spirit assures us of eternal life because he is eternal life and because he has been given to us here and now.

The Seal of the Holy Spirit

Thomas Goodwin, in his exposition of Ephesians 1:13–14, argued that when Paul writes that believers have been sealed with the Holy Spirit of promise, he is referring to a special experience of the Spirit that grants someone a direct assurance of the person's final salvation. This experience is postconversion and is not common to all believers. To receive it, it is necessary to "sue God for it" by persistent and importunate prayer. This reading was based on the aorist participle *pistuesantes,* with an English translation of "after you believed, you were sealed with the Holy Spirit."[20]

This view has been popularized in various holiness and pietist circles through the years in support of a "second blessing" theology. In such groups, it is asserted that God intends us to rise above the usual, humdrum Christian life in which we are living effectively a second-rate spiritual existence. This great postconversion effusion of the Spirit will empower us to live far more effectively for God. In the last century, a notable exponent of this position was the great preacher Dr. Martyn Lloyd-Jones. In his published sermons on Romans, Lloyd-Jones argued strongly, using Goodwin's exposition as a benchmark, in order to extol this extra dimension of Christian experience as a desirable goal. In particular, he drew attention to a range of preachers, often in Wales, whose ministries were transformed overnight by a sudden and overpowering experience of the Holy Spirit. While Lloyd-Jones uses Goodwin, most of his case rests on these historical examples.[21] He cites, among very many others, Charles Simeon, who wrote that the seal of the Spirit was given "to many in the church at Ephesus" and that "there shall always be some in the church who possess and enjoy it."[22] In what follows, I am not in the least wanting to downplay the need to seek the blessing of the Holy Spirit on our persons and endeavors. Nor am I wanting to detract from the reality of the experiences that Lloyd-Jones mentions.[23] We are commanded to be filled with the Spirit

20. Thomas Goodwin, *The Works of Thomas Goodwin* (Edinburgh: James Nichol, 1864), 1:233–48.

21. D. Martyn Lloyd-Jones, *Romans: An Exposition of Chapter 8:5–17: The Sons of God* (Edinburgh: Banner of Truth, 1972), 311–14.

22. Quoted in D. Martyn Lloyd-Jones, *Joy Unspeakable: The Baptism with the Holy Spirit* (Eastbourne, UK: Kingsway Publications, 1984), 150.

23. His treatment of Romans 8:15–16 alone takes up nearly two hundred pages, overwhelmingly based on reports of spiritual experience. Lloyd-Jones, *Sons of God,* 206–399.

(Eph. 5:18). But not only is this reading exegetically implausible, but the conclusions drawn from it are theologically indefensible and, in practical terms, dangerous and damaging. Besides, basing doctrine on personal experiences is at best a highly subjective undertaking.

First, it is exegetically implausible. Goodwin's reading supports the idea that the seal of the Spirit is a particular work that the Spirit effects. He seals. Moreover, he does this for some believers, not for all. It normally happens sometime after conversion, at an indefinite interval. Some may never be sealed in the way Goodwin describes. He urges his readers to plead with God for it.[24]

This reading, however, proceeds on the assumption that the aorist participle in Ephesians 1:13, mentioned above, refers to an event preceding the main verb. The main verb is ἐσφραγίσωητε, "you were sealed," the participle locating the sealing as πιστεύσαντες, "after you believed." While it is possible that the aorist participle refers to an event significantly preceding the main verb, there are a large number of circumstances in which, if that were the case, the temporal distance would be negligible. Moreover, the participle can be the means by which the action of the main verb is accomplished. In both such instances, the sealing and the believing would be more or less simultaneous. While the previous aorist participle, *akousantes*, "having heard," normally requires some temporal distance from the main verb, this is not necessarily the case with our participle and is by no means demanded. At the very best, this would be an ambiguous reading. Lloyd-Jones recognized this, although he concluded that his preferred reading meant the same thing. "Believing is one thing but being sealed by the Spirit is another. They do not happen, of necessity, at the same time," he wrote.[25] It is wrong for two reasons. It assumes that the aorist tense refers to the past, whereas it has no necessary relation to time. The participle is most likely one of attendant circumstance, referring to an event associated with the main verb rather than one preceding it to a significant degree.[26]

24. Goodwin, *Works*, 1:233–48.

25. Lloyd-Jones, *Sons of God*, 312.

26. On the "coincident" use of the aorist participle, see Albert Rijksbaron, *The Syntax and Semantics of the Verb in Classical Greek*, 3rd ed. (Chicago: University of

It is also wrong on a wider exegetical basis, as well as on theological grounds. The seal involved here is described as the "Holy Spirit." *The Spirit himself* is the seal, the mark of ownership by which we are identified as belonging to God and as having received the great blessings listed in the entire section from Ephesians 1:3. Indeed, those who are sealed are identical with the ones who were elected before the foundation of the world (v. 4), foreordained to adoption (v. 5), and redeemed by the blood of Christ (v. 7) and who are heirs to the future inheritance (vv. 14, 17–18). This is reinforced later when Paul urges his readers, "Do not grieve the Holy Spirit of God, by whom you were sealed for the day of redemption" (4:30). There is not the slightest hint or possibility that this sealing is restricted to a smaller group than the whole of those to whom the letter was addressed. It is equally clear, in 2 Corinthians 1:21–22, that Paul considers all believers to have received the Spirit as a seal of their inheritance. Throughout his writings, Paul, with the rest of the New Testament, asserts that the Spirit has been given to all who believe (Rom. 8:9–11; 1 Cor. 12:13; see also John 14:16–23; 1 John 3:21–24). Ephesians 1:13 cannot be pressed into service for a second-blessing experience to which some, possibly most, believers are strangers. The Holy Spirit himself has been given to us. He seals us himself, guaranteeing that we belong to God (v. 14), that we "are not our own but belong, body and soul, in life and in death to [our] faithful Savior, Jesus Christ."[27] As John Owen writes on this statement in Ephesians, opposing and correcting Goodwin, "it is indeed not any act of the Spirit in us that is the ground of our assurance, but the communication of the Spirit unto us. . . . I judge that it is the communication of the Spirit himself unto us that is here intended."[28]

Chicago Press, 2007), 125 (§ 38, ¶ 384); Evert van Emde Boas, Albert Rijksbaron, Luuk Huitink, and Mathieu de Bakker, *The Cambridge Grammar of Classical Greek* (Cambridge: Cambridge University Press, 2019), 52.42. I am grateful to Dr. Steffen Jenkins for these references.

27. Heidelberg Catechism 1, in Philip Schaff, *The Creeds of Christendom* (Grand Rapids: Baker, 1966), 3:307–8.

28. John Owen, *A Discourse on the Holy Spirit as a Comforter* (1693), in *The Works of John Owen*, ed. William H. Goold (London: Banner of Truth, 1965–68), 4:405. See also: "God gives who God is, not just something else that might be accumulated

Second, from this it is clear that the claims of Lloyd-Jones and those influenced by him are theologically insupportable. In practice, the interpretation creates a spiritual elite of those who have received "the blessing." Paul would then have written to the church in Ephesians 1 intending to say that "you were all chosen in Christ before the foundation of the world, all of you were foreordained to adoption in Christ, all of you were redeemed by the blood of Christ, all of you are heirs to a great inheritance, and some—probably a few of you—were sealed by the Holy Spirit." This divides the church. The Nicene Creed includes the statement that "we believe in one holy, catholic and apostolic Church." This has been confessed for over sixteen hundred years by Orthodox, Catholic, and Protestant alike and, as the Thirty-Nine Articles assert, "ought most thoroughly to be received and believed, since [it] may be proved by most certain warrants of holy Scripture."[29] Ephesians 2:11–22 underlies it.[30] This view undermines the unity of the church of Jesus Christ taught, *inter multa alia*, in Ephesians itself.

Third, this teaching is dangerously misleading and can do great damage. By its divisiveness, therefore, it has the effect of repeating the Corinthian heresy that Paul so strenuously opposed. How many preachers, influenced by this thinking, have considered themselves second-rate and their ministries subpar, since the blessed sealing of the Spirit, as they were taught it, has passed them by? In this particular case, for Lloyd-Jones particular experiences determine exegesis and theology. It is an experience traveling in search of an exegetical justification and a theological rationale and arriving at the wrong destination.

The Holy Spirit, Creation, and Providence

As Yves Congar remarks, there is a close bond between the Spirit who indwells us and his cosmic role. He is Creator of the universe

---

and discarded." Amos Yong, *Spirit of Love: A Trinitarian Theology of Grace* (Waco, TX: Baylor University Press, 2012), 163.

29. Article 8, in Schaff, *Creeds*, 3:392.

30. Robert Letham, "Catholicity Global and Historical: Constantinople, Westminster, and the Church in the Twenty-First Century," *WTJ* 72, no. 1 (2010): 43–57.

(Gen. 1:2) and inaugurator of the new creation in Christ (John 3:3; 4:14; Rom. 8:17; Gal. 4:7).[31] Paul develops this at some length in Romans 8:19–25, continuing to verse 30. The experience of the faithful mirrors that of the universe. There is intense pain, a subjection to futility. The pain is akin to the labor pains of a pregnant woman. Intense expectation is mingled with anguish. This keen anticipation will reach fruition at the return of Christ when not only the church but the whole creation will be completely liberated to realize the ultimate purpose for which God intended it.[32] At the present time, this for us is a mystery. It lies beyond our current knowledge and experience. As Congar writes, "we simply do not know the frontiers of the Spirit's activity in this world, nor the ways in which he acts. We can only be sure that they are related to Christ, whose spiritual body is formed with men by the Spirit."[33]

One way in which this may be evident here and now is God's providential direction of human affairs in the interests of his church and the spread of the gospel. Throughout the history of the church, it is remarkable that its growth has been fostered by the world powers of the day. The first few centuries of the church's existence were immensely helped by the hegemony of the Roman Empire, its advanced system of communications through its road networks, and the presence of a common commercial language in Greek. Following its demise, the rise of the Frankish Empire, and the policies of Charles the Great, enabled the preservation of much of the Greek and Latin literature of the church fathers and provided a stable context for the work of preaching. In later centuries, the Renaissance, the rediscovery of Greek texts, the attention to primary sources, and the invention of the printing press facilitated a renewed interest in the original languages of Scripture, literacy, and education, all of which provided fuel for the Reformation. The control of the seas exerted by the British Empire in the nineteenth century enabled worldwide mission activity to mushroom and flourish,

31. Yves M. J. Congar, *The Word and the Spirit*, trans. David Smith (London: Geoffrey Chapman, 1986), 21–22.

32. Congar, *Word and Spirit*, 122–25.

33. Congar, *Word and Spirit*, 126.

while American hegemony in the twentieth century advanced this process further. Throughout, the Holy Spirit used the channels of communication brought about by the superpowers of the day as means for spreading the gospel.[34] It is interesting how church growth has recently accelerated in China and India.

The Holy Spirit and the Resurrection

Perhaps the most far-reaching treatment of the Holy Spirit's work that we find in the Bible is Paul's discussions of the resurrection body. In the first instance, this refers to the resurrection body of Christ, but it also has a direct bearing on our own resurrection. This is because Christ's resurrection and ours are one reality (1 Cor. 15:12–19) due to his union with us and ours with him. Since we are united to Christ, we share in his resurrection. Paul makes it very clear that the two are inseparable. Christ took our humanity into union with himself, lived and died in our flesh, and in our flesh rose from the dead. Since we are united to him, we died with him and are resurrected with him (Rom. 6:1–9). Here there is analogy with the Einstein-Podolsky-Bell theory. First postulated by Albert Einstein, and later confirmed by John Stewart Bell's experiment in 1964, a subatomic particle, a prion, divided in two and separated by infinite space, behaves identically in both parts.[35] The resurrection, the one reality—separated by indefinite time—also behaves identically in both aspects.

Christ's resurrection, as the firstfruits, has a temporal priority, and it also is the guarantee of the full harvest at his return, for it is of the same kind as the rest (1 Cor. 15:20).[36] Christ, as the second or last Adam, conquered death in our flesh. In union with him, we share in

34. We noted earlier how Frank D. Macchia has drawn attention to the cosmic work of the Spirit.

35. Arthur Fine, "The Einstein-Podolsky-Rosen Argument in Quantum Theory," in *The Stanford Encyclopedia of Philosophy*, ed. Edward N. Zalta, Winter 2017, https://plato.stanford.edu/archives/win2017/entries/qt-epr/.

36. Anthony C. Thiselton, *The First Epistle to the Corinthians: A Commentary on the Greek Text* (Grand Rapids: Eerdmans, 2000), 1223–24; Joseph A. Fitzmyer, *First Corinthians: A New Translation with Introduction and Commentary*, Anchor Yale Bible 32 (New Haven, CT: Yale University Press, 2008), 569; Gordon D. Fee, *The First Epistle to the Corinthians* (Grand Rapids: Eerdmans, 1987), 748–49.

his resurrection life and at his return will participate in union with him in the resurrection of the body (vv. 21–22). This, as with all the other works of God, is a Trinitarian event. The Father raised Jesus Christ, his Son, from the dead by his Spirit. The Father will raise us from the dead in union with Christ, also by his Spirit. The Father's Spirit, who raised Christ from the dead and who will raise us from the dead in Christ, dwells in us now (Rom. 8:10–11). Our present experience of the Spirit is of the same order as in the resurrection, different in degree but not in kind.

When this occurs, Christ will hand over the kingdom to God the Father in completion of his redemptive work, the work for which the Father sent him, having rendered inoperative all hostile powers and subjected all his enemies to his rule. This is necessary (δεῖ γὰρ αὐτὸν βασιλεύειν [*dei gar auton basileuein*]), and is already happening, but will reach its consummation at his return (1 Cor. 15:24–27). The last enemy to be destroyed, or rendered inoperative, is death (v. 26), at Christ's return when the dead are raised. The verb καταργεῖται (*katargeitai*) is in the present indicative, a prophetic present; death is already being destroyed, the final blow to be administered when Christ appears in glory. The process of annihilation of death began at Christ's resurrection and is completed at his parousia. This entire process, together with the climactic event of the resurrection, is attributable to the Holy Spirit, working with the Father and the Son.

The Holy Spirit and the Resurrection Body

In his discussion of the resurrection body, Paul directs attention to continuities with our present bodies but, to a greater extent, its vast discontinuity (1 Cor. 15:35–49). In each of the details he provides (seen in the following contrasts: a seed sown and a seed coming to life; weak and powerful; a corruptible body and an incorruptible one; mortal and immortal; perishable and imperishable; dishonorable and glorious; natural and spiritual; earthly and heavenly), the differences ultimately relate to a body produced by natural processes and governed by those processes, and one under the sovereign and pervasive direction of the Holy Spirit. This is represented by the first Adam, who was a living being, on the one hand, and the risen

Christ, who is a life-giving spirit, on the other. As Anthony Thiselton remarks, "the manifestation of Christ's raised body occurred *within the conditions of this world*. We still cannot have a *comprehensive* view of this 'body,' which is *more than* 'physical' but *not less than* 'physical.'"[37] It is not static; it is a dynamic flourishing and fullness of life, "an ever-increasing condition."[38]

This places the resurrection body in a different category from our present bodies. Of course, the continuities are clear. Jesus himself was recognized, was mistaken for another person, talked with the disciples, ate broiled fish, and still had the marks of the nails from the cross on his hands and feet. Paul writes that "*this perishable body* must put on the imperishable, and *this mortal body* must put on immortality" (1 Cor. 15:53–54). Elsewhere he describes it as akin to putting on an outer garment (2 Cor. 5:1–4) or our lowly body's being transformed to be like the glorified Christ (Phil. 3:21). It is resurrection and transformation, not replacement or metamorphosis. Since this change is described as glorification—and glory is distinctive of God—this can only be due to the power of the Spirit of glory.

As Thiselton remarks, it will be a body no less physical, but it will be more than physical, constituted by the Spirit. It will be "able to do all that we seek to do,"[39] enhanced above and beyond its present limitations. It will be a body for the new creation, the realm of the Holy Spirit, which includes the physical. The resurrection is not a return to this present life. It is a quantum leap beyond our current imagination, a new creation (2 Cor. 5:17), unfettered life in the Holy Spirit.

The Life of the World to Come

The life of the consummate age is under the aegis of the Spirit. The resurrection body is *kata pneuma*, in the domain of and under the government of the Holy Spirit. Earlier we considered *theosis* and how we will be changed to be like the glorified Christ, partakers

37. Anthony C. Thiselton, *The Last Things: A New Approach* (London: SPCK, 2012), 90.

38. Thiselton, *Last Things*, 121.

39. Thiselton, *Last Things*, 121.

of the divine nature as fulfilled humans (John 14:16–24; Rom. 8:29; 2 Cor. 3:18; 2 Peter 1:4; 1 John 3:1–2). This at last will reach its eternal apex.

Even now we know that our experience of the world is limited. Thiselton points to the dimensions of this world that are outside our present experience.[40] Animals have ranges of perception that are beyond us—the hearing of dogs, the flight of bats, the bird that flies in its migration down the center of North America by hearing the waves beat on the shores of the Atlantic and Pacific simultaneously.

The nature of Christ's resurrection, insofar as it is revealed in the New Testament, indicates that human powers will be greatly enhanced. He passed through closed doors (Luke 24:36; John 20:19, 26) and knew of Thomas's questions even though he had not been physically present when Thomas voiced them (John 20:24–29). Since our resurrection shares the characteristics of his, there will be dimensions of human activity that transcend our present experience (1 Cor. 2:7–10). This will be under the sway of the Spirit, in whose "circumambient atmosphere" we will live[41] and in the eternally unbroken company of the Lord.

Key Terms

attributes
being
deification
essence
hypostatically
nature
ontological
pantheism
participation

Questions for Reflection

1. The church today lives in the "circumambient atmosphere" of the Holy Spirit, as Geerhardus Vos put it. Greater things are to come; how do we know this?
2. When Peter writes that we are "partakers of the divine nature" (2 Peter 1:4), what might he mean, and what does he not mean?

40. Thiselton, *Last Things*, 212.
41. Geerhardus Vos, *The Pauline Eschatology* (Grand Rapids: Eerdmans, 1972), 163.

For Further Reading for Part 2: Chapters 5–10

Commentaries, including those cited in these chapters, on relevant biblical passages.

Owen, John. *A Discourse concerning the Holy Spirit*. In *The Works of John Owen*. Edited by William H. Goold. Vol. 3. London: Banner of Truth, 1965–68.

Russell, Norman. *The Doctrine of Deification in the Greek Patristic Tradition*. Oxford: Oxford University Press, 2004.

Thiselton, Anthony C. *The Holy Spirit—In Biblical Teaching, through the Centuries, and Today*. London: SPCK, 2013.

Vos, Geerhardus. *The Pauline Eschatology*. Grand Rapids: Eerdmans, 1972.

11

Discerning the Spirit's Redemptive Work

What are the characteristics of the work of the Holy Spirit? How are we to discern when he is at work redemptively? Some might think that we have adopted a highly skeptical attitude to the presence and work of the Spirit in the church and the world. This would be entirely wrong. To take such a view would be monstrous. The evidence of the whole of Scripture, and the testimony of the church through the centuries, is that the Spirit has been poured out on all flesh, effecting the worldwide spread of the gospel and the gathering of a vast crowd of people from every continent and island. Moreover, as I have written here and elsewhere, we can expect more, much more.[1]

We are to expect great and amazing things from the Holy Spirit in the worship of the church and in the means of grace. The Spirit has given us his Word. The Spirit empowers the preaching of the gospel and the faithful exposition of his Word. The Spirit enables us to commune with the ascended Christ, to feed on him by faith. The Spirit sustains us in our human weakness. The Spirit helps us in our inability to pray. Every time the church meets to worship or to pray, the Spirit is at work, sometimes dramatically, most often quietly and unobtrusively, in keeping with his ministry of speaking

1. Robert Letham, *Systematic Theology* (Wheaton, IL: Crossway, 2019), 835–41.

to us of Christ. We are, in the words of William Carey, to expect great things; that is the basis for attempting great things.

Where Christ Is Glorified

The Holy Spirit is not embodied as the Son is. He works inseparably with the Father and the Son, but for the vast majority of the time, we can observe only the effects of his work. Principally, he glorifies Jesus Christ (John 16:12–15). This appears to me to rule out the celebrity culture that has insinuated its way into some sections of the church, the dynamic leader who allows no divergence from his ideas, who draws attention to himself.

Yves Congar points to the confession that Jesus is Lord as the prime criterion for recognizing that the Spirit is at work, for in his citation of Thomas Aquinas, "the Spirit is the Spirit of the Word, of the Lord, of the Son, of Christ."[2] Since the Word and sacraments focus on Christ, it is here that the Spirit mainly operates to draw people to salvation and nurture them there (WSC 88).

From this, the conclusion follows that evidence for the presence and working of the Holy Spirit is to be located in the context of orthodox **Christology** and Trinitarianism. Scripture bears this out. John indicates that the marks of the Spirit's presence include correct doctrine concerning Jesus Christ. In his day, John was forced to confront a movement that disparaged the material world and could not accept that the Son could have taken a full human nature into union. He replied by asserting that a denial of the reality of his incarnation establishes that a godless mindset is at work (1 John 4:1–6).

It follows that the nature of the Spirit's work underlines the classic Trinitarian **order**, expressed in the baptismal formula, from the Father through the Son by the Spirit, with its reverse response from our side, by the Spirit through the Son to the Father (Matt. 28:19; Eph. 2:18). We expressed misgivings earlier about Spirit Christology for infringing on this hypostatic order. It is true that other orders are expressed in the New Testament, but these can best be understood as

2. Yves M. J. Congar, *The Word and the Spirit*, trans. David Smith (London: Geoffrey Chapman, 1986), 61–62.

affirming the equality of the three ***hypostases*** and the indivisibility of the divine **being**.

Where the Biblical Gospel Is Preached, Taught, Believed, and Confessed

The Spirit speaks in and through the Word he has authored. That is where he is primarily at work redemptively. In that Word he attests that the salvation of the sinner is found exclusively in Jesus Christ, and that the same Christ is the one who will reconstitute and renew the entire created order at his parousia.

This entails a central role for the Word and sacraments, the preached Word and the visible words.[3] Where does the Holy Spirit speak today? In his Word, the Scriptures, which he breathed out (2 Tim. 3:16; 2 Peter 1:20–21), through the proclamation of that Word in preaching (1 Cor. 1:18–2:16; 1 Thess. 1:5; 2:13; James 1:18; 1 Peter 1:23), in baptism (Matt. 28:19; Rom. 6:1–9; 1 Cor. 12:13; Titus 3:5), and in the Lord's Supper (John 6:47–58; 1 Cor. 10:16–17; 11:23–26).

Where the Fruit of the Spirit Is Evident

Where the Holy Spirit indwells, he produces results. As God promised, he replaces a heart of stone with a heart of flesh (Ezek. 36:26). Paul states that "the fruit of the Spirit is love, joy, peace, patience, kindness, goodness, faithfulness, gentleness, self-control" (Gal. 5:22–23). When these are developing, we can have confidence that the Spirit is present.

Some people have temperaments that are more naturally disposed to some of these virtues rather than others. Here the Spirit will develop these further and, over time, enhance those other characteristics that come less readily. On the other hand, some may start from a low base and have a naturally sour disposition. I recall one man who was notorious in many respects. A wise pastor told me, however, that I should see his relatives, who were far worse. In short, we are all works in progress, and it is not in our capabilities to determine with exactitude where other individuals stand (Matt. 7:1–5).

3. Augustine, *On the Gospel of John*, 26.11; *NPNF*[1], 7:171.

Yet some things are very clear. In 1994, people flocked to Toronto from all over the world to observe the dramatic phenomena of the Toronto Blessing, marked by sustained and uncontrollable laughter and people's making animal sounds. How many will cross the globe to see a community that is patient, kind, and gentle? What international pilgrimages will be held to observe a congregation that is self-controlled? But that is where the Spirit is preeminently at work, changing people to be conformed to the image of Christ. The Spirit engenders love, with all the variegated fruit that flows from it, expressed in each member of the body of Christ looking not to his or her own interests but to those of others. Visiting the sick, ministering to the needy, faithfully proclaiming and teaching the gospel of Christ, caring for one another, not being easily provoked, welcoming the outcasts of society—that is where the Spirit is preeminently at work. Self-control rules out uncontrolled spontaneous, ecstatic phenomena such as protracted hysterical laughter, barking like dogs, and howling like hyenas. Such things are expressly contrary to the mind of the Holy Spirit expressed in the Word of God that he himself has breathed out. Those who value them are seriously and dangerously deluded.

I had a striking experience while I was serving as senior minister of a congregation located in an area with the highest per capita concentration of PhDs anywhere in the world, with research scientists, corporate managers, and attorneys by the bucketload. A few doors away, a halfway house opened with residents released from the state mental hospital living in monitored accommodation. Several made their way to the church, and two became communicant members. One man, because of his medical conditions, sometimes inadvertently urinated in his chair. When the Holy Spirit is active, where must the focus of the church lie? With the rich and powerful? With the CEO of an international corporation who for a while attended before retiring elsewhere? Or with the man who has nothing whatever of this world's goods, who sits and urinates in the chair during a church service? It should be a no-brainer; you are to treat the incontinent and helpless as you would Jesus Christ (Matt. 25:31–46). That will be evidence of the work of the Spirit. If that is not done, no words could convey the opprobrium. Read carefully Matthew 25:31–46 and James 2 if you are inclined to disagree. How many on the day of judgment will hang their heads in shame?

Where There Is Love, Demonstrated in Service of Others

The Pentecostal theologian Amos Yong correctly states, "The most important criterion for discerning the Spirit is Christ . . . but another criterion must surely be love."[4] Love is not to be construed as a fuzzy emotional response. In this context, it refers to serving others, to active deeds. Paul wrote that we are to look not to our own interests but to the interests of others (Phil. 2:1–4). Love is seen in action. It is produced by the Holy Spirit. It relates to how we treat other people. In a severe pandemic, it will ask first and foremost how our actions can best protect the vulnerable, preserve and support the weak and infirm. When there is evidence of service to other people, we may conclude that effusions of the Spirit have been received (James 1:27). Love covers a multitude of sins.

How many times in recent years have I heard Christians, even those in positions of influence or in office, boasting of their achievements, even extolling the fact that they are not patient or kind? Or setting a strategic direction and expecting everyone to bow to their dictates? This is particularly a problem in parachurch organizations, where of necessity distinctive teachings or emphases must be stressed so as to justify their existence. But it is by no means unknown in churches whose leaders want to build an empire for themselves or where the impact of corporate culture and business-management theory has been allowed to dominate. It fits the contemporary climate in which, in order to advance, people must project themselves as skilled and dynamic, with a curriculum vitae full of achievements.

In stark contrast, Jesus came among us as one who serves. He took the lowest place, washing the disciples' feet, the action of a Gentile slave, the lowest of the low (Matt. 20:20–28; Mark 10:45). This is the mode into which the Spirit is conforming us. Paul writes of being

4. Amos Yong, *Spirit of Love: A Trinitarian Theology of Grace* (Waco, TX: Baylor University Press, 2012), 164.

conformed to the image of Christ's death (Phil. 3:10). Peter, in 1 Peter 5:1, although an apostle, calls himself a fellow elder (addressing elders) and a witness of the sufferings of Christ. He witnessed them, all right, by denying him, but he points to his failings and so demonstrates our absolute need for the grace and strength of the Spirit, as he reflects later about being restored and strengthened (v. 10). This is the kind of strong leadership that the church so sorely needs.

Where There Is Hard Work

Paul, forced to defend his apostolic authority, writes that the grace of God was more evident in him because he worked harder than anyone else (1 Cor. 15:10). We are called to do good works, prepared for us by God the Father, the Son, and the Holy Spirit (Eph. 2:10). We are justified on the ground of Christ's obedience and blood, received by faith apart from works, but we cannot be saved without works. Justification is only by faith; salvation, viewed as a whole, is with works.[5]

There is no requirement in the Bible for us to seek mystical ecstasy, none whatsoever. God expects you to use your mind. We live by faith, not by sight. There is no premium on dramatic and exciting miracles. The most dramatic events have already happened, and none can transcend them—the creation of the universe, the incarnation of the Son of God, his resurrection and ascension, the gift of the person of the Holy Spirit. Nor is there a biblical mandate for us to sit back and wait for revival to come. "Get up! Why have you fallen on your face?" Yahweh said to Joshua when he was having a prayer meeting instead of discharging his responsibilities (Josh. 7:10). Hard work is needed. It has been written that the ultimate success of the early church lay in its outthinking its opponents.[6] These things are performed by the impelling power of the Holy Spirit.

According to Paul, spiritual warfare begins in the library (2 Cor. 10:3f.), as the base from which the godless opinions of the world can

5. Francis Turretin, *Institutes of Elenctic Theology*, ed. James T. Dennison Jr., trans. George Musgrave Giger (Phillipsburg, NJ: P&R Publishing, 1992), 2:702–5.

6. This has been commonly attributed to Adolf von Harnack, but I have been unable to locate it.

be cast down and those who hold them brought into submission to Christ. It does not end there, since we are actively sent out to disciple the nations and subvert opposing claims. It is the enabling strength of the Holy Spirit that accomplishes this.

> And every virtue we possess
> and every victory won,
> and every thought of holiness,
> are his alone.[7]

Key Terms

being
Christology
hypostases
order

Question for Reflection

Thoughtfully evaluate the significance of the fruit of the Spirit. How is this best cultivated?

For Further Reading

No particular reading is relevant at this point. The onus is on us to live for Christ and, by the power of the Holy Spirit, to turn from sin, looking not to our own interests but to the interests of others.

7. Harriet Auber (1773–1862), "Our Blest Redeemer, Ere He Breathed," in *The English Hymnal with Tunes* (Oxford: Oxford University Press, 1933), no. 157.

Appendix: Pentecostalism and the Charismatic Renewal

Historical Background

Current estimates of the size of global Pentecostalism range from upward of 650 million, a huge portion of the world's confessing Christian population. Moreover, it is also by far the fastest-growing segment of Christianity worldwide. Leading representatives state that it is neither Protestant nor Western. The latter is obvious, since the lion's share of the total is found in Africa, South and Central America, and Asia; the former follows from its origins long post-dating the Reformation. Moreover, strong elements within global Pentecostalism bypass or relativize the classic Protestant doctrine of justification. The following historical summary is, because of space limits, grossly incomplete and superficial, intended merely to identify the main strands. Much debate surrounds the details of its emergence.

Azusa Street

While its exact origins are now disputed, Pentecostalism has traditionally traced its genesis to the revival at Azusa Street in Los Angeles that started in April 1906. A group, gathered for prayer, began to speak in tongues. Before long, huge crowds gathered in the thousands. Speaking in tongues and healings were commonplace during this time. At the heart of this movement was William J. Seymour, who taught that after the new birth and entire sanctification—indicating origins in Wesleyan holiness sources—the baptism with the Holy Spirit was a third work of grace, giving empowerment to witness and evidenced by tongues-speaking. Another prominent figure was Charles Parham, who had strongly influenced Seymour. Many congregations sprang up elsewhere in the USA, largely composed of immigrants and ethnic minorities, and also overseas.

Shortly after the emergence of Pentecostalism and its rapid spread, the movement splintered, as human movements often do. Differences emerged over the necessity of tongues and whether the baptism of the Holy Spirit was a postconversion phenomenon or definitive of a Christian. Anthony Thiselton remarks: "I cannot help wondering, since they claimed no system of doctrine, how many of these 'divisions' were grouped around strong personalities who gave rise to power struggles, just as these occurred at Corinth. Strangely, 'the unity of the Spirit' did not seem to matter."[1]

Oneness Pentecostalism

The most significant early division surrounded the "New Issue" controversy, as it was called, which began obscurely at a conference in 1913 when a speaker remarked that most baptisms in the New Testament were simply in the name of Jesus. This idea caught on and spread.[2] It was a debate wider than the baptismal formula alone. Acts 2:38 was crucial. Some held that the name of the Father, the Son, and the Holy Spirit is Jesus Christ.[3] This has certain similarities to the views of the Socinians in the post-Reformation era, who held that the triune name referred to the Father.[4] In 1916, at the fourth general council of the Assemblies of God, the Trinitarians won by 429 to 156.[5] The advocates of the New Issue claimed that their doctrine was based exclusively on

1. Anthony C. Thiselton, *The Holy Spirit—In Biblical Teaching, through the Centuries, and Today* (London: SPCK, 2013), 451.

2. Thomas A. Fudge, *Christianity without the Cross: A History of Salvation in Oneness Pentecostalism* (Parkland, FL: Universal Publications, 2003), 45f.

3. Fudge, *Christianity without the Cross*, 50–53.

4. Faustus Socinus, *Explicatio Primae Partis Primi Capitis Iohannis* (Racoviae: Typis Sebastiani Sternacii, 1618), 17; Valentin Smalcius, *Racovian Catechism*, English trans. (Amsterdam: For Brouer Janz, 1652), 14–23.

5. Fudge, *Christianity without the Cross*, 56–57.

Scripture but came by revelation. They argued that it was found in the primitive church and had been passed down historically by Christ.[6] In reality, it was nothing new, merely a rehash of **modalism** and Arianism. Its basic premises were similar to the Socinians'—a stress on the Bible alone, interpreted literally, to the exclusion of the ecumenical councils.

Since then, this movement has continued. According to one of its leading advocates, David Bernard, it holds that "(1) There is one indivisible God with no distinction of **persons** in God's eternal **essence**. (2) Jesus Christ is the manifestation, human personification, incarnation of the one God. . . . All names and titles of deity properly apply to him. God's manifestations as Father, Son, and Holy Spirit reveal God's work in salvation history but do not represent different centers of consciousness or personalities. The scriptural distinction between Father and Son does not describe two divine persons but the transcendent, eternal deity and the deity's manifestation in flesh as the man Christ Jesus."[7] This rests on a methodology effectively identical to that of the Socinians, as found in John Biddle, the Racovian Catechism, and Faustus Socinus himself.[8] It claims a basis in the apostolic writings of the New Testament to the exclusion of the fourth-century theologians. Effectively it privileges its own exegesis over that of a millennium and a half of the church. For oneness theology, "God has revealed himself in three significant manifestations": as the Father, the source of all life; as the Son, in human identity; and as the Holy Spirit, as God in presence and action. These are purely economic and redemptive manifestations of the one God.[9] This is a vivid repristinization of ancient modalism. Again, Bernard writes

6. Fudge, *Christianity without the Cross*, 65.

7. David K. Bernard, "Oneness Theology: Restoring the Apostolic Faith," in *The Routledge Handbook of Pentecostal Theology*, ed. Wolfgang Vondey (London: Routledge, 2020), 195–205, here 199. See also Edward L. Dalcour, *A Definitive Look at Oneness Theology: Defending the Tri-Unity of God* (Lanham, MD: University Press of America, 2005), 3.

8. Socinus, *Explicatio Primae Partis Primi Capitis Iohannis*, 8–45; Smalcius, *Racovian Catechism*, 1–24; John Biddle, *Twelve Arguments Drawn Out of the Scripture: Wherein the Commonly-Received Opinion Touching the Deity of the Holy Spirit, Is Clearly and Fully Refuted* (London, 1647); John Biddle, *A Twofold Catechism* (London: J. Cottrel for Ri. Moone, at the Seven Stars in Paul's Church-Yard, Neer the Great North-Door, 1654).

9. Bernard, "Oneness Theology," 200–201.

that "modalistic **monarchianism** can be defined as the belief that the Father, Son, and Holy Spirit are manifestations of the one God with no distinctions of person being possible. Furthermore, the one God is expressed fully in the person of Jesus Christ."[10] The title "Son of God" refers to the humanity of Jesus only. In turn, references to Jesus as God are to the Father, the divine **nature**. Jesus did not exist before Bethlehem as a distinct conscious self, since only the Father is eternal and there is no distinct person of the Son.[11] This view cannot be identified with Christianity. From now on, we will discuss Pentecostalism as it exists within the bounds of Trinitarian orthodoxy.[12]

Charismatic Renewal

In the late 1950s and through the 1960s and beyond, a distinct movement emerged and eventually spread through most denominations, Protestant and Roman Catholic alike. In general, it was marked by a claim that the extraordinary gifts of the New Testament had been restored and by a more spontaneous form of worship. While it was for the most part a development within existing church bodies, it was not confined to those by any means, but also included more informal house churches. Having started in the USA, most notably in Episcopal circles in California, the movement was soon evident in the UK and elsewhere. In Britain, one notable figure was Michael Harper, curate to John Stott at the influential All Souls, Langham Place, in the heart of London. Stott wrote his book *The Baptism and Fullness of the Holy Spirit* (1964) in critical response to the fast-growing developments—developments that had the sympathetic support of Dr. Martyn Lloyd-Jones. Stott stressed that all believers have been baptized in the Spirit, so that there is no spiritual hierarchy in the church.

10. David K. Bernard, *The Oneness of God* (Hazelwood, MO: Word Aflame Press, 1983), 252, quoted in Dalcour, *Oneness Theology*, 7. See also Anthony Buzzard and Charles F. Hunting, *The Doctrine of the Trinity: Christianity's Self-Inflicted Wound* (Lanham, MD: Rowman & Littlefield, 1998).

11. Dalcour, *Oneness Theology*, 8.

12. For a more gracious and kind evaluation of oneness Pentecostalism but one that reaches the same conclusions, see Fred Sanders, "A Theological Analysis of Oneness Pentecostalism" (unpublished paper), https://www.academia.edu/16238613/Analysis_of_Oneness_Pentecostalism.

Over the succeeding decades, the initial growth and militancy of the movement has subsided, but its impact remains. Its chorusology and modes of worship have had pervasive impact and have changed the way that churches worship, moving toward more informal styles. Much of the sung elements have focused on worshiping God in his glory, to the neglect of creation, the sacraments, and suffering. Tony Lane makes a similar observation: "A quick comparison of a traditional hymn book with a book of modern worship songs shows a similar trend. The majority of modern choruses and worship songs emphasise themes like glory and power, with relatively little mention of sin and its cure. Even worse, in many of them we sing about ourselves and our feelings, rather than who God is and what he has done. A proper balance is required between all these aspects, or we risk betraying the gospel."[13]

Third Wave

In the late seventies and eighties, an allied movement sprang into view. In Britain, it became known as the Restoration movement, sharing an emphasis with those in North America on the presence of "signs and wonders." John Wimber's Vineyard movement was prominent. Wimber had a strong stress on "power healing" and "power evangelism."[14] Peter Wagner, of Fuller Seminary, was a prominent spokesman. This was a more radical movement than the charismatic renewal, going beyond the immediate teaching on the Spirit to envisage a thorough transformation of church life by the Spirit. It is largely located in rapidly growing networks of independent churches. Still maintaining the focus on extraordinary gifts, attention was more eschatologically oriented, with claims that we are in or approaching "the end times" with the idea of "the latter rain," an extraordinary outpouring of the Spirit as a precursor to the return of Christ, prominent.[15] In the UK, some

13. Tony Lane, *Sin and Grace: Evangelical Soteriology in Historical Perspective* (London: Apollos, 2020), 270.

14. But not, regrettably, on power scholarship.

15. For a fascinating account of the charismatic renewal and particularly the background and early development of the house-church movement in the UK, see

of these networks are broadly sympathetic in varying degrees to Reformed theology.

Meanwhile, each strand in this family of movements has spread rapidly, none more so than in South America, Africa, and Asia, to the extent that estimated numbers in Pentecostal or related churches worldwide are close to one billion, far outnumbering adherents of Orthodoxy and Protestantism. Among these churches, however, particularly in the Global South but not confined to there, is a strong presence of prosperity-gospel advocates. Reflecting on this global spread, Dale Coulter and Amos Yong point out that "classical Pentecostal streams now flow into and out of many others."[16] Largely for this reason, much of what follows consists of broad generalizations, from which there are inevitably many variations, exceptions, and differences.

The Theology of Pentecostalism

Allan Anderson

According to Allan Anderson, widely acknowledged as one of the most authoritative chroniclers of the movement, the common denominator of Pentecostal and charismatic circles is an experience,[17] sometimes identified with **xenolalia** but more often **glossolalia**. Anderson's work is theologically lightweight, almost entirely descriptive and noncommittal. In such theological discussion as it has, it focuses on Western charismatic theology, particularly on the disputed question whether the gift of tongues is normal or normative, whether it is to be expected at conversion or subsequently, and the like.

Anderson agrees with Yong that "the Pentecostal and Charismatic experience 'demands interpretation of the existential dimension of spirituality over and against an emphasis on textuality in religious

---

Andrew Walker, *Restoring the Kingdom* (London: Hodder and Stoughton, 1989). A later edition was released by Eagle in 1998.

16. Dale M. Coulter and Amos Yong, "Between East and West—From North and South," *Pneuma* 36, no. 3 (2014): 351–54, here 352.

17. Allan Heaton Anderson, *An Introduction to Pentecostalism: Global Charismatic Christianity* (Cambridge: Cambridge University Press, 2014), 179–82.

life.'"[18] This would place it squarely in the camp of mysticism. This claim sidelines the Bible and marginalizes the ecumenical councils of the church. Yet we must bear in mind the huge and disparate nature of the movements; there are many elements that insist on a creedal and doctrinal foundation.[19]

Moreover, Anderson, as a historian of missions, writes descriptively. His approach is phenomenological, that of a chronicler of religious and theological opinion.[20] Classic Christian teaching is labeled as "Western" (Anderson's text is liberally sprinkled with quotation marks so that Anderson can reduce "ideas" to a socially constructive level). In fact, contrary to Anderson, "theological orthodoxy" is not Western; if anything, it is "Middle Eastern." Anderson is also noncommittal on oneness Pentecostalism, which we saw to be effectively a revival of ancient modalism. For Anderson, it is one of the phenomena of global charismatic experience and so equally valid with "orthodox Christianity."

Missions is central to Pentecostalism. Here the emphasis is not on the great apostolic commission as in evangelicalism but on the leading of the Spirit, with dependence on that rather than formal structures. Because of this and the fact that each believer is filled with the Spirit, each believer is a minister. So, generally, there has not been formal theological education for ministers and missionaries. This has enabled a quick transition to churches led by indigenous people.[21] "Charismatic leaders became catalysts in what has been called in the African context 'a primary movement of mass conversion.'"[22]

Worship is generally spontaneous in global Pentecostalism, with dancing and clapping in contrast to "rationalistic written liturgies presided over by a clergyman."[23] Anderson, recognized as one of Pentecostalism's most distinguished international spokespersons,

18. Anderson, *Pentecostalism*, 193.

19. See the discussion in Leopoldo A. Sánchez M., *T&T Clark Introduction to Spirit Christology* (London: T&T Clark, 2022), esp. 121–41.

20. A similar approach, full of sociological jargon, is evident in Coulter and Yong, "Between East and West."

21. Anderson, *Pentecostalism*, 198–200.

22. Anderson, *Pentecostalism*, 213.

23. Anderson, *Pentecostalism*, 204.

demonstrates a view of worship defined sociologically rather than theologically, dismissive of the great tradition of the church. If the confession of sins—integral to the historic liturgies—is rationalistic, it is questionable whether Anderson is advocating the Christian faith. This follows from Anderson's point that the interpretation of Scripture in Pentecostal circles is oriented not to understanding the text but to what the Spirit is saying to me.[24] In its relativization of Scripture and its prominent individualism, this veers strongly in the direction of subjectivity.

Main Distinguishing Features

Pentecostalism has no uniform theology or agreement on the details. The movement is so huge, and without an authoritative magisterium, it is unlikely that complete agreement will ever be found. The same could be said for some other branches of the church; the contemporary Church of England comes to mind. Anderson remarks that "when we speak of 'Pentecostal' theology, standardization is precarious, if not impossible," since it is not doctrinal but experiential.[25] There is no single Pentecostal theology, since there is no single Pentecostal church, which is a reality applying to charismatic and "third-wave" congregations worldwide. Consequently, "universal statements of Pentecostal theology will not do," Anderson continues.[26] Harold Hunter reflects that global Pentecostals are neither Protestants nor Western, a fact that will become apparent as we proceed. The largest Pentecostal organization is the Pentecostal World Fellowship (PWF) founded in 1947, with around fifty denominations internationally and with no jurisdiction over member bodies. It extends deep into the Global South.[27] There is no one leader, the emphasis being pneumatic.[28] There is a wide diversity in ecclesiology, such that there

24. Anderson, *Pentecostalism*, 222–23.

25. Allan Anderson, "Pentecostal Theology as a Global Challenge: Contextual Theological Constructions," in *The Routledge Handbook of Pentecostal Theology*, ed. Wolfgang Vondey (London: Routledge, 2020), 18–28, here 19.

26. Anderson, "Pentecostal Theology," 22.

27. Harold Hunter, "Pentecostal Reflections on Apostolicity," *JEPTA* 33, no. 1 (2013): 1–13, here 1–2.

28. Hunter, "Pentecostal Reflections," 3.

is "no agreement on global Pentecostal identity." No one person can speak authoritatively on it, since there is "no uniform ecclesiastical polity."[29] Hunter thinks this reflects the New Testament. The one common feature is that local churches are encouraged to be alive and "to carry the flame."[30] This begs the question as to exactly what flame it is that is carried. It should also sound a caveat to Anderson's disclaimer of a uniform theology in the sense that there are common, almost universal, characteristics that, while experiential in nature, in effect create their own theology, however disparately it may be expressed.

The main factors in common are the following:[31]

Focus on the Holy Spirit

Some continue to claim that the baptism of the Spirit is individualistic and is a postconversion experience to which many if not most believers are strangers. Others of these, a small minority, maintain that it is an identity marker for Christians and that those who lack it are not Christians. There is a growing awareness among some prominent theologians that a corporate understanding of the baptism with the Spirit is needed. It is claimed that miraculous gifts evident in the New Testament are of ongoing existence—especially tongues, interpretation of tongues, prophecy, gifts of knowledge, discernment of spirits, and healing. There is a common focus on the spiritual experience of the individual, with pietism and mysticism the result.

This focus on the Holy Spirit comes close to breaking one of the axioms of Trinitarian theology—the indivisibility of the Trinity and the inseparability of the works. Furthermore, it goes against the **hypostatic** character of the Spirit, whom Scripture declares to be anonymous, reticent, witnessing to Christ, not himself (John

29. Hunter, "Pentecostal Reflections," 5.

30. Hunter, "Pentecostal Reflections," 6.

31. In this we are focusing on Pentecostal and charismatic treatments of the Spirit and his work. This is not an analysis of its theology as a whole or other aspects of it. This can best be done by reference to Wolfgang Vondey, ed., *The Routledge Handbook of Pentecostal Theology* (London: Routledge, 2020). At the time of writing, this volume costs £190 ($250) in hardback but much less on Kindle.

15:26; 16:12–15). It also appears to neglect the person of Christ. According to William Atkinson, a prominent evangelical Pentecostal theologian, important recent summaries of Pentecostal theology have no chapters or entries on Christ.[32] At the same time, before the emergence of the Pentecostal movement, a focus in many circles on "Jesus only" was equally misplaced and may have encouraged a works-based religion.[33]

Baptism in or with the Holy Spirit

The Claim That the Baptism with the Spirit Is a Postconversion Experience

While we note other views, and that these are growing, the most dominant idea since the emergence of Pentecostalism has been that baptism with the Holy Spirit is an experience for the individual after conversion that is received by some but not all. It is very frequently associated with speaking in tongues.

Some evangelicals who are not part of Pentecostal denominations or formally identified with the charismatic movement or later developments have also identified the baptism with the Holy Spirit with an individual experience that is not common to all believers. Most prominent in the UK was Dr. Martyn Lloyd-Jones. While in no way a Pentecostal and not identified with the charismatic movement, he gave private support and encouragement to the latter in its early days.[34] In his own congregation, he gave powerful stress to the baptism of the Spirit as a postconversion experience to which some are strangers. In that setting he presents those who differ as saying:

> "I am already baptized with the Spirit, it happened when I was born again, it happened at my conversion; there is nothing more

32. He refers to *Pentecostal Doctrine*, published in the UK in 1976, and to *The New International Dictionary of Pentecostal and Charismatic Movements*. William P. Atkinson, "Christology: Jesus and Others: Jesus and God," in *The Routledge Handbook of Pentecostal Theology*, ed. Wolfgang Vondey (London: Routledge, 2020), 216–25, here 220.

33. I am thankful to Tony Lane for this observation.

34. Andrew Atherstone and David Ceri Jones, eds., *Engaging with Martyn Lloyd-Jones: The Life and Legacy of "The Doctor"* (Nottingham, UK: Apollos, 2011), 115–18; Timothy Dudley-Smith, *John Stott: A Global Ministry: A Biography: The Later Years* (Downers Grove, IL: InterVarsity Press, 2001), 37–38.

> for me to seek, I have got it all." Got it all? Well, if you have "got it all" I simply ask, in the name of God, why are you as you are? If you have got it all, why are you so unlike these Apostles, why are you so unlike the New Testament Christians? Got it all! Got it at your conversion! Well, where is it, I ask?[35]

The obvious riposte is to ask, unlike *which* New Testament Christians? Those at Corinth who were consorting with prostitutes? The ones at Colossae who were venerating angels? The Galatians, who had fallen for legalism? The Christians at Crete who were evil beasts, lazy gluttons? Or perhaps at Laodicea, lukewarm to the point at which Christ was about to spew them out of his mouth in disgust? How about those at Ephesus, who had lost their first love? Or the people to whom the author of the letter to the Hebrews wrote, who were thinking of committing apostasy? Which of these should we emulate? If we are so unlike these "New Testament Christians," I would have thought it a matter for thanksgiving to God for his grace in keeping us from such dire conditions. Leaving this aside, Lloyd-Jones presents at best an unfortunate caricature of those who beg to differ from him. Moreover, his case is overwhelmingly grounded on special experiences of remarkable effusions of the Spirit on past figures rather than on sustained theological argument or an engagement with redemptive history.[36]

35. D. Martyn Lloyd-Jones, "Quenching the Spirit," *Westminster Record* 39, no. 9 (September 1964): 129–43, here 136. Additionally, in the mid-sixties, he gave a number of private addresses to his congregation on "The Biblical Doctrine of the Baptism with the Holy Spirit" in which he forcefully urged his hearers to seek this experience of the Spirit that, he claimed, went over and beyond normal Christian experience. He even used the expression "higher life." This is according to a typed record by a congregation member, Anthony Beaurepaire, who was described to me as "extremely reliable." The addresses largely consisted of a wide range of biblical references taken out of context, without consideration of interpretative questions. I am grateful to Ian R. Hepburn, a member of Westminster Chapel at the time, for granting me access to these documents.

36. See D. Martyn Lloyd-Jones, *Romans: An Exposition of Chapter 8:5–17: The Sons of God* (Edinburgh: Banner of Truth, 1972), 280; D. Martyn Lloyd-Jones, *God's Ultimate Purpose: An Exposition of Ephesians 1:1–23* (Edinburgh: Banner of Truth, 1978), 243–300; D. Martyn Lloyd-Jones, *Joy Unspeakable: The Baptism with the Holy Spirit* (Eastbourne, UK: Kingsway Publications, 1984), 146–79, esp. 148–50.

One-Stage Reception of the Spirit

Many other thinkers have moved away from the dominant two-stage doctrine. Max Turner, who seeks middle ground between Pentecostal and charismatic positions on the one hand and mainstream evangelicalism on the other, is a leading New Testament scholar who has written extensively in this area. Turner is correct that Paul rubs out the possibility of a second-stage gift of the Spirit by his failing to articulate any theologically distinct second gift. Citing Gordon Fee, Turner maintains that passages such as 1 Corinthians 12:13 and Galatians 4:6 concern ongoing activities of the Spirit that had been received at conversion, not later distinct grantings of the Spirit.[37] Indeed, we may add, it is questionable whether Paul writes in individual terms at all, since he says that we *all* were baptized into Christ by the Spirit.

Turner argues for a one-stage reception of the Spirit[38] as inherent to Paul and John. He also claims that Luke is the same.[39] "Neither Paul nor Luke uses 'to receive (the gift of) the Spirit' of some definite second experience—they use such expressions only in connection with the conversion-initiation complex."[40] He adds that "there is simply no clear exegetical evidence to suggest that Luke, Paul or John envisaged the possibility that there were in the post-Easter church two classes of Christians, distinguished by whether or not they had received the Pentecostal gift of the Spirit."[41] Turner rejects two-stage constructions.[42]

A More Comprehensive View

Frank Macchia concentrates on the baptism of the Holy Spirit (BHS) in a much wider context than had been previously done. Because his is a highly sophisticated account, I will consider it in

37. Max Turner, *The Holy Spirit and Spiritual Gifts* (Carlisle, UK: Paternoster, 1996), 151–53.

38. Turner, *Holy Spirit*, 154.

39. Turner, *Holy Spirit*, 154–55.

40. Turner, *Holy Spirit*, 155–56.

41. Turner, *Holy Spirit*, 156.

42. Turner, *Holy Spirit*, 158–59.

some detail. He is one of the leading exponents of the more recent idea that the BHS is to be understood in corporate terms. He also questions the historical stress on a postconversion experience. He recognizes that in the early development of Pentecostalism and its later progress, the most common understanding of the BHS was that it was a postconversion experience with which speaking in tongues was associated. Frequently the latter was regarded as an indispensable sign of the baptism. Latterly, however, the BHS is no longer the focal point of the writings of Pentecostal theologians.[43] Yet "enough have understood Spirit-baptism as a postconversion charismatic experience to make this view of the doctrine distinctly Pentecostal."[44] Notwithstanding, this is not the case with the charismatic renewal in the mainstream denominations or with the Third Wave churches. Nevertheless, the BHS is, Macchia contends, "the crown jewels of Pentecostal distinctives" that the wider charismatic movement shares together with an emphasis on the charisms of the Holy Spirit.[45] Macchia wants to recover this emphasis on the BHS, but with a much wider reach to it, as signaling the work of the Spirit in renewing not only the church but the entire cosmos. He argues for the theme of the kingdom of God as central to the message of the New Testament, with Jesus as the one who is baptized in the Spirit and baptizes with the Spirit. This message, anticipated in the Old Testament and fulfilled in Jesus and the outpouring of the Spirit that he enacted, encompasses the world, the church, and the individual within it. This wider context is to be welcomed. But we will see that as Macchia presents it, it comes with a price. Whereas Turner operates clearly within the historic Reformation theology, while being sympathetic to and supportive of the claims of ongoing charisms, Macchia is outside these parameters.

43. Frank D. Macchia, *Baptized in the Spirit: A Global Pentecostal Theology* (Grand Rapids: Zondervan, 2006), 19–60. See also Frank D. Macchia, "Spirit Baptism: Initiation in the Fullness of God's Promises," in *The Routledge Handbook of Pentecostal Theology*, ed. Wolfgang Vondey (London: Routledge, 2020), 247–56, an excellent summary.

44. Macchia, *Baptized in the Spirit*, 20.

45. Macchia, *Baptized in the Spirit*, 20–21.

Macchia remarks that "there is no universal agreement among Pentecostals worldwide" about questions on the relationship of the Spirit to baptism, initial faith in Christ, or speaking in tongues.[46] While "subsequence," the idea that the BHS is a second blessing for the individual Christian, is perhaps regarded as the distinctive Pentecostal teaching, the underlying factor is that the movement is based on experience rather than doctrine, and "Paul Lees' exaggerated statement that there appears an almost 'infinite variety' of views within and outside Pentecostalism on the nature of Spirit baptism certainly contains an element of truth."[47] This global diversity has led some to question what meaning there is to having a doctrine in common if there is no agreement in it.[48] Macchia indicates that many recognize that "doctrinal conceptions among Pentecostals are too diverse to provide us with that which is theologically distinctive to the movement."[49] In keeping with our earlier observations, it appears to me to be problematic to think of a single identifiable movement if there is no coherently recognizable theology or church polity.

Latterly, Macchia proceeds, and in the wake of newer movements within denominations and in the Third Wave, attention has turned more to eschatology. Here there is a belief that the "latter rains" will precede the imminent return of Christ, with the outpouring of the Spirit a precursor. This is part of a belief that we are in the "end time," a characteristically premillennial and often dispensationalist feature. This premillennialism is widespread throughout, from old-style Pentecostalism on to the more recent elements, and is present on a global scale, not limited to the West.[50] Here, perhaps, it is a unifying theme, although not a distinctive one, since it is shared with noncharismatic and non-Pentecostal fundamentalists.

46. Macchia, *Baptized in the Spirit*, 34.
47. Macchia, *Baptized in the Spirit*, 35.
48. Macchia, *Baptized in the Spirit*, 37.
49. Macchia, *Baptized in the Spirit*, 50.
50. Macchia, *Baptized in the Spirit*, 38–40. As Peter Althouse comments, it is "a major building block throughout Pentecostal theology." Peter Althouse, "Eschatology: The Always Present Hope," in *The Routledge Handbook of Pentecostal Theology*, ed. Wolfgang Vordey (London: Routledge, 2020), 268.

Macchia wants to extend the doctrine of the BHS to include sanctification and eschatology, with the kingdom of God the theme that will bind these elements together. Narrative and dramatic theology prevail in the worldwide movement, and a theology of the Spirit "cannot neglect aspects of experience in Christ that lie outside the limits of rational discourse."[51] If so, one suggests, it may spell the end of reasoned discourse. For Macchia, "telling stories and dancing within the world of the larger narrative of Scripture"[52] is the way forward. With the BHS, "we do not relate to God as an object of reflection; rather, we are baptized into God as a powerful field of experience, which opens up wonders and joys as a daily experience."[53] This reinforces my suggestion that mysticism is a main common characteristic.

Macchia operates with an assumption that the BHS is separate from "water baptism,"[54] although he does eventually qualify this by agreeing that there is one baptism and that baptism with water and baptism with the Spirit are intimately related.[55] Yet even an intimate connection entails two separable entities; Macchia has not seriously considered the possibility that they are two sides of the same coin.[56]

Macchia acknowledges that Spirit baptism "is somewhat ambiguous as a metaphor and fluid in its meaning throughout the New Testament, because it is an **eschatological** metaphor."[57] Yet, Macchia adds, it is "decisive for the identity of Jesus in the New Testament as the Savior and Bestower of life."[58] How, we ask, can a metaphor be fluid and ambiguous and yet decisive for the identity of Jesus without reducing the identity of Jesus to fluidity and ambiguity? The mistake—a cardinal one—is basing Jesus' identity on what he does

51. Macchia, *Baptized in the Spirit*, 52.
52. Macchia, *Baptized in the Spirit*, 52.
53. Macchia, *Baptized in the Spirit*, 56.
54. Macchia, *Baptized in the Spirit*, 64–65, 72–73.
55. Macchia, *Baptized in the Spirit*, 73.
56. Sarah Hinlicky Wilson, "Water Baptism and Spirit Baptism in Luke-Acts: Another Reading of the Evidence," *Pneuma* 38, no. 4 (2016): 476–501.
57. Macchia, *Baptized in the Spirit*, 87.
58. Macchia, *Baptized in the Spirit*, 90.

rather than who he is. It follows the panentheist trend in Macchia's theology, to which we will shortly refer.

In all this, Macchia has some fine things to say. He writes that "the line between the ordinary and the extraordinary is fine indeed, not because there is no such thing as signs and wonders, but because all of creation is graced by God's Spirit in ways unknown to us."[59] For Luke, Spirit baptism cleanses, fills the temple with God's holy presence, sanctifies, and empowers for witness.[60] Christ's ascension and the gift of the Spirit have as their ultimate goal that Christ fill the whole universe with his presence.[61] It points to the final deliverance of creation from the dominion of death.[62] The kingdom of God is the kingdom of Christ because he is the incarnate Word and the bearer of the Spirit.[63]

Macchia uses Jürgen Moltmann favorably and, sharing the latter's **panentheism**, is committed to divine passibility.[64] He leaves the incarnation out of consideration in this context. Although he has a clear Trinitarian basis for his argument—from the Father through the Son in the Spirit, with a return pattern from our side, by the Spirit through the Son to the Father[65]—he shares Moltmann's panentheism and incipient **inclusivism**.[66] As we will see, this impacts his doctrine of justification.

Macchia underlines the point that Pentecostal theology cannot be identified with Protestantism. It is a new and different form of Christianity in addition to Rome, Orthodoxy, and Protestantism. Nowhere is this clearer than in his discussion of justification in relation to the BHS and the kingdom: "We need to define the righteousness of

59. Macchia, *Baptized in the Spirit*, 96.

60. Macchia, *Baptized in the Spirit*, 100.

61. Macchia, *Baptized in the Spirit*, 102.

62. Macchia, *Baptized in the Spirit*, 103.

63. Macchia, *Baptized in the Spirit*, 106. I have argued elsewhere that the theme of the kingdom of God in the Gospels and Acts, which recedes from view in the Epistles, is absorbed into the mediatorial kingdom of Christ, since Christ is one with the Father from eternity. Robert Letham, *The Work of Christ* (Leicester, UK: Inter-Varsity Press, 1993), 57–74.

64. Macchia, *Baptized in the Spirit*, 112–13, 125–27, 263–64.

65. Macchia, *Baptized in the Spirit*, 117.

66. Macchia, *Baptized in the Spirit*, 128.

justification as kingdom righteousness, the righteousness inspired by the Spirit in the work of Christ in fulfillment of the will of the Father." He continues:

> Justification literally means to be "righteoused" by God. It is my conviction that *Spirit baptism* as the fulfillment of the "kingdom of God and its righteousness" provides us with a richer framework for understanding justification by faith than is possible within the narrow confines of a forensic notion of justification read from select Pauline texts.[67]

We must ask here what exactly "to be righteoused" means.[68] Macchia contrasts it from a forensic declaration. Thus, it appears to be a rejection of the classic Protestant doctrines of justification. Rather, Macchia adds, it is "an eschatological gift of new creation through the Spirit of God," a statement drawn from Ernst Käsemann. Indeed, Macchia agrees with Moltmann's shift from justification to the kingdom of God, a shift from Paul to the Gospels.[69] This was a characteristic emphasis of classic liberal theology. Furthermore, Macchia proposes a shift in the *meaning* of justification rather than, as with Moltmann, a shift of focus. It is important for us to grasp that a shift to Spirit **Christology** and **pneumatocentrism** in general is a move away from classic Trinitarianism and has the effect of redefining the rest of theology as well. Macchia's move cannot be identified with Protestantism, let alone evangelical or Reformed theology, and its biblical provenance is at best highly questionable. Indeed, he explicitly rejects the Reformation doctrine, although much of it rests on a caricature when he talks about a transfer of merits from Christ to us.[70] Macchia is mistaken in arguing that

67. Macchia, *Baptized in the Spirit*, 130.

68. A term dependent on E. P. Sanders, *Paul, the Law, and the Jewish People* (Philadelphia: Fortress Press, 1983), 6, and his suggestion that "righteousing" is the best way to consider justification as a gift, putting people into a right relationship with God and one another.

69. Macchia, *Baptized in the Spirit*, 131.

70. Macchia, *Baptized in the Spirit*, 137–38.

the Reformation teaching entails such a transfer, since, because of union with Christ, we are incorporated in him and his merit is ours in reality.[71]

In his predilection for the Finnish school of Luther scholarship, Macchia adopts Tuomo Mannermaa's use of a stray comment from Martin Luther—*in ipsa fide Christus adest* ("in faith itself Christ is present")—to argue that Christ is not only the object of faith but its subject also.[72] In this, Macchia ignores the point that Luther wrote this early in his career in pre-Reformation days, and moreover, he uses it as paradigmatic, just as Mannermaa has done.[73] In this Macchia again follows Moltmann in cherry-picking quotations from here and there, often out of context, that appear to support his thesis. He expressly states that his proposals take both Catholic and Protestant doctrines to a pneumatological understanding of justification. This is a specious claim, since it is in effect a rejection of the Protestant doctrine, as he has made clear earlier.[74] Moreover, he ignores searching criticisms of the Finnish school.[75]

71. In all this, Macchia is echoed by Veli-Matti Kärkkäinen in his attempt to relativize what he terms "the Protestant doctrine of justification," despite not referring to any primary sources or differentiating between the Lutheran insistence on justification as central and dominant, and the Reformed location of the doctrine in the context of covenant. Kärkkäinen's argument is grounded on uncritical readings of favored sources, such as those from the school of Pauline interpretation associated with E. P. Sanders, and from Kärkkäinen's doctoral supervisor, Tuomo Mannermaa, about whom see below. See Veli-Matti Kärkkäinen, "'By the Washing of Regeneration and Renewal in the Holy Spirit': Towards a Pneumatological Theology of Justification," in *The Spirit and Christ in the New Testament and Christian Theology: Essays in Honor of Max Turner*, ed. I. Howard Marshall, Volker Rabens, and Cornelis Bennema (Grand Rapids: Eerdmans, 2012), 303–22.

72. Macchia, *Baptized in the Spirit*, 138–39; Tuomo Mannermaa, "Justification and Theosis in Lutheran-Orthodox Perspective," in *Union with Christ: The New Finnish Interpretation of Luther*, ed. Carl E. Braaten (Grand Rapids: Eerdmans, 1998), 25–41.

73. See Stephen Ozment, *The Age of Reform 1250–1550* (New Haven, CT: Yale University Press, 1980), 240–41, who argued that after 1518, Luther showed little interest in the writings of the German mystics.

74. Macchia, *Baptized in the Spirit*, 139.

75. Paul Louis Metzger, "Mystical Union with Christ: An Alternative to Blood Transfusions and Legal Fictions," *WTJ* 65, no. 2 (2003): 201–13; Mark A. Seifrid, "Paul, Luther, and Justification in Gal 2:15–21," *WTJ* 65, no. 2 (2003): 215–30; Carl R. Trueman, "Is the Finnish Line a New Beginning? A Critical Assessment of the Reading of Luther Offered by the Helsinki Circle," *WTJ* 65, no. 2 (2003): 231–44.

In keeping with his redefinition of justification, Macchia calls into question "the logical distinction traditionally made in Protestant dogmatics between justification and sanctification."[76] Macchia argues that the difference is one of emphasis rather than between objective and subjective "because of the obvious pneumatological and transformationist understanding of justification just noted from the Scriptures."[77] He states, correctly, that sanctification is just as objective as justification because it is also based on the grace of God alone. The sanctifying work of the Spirit "needs to be released in life through powerful experiences of renewal and charismatic enrichment that propel us toward vibrant praise, healing reconciliations, enriched koinonia, and enhanced gifting for empowered service."[78]

On extraordinary gifts of the Spirit, Macchia insists that we do not have the option of deciding that they are irrelevant. In most cultures in the Southern Hemisphere, where the church is growing fastest, such an attitude is regarded as unthinkable. These assumptions are "culturally provincial and even presumptuous."[79] Reflecting Romans 8:26–27, Macchia understands that "in tongues we groan for a liberty in the Spirit that is not yet fulfilled."[80] He claims that "tongues are the language of love, not reason."[81] Love is God's supreme gift, for it transcends all emotion and conceptuality and action.[82] The **substance** of the Christian life is God's love.[83] Here, we reply, the assumption that love is detached from reason needs to be reconsidered. Macchia seems to view love as emotive; the Bible sees it as evidenced in action whereby we serve the interests of others.

In contrast, Richard Gaffin recognizes that in Pentecostal and charismatic circles, baptism in the Holy Spirit has generally been seen individualistically rather than in corporate terms or in its redemptive-historical setting. He establishes that the cross, the

76. Macchia, *Baptized in the Spirit*, 140.
77. Macchia, *Baptized in the Spirit*, 140.
78. Macchia, *Baptized in the Spirit*, 145.
79. Macchia, *Baptized in the Spirit*, 149.
80. Macchia, *Baptized in the Spirit*, 281.
81. Macchia, *Baptized in the Spirit*, 257.
82. Macchia, *Baptized in the Spirit*, 259.
83. Macchia, *Baptized in the Spirit*, 259.

resurrection, the ascension, and Pentecost are integrally related as one redemptive event. Consequently, as Christ is never again to be crucified, so Pentecost is never to be repeated. Baptism with the Holy Spirit is the once-for-all act establishing the church in union with Christ. It is not an individual experience but a corporate one.[84] This might be held by some to beg the question whether it means that the Spirit is never again outpoured. Is not Pentecost the beginning of the age of the Spirit, when what marks the church is that the Spirit is poured out liberally, extravagantly, on it? This latter point is undoubtedly the case, but it does not follow from this that Pentecost itself is a repeatable event.

Assumption That the Distinctive Charismatic Phenomena Are the Same as in the New Testament

In common with most, if not all, of the Pentecostal and charismatic writers I have read, Anderson assumes that the phenomena evident in global charismatic churches, in all their diversity, are the same as were present in the New Testament. He produces no evidence in support, nor does he show any awareness of the crucial nature of such an unproven assumption. Rather, he asserts that "the early church was a community of the Holy Spirit, and the freedom of expression and spontaneity of its worship may not have been very different from that of many Pentecostal and Charismatic churches today."[85] He proceeds to claim, "Some of the characteristic features and ecstatic phenomena of Pentecostalism like prophecy, healing and speaking in tongues were common."[86] This assumption that the phenomena are the same is uniform among Pentecostal and charismatic advocates. In view of our argument that it is crucial to understand the ongoing work of the Spirit in the theological context of the New Testament and the apostolic ministry, with its unique place in redemptive history, such assumptions beg the question. Thiselton remarks, in relation to

84. Richard B. Gaffin Jr., *Perspectives on Pentecost: Studies in New Testament Teaching on the Gifts of the Holy Spirit* (Phillipsburg, NJ: Presbyterian and Reformed, 1979), *passim*.

85. Anderson, *Pentecostalism*, 19.

86. Anderson, *Pentecostalism*, 19.

prophecy, "A number of specialist writers on 'prophecy' conclude after many pages of discussion that (a) we cannot be entirely certain of its scope; and (b) we have no hermeneutical entitlement simply to read *into* the use of the term in Corinth and by Paul modes of popular understanding of the term today."[87] Since we do not have immediate evidence of the nature of the phenomena in the New Testament, and because of the uncertainty surrounding them, the conclusions that Pentecostal and charismatic advocates advance cannot be sustained.

Moreover, to say that such worship and the accompanying events were "common" at that time is questionable. As John-Christian Eurell remarks, the only explicit instances we have that record speaking with tongues, whatever the nature of tongues may have been, are recorded by Luke and Paul. Apart from Pentecost and other related events, it is recorded in only one church, at Corinth, a church marked by serious disorder that Paul attempted vigorously to correct. We read nothing of it elsewhere in the New Testament, neither at Rome, nor at Ephesus, Galatia, Philippi, Colossae, Thessalonica, or the churches of Crete and Asia Minor.[88] Given the paucity of references, it must be concluded that the phenomena at Corinth were exceptional, even in the context of the New Testament. Even if they were more extensive than I am suggesting, there is no evidence that the apostles expected their churches to exhibit these phenomena. Given that, they are not to be regarded as necessary or desirable today.

Bearing in mind this uncertainty, even ignorance, we recall our earlier observation that there is considerable division among scholars over exactly what were the phenomena in the New Testament. This applies especially to prophecy, tongues, and interpretation of tongues.

Here the Orthodox theologian Constantinos Dragkiotis's explanation is both confused and contradictory. He argues that tongues in Acts 10 and Acts 11:17 are the same gift as in Acts 2.[89] Yet in relation to

87. Anthony C. Thiselton, *The First Epistle to the Corinthians: A Commentary on the Greek Text* (Grand Rapids: Eerdmans, 2000), 901.

88. John-Christian Eurell, "The Nature of Pauline Glossolalia and Its Early Reception," *SJT* 72, no. 2 (2019): 182–90.

89. Constantinos Dragkiotis, "Emptiness, as a Prerequisite for Being Filled in the Holy Spirit," *JEPTA* 34, no. 2 (2014): 184–99, here 193–94.

tongues, he states that a private conversation with God automatically implies being filled with the Holy Spirit. But the events recorded in Acts were hardly private conversations with God; they were as public as could be. Dragkiotis asserts that no one else can understand what the tongues-speaker is saying; in Acts 2, however, they clearly could understand! He assumes an identity in the tongues at Pentecost and in the house of Cornelius on the one hand, an identity attested by Peter and Luke (Acts 10:44–48; 11:17–18), with the phenomena discussed by Paul in 1 Corinthians 14:4. If that is so, understanding of the tongues would be entailed, given the presence of an interpreter or someone to put into words what had been uttered in the latter instance.[90] While Dragkiotis cites a range of fathers and medievals in support of the continuation of these gifts, he cannot establish with any degree of confidence what these gifts were, nor does he attempt the task.[91]

From the uncertainty surrounding the New Testament phenomena, the Pentecostal scholar Gordon Fee recognizes that it cannot be asserted with any authority whether the phenomena present today are the same as those that occurred in the New Testament. He writes that "the question as to whether the 'speaking in tongues' in contemporary Pentecostal and charismatic communities is the same in kind as that in the Pauline churches is moot—and probably irrelevant. There is simply no way to know."[92] Arie Zwiep remarks that when a Pentecostal Christian utters unintelligible sounds, it is readily believed that the Holy Spirit has inspired it, but that when an agnostic or psychiatric patient does so, it is explained differently.[93]

90. Unless the miracle in Acts 2 was a miracle of hearing, which most have discounted.

91. For example, on tongues, Irenaeus, *Adversus Haereses*, 5.6.1; on other languages "for the general benefit," *Adversus Haereses*, 5.8.1–10; Tertullian, *Adversus Marcion*, 5.8.1–10; Hilary, *De Trinitate*, 10, who writes of "various tongues" "for everyone's edification," implying languages; Ambrose, *On the Holy Spirit*, 14, "various types of tongues"; Nicholas Kavasilas, *Life in Christ*, who remarks that these occurred in the early years, but "even in our days"; and Symeon the New Theologian, *Thanksgiving to God*, 1.14, in relation to Paul and "mystical voices" (2 Cor. 12); Dragkiotis, "Emptiness," 195–97.

92. Gordon D. Fee, *Paul, the Spirit and the People of God* (London: Hodder and Stoughton, 1996), 169.

93. Arie W. Zwiep, *Christ, the Spirit and the Community of God: Essays on the Acts of the Apostles* (Tübingen: Mohr Siebeck, 2010), 100–101.

Nature of the Extraordinary Phenomena

It will be more than helpful to recall our discussion on gifts of the Spirit in the New Testament, as we presented it in chapter 9. Here we consider how a few of the claimed gifts today are understood by those who maintain an identity of these phenomena with those in the New Testament.

Discernment of Spirits

Kärkkäinen recognizes that there has been little careful theological reflection on this gift. He acknowledges that Pentecostals are better known for claiming "a word from the Lord." This often affects major life decisions and is used in controversy against other Christian groups, including Pentecostal ones.[94] Is discernment a distinctive gift? he asks. Or is it a Spirit-aided capacity? Or both? There have been no major systematic discussions. It is assumed that it exists.

Some think that purely practical advice was given in prophecies.[95] Yet New Testament texts indicate that discernment may relate to doctrinal and ethical issues, he writes (1 Cor. 14:21; 1 Thess. 5:19–21; 1 John 4:1–6). The key criteria for Pentecostals are adherence to scriptural teaching; a "controlled" use of the gift; and the moral character of the one doing the discernment. Beyond that, Kärkkäinen rightly suggests, there is something more—we must be guided by the biblical teaching on Christology in particular and the Trinity in general.

Kärkkäinen argues that in a religiously pluralistic world, the question is not whether the Holy Spirit is at work among people of other faiths—Kärkkäinen appears to assume that this is the case—but rather how to discern the Spirit's presence and work. Quoting Paul

94. Veli-Matti Kärkkäinen, "The Challenge of Discerning between the Genuine and Counterfeit 'Signs of the Spirit': Toward a Pentecostal Theology of the Discernment of the Spirit(s)," *JEPTA* 39, no. 2 (2019): 165–83, https://doi.org/10.1080/18124461.2019.1627510. I read this and what follows from the online edition, in which there are no page numbers and which is available only on a subscription basis.

95. Kärkkäinen refers to Stephen Parker, *Led by the Spirit: Toward a Practical Theology of Pentecostal Discernment and Decision Making* (Cleveland, TN: CPT Press, 2015), 31.

Hiebert, he indicates that it is widely agreed among Pentecostals that there are "no simple phenomenological criteria by which we can test the presence of the Holy Spirit."[96] Christology is the key, Kärkkäinen continues (1 John 4:1–6), since looking at the Holy Spirit is looking at Christ. Moreover, citing J. S. Ukpong, divine activity transcends human understanding.[97] He also cites Macchia, who argues that this needs to be placed in the context of the person and work of Christ, in the context of the biblical canon.[98] For example, how does the prosperity gospel relate to the poverty of the cross? Furthermore, Kärkkäinen concludes, we need to remember that all discernment is human discernment and liable to mistakes and misuse.

Charismata of the Spirit

After extensive analysis, Max Turner concludes that *charismata* has the meaning of "gracious gift" and does not mean "supernatural gift." In the context, Paul wants to curb the Corinthians' hubris and so uses a word that has a general sense.[99] *All* who confess that Jesus is Lord are the *pneumatikoi*.[100] Paul broadens the list of gifts to include those that the spiritual elitists would overlook—helps, government, and so on.[101] In terms of a possible distinction between spiritual and natural gifts, prophecy, tongues, and healings are clearly not natural, but teaching and other gifts are based on natural abilities and experience.[102] In the latter case, the Spirit enhances a natural gift, whereas in the former there is an incursion by the Spirit, gifting an ability that the person has not previously had. As for a distinction between gifts of the Spirit and the fruit of the Spirit, this is not sharp at all. The

96. Paul G. Hiebert, "Discerning the Work of God," in *Charismatic Experiences in History*, ed. Cecil M. Robeck Jr. (Peabody, MA: Hendrickson, 1985), 147–63, here 151.

97. J. S. Ukpong, "Pluralism and the Problem of the Discernment of Spirits," *Ecumenical Review* 41, no. 3 (1989): 416–25.

98. Frank D. Macchia, "A Call for Careful Discernment: A Theological Response to Prosperity Teaching," in *Pentecostalism and Prosperity: The Socio-Economics of the Global Charismatic Movement*, ed. Katherine Attanasi and Amos Yong (New York: Palgrave Macmillan, 2012), 225–37.

99. Turner, *Holy Spirit*, 260.

100. Turner, *Holy Spirit*, 262.

101. Turner, *Holy Spirit*, 263.

102. Turner, *Holy Spirit*, 271.

exception is that the fruit of the Spirit is to be present in all to whom Paul wrote, whereas not all have this gift or that.[103]

On Cessationism

After a critical attack on B. B. Warfield (with which many if not most cessationists might be in some degree of sympathy), Turner acknowledges that "we have implied that it is not possible to answer the question whether any of the prototypical gifts ceased. All that we can say is that claims to them were made, even if relatively sparsely."[104] He continues: "The only claim that can be made with confidence is that our prototypical gifts gradually became marginalized. But it would be very unwise to give a single and theological reason for this." Again, "as for incomprehensible 'tongues,' they had little built-in survival value," and he concludes that "searching before God for personalized spiritual experiences . . . is characteristically a phenomenon of the church in periods of insecurity, introspection and historical instability, rather than in those of consolidation and self-confidence."[105]

Evaluation

Significant Problems

In what follows I do not intend to claim that all these features are invariably present in every Pentecostal or charismatic writer, nor that most of them are. These are put forward as general tendencies that appear to follow from the stance taken by spokespersons in the movement, such as it is. We must also bear in mind that Pentecostalism and the charismatic renewal and all that follows are

103. Turner, *Holy Spirit*, 272.

104. Turner, *Holy Spirit*, 292.

105. Turner, *Holy Spirit*, 293. Arguing against the idea of cessationism and in favor of continuance is Jon Ruthven, *On the Cessation of the Charismata: The Protestant Polemic on Post-Biblical Miracles*, JPT Supplement Series 3 (Sheffield, UK: Sheffield Academic Press, 1993). Writing from a cessationist position is Gaffin, *Perspectives*. See also Wayne A. Grudem, ed., *Are Miraculous Gifts for Today? 4 Views*, Counterpoints: Bible and Theology (Grand Rapids: Zondervan, 2011). I have argued that the term *cessationism* is not helpful, since it assumes that there was a prior state of continuance and that the miraculous was in some sense the norm. Robert Letham, *Systematic Theology* (Wheaton, IL: Crossway, 2019), 203–6.

recognized by those who are part of them as too diverse to identify as a single movement with a clear and distinctive theology. It rather exemplifies a mystical, "experiential" perspective that is difficult, if not impossible, to pin down.

Thiselton draws attention to some dangerous hermeneutical strategies that effectively close discussion. One such strategy is to argue on the basis of presuppositions. "It appears to promote an opt-out clause from genuine dialogue."[106] Others adopt reader-response theory, in which meaning is the response of the reader. This precludes any criticism from outside. Third is reliance on postmodern **hermeneutics**. This can take the form of an abuse of Thomas Kuhn's argument for paradigms, leading to the claim that different paradigms are incommensurable. From this, some take the position that there is no possibility of agreement and that any attempt to agree is an attempted exertion of power by one side over the other.[107]

Is There Something Additional to Christ?

Frederick Dale Bruner's negative assessment needs to be taken seriously.[108] He argues that the Pentecostal narrative follows the errors at Corinth by insisting on something more in addition to Christ and his finished work. It is an attack on the perfection, completion, and efficacy of the work of Christ. In contrast, the Bible states that the Spirit baptizes all believers into Christ. The Spirit works inseparably with the Father and the Son. The incarnation and Pentecost are inseparably distinct elements of the one movement of God's grace in Christ in which all three persons are inseparably active.

Moreover, Bruner indicates, an inevitable corollary in the Pentecostal and charismatic theology is that there is something that believers themselves must do in order to receive the full blessing of the Spirit. This may entail a deliberate seeking of the Spirit's power, surrender to the Spirit's operations, or some such qualifying criterion. In addition to entailing that Christ is not sufficient, it introduces

106. Thiselton, *Holy Spirit*, 96.

107. Thiselton, *Holy Spirit*, 95–101.

108. Frederick Dale Bruner, *A Theology of the Holy Spirit: The Pentecostal Experience and the New Testament Witness* (Grand Rapids: Eerdmans, 1970), 225–84.

legalism. The charismatics and Pentecostalists argue that we must do something ourselves to make us fit to receive the Spirit. This replaces grace by works. It fosters self-righteousness on the one hand by those who receive the blessing and the endowments and despair on the other.[109] It can also create a division in the church based on claimed experiences to which many are strangers. In contrast, the New Testament teaches that the Holy Spirit is a gift of grace to sinners.

The Orthodox theologian Dragkiotis falls into this trap.[110] In order to be filled with the Spirit, he says, we must empty ourselves of everything that has to do with our ego. This is in line with the Palamite claim, stemming from Dionysius the Areopagite, that God is beyond knowledge so that the essence of piety is to empty our minds and ascend to the darkness of total ignorance.[111] This emptying, Dragkiotis claims, has three stages. The prerequisite is the direction that must be followed to attain the filling, the trajectory of self-emptying to which we must commit ourselves. Then comes emptiness itself, which entails fighting against one's earthly self, its will and desires. Eventually, there is the filling, with manifestations of the Holy Spirit in daily life.[112] The argument runs that in order to be filled, first there must be an emptying, with Jesus Christ as the ultimate example. This is false. Jesus grew in all the aspects of human life (Luke 2:52). This was not a relinquishing of his human desires but, being sanctified, a growth in them. Nor is there the slightest hint, in fact the reverse, that he ever had to engage in such a process, that he ever had desires that he was compelled to deny.

Dragkiotis continues by asserting, with Paul (Phil. 3:13), that there must be a rejection of anything "previous." The worship of God requires that we do not have anything on our mind, and are rid of worldly concerns. "The one who seeks God must first believe absolutely in the Lord, then surrender entirely to his commandments,

109. See particularly Bruner, *Theology of the Holy Spirit*, 281–84, 323–41.

110. Dragkiotis, "Emptiness."

111. Vladimir Lossky, *The Mystical Theology of the Eastern Church* (London: James Clarke, 1957), 23–43; John A. McGuckin, "On the Mystical Theology of the Eastern Church," *SVTQ* 58, no. 4 (2014): 373–99, here 393.

112. Dragkiotis, "Emptiness," 184.

be distant from all those things that bind human beings to the world. . . . In this way the Lord himself can become a dwelling place for the soul." This does not mean deadening the passions, but rather transforming them.[113] This argument supports Bruner's case; reception of the Spirit, for Dragkiotis, is based on prior human qualifying actions. With such a mindset, one can never be sure that one has properly fulfilled the conditions. It misses the point, prominent in the letter to the Hebrews, that Christ has opened the way to the Father and that all believers have access through his blood (Heb. 10:19) and can approach the throne of grace with confidence (4:14–16). It is contrary to Paul's observation that we have all been baptized by the Spirit and have been given the Spirit to drink (1 Cor. 12:12–13). It is contrary to the biblical teaching that the creation, and this world, is inherently good.

Mysticism

At root, the Pentecostal and charismatic movements are mystical. Experience rather than doctrine is the determining factor, sometimes experience unchecked by doctrine. Anderson agrees with Amos Yong that "the Pentecostal and Charismatic experience 'demands interpretation of the existential dimension of spirituality over and against an emphasis on textuality in religious life.'"[114] Andrew Gabriel remarks that "the theological symbol of Pentecost and the experience of the Spirit are foundational for Pentecostal theology as a whole," although he acknowledges that the biblical texts provide the primary foundation.[115] Anderson is close to the mark when he cites Harvey Cox, who suggests that tongues-speaking is a response to "an ecstasy deficit" in the modern world.[116] This places it squarely in the camp of mysticism. This claim sidelines the Bible and the ecumenical councils of the church and can relativize reasoned discourse.

113. Dragkiotis, "Emptiness," 188–89.

114. Anderson, *Pentecostalism*, 193.

115. Andrew K. Gabriel, "Pneumatology: Eschatological Intensification of the Presence of God," in *The Routledge Handbook of Pentecostal Theology*, ed. Wolfgang Vondey (London: Routledge, 2020), 206–15, here 206.

116. Harvey Cox, *Fire from Heaven* (London: Cassell, 1996), 81–88, 91–92, 96, quoted in Anderson, *Pentecostalism*, 192.

While, in a movement so vast and diverse, this emphasis is not necessarily uniform, for there are very many exceptions, it leads one to ask what the sources of these experiences are. Is the movement a work of the Spirit? Alternatively, is it predominantly a means of emotional and psychological release? Are demonic influences to be taken into account? Is it, as a whole, a mixed picture?

The theology of Pentecost is vital to grasp because it is crucial to an understanding of contemporary claims. As we saw in chapter 7, Pentecost has to be understood in redemptive-historical terms. Thus, it is a unique event. It can no more be repeated than can the death and resurrection of Christ or his ascension to the right hand of the Father. In view of its uniqueness, it cannot be made a yardstick for contemporary phenomena.

Individualism

Yves Congar sees prophecy as a corporate matter rather than an individualistic one. It always depends on the judgment of the church.[117] In an excellent argument, he establishes that prophets were inspired interpreters of Scripture.[118] Prophecy entailed understanding of the depth of Scripture and the divine mysteries. The whole body of the church is prophetic, since prophecy subsists in the church.[119] Congar states, however, that prophecy as it was recorded in the New Testament in 1 Corinthians 14 is now practiced in the charismatic renewal. Even he gives no evidence to establish this claim,[120] other than to assert that the Spirit displays something new, but within the fullness given once for all by God in Christ.[121]

This corporate context is vital. It is striking how in the New Testament the apostles acted for the most part in concert with others and expected the church to do the same. When issues arose, councils

117. Yves M. J. Congar, *The Word and the Spirit*, trans. David Smith (London: Geoffrey Chapman, 1986), 64, where he cites C. Perrot, Prophètes et Prophêtisme dans le Nouveau Testament, *Lumière et Vie* (November–December 1973): 25–39.

118. Congar, *Word and Spirit*, 65.

119. Congar, *Word and Spirit*, 68. See John Henry Newman, *Essays 1: Apostolic Tradition* (London, 1836), 125f.

120. Congar, *Word and Spirit*, 70.

121. Congar, *Word and Spirit*, 71.

were called (Acts 11:1–18; 15:1–35). Paul was rarely alone, taking Barnabas, Silas, and Timothy with him on his journeys. On occasions when his companions were delayed, he was anxious and refrained from overt action (2 Cor. 2:12–13). He gave instructions for the leadership of congregations to be in the hands of a plurality of elders (Acts 14:23; Titus 1:5). When the offering for the poor in Jerusalem was made, he arranged for a team to transport it there (1 Cor. 16:1–4). In this, the precedent had been set by Jesus, who sent his disciples out two by two (Matt. 10:1–42; Mark 6:7–13, 30–31). This collective principle is particularly the case when considering the baptism of the Holy Spirit and the claims made in recent decades.

In this, we in the Western world are prone to misunderstandings occasioned by the imposition of post-Kantian individualism. We think mainly in terms of the individual person rather than the group. Consequently, the inevitable tendency is to interpret biblical texts as referring to individual believers, to me personally, when in fact they are addressed to the church. This dominating focus was set in order by the invention of the printing press, which enabled the mass production of Bibles. With this, individuals could have their own copy rather than relying on the public reading of Scripture in the church, as had been the norm in the preceding centuries. It also encourages the reader (note the singular) to assume that the biblical documents are addressed directly to himself or herself.[122]

The hitherto-dominant emphasis on the baptism of the Spirit as a postconversion experience and thus not common to all believers throws the whole focus onto the individual and his or her spiritual experience. This is in line with the holiness movement from which the original Pentecostalism traces its roots and with which much of the later developments in the charismatic renewal and the third wave resonate. Beginning with the eighteenth-century revivals, and feeding into such things as the Keswick movement of the nineteenth and twentieth centuries, the prevailing stress was on the individual believer and the claim that some process or experience can lift one

122. This should be taken neither to undermine Bible reading by individuals nor to encourage uncritical following of church teachings (Acts 17:11).

out of the mundane level of regular Christian living and transform one's life. This mindset fitted comfortably into the West's post-Enlightenment concentration on the individual. This individualism is common throughout both church and society and is by no means confined to Pentecostal or charismatic circles. Indeed, as we have noted, many Pentecostal theologians are emphatically stressing the corporate and cosmic dimensions of the kingdom of God and so are seeking to avoid these forces. But while the focus on postconversion experiences or on such claimed effusions of the Spirit continues, this individualistic stress will remain a feature.

The Claims for the Continuation of Special Gifts Are Impossible to Establish and Are Theologically Irrelevant

Since there is considerable uncertainty about the nature of the extraordinary New Testament phenomena, it is impossible to maintain that those evident today are identical to them. This of itself does not establish that the present manifestations are invalid. Yet the unique events of the resurrection, the ascension, and Pentecost mean that even if an identity between the two sets of phenomena were established, their function and significance could not be the same.

That does not of itself mean that the Holy Spirit is not at work in such contexts. It is normal that "God uses crooked sticks to draw straight lines," for we are all jars of clay, beset by weakness (2 Cor. 4:7). While the evidence points to the current phenomena as a form of psychological release, this can take a number of different forms. It can be release from the stresses of modern life. It may coalesce with experiences that may or may not be positive, adverse, or neutral, or any combination of these. More positively, in expressing the deep yearning for the completion of redemption, it may exhibit the working of the Holy Spirit in the deepest recesses of the human heart (Rom. 8:26–27). If that is the case, it is the yearning for redemption that is significant, rather than the form that such yearning takes. Such a variety of features can be found in any movement in the church; where the Spirit is at work, there may be a range of human factors to take into account. Furthermore, it is possible that demonic forces are active in some cases, whether the overall focus is mystical and emotional, cultural, or intellectual. The real issue is whether this or that is faithfully in accord with God's revelation in Christ and in Scripture.

Slaying in the Spirit

In certain circumstances, the Pentecostal and charismatic manifestations could exhibit more sinister sources. Slaying in the Spirit goes against the regular pattern of encounters with God or his angelic emissaries recorded in the Bible. When a person encounters a theophanic vision or, in the case of Saul of Tarsus and John, the glorified Christ, in each case he falls on his face. In slaying in the Spirit, the person falls on his back. The event is prearranged; someone is normally standing behind to catch the person as he falls.[123] If events such as these are prearranged, it immediately raises questions about their **efficient cause** and their motivation.

There is a good reason why the persons in the Bible in such cases slumped forward. Humans have a natural reaction when falling forward by which they use their arms to cushion their fall and prevent serious injury; no such safety mechanism exists when falling backward, which can pose a harmful and even life-threatening danger. The Holy Spirit is the Spirit of life, the author and giver of life. His actions promote life, health, and well-being. Except in cases of judgment, he does not facilitate events in which people fall backward to their harm or even death.

One can only suggest that "slaying in the Spirit" in this manner is most likely occasioned by one or both of two sources. The first is a preplanned human action that claims to be from the Holy Spirit but that does not go with the grain of the Spirit's actions. Such an event is a fraud or an attempt to manipulate the Holy Spirit—which

123. John Stott was critical of the Toronto Blessing and other similar features on the grounds of their anti-intellectualism, contrary to the gospel's address to the mind; people barking like dogs and howling like hyenas, inverting the created relationship between humans and the animals; uncontrolled laughter, in the face of self-control as the fruit of the Spirit; and slaying in the Spirit, in which people fall backward, contrary to encounters with God recorded in Scripture. See Dudley-Smith, *John Stott: A Global Ministry*, 412–13.

is a heinous sin (Acts 8:14–24). The second possibility, not exclusive of the first, is that it arises from evil sources.

Prophecy and the Sufficiency of Scripture

Ultimately the claim to continued prophecy inevitably collides with the sufficiency of Scripture. This is the case in relation to Wayne Grudem's theories, even though he defends the doctrine himself. There seem to me to be only three alternatives. First, the prophecy contradicts Scripture, in which case it is false and must be rejected. Or else it repeats the words of Scripture, rendering it superfluous, for the Bible has already spoken on the matter. This probably accounts for the majority of contemporary prophecies and reduces the original utterance to the banal. Or, third, it adds to Scripture, contradicting the words of the apostle that Scripture has been given "that the man of God may be *artios* [complete, capable], equipped for every good work" (2 Tim. 3:17), and entailing that the Bible is not sufficient to guide us. Stephen Land, a renewal theologian, writes that the Spirit has more to say than Scripture.[124]

Congar refers to the 1907 papal syllabus decree *Lamentabili sane*, which asserted that revelation has closed. Since then, Catholic treatises have had to include a paragraph on the closure of revelation upon the death of the last apostle. The decree rejected the claim that "revelation, which constitutes the object of Catholic faith, was not completed with the apostles."[125] This decree was propounded in opposition to Alfred Loisy (1857–1940), who maintained that revelation is situated in human religious intuitions, and to George Tyrell (1861–1909), who identified revelation with the human consciousness, although Tyrell did agree that the apostolic revelation contained all that is necessary for the Christian life.[126] Later theologians, such as Henri De Lubac (1896–1991), Karl Rahner (1904–84), and Eduard Schillebeeckx (1914–2009), connect the closure of revelation

124. Stephen J. Land, *Pentecostal Spirituality: A Passion for the Kingdom*, JPT Supplement 1 (Sheffield, UK: Sheffield Academic Press, 1993), 100, quoted in Gabriel, "Pneumatology," 208.

125. Congar, *Word and Spirit*, 55–56.

126. Congar, *Word and Spirit*, 56.

with fulfillment by Christ, leaving room for private and limited revelations.[127] This Roman Catholic assertion of 1907 is, to the extent we have mentioned, in harmony with the Westminster Confession of Faith, in its assertion that the whole counsel of God for God's glory and our salvation, faith, and life either is expressly set down in Scripture or by good and necessary consequence can be deduced from Scripture (WCF 1.6).

The claims of Grudem and charismatics also raise questions about the extraordinary gifts of the Spirit. This is conventionally discussed as *cessationism versus continuationism*. The exponents of continuationism argue that the special gifts of the Spirit mentioned in the New Testament are of ongoing validity and exist in the church today. Those in the cessationist camp maintain that they ceased with the passing of the apostles, since they were "the signs of a true apostle" (2 Cor. 12:12).

The choice of nomenclature can easily prejudice a case. The term *cessationism* implies that these gifts were, to varying degrees, normally present in the covenant community on an ongoing basis but suddenly stopped. They ceased. Implied in cessation is a previous ongoing presence and operation. The hiatus requires explanation, and the burden of proof lies there.

But any idea that extraordinary gifts had been the norm for the covenant community is untenable. Miracles and similar phenomena never happened on an ongoing basis. They occurred only at particular points in the history of redemption: in the exodus and the conquest, at or following the ministry of Moses; at the beginning of the prophetic period with Elijah and Elisha; and again with the ministry of Jesus and the apostles. Talk of *continuationism* and *cessationism* is misleading and needs some qualification, for the norm was absence, not presence. Only at three key hinges of redemptive history did the miraculous punctuate the narrative. The terms of the discussion are misplaced and need to be recalibrated.

Following the ascension of Christ and the apostolic foundation of the church, there are no significant redemptive-historical events

127. Congar, *Word and Spirit*, 57.

to precede the parousia. God has spoken in Christ (Heb. 1:1–4). Christ is his definitive Word; there is nothing more that God can say—not because he is incapable, which would be patently false, but since he has said it all. The ministry of Christ and the apostles, under the direction of the Spirit, accompanied by the signs and wonders appropriate to the clinching action of God in the cross, resurrection, and ascension, is the last word. This is definitively interpreted to us in the New Testament. The next item on the agenda is the consummation of salvation at the parousia. No theological or redemptive significance can attach to any unusual happenings that have occurred since, are occurring, or may occur in the future. God has given us all we need to reach our eschatological destiny: the Spirit's empowering the Word, the sacraments, and prayer, the means he has given for that purpose (WSC 88).[128]

Concluding Suggestions

We noted that the same overall alternatives (the Spirit, emotional origins, human manipulation, evil influences) could be said to exist for any range of human experiences when in contact with the gospel. People are attracted to the gospel for a variety of reasons. Many come to faith, others endure for a while and fall away, while others, sadly, think it is a means to their own temporal benefit. Many Pentecostal and charismatic churches hold firmly to the apostolic gospel. Nevertheless, a movement that has no discernible distinctive theology and is based not on the textuality of the Bible but rather in experience cannot, *as such*, be judged to be in harmony with the biblical gospel and the Christian tradition. Despite the very many exceptions, such misgivings remain.[129]

Key Terms

Christology	essence
efficient cause	glossolalia
eschatological	hermeneutics

128. Letham, *Systematic Theology*, 200–206.

129. Amos Yong, *Spirit of Love: A Trinitarian Theology of Grace* (Waco, TX: Baylor University Press, 2012), 163.

hypostatic
inclusivism
modalism
modalistic monarchianism
nature
panentheism
persons
pneumatocentrism
substance
xenolalia

For Further Reading

The following are recent major scholarly works from a Pentecostal or charismatic perspective.

Levison, John R. *Filled with the Spirit*. Grand Rapids: Eerdmans, 2009.

Macchia, Frank D. *Jesus the Spirit Baptizer: Christology in the Light of Pentecost*. Grand Rapids: Eerdmans, 2018.

Turner, Max. *The Holy Spirit and Spiritual Gifts*. Carlisle, UK: Paternoster, 1996. This is a book adopting a mediating position, supportive but nevertheless critical of aspects of charismatic theology and practice.

The following adopt a critical approach while seeking to maintain a biblical irenicism.

Bruner, Frederick Dale. *A Theology of the Holy Spirit: The Pentecostal Experience and the New Testament Witness*. Grand Rapids: Eerdmans, 1970.

Ferguson, Sinclair B. *The Holy Spirit*. Leicester, UK: Inter-Varsity Press, 1996.

Gaffin, Richard B., Jr. *Perspectives on Pentecost: Studies in New Testament Teaching on the Gifts of the Holy Spirit*. Phillipsburg, NJ: Presbyterian and Reformed, 1979.

Glossary

accidents. Characteristics of an entity that may be present but are not intrinsic to what it is but merely adventitious. A male human being is a man, but the fact that he may be a father is not necessary to who he is, since not all men are fathers.

accompanying cause. An entity or factor that is associated in some way with the effecting of a motion or change, without being the **efficient cause** or necessarily the **instrumental cause**.

adoptionism. An early heresy relating to the **person** of Christ that claimed that the human Jesus was elevated to divine status at his ascension.

anthropological. Relating to a focus on humanity.

appropriations. Works of the triune God ascribed to particular **persons**. Since God is one, all three persons act together in all of God's works. Yet each work is particularly attributable (appropriated) to one person. Only the Son became incarnate; only the Holy Spirit came at Pentecost. This does not deny that the other two persons were also involved in these acts.

Arians. Those who held the same or a similar view as **Arius**. Cf. **Homoian Arian.**

Arius (c. 276–337). Priest who taught that the Son was a creature who came into being at some point, and was the agent through whom the world was made, but was neither coeternal with the Father nor of the same **being**. Cf. **Eunomius.**

attributes. Particular characteristics of God, such as holiness, sovereignty, justice, goodness, mercy, and love. See **nature of God.**

begetting (eternal). See **generation; unbegotten.**

begotten. See **unbegotten.**

being. Something that *is*, an existent. See **essence; *ousia*.**

Christocentric. Of a theology, centered in Christ.

Christology. Teaching relating to the **person** of Christ.

consubstantiality. The dogma that the Son and the Holy Spirit are of the same **substance** as the Father. This means that all three **persons** are fully God, and the whole God.

creation *ex nihilo*. The teaching, based on biblical revelation, that God created the entire universe, there being no preexisting materials. Consequently, he brought into existence all entities other than himself.

Cyprian. Bishop of Carthage who lived from c. 200 to 258.

deification. According to the Eastern church, the goal of salvation, which is to be made God. The Holy Spirit effects deification in us. It involves no blurring of the Creator-creature distinction, but rather focuses on the union and communion that we are given by God in which, as Peter says, we are made partakers of the divine **nature** (2 Peter 1:4). Cf. **participation.**

Docetism. The early heresy that Christ's humanity was apparent and not real. The term is a derivative of the Greek verb *dokein*, "to seem" or "appear." This view is heretical because if Christ were not fully man, we could not be saved, since only a perfect, sinless man can atone for the sins of man.

dualism. A positing of two separate realms that can have the effect of dividing an entity.

efficient cause. An agent that brings about a motion or change in a series of effects. Cf. **accompanying cause; instrumental cause.**

emanation. The idea, prevalent in **gnosticism**, that **beings** flowed out of a higher being as from a source.

energies. God's powers at work in the creation. According to Gregory Palamas, the **essence** of God is unknowable. We have to do with God's energies. —**energy**, sing.

eschatological. Relating to the last things, from the Greek word *eschatos* ("last"). —**eschatology,** n. —**eschatologically,** adv.

essence (of God). What God *is*, his **being** (from *esse*, "to be").

eternal generation. See **generation.**

Eunomius. A fourth-century heretic who, like **Arius**, believed that the Son was created and so was not of the same **being** as the Father.

filioque. The phrase "and the Son" added by the Western church to the Niceno-Constantinopolitan Creed (A.D. 381). That creed stated that the Holy Spirit proceeds "from the Father." Later the Western church added the *filioque* clause, which has been the source of ongoing controversy and division ever since.

generation (eternal). The unique **property** of the Son in relation to the Father. Since God is eternal, the **relations** between the Father and the Son are eternal. This is not to be understood on the basis of human generation or begetting, since God is spiritual. It is beyond our capacity to understand. See **unbegotten.**

glossolalia. Utterances in sounds or language unknown to humans.

gnosticism. A movement prominent in the early centuries of the church that combined elements of various religions and philosophies into a worldview that posited a chain of **being** from an ineffable source by way of **emanations** to lower entities, with the material world as a lower and inferior level.

hermeneutics. A principle of interpretation that governs how texts or realities are to be understood.

Heterousians. A group in the fourth century that maintained that the Son is different in **being** from the Father.

Homoian Arian. One of a group in the late fourth century that thought that the Son is simply "like" the Father but not eternally one in **being** with him. Cf. **Arians.**

homoousios. Greek for "of the same being," meaning that the Son and the Holy Spirit are of the same identical **being** as the Father.

hypostasis. Greek for "something with a concrete existence." In terms of the Trinity, it came to mean ***person***. Thus, by the end of the fourth-century controversy, it referred to what is distinct in God, the way in which he is three, while ***ousia*** was reserved for the one **being** of God. —**hypostatic,** adj. —**hypostatically,** adv.

hypostatic union. The union formed in the incarnation by the ***hypostasis*** of the Son in assuming a human nature.

immanent Trinity. The Trinity in itself, or the three **persons** as they relate to one another without regard to creation.

incomprehensible. Relating to the idea that humans cannot exhaustively understand God, who is infinite and transcends the creation he has made. *Inter multa alia,* Psalm 139:1–12 and Romans 11:33–36 reflect this idea.

instrumental cause. The means or tool used to bring about an effect. Cf. **accompanying cause; efficient cause.**

Macedonians. The putative followers of Macedonius, Bishop of Constantinople from 342 until his deposition in 360, who denied the deity of the Holy Spirit. Macedonius himself may not have shared these views.

Manichaeism. An extreme form of ontological **dualism**, holding that there are two coequal realities, good and evil. Cf. **ontology.**

Maximus. Perhaps the most significant theologian of the seventh century. Maximus the Confessor (A.D. 580–662) was instrumental in opposing the Monothelites, who held that Christ had only one will. He suffered mutilation for his stand for the truth.

missions. The particular **relations** of the three Trinitarian ***hypostases*** in terms of the work of God outside himself, in creation, providence, and grace. In these the Father sends the Son, while the Father and the Son (according to the Western church) send the Spirit. These relations are never reversed. They reflect the internal relations in the Trinity, whereby the Father begets the Son, while the Father (and the Son, according to the Latin church) spirates the Spirit. See **processions; spiration; unbegotten.**

modalism. The blurring or erasing of the real, eternal, and irreducible distinctions between the three **persons** of the Trinity. This danger can arise when the unity of God, or the identity in **being** of the three, is overstressed at the expense of the personal distinctions. It can also surface when there is a pervasive stress on salvation history, so as to eliminate any reference to eternal realities. When that is so, God's revelation in human history as the Father, the Son, and the Holy Spirit is no longer held to reveal who he is eternally in himself.

monarchy/monarchianism. Sole rule, the rule of one. It refers to the unity of God, his oneness (cf. Deut. 6:4). In the Eastern church, it was common to base the monarchy in the Father. Yet this could often lead to the subordination of the Son and the Holy Spirit, or else to **modalism** by which the other **persons** were reduced to little more than **attributes**. See **subordinationism.**

monopatrist. Someone who adheres to the idea that the Holy Spirit proceeds from the Father alone.

nature of God. What God is *like* (love, just, holy, omnipotent, et al.). These particular aspects of his nature are termed **attributes**. In the fourth century, *nature of God* was sometimes used as a synonym for God's **essence** or **being**.

Nestorianism. A heresy propounded by the followers of Nestorius. The Nestorians, concerned to stress the reality of Christ's humanity, undermined the unity of his **person**. By focusing excessively on the two natures of Christ, it appeared that deity and humanity were separate, side by side, with no union between them, and so no incarnation. Nestorius was condemned as a heretic at the Council of Ephesus (A.D. 431). —**Nestorian,** n. & adj.

ontology. The study relating to **being**, that which is. —**ontological,** adj. —**ontologically,** adv.

order (*taxis*). The irreversible order disclosed by the **relations** among the three **persons**. In eternity, the Father begets the Son and sends the Holy Spirit in or through the Son.

original cause. God, since he governs all things. Also called *first cause*; *primary cause*. See **secondary causes.**

***ousia*.** **Being** (that which is). Since there is only one God, he is only one *ousia*. The word refers to the one being of God. Before the Trinitarian crisis of the fourth century was resolved, however, this word had a range of meanings, and so there was much confusion. See chapter 1.

panentheism. The idea that God and the creation are mutually interdependent, God being in the creation and the creation in God.

pantheism. The idea that the creation is divine, that God and the creation are identical.

participation. The notion that believers, united to Christ, participate in the divine **nature** (2 Peter 1:4), since they are indwelt by the Spirit. This does not mean that the Creator-creature distinction is blurred or eclipsed, but expresses the unbreakable closeness of this union. Athanasius, for one, distinguished Christ, who is *proper* to the Father's **being**, since he is one in being with him from eternity, with our being *participants* in the divine nature. Cf. **deification.**

perichorēsis. The mutual indwelling of the three **persons** of the Trinity in the one **being** of God.

persons. The Father, the Son, and the Holy Spirit. There has been much debate about whether *persons* is an appropriate or adequate term for the three, in view of its modern usage, which entails separate individuals. But none of the proposed alternatives has succeeded in establishing itself, for those alternatives invariably yield a less-than-personal view of God. See **consubstantiality.**

phūsis. Greek for "nature."

pneumatocentric. Relating to a theology that is centered on the Holy Spirit. —**pneumatocentrism,** n.

pneumatomachii. The "fighters against the Spirit" who, while accepting the deity of the Son, did not hold that the Holy Spirit is God. Their rise to prominence in the fourth century occasioned the Council of Constantinople (381), which resolved the Trinitarian crisis and declared this view heretical.

procession (eternal). The eternal **relation** of the Holy Spirit to the Father (and to the Son, under Western eyes).

processions. The eternal begetting of the Son and eternal **procession** of the Holy Spirit. These are matched by the **missions**, the historical sending of the Son and the Spirit. The Eastern church considers it an error to call the Father's begetting of the Son a *procession*. For the East, this is a typically Western confusion of the Father and the Son. See **generation; unbegotten.**

properties. Paternity, filiation, active **spiration**, passive spiration, innascibility.

relations. The relationships in the invisible Trinity among the Father and the Son, the Son and the Father, the Father / the Son and the Holy Spirit, and the Holy Spirit and the Father / the Son. These are considered differently in the Eastern church than in the West. The relations among the three **persons** differ, in that the Father is first, the Son second, the Spirit third. The Father begets the Son and spirates the Spirit, but neither is begotten nor proceeds; the Son is begotten and (according to the West) shares with the Father in the **spiration** or sending of the Spirit, but does not proceed; the Spirit proceeds from the Father and (or through) the Son, but neither begets nor is begotten. These relations are irreversible. See **missions; order; relative opposition; unbegotten.**

relative opposition. Within the Trinity, the **relations** of the three ***hypostases*** that are each distinguished by irreversible characteristics in opposition to each other. The Father begets the Son and spirates the Spirit, but neither is begotten nor proceeds. The Son is begotten and (according to the West) shares with the Father in the **spiration** or sending of the Spirit, but does not proceed. The Spirit proceeds from the Father and (or through) the Son, but neither begets nor is begotten. See **missions; order; unbegotten.**

Sabellianism. The heresy of the third-century priest Sabellius, who taught that the Father, the Son, and the Holy Spirit were merely three ways in which the one God revealed himself.

secondary causes. Under the sovereign action of God, created powers or entities that contribute to a particular outcome. God (the first or primary cause) determines that it should rain today, and he brings about this event through the combination of temperature, wind, and relative humidity (secondary causes). See **original cause.**

semi-Pelagianism. The teaching that humans, after the fall, retain the ability to respond to the gospel while also needing the grace of God. In effect, humans take the first step, and the Holy Spirit takes over at that point. It could be summed up in the popular saying that God helps those who help themselves.

simplicity. God's state of being one and indivisible. He cannot be divided into parts. See **subsistence.**

social Trinitarianism. An understanding of the Trinity that sees the three **persons** as a community, interacting with one another. Its basic premise is the priority of the three persons over the one **being** (**essence**).

spiration. The defining characteristic of the Holy Spirit, who proceeds from (or is breathed out by) the Father. The West insists that the Spirit also proceeds from the Son (the ***filioque*** clause).

subordinationism. A teaching that the Son and the Holy Spirit are of lesser **being** or status than the Father. See **monarchy.**

subsistence. The manner by which the three ***hypostases*** are related to the one simple divine **essence**. This is not a real distinction (that is, a distinction between a thing and a thing), or else there would be a quarternity, not a Trinity. Nor is the distinction merely formal, or it would be purely in our own minds. Rather, it is modal, between a thing (the indivisible **being** of God) and the manner in which the thing is. Thus, while the three *hypostases* are distinct in real terms (the Father is not the Son, etc.), each is identical with the one indivisible divine being, the three subsisting in the one divine essence. See **simplicity.**

substance. (1) What a thing is in itself. (2) What God is, the one identical **being** of the Father, the Son, and the Holy Spirit. See **consubstantiality.**

theophany. A temporary appearance of God in the form of a human or some other created entity.

tritheism. The belief that there are three Gods. An exaggerated stress on the three **persons** can, it is claimed, lead to a belief that there are three Gods, not one.

unbegotten; begotten. Properties of, respectively, the Father and the Son. The property of the Son is that he is begotten by the Father from eternity. The Father is unbegotten. Begetting is qualitatively different from creation, refers to the eternal **relations** of the Father and the Son, distinguishes the Son from the creatures, and is beyond our capacity to understand. See **generation; processions.**

unitarian. The belief that there is one god that is an undifferentiated monad.

universalism. The belief that all people will eventually be saved.

univocal. Relating to an exact correspondence between our knowledge and God's knowledge.

xenolalia. An utterance made in an existing human language that is unknown to the speaker.

Bibliography

Alexander, Kimberly E. *Pentecostal Healing: Models in Theology and Practice*. Journal of Pentecostal Theology Supplement 29. Blandford Forum, UK: Deo, 2006.

Althouse, Peter. "Eschatology: The Always Present Hope." In *The Routledge Handbook of Pentecostal Theology*, edited by Wolfgang Vordey, 268–78. London: Routledge, 2020.

Anastos, Milton V. "Basil's *Kata Eunomiou*: A Critical Analysis." In *Basil of Caesarea: Christian, Humanist, Ascetic: A Sixteen-Hundredth Anniversary Symposium*, edited by Paul Jonathan Fedwick, 67–136. Toronto: Pontifical Institute of Medieval Studies, 1981.

Anderson, Allan Heaton. *An Introduction to Pentecostalism: Global Charismatic Christianity*. Cambridge: Cambridge University Press, 2014.

———. "Pentecostal Theology as a Global Challenge: Contextual Theological Constructions." In *The Routledge Handbook of Pentecostal Theology*, edited by Wolfgang Vondey, 18–28. London: Routledge, 2020.

Anselm. *De Incarnatione Verbi*.

———. *De Processione Spiritus Sancti Contra Graecos*.

Aquinas, St. Thomas. *Commentary on the Gospel of John Chapters 9–21*. Translated by Fabian R. Larcher. Lander, WY: Aquinas Institute for the Study of Sacred Doctrine, 2013.

———. *Commentary on the Gospel of St. John*. Albany, NY: Magi Books, 1980.

———. *Summa contra Gentiles*.

———. *Summa Theologia*.

Athanasius. *Against the Arians.*
———. *Defence of Dionysius.*
———. *Letters to Serapion on the Holy Spirit.*
———. *On the Incarnation.*
Atherstone, Andrew, and David Ceri Jones, eds. *Engaging with Martyn Lloyd-Jones: The Life and Legacy of "The Doctor."* Nottingham, UK: Apollos, 2011.
Atkinson, William P. "Christology: Jesus and Others: Jesus and God." In *The Routledge Handbook of Pentecostal Theology*, edited by Wolfgang Vondey, 216–25. London: Routledge, 2020.
Augustine. *De Trinitate.*
———. *Letter 169.*
———. *On the Gospel of John.*
Aune, David E. *Prophecy in Early Christianity and the Ancient Mediterranean World*. Grand Rapids: Eerdmans, 1983.
Ayres, Lewis. *Augustine and the Trinity*. Cambridge: Cambridge University Press, 2010.
———. "Innovation and Ressourcement in Pro-Nicene Pneumatology." *AugStud* 39, no. 2 (2008): 187–205.
———. *Nicaea and Its Legacy*. Oxford: Oxford University Press, 2004.
Ayres, Lewis, and Michel R. Barnes. "Conclusion." *AugStud* 39, no. 2 (2008): 235–36.
Baker, Matthew. "The Eternal 'Spirit of the Son': Barth, Florovsky, and Torrance on the *Filioque*." *International Journal of Systematic Theology* 12, no. 4 (October 2010): 382–403.
Barnes, Michel René. "Augustine's Last Pneumatology." *AugStud* 39, no. 2 (2008): 223–34.
———. "The Beginning and End of Early Christian Pneumatology." *AugStud* 39, no. 2 (2008): 169–86.
———. "Irenaeus's Trinitarian Theology." *Nova et Vetera* 7, no. 1 (2009): 67–106.
Barrett, C. K. *A Commentary on the First Epistle to the Corinthians*. London: Adam & Charles Black, 1968.
Barth, Karl. *Church Dogmatics*. Edited by Thomas F. Torrance. Translated by Geoffrey W. Bromiley. 14 vols. Edinburgh: T&T Clark, 1956–77.

Barth, Markus. *Ephesians: Translation and Commentary on Chapters 4–6*. Anchor Bible 34A. New York: Doubleday, 1974.

Basil of Caesarea. *The Hexaemeron*.

———. *Letters*.

———. *On the Holy Spirit*. Translated by Stephen Hildebrand. Yonkers, NY: St. Vladimir's Seminary Press, 2011.

Bavinck, Herman. *The Doctrine of God*. Translated, edited, and outlined by William Hendriksen. Edinburgh: Banner of Truth, 1977.

Beasley-Murray, G. R. *Baptism in the New Testament*. Exeter, UK: Paternoster Press, 1972.

———. *John*. Word Biblical Commentary 36. Waco, TX: Word, 1987.

Beeley, Christopher A. *Gregory of Nazianzus on the Trinity and the Knowledge of God: In Your Light Shall We See Light*. Oxford: Oxford University Press, 2008.

———. "The Holy Spirit in the Cappadocians: Past and Present." *Modern Theology* 26, no. 1 (January 2010): 90–119.

Behr, John. *The Formation of Christian Theology*. Vol. 2, *The Nicene Faith*. Pt. 2, *One of the Holy Trinity*. Crestwood, NY: St. Vladimir's Seminary Press, 2004.

Bennema, Cornelis. "The Giving of the Spirit in John 19–20: Another Round." In *The Spirit and Christ in the New Testament and Christian Theology: Essays in Honor of Max Turner*, edited by I. Howard Marshall, Volker Rabens, and Cornelis Bennema, 86–104. Grand Rapids: Eerdmans, 2012.

Bernard, David K. *The Oneness of God*. Hazelwood, MO: Word Aflame Press, 1983.

———. "Oneness Theology: Restoring the Apostolic Faith." In *The Routledge Handbook of Pentecostal Theology*, edited by Wolfgang Vorney, 195–205. London: Routledge, 2020.

Biddle, John. *Twelve Arguments Drawn Out of the Scripture: Wherein the Commonly-Received Opinion Touching the Deity of the Holy Spirit, Is Clearly and Fully Refuted*. London, 1647.

———. *A Twofold Catechism*. London: J. Cottrel for Ri. Moone, at the Seven Stars in Paul's Church-Yard, Neer the Great North-Door, 1654.

Bierma, Lyle D. *Font of Pardon and New Life: John Calvin and the Efficacy of Baptism*. New York: Oxford University Press, 2021.

Blaylock, Richard M. "Towards a Definition of New Testament Prophecy." *Them* 44, no. 1 (2019): 41–60.

Blowers, Paul M. *Maximus the Confessor: Jesus Christ and the Transfiguration of the World*. Oxford: Oxford University Press, 2016.

Bobrinskoy, Boris. *The Mystery of the Trinity: Trinitarian Experience and Vision in the Biblical and Patristic Tradition*. Translated by Anthony P. Gythiel. Crestwood, NY: St. Vladimir's Seminary Press, 1999.

Bouton-Touboulic, Anne-Isabelle. "Consonance and Dissonance: The Unifying Action of the Holy Ghost in Saint Augustine." *StPatr* 61 (2013): 31–51.

Brand, Thomas. "A Trinitarian Christology of the Fourth Word from the Cross: The *Communicatio Idiomatum*, the Modal Distinction, and the Forsakenness of Christ." PhD diss., University of Durham, 2020.

Bray, Gerald. *The Doctrine of God*. Leicester, UK: Inter-Varsity Press, 1993.

Bromiley, Geoffrey W. *An Introduction to the Theology of Karl Barth*. Grand Rapids: Eerdmans, 1979.

Bruce, Robert. *The Mystery of the Lord's Supper: Sermons on the Sacrament Preached in the Kirk of Edinburgh in A.D. 1589*. Edited and translated by Thomas F. Torrance. London: James Clarke, 1958.

Bruner, Frederick Dale. *A Theology of the Holy Spirit: The Pentecostal Experience and the New Testament Witness*. Grand Rapids: Eerdmans, 1970.

Bulgakov, Sergei Nikolaevich. *Le Paraclet*. Translated by Constantin Andronikof. Paris: Aubier, 1946.

Butin, Philip Walker. *Revelation, Redemption, and Response: Calvin's Trinitarian Understanding of the Divine-Human Relationship*. New York: Oxford University Press, 1995.

Buzzard, Anthony, and Charles F. Hunting. *The Doctrine of the Trinity: Christianity's Self-Inflicted Wound*. Lanham, MD: Rowman & Littlefield, 1998.

Cabasilas, Nicholas. *Life in Christ*. Translated by Margaret I. Lisney. London: Janus, 1995.

Calvin, John. *Calvini Opera (Opera quae supersunt omnia)*. Edited by Guilelmus Baum, Eduardus Cunitz, and Eduardus Reuss. 59 vols. *Corpus Reformatorum* 29–87. Brunswick: 1863–1900.

———. *Calvin's Commentaries: The Epistle of Paul the Apostle to the Hebrews; and the First and Second Epistles of St Peter*. Edited by Thomas F. Torrance and David W. Torrance. Translated by William B. Johnston. Grand Rapids: Eerdmans, 1963.

———. *Calvin's Commentaries: The Epistles of Paul the Apostle to the Galatians, Ephesians, Philippians and Colossians*. Edited by Thomas F. Torrance and David W. Torrance. Translated by T. H. L. Parker. Grand Rapids: Eerdmans, 1965.

———. *Calvin's Commentaries: The First Epistle of Paul the Apostle to the Corinthians*. Edited by Thomas F. Torrance and David W. Torrance. Translated by John W. Fraser. Grand Rapids: Eerdmans, 1960.

———. *Calvin's Commentaries: The Gospel according to St. John 11–21 and the First Epistle of John*. Edited by Thomas F. Torrance and David W. Torrance. Translated by T. H. L. Parker. Grand Rapids: Eerdmans, 1959.

———. *Calvin's Commentaries: The Second Epistle of Paul to the Corinthians and the Epistles to Timothy, Titus, and Philemon*. Edited by David W. Torrance and Thomas F. Torrance. Translated by T. A. Smail. Grand Rapids: Eerdmans, 1964.

———. *Calvin: Theological Treatises*. Translated by J. K. S. Reid. London: Westminster Press, 1954.

———. *Commentarii in Epistolas Canonicas*. Ioannis Calvini Opera Omnia. Genève: Librairie Droz, 2009.

———. *Commentarii in Pauli Epistolas*. Ioannis Calvini Opera Omnia. Genève: Librairie Droz, 1992.

———. *In Evangelium Secundum Johannem Commentarius Pars Altera*. Genève: Librairie Droz, 1998.

———. *Institutes of the Christian Religion*. Edited by Ford Lewis Battles. Translated by John T. McNeill. Philadelphia: Westminster Press, 1960.

Canlis, Julie. *Calvin's Ladder: A Spiritual Theology of Ascent and Ascension*. Grand Rapids: Eerdmans, 2010.

Carson, D. *The Gospel according to St John*. Leicester, UK: Inter-Varsity Press, 1991.

Catechism of the Catholic Church. London: Geoffrey Chapman, 1994.

Church of Scotland. *The Confession of Faith, the Larger and Shorter Catechisms with the Scripture Proofs at Large, Together with The Sum of Saving Knowledge*. Applecross: Publications Committee of the Free Presbyterian Church of Scotland, 1970.

Ciampa, Roy E., and Brian S. Rosner. *The First Letter to the Corinthians*. Grand Rapids: Eerdmans, 2010.

Claunch, Kyle. "The Son and the Spirit: The Promise and Peril of Spirit Christology." *Southern Baptist Journal of Theology* 19, no. 1 (2015): 91–112.

Clowney, Edmund P. *The Church*. Downers Grove, IL: InterVarsity Press, 1995.

Congar, Yves M. J. *I Believe in the Holy Spirit: The Complete Three Volume Work in One Volume*. Translated by David Smith. New York: Crossroad, 1997.

———. *The Word and the Spirit*. Translated by David Smith. London: Geoffrey Chapman, 1986.

Conticello, V. S. "Pseudo-Cyril's De Sacrosancte Trinitate: A Compilation of Joseph the Philosopher." *Orientalia Christiana Periodica* 61 (1995): 117–29.

Coulter, Dale M., and Amos Yong. "Between East and West—From North and South." *Pneuma* 36, no. 3 (2014): 351–54.

Cranfield, C. E. B. *A Critical and Exegetical Commentary on the Epistle to the Romans*. Edinburgh: T&T Clark, 1979.

Cross, Anthony R. "Baptism in the Theology of John Calvin and Karl Barth." In *Calvin, Barth and Reformed Theology*, edited by Neil B. MacDonald, 57–87. Eugene, OR: Wipf & Stock, 2008.

Cyril of Alexandria. *Commentary on John*. Library of Fathers of the Holy Catholic Church 2. Online. Members of the English Church. London: Walter Smith, 1874/1885.

Dalcour, Edward L. *A Definitive Look at Oneness Theology: Defending the Tri-Unity of God*. Lanham, MD: University Press of America, 2005.

Davies, Brian. *The Thought of Thomas Aquinas*. Oxford: Clarendon Press, 1992.

Davies, Brian, and G. R. Evans. *Anselm of Canterbury: The Major Works*. Oxford: Oxford University Press, 1998.

DelCogliano, Mark, Andrew Radde-Gallwitz, and Lewis Ayres. *Works on the Spirit: Athanasius the Great and Didymus the Blind*. Yonkers, NY: St. Vladimir's Seminary Press, 2011.

de Margerie, Bertrand. *The Christian Trinity in History*. Translated by Edmund J. Fortman. Studies in Historical Theology 1. Petersham, MA: St. Bede's Publications, 1982.

Didymus the Blind. *On the Holy Spirit*.

Dragkiotis, Constantinos. "Emptiness, as a Prerequisite for Being Filled in the Holy Spirit." *JEPTA* 34, no. 2 (2014): 184–99.

Drecoll, Volker Henning. *Die Entwicklung der Trinitätslehre Des Basilius von Cäsarea*. Göttingen: Vandenhoeck & Ruprecht, 1996.

Dudley-Smith, Timothy. *John Stott: A Global Ministry: A Biography: The Later Years*. Downers Grove, IL: InterVarsity Press, 2001.

Dunn, James D. G. *Baptism in the Holy Spirit: A Re-Examination of the New Testament Teaching on the Gift of the Holy Spirit in Relation to Pentecostalism Today*. London: SCM, 1970.

———. *Jesus and the Spirit: A Study of the Religious and Charismatic Experience of Jesus and the First Christians as Reflected in the New Testament*. London: SCM, 1975.

———. "'The Lord, the Giver of Life': The Gift of the Spirit as Both Life-Giving and Empowering." In *The Spirit and Christ in the New Testament and Christian Theology: Essays in Honor of Max Turner*, edited by I. Howard Marshall, Volker Rabens, and Cornelis Bennema, 1–17. Grand Rapids: Eerdmans, 2012.

Emery, Gilles. *The Trinitarian Theology of St. Thomas Aquinas*. Translated by Francesca Aran Murphy. Oxford: Oxford University Press, 2007.

Eurell, John-Christian. "The Nature of Pauline Glossolalia and Its Early Reception." *SJT* 72, no. 2 (2019): 182–90.

Evans, G. R. *Anselm*. London: Geoffrey Chapman, 1989.

Everts, Janet (Jenny) Meyer. "Filled with the Spirit from the Old Testament to the Apostle Paul." *Pneuma* 33, no. 1 (2011): 63–68.

Farrow, Douglas. *Ascension and Ecclesia: On the Significance of the Ascension for Ecclesiology and Christian Cosmology*. Edinburgh: T&T Clark, 1999.

Fee, Gordon D. *The First Epistle to the Corinthians*. Grand Rapids: Eerdmans, 1987.

———. *God's Empowering Presence: The Holy Spirit in the Letters of Paul*. Carlisle, UK: Paternoster, 1994.

———. *Paul, the Spirit and the People of God*. London: Hodder and Stoughton, 1996.

Ferguson, Sinclair B. *The Holy Spirit*. Leicester, UK: Inter-Varsity Press, 1996.

Fine, Arthur. "The Einstein-Podolsky-Rosen Argument in Quantum Theory." In *The Stanford Encyclopedia of Philosophy*. Edited by Edward N. Zalta. Winter 2017. https://plato.stanford.edu/archives/win2017/entries/qt-epr/.

Fitzgerald, Allan G., ed. *Augustine through the Ages: An Encyclopedia*. Grand Rapids: Eerdmans, 1999.

Fitzmyer, Joseph A. *First Corinthians: A New Translation with Introduction and Commentary*. Anchor Yale Bible 32. New Haven, CT: Yale University Press, 2008.

———. *The Gospel according to Luke (I–IX)*. Anchor Bible 28. New York: Doubleday, 1970.

Flavel, John. *The Mystery of Providence*. 1678. Reprint, London: Banner of Truth, 1963.

Fudge, Thomas A. *Christianity without the Cross: A History of Salvation in Oneness Pentecostalism*. Parkland, FL: Universal Publications, 2003.

Gabriel, Andrew K. "Pneumatology: Eschatological Intensification of the Presence of God." In *The Routledge Handbook of Pentecostal Theology*, edited by Wolfgang Vondey, 206–15. London: Routledge, 2020.

Gaffin, Richard B., Jr. *The Centrality of the Resurrection: A Study in Paul's Soteriology*. Grand Rapids: Baker, 1978.

———. *Perspectives on Pentecost: Studies in New Testament Teaching on the Gifts of the Holy Spirit*. Phillipsburg, NJ: Presbyterian and Reformed, 1979.

Gaiser, Frederick J. *Healing in the Bible: Theological Insight for Christian Ministry*. Grand Rapids: Baker Academic, 2010.

Gempf, Conrad. "Apollos and the Ephesian Disciples: Befores and Afters (Acts 18:24–19:7)." In *The Spirit and Christ in the New*

Testament and Christian Theology: Essays in Honor of Max Turner, edited by I. Howard Marshall, Volker Rabens, and Cornelis Bennema, 119–37. Grand Rapids: Eerdmans, 2012.

Gillespie, Thomas W. *The First Theologians: A Study in Early Christian Prophecy*. Grand Rapids: Eerdmans, 1994.

Giulea, Dragos A. "Divine Being's Modulations: *Ousia* in the Pro-Nicene Context of the Fourth Century." *SVTQ* 59, no. 3 (2015): 307–37.

Goldingay, John. "The Holy Spirit and the Psalms." *JPT* 27, no. 1 (2018): 1–13.

Goodwin, Thomas. *The Works of Thomas Goodwin*. Edinburgh: James Nichol, 1864.

Green, Joel B. *The Gospel of Luke*. Grand Rapids: Eerdmans, 1997.

Grégoire, J. "La Relation Éternelle de l'Esprit au Fils d'aprés les Écrits de Jean de Damas." *Revue d'Histoire Ecclésiastique* 64, no. 3/4 (1969): 713–55.

Gregory of Nazianzus. *Oration 1*.

———. *Oration 12*.

———. *Oration 25*.

———. *Oration 28*.

———. *Oration 31*.

———. *Oration 33*.

———. *Oration 41*.

———. *Oration 43*.

———. *Oration on the Holy Lights*.

———. *Oration on the Theophany, or Birthday of Christ*.

Gregory of Nyssa. *Against Eunomius*.

———. *Against the Macedonians*.

———. *On "Not Three Gods" to Ablabius*.

———. *On the Holy Spirit against the Followers of Macedonius*.

———. *On the Holy Trinity and of the Godhead of the Holy Spirit to Eustathius*.

———. *To the Greeks (about Common Notions)*.

Grudem, Wayne A., ed. *Are Miraculous Gifts for Today? 4 Views*. Counterpoints: Bible and Theology. Grand Rapids: Zondervan, 2011.

———. *The Gift of Prophecy in 1 Corinthians*. Lanham, MD: University Press of America, 1982.

———. *The Gift of Prophecy in the New Testament and Today*. Westchester, IL: Crossway, 1988.

———. *Systematic Theology*. Grand Rapids: Zondervan, 1994.

Guthrie, Donald. *New Testament Theology*. Leicester, UK: Inter-Varsity Press, 1981.

Habets, Myk. *Anointed Son: Toward a Trinitarian Spirit Christology*. Eugene, OR: Pickwick, 2010.

———. ed. *Ecumenical Perspectives on the* Filioque *for the 21st Century*. London: Bloomsbury, 2014.

Haight, Roger. "The Case for Spirit Christology." *Theological Studies* 53, no. 2 (1992): 257–87.

Hanson, R. P. C. *The Search for the Christian Doctrine of God: The Arian Controversy 318–81*. Edinburgh: T&T Clark, 1988.

Harrison, Verna. "Perichoresis in the Greek Fathers." *SVTQ* 35, no. 1 (1991): 53–65.

Haugh, R. M. *Photius and the Carolingians: The Trinitarian Controversy*. Belmont, MA: Norland, 1975.

Hiebert, Paul G. "Discerning the Work of God." In *Charismatic Experiences in History*, edited by Cecil M. Robeck Jr., 147–63. Peabody, MA: Hendrickson, 1985.

Hill, David. *New Testament Prophecy*. London: Marshall, 1979.

Hillis, Gregory K. "Pneumatology and Soteriology according to Gregory of Nazianzus and Cyril of Alexandria." *StPatr* 61 (2013): 187–97.

Hodge, Charles. *A Commentary on the Epistle to the Ephesians*. London: Banner of Truth, 1964.

———. *A Commentary on the First Epistle to the Corinthians*. London: Banner of Truth, 1958.

Holland, Tom. *Contours of Pauline Theology: A Radical New Survey of the Influences on Paul's Biblical Writings*. Fearn, Scotland: Mentor, 2004.

Holmes, Christopher R. J. *The Holy Spirit*. Grand Rapids: Zondervan, 2015.

Hopkins, Jasper, and Herbert Richardson. *Anselm of Canterbury*. Vol. 3. Toronto: Edwin Mellen Press, 1976.

Hughes, Philip Edgcumbe. *A Commentary on the Epistle to the Hebrews*. Grand Rapids: Eerdmans, 1977.

Hünermann, Peter. *Heinrich Denzinger: Kompendium der Glaubensbekentnisse und Kirchlichen Lehrentscheidungen*. Aktualisierte Auflage 38. Freiburg im Breisgau: Herder, 1999.

Hunter, Harold. "Pentecostal Reflections on Apostolicity." *JEPTA* 33, no. 1 (2013): 1–13.

Irenaeus. *Against Heresies*.

———. *The Demonstration of the Apostolic Preaching*.

John of Damascus. *On the Orthodox Faith*.

Jüngel, Eberhard. *The Doctrine of the Trinity: God's Being Is in His Becoming*. Edinburgh: T&T Clark, 1976.

Kärkkäinen, Veli-Matti. "'By the Washing of Regeneration and Renewal in the Holy Spirit': Towards a Pneumatological Theology of Justification." In *The Spirit and Christ in the New Testament and Christian Theology: Essays in Honor of Max Turner*, edited by I. Howard Marshall, Volker Rabens, and Cornelis Bennema, 303–22. Grand Rapids: Eerdmans, 2012.

———. "The Challenge of Discerning between the Genuine and Counterfeit 'Signs of the Spirit': Toward a Pentecostal Theology of the Discernment of the Spirit(s)." *JEPTA* 39, no. 2 (2019): 165–83. https://doi.org/10.1080/18124461.2019.1627510.

Kaspar, Walter, ed. *Lexicon Für Theologie und Kirche*. Freiburg: Herder, 1999.

Kelly, J. N. D. *Early Christian Doctrines*. London: Adam & Charles Black, 1968.

Kidd, B. J. *Documents Illustrative of the Continental Reformation*. Oxford: Clarendon Press, 1911. Reprint, 1967.

Kopecek, Thomas A. *A History of Neo-Arianism*. 2 vols. Cambridge, MA: Philadelphia Patristic Foundation, Ltd., 1979.

Kuyper, Abraham. *The Work of the Holy Spirit*. Translated by Henri De Vries. Grand Rapids: Eerdmans, 1900.

Laats, Alar. *Doctrines of the Trinity in Eastern and Western Theologies: A Study with Special Reference to K. Barth and V. Lossky*. Frankfurt am Main: Peter Lang, 1999.

Lampe, G. W. H. *God as Spirit: The Bampton Lectures, 1976*. Oxford: Clarendon Press, 1977.

———, ed. *A Patristic Greek Lexicon*. Oxford: Clarendon Press, 1961.

Land, Stephen J. *Pentecostal Spirituality: A Passion for the Kingdom*. JPT Supplement 1. Sheffield, UK: Sheffield Academic Press, 1993.

Lane, Anthony N. S. "Cyril of Alexandria and the Incarnation." In *The Spirit and Christ in the New Testament and Christian Theology: Essays in Honor of Max Turner*, edited by I. Howard Marshall, Volker Rabens, and Cornelis Bennema, 285–302. Grand Rapids: Eerdmans, 2012.

———. *Exploring Christian Doctrine*. London: SPCK, 2013.

———. *Sin and Grace: Evangelical Soteriology in Historical Perspective*. London: Apollos, 2020.

Larson, Mark J. "A Re-Examination of *De Spiritu Sancto*: Saint Basil's Bold Defence of the Spirit's Deity." *Scottish Bulletin of Evangelical Theology* 19, no. 1 (Spring 2001): 65–84.

Lebreton, Jules. *History of the Dogma of the Trinity: From Its Origins to the Council of Nicæa*. Translated by Algar Thorold. 8th ed. London: Burns, Oates & Washbourne, 1939.

Legge, Dominic. *The Trinitarian Christology of St. Thomas Aquinas*. Oxford: Oxford University Press, 2017.

Letham, Robert. "Catholicity Global and Historical: Constantinople, Westminster, and the Church in the Twenty-First Century." *WTJ* 72, no. 1 (2010): 43–57.

———. *The Holy Trinity: In Scripture, History, Theology, and Worship*. Rev. and expanded ed. Phillipsburg, NJ: P&R Publishing, 2019.

———. *The Lord's Supper: Eternal Word in Broken Bread*. Phillipsburg, NJ: P&R Publishing, 2001.

———. "The Person of Christ." In *Reformation Theology: A Systematic Summary*, edited by Matthew Barrett, 313–45. Wheaton, IL: Crossway, 2017.

———. *Systematic Theology*. Wheaton, IL: Crossway, 2019.

———. *Union with Christ: In Scripture, History, and Theology*. Rev. and expanded ed. Phillipsburg, NJ: P&R Publishing, 2011.

———. *The Westminster Assembly: Reading Its Theology in Historical Context*. Phillipsburg, NJ: P&R Publishing, 2009.

———. *The Work of Christ*. Leicester, UK: Inter-Varsity Press, 1993.

Levering, Matthew. *Engaging the Doctrine of the Holy Spirit: Love and Gift in the Trinity and the Church*. Grand Rapids: Baker Academic, 2016.

Levison, John R. *Filled with the Spirit*. Grand Rapids: Eerdmans, 2009.

———. "*Filled with the Spirit*: A Conversation with Pentecostal and Charismatic Scholars." *JPT* 20, no. 2 (2011): 213–31.

———. *The Holy Spirit before Christianity*. Waco, TX: Baylor University Press, 2019.

———. "Recommendations for the Future of Pneumatology." *Pneuma* 33, no. 1 (2011): 79–93.

Lloyd-Jones, D. Martyn. *God's Ultimate Purpose: An Exposition of Ephesians 1:1–23*. Edinburgh: Banner of Truth, 1978.

———. *Joy Unspeakable: The Baptism with the Holy Spirit*. Eastbourne, UK: Kingsway Publications, 1984.

———. "Quenching the Spirit." *Westminster Record* 39, no. 9 (September 1964): 129–43.

———. *Romans: An Exposition of Chapter 8:5–17: The Sons of God*. Edinburgh: Banner of Truth, 1972.

Lossky, Vladimir. *The Mystical Theology of the Eastern Church*. London: James Clarke, 1957.

Macchia, Frank D. *Baptized in the Spirit: A Global Pentecostal Theology*. Grand Rapids: Zondervan, 2006.

———. "Baptized in the Spirit: A Pentecostal Reflection on the *Filioque*." In *Ecumenical Perspectives on the* Filioque *for the Twenty-First Century*, edited by Myk Habets, 141–56. London: Bloomsbury, 2014.

———. "A Call for Careful Discernment: A Theological Response to Prosperity Teaching." In *Pentecostalism and Prosperity: The Socio-Economics of the Global Charismatic Movement*, edited by Katherine Attanasi and Amos Yong, 225–37. New York: Palgrave Macmillan, 2012.

———. "Groans Too Deep for Words: Towards a Theology of Tongues as Initial Evidence," *Asian Journal of Pentecostal Studies* 1, no. 2 (1998): 149–73.

———. *Jesus the Spirit Baptizer: Christology in the Light of Pentecost*. Grand Rapids: Eerdmans, 2018.

———. "Spirit Baptism: Initiation in the Fullness of God's Promises." In *The Routledge Handbook of Pentecostal Theology*, edited by Wolfgang Vondey, 247–56. London: Routledge, 2020.

Mannermaa, Tuomo. "Justification and Theosis in Lutheran-Orthodox Perspective." In *Union with Christ: The New Finnish Interpretation of Luther*, edited by Carl E. Braaten, 25–41. Grand Rapids: Eerdmans, 1998.

McCormack, Bruce L. *For Us and Our Salvation: Incarnation and Atonement in the Reformed Tradition*. Studies in Reformed Theology and History 1, no. 2. Princeton, NJ: Princeton Theological Seminary, 1993.

McGuckin, John A. "On the Mystical Theology of the Eastern Church." *SVTQ* 58, no. 4 (2014): 373–99.

———. *St. Gregory of Nazianzus: An Intellectual Biography*. Crestwood, NY: St. Vladimir's Seminary Press, 2001.

Meredith, Anthony. "The Idea of God in Gregory of Nyssa." In *Studien zur Gregor von Nyssa und der Christlichen Spätantike*, edited by Hubertus R. Drobner and Christophe Klock, 127–47. Supplements to Vigiliae Christianae 12. Leiden: Brill, 1990.

Metzger, Paul Louis. "Mystical Union with Christ: An Alternative to Blood Transfusions and Legal Fictions." *WTJ* 65, no. 2 (2003): 201–13.

Molnar, Paul D. *Divine Freedom and the Doctrine of the Immanent Trinity: In Dialogue with Karl Barth and Contemporary Theology*. London: T&T Clark, 2002.

Moltmann, Jürgen. *The Spirit of Life: A Universal Affirmation*. Minneapolis: Fortress Press, 1992.

———. *The Trinity and the Kingdom: The Doctrine of God*. London: SCM, 1991.

Morales, Xavier. "Basile de Césarée est-il l'introducteur du concept de relation en théologie trinitaire?" *Revue des Études Augustiniennes* 63 (2017): 141–80.

Murray, John. "Definitive Sanctification." *Calvin Theological Journal* 2, no. 1 (1967): 5–21.

———. *The Epistle to the Romans*. Grand Rapids: Eerdmans, 1965.

———. *Select Lectures in Systematic Theology*. Vol. 2 of *Collected Writings of John Murray*. Edinburgh: Banner of Truth, 1977.

Newman, John Henry. *Essays 1: Apostolic Tradition*. London, 1836.

Owen, John. *The Works of John Owen*. Edited by William H. Goold. London: Banner of Truth, 1965–68.

Ozment, Stephen. *The Age of Reform 1250–1550*. New Haven, CT: Yale University Press, 1980.

Pannenberg, Wolfhart. *Systematic Theology*. Grand Rapids: Eerdmans, 1991.

Perrot, C. "Prophètes et Prophêtisme dans le Nouveau Testament." *Lumière et Vie* (November–December 1973): 25–39.

[Photios]. *On the Mystagogy of the Holy Spirit by Saint Photios Patriarch of Constantinople*. Translated by Holy Transfiguration Monastery. N.p.: Studion Publishers, 1983.

Polyander, Johannes. *Synopsis Purioris Theologiae, Disputationibus Quinquaginta Duabus Comprehensa*. Leiden: Ex officina Elzeverianus, 1625.

Poythress, Vern S. "The Boundaries of the Gift of Tongues: With Implications for Cessationism and Continuationism." *Them* 44, no. 1 (2019): 61–69.

Prestige, G. L. *God in Patristic Thought*. London: SPCK, 1959.

Quasten, Johannes. *Patrology*. 4 vols. Westminster, MD: Christian Classics, 1992.

Radde-Gallwitz, Andrew. *Gregory of Nyssa's Doctrinal Works: A Literary Study*. Oxford: Oxford University Press, 2018.

Ridderbos, Herman N. *Paul: An Outline of His Theology*. Grand Rapids: Eerdmans, 1975.

Ritschl, Dietrich. "Historical Development and the Implications of the *filioque* Controversy." In *Spirit of God, Spirit of Christ*, edited by Lukas Vischer, 46–65. London and Geneva: SPCK, 1981.

Robertson, Archibald, and Alfred Plummer. *A Critical and Exegetical Commentary on the First Epistle of St Paul to the Corinthians*. Edinburgh: T&T Clark, 1999.

Rousseau, Philip. *Basil of Caesarea*. Berkeley: University of California Press, 1994.

Routledge, Robin. "'My Spirit' in Genesis 6:4." *JPT* 20, no. 2 (2011): 232–51.

Russell, Norman. *The Doctrine of Deification in the Greek Patristic Tradition*. Oxford: Oxford University Press, 2004.

Ruthven, Jon. *On the Cessation of the Charismata: The Protestant Polemic on Post-Biblical Miracles*. JPT Supplement Series 3. Sheffield, UK: Sheffield Academic Press, 1993.

Sánchez M., Leopoldo A. *T&T Clark Introduction to Spirit Christology*. London: T&T Clark, 2022.

Sanders, E. P. *Paul, the Law, and the Jewish People*. Philadelphia: Fortress Press, 1983.

Schaff, Philip. *The Creeds of Christendom*. Grand Rapids: Baker, 1966.

Scheeben, Matthias Joseph. *The Mysteries of Christianity*. Translated by Cyril Vollert. Orig. published 1946. New York: Crossroad, 2006.

Seifrid, Mark A. "Paul, Luther, and Justification in Gal 2:15–21." *WTJ* 65, no. 2 (2003): 215–30.

Siecienski, A. Edward. *The Filioque: History of a Doctrinal Controversy*. Oxford: Oxford University Press, 2010.

Skinner, Quentin. "Meaning and Understanding in the History of Ideas." In *Visions of Politics*, vol. 1, *Regarding Method*, 59–97. Cambridge: Cambridge University Press, 2002.

Smalcius, Valentin. *Racovian Catechism*. English trans. Amsterdam: For Brouer Janz, 1652.

Smith, Shawn C. "The Insertion of the *Filioque* into the Nicene Creed and a Letter of Isidore of Seville." *Journal of Early Christian Studies* 22, no. 2 (2014): 261–86.

Socinus, Faustus. *Explicatio Primae Partis Primi Capitis Iohannis*. Racoviae: Typis Sebastiani Sternacii, 1618.

Stead, G. Christopher. "Why Not Three Gods? The Logic of Gregory of Nyssa's Trinitarian Doctrine." In *Studien zur Gregor von Nyssa und der Christlichen Spätantike*, edited by Hubertus R. Drobner and Christophe Klock, 149–63. Supplements to Vigiliae Christianae 12. Leiden: Brill, 1990.

Stott, John R. W. *The Message of 1 Timothy and Titus: The Life of the Local Church*. Leicester, UK: Inter-Varsity Press, 1996.

Studebaker, Steve M. "The Spirit and the Fellowship of the Triune God." In *The Routledge Handbook of Pentecostal Theology*, edited by Wolfgang Vondey, 185–94. London: Routledge, 2020.

Studer, Basil. *Trinity and Incarnation: The Faith of the Early Church*. Edited by Andrew Louth. Translated by Matthias Westerhoff. Collegeville, MN: Liturgical Press, 1993.

Stylianopoulos, Theodore G. "The Biblical Background of the Article on the Holy Spirit in the Constantinopolitan Creed." In *Études Theologiques: Le Ile Concile Oecuménique*. Chambésy-Genève: Centre Orthodoxe Du Patriarcat Oecuménique, 1982.

———. *Spirit of Truth: Ecumenical Perspectives on the Holy Spirit: Papers of the Holy Spirit Consultation, October 24–25, 1985, Brookline, Massachusetts*. Brookline, MA: Holy Cross Orthodox Press, 1986.

Swete, Henry Barclay. *The Holy Spirit in the Ancient Church: A Study of the Christian Teaching in the Age of the Fathers*. London: Macmillan, 1912.

Tanner, Kathryn. "Beyond the East/West Divide." In *Ecumenical Perspectives on the* Filioque *for the 21st Century*, edited by Myk Habets, 198–210. London: Bloomsbury, 2014.

———. *Christ the Key*. Cambridge: Cambridge University Press, 2010.

Thiselton, Anthony C. *The First Epistle to the Corinthians: A Commentary on the Greek Text*. Grand Rapids: Eerdmans, 2000.

———. *The Holy Spirit—In Biblical Teaching, through the Centuries, and Today*. London: SPCK, 2013.

———. *The Last Things: A New Approach*. London: SPCK, 2012.

Thomas, John Christopher. "Frederick J. Gaiser, *Healing in the Bible: Theological Insight for Christian Ministry* (Grand Rapids: Baker Academic, 2010)—An Appreciative Engagement." *JPT* 21, no. 1 (2012): 16–26.

Toon, Peter. *Our Triune God: A Biblical Portrayal of the Trinity*. Wheaton, IL: Bridgepoint, 1996.

Torrance, Thomas F. *The Christian Doctrine of God: One Being, Three Persons*. Edinburgh: T&T Clark, 1996.

———. *Incarnation: The Person and Life of Christ*. Milton Keynes, UK: Paternoster, 2008.

———. *Theology in Reconciliation: Essays towards Evangelical and Catholic Unity in East and West*. Grand Rapids: Eerdmans, 1975.

———. *Trinitarian Perspectives: Toward Doctrinal Agreement*. Edinburgh: T&T Clark, 1988.

Trueman, Carl R. "Is the Finnish Line a New Beginning? A Critical Assessment of the Reading of Luther Offered by the Helsinki Circle." *WTJ* 65, no. 2 (2003): 231–44.

Turcescu, Lucian. *Gregory of Nyssa and the Concept of Divine Persons*. Oxford: Oxford University Press, 2005.

Turner, Max. *The Holy Spirit and Spiritual Gifts*. Carlisle, UK: Paternoster, 1996.

———. "Levison's *Filled with the Spirit*: A Brief Appreciation and Response." *JPT* 20, no. 2 (2011): 193–200.

———. "Spiritual Gifts and Spiritual Transformation in 1 Corinthians and Ephesians." *Journal of Pentecostal Theology* 22, no. 2 (2013): 187–205.

Turretin, Francis. *Institutes of Elenctic Theology*. Edited by James T. Dennison Jr. Translated by George Musgrave Giger. 3 vols. Phillipsburg, NJ: P&R Publishing, 1992–97.

Twombly, Charles C. *Perichoresis and Personhood: God, Christ, and Salvation in John of Damascus*. Eugene, OR: Pickwick, 2015.

Ukpong, J. S. "Pluralism and the Problem of the Discernment of Spirits." *Ecumenical Review* 41, no. 3 (1989): 416–25.

Van Nieuwenhove, Rik. *An Introduction to Medieval Theology*. Cambridge: Cambridge University Press, 2012.

Vischer, Lukas, ed. *Spirit of God, Spirit of Christ: Ecumenical Reflections on the Filioque Controversy*. London: SPCK, 1981.

Vollert, Cyril O. Foreword to *Nature and Grace* (*Natur und gnade* [1861]), by Matthias Joseph Scheeben. Translated by Cyril Vollert. St. Louis: Herder, 1954.

Vondey, Wolfgang, ed. *The Routledge Handbook of Pentecostal Theology*. London: Routledge, 2020.

Vos, Geerhardus. "The Eschatological Aspect of the Pauline Conception of the Spirit." In *Biblical and Theological Studies*, edited by the members of the faculty of Princeton Theological Seminary, 209–59. New York: Charles Scribner's Sons, 1912.

———. *The Pauline Eschatology*. Grand Rapids: Eerdmans, 1972.

Wainwright, Arthur. *The Trinity in the New Testament*. London: SPCK, 1963.

Walker, Andrew. *Restoring the Kingdom*. London: Hodder and Stoughton, 1989.

Warfield, Benjamin Breckinridge. "Calvin's Doctrine of the Knowledge of God." In *Calvin and Augustine*, edited by Samuel G. Craig, 29–130. Nutley, NJ: Presbyterian and Reformed, 1974.

———. "Calvin's Doctrine of the Trinity." In *Calvin and Augustine*, edited by Samuel G. Craig, 187–284. Nutley, NJ: Presbyterian and Reformed, 1974.

———. "The Spirit of God in the Old Testament." In *Biblical and Theological Studies*, edited by Samuel G. Craig, 127–56. Philadelphia: Presbyterian and Reformed, 1952.

Weinandy, Thomas G. *The Father's Spirit of Sonship: Reconceiving the Trinity*. London: T&T Clark, 1995.

Williams, Frederick, and Lionel Wickham. *St. Gregory of Nazianzus: On God and Christ*. Crestwood, NY: St. Vladimir's Seminary Press, 2002.

Williams, Rowan. "Barth on the Triune God." In *Karl Barth: Essays in His Theological Method*, edited by S. W. Sykes, 147–93. Oxford: Clarendon Press, 1979.

———. "De Trinitate." In *Augustine through the Ages: An Encyclopedia*, edited by A. Fitzgerald, 845–51. Grand Rapids: Eerdmans, 1999.

Wilson, Sarah Hinlicky. "Water Baptism and Spirit Baptism in Luke-Acts: Another Reading of the Evidence." *Pneuma* 38, no. 4 (2016): 476–501.

Yong, Amos. *Spirit of Love: A Trinitarian Theology of Grace*. Waco, TX: Baylor University Press, 2012.

Zwiep, Arie W. *Christ, the Spirit and the Community of God: Essays on the Acts of the Apostles*. Tübingen: Mohr Siebeck, 2010.

Index of Scripture

Acts

Romans

1 Corinthians

Index of Names

Index of Subjects

Also from P&R Publishing

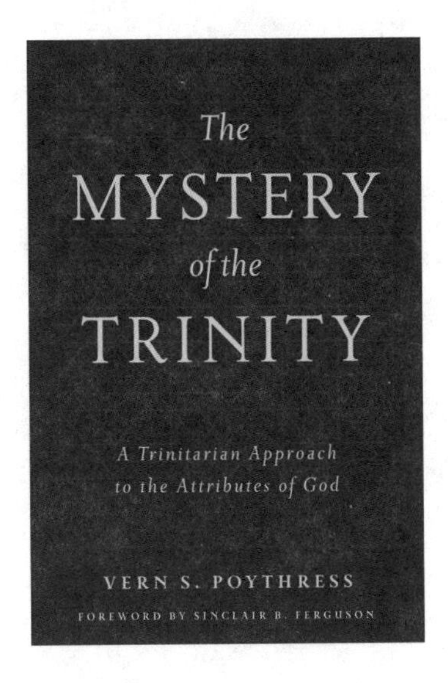

Starting with the doctrine of the Trinity, Vern Poythress addresses six challenges concerning the compatibility of God's independence with his activities in the world. The eternal activities among the persons of the Trinity offer a foundation for God's activities in the world. Alternative metaphysical frameworks for explaining God's transcendence and immanence run the danger of overriding the truths in biblical revelation.

"Dr. Poythress applies his deep knowledge of Scripture, his well-informed knowledge of historical theology, and his brilliant mind to some of the most difficult controversies in the theology of the divine attributes."
—Philip Graham Ryken

"A stimulating and fascinating book. . . . Poythress raises important questions that need addressing and offers many incisive and challenging insights."
—Robert Letham